Teaching Emotionally
Disturbed Children

Teaching Emotionally Disturbed Children

Edited by

RICHARD L. McDOWELL
University of New Mexico

GARY W. ADAMSON
University of New Mexico

FRANK H. WOOD
University of Minnesota

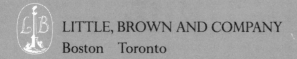

LITTLE, BROWN AND COMPANY
Boston   Toronto

Library of Congress Catalog Card No. 81–82313

ISBN 0–316–555576

9 8 7 6 5 4 3 2 1

MV
Published simultaneously in Canada
by Little, Brown & Company (Canada) Limited

Printed in the United States of America

Preface

As a result of popular concern and governmental action at local, state, and federal levels, emotionally disturbed children are now enrolled in regular classrooms. In fact, in most communities around the country, the public school program is the only educational service these children receive. It is imperative, therefore, that school personnel provide the best possible programs for these students. It is to teachers, future teachers, and other professionals who are entrusted with the challenge of creating and implementing educational services for the emotionally disturbed that we address this book. Our overriding purpose in writing this text was to provide a framework from which effective educational programs can be established.

The order in which the topics are presented reflects a logical sequence in the process of devising and carrying out educational programs. In Part I we present the theoretical foundations. The behavioral (Chapter 1), the psychoeducational (Chapter 2), and the ecological (Chapter 3) approaches are discussed. Part II, written from the behavioral and psychoeducational perspectives, addresses two key issues — the management of behavior and the measurement of behavior change. The two chapters in Part III are concerned with the development of appropriate curriculum. Again, the behavioral model (Chapter 6) and the psychoeducational model (Chapter 7) are used as frameworks for describing curriculum interventions. In Part IV we look at applied strategies. The use of social learning principles and developmental therapy are discussed in Chapters 8 and 9. The book closes with a chapter on working with parents of emotionally disturbed children and youth.

When we first considered undertaking a project of this magnitude, we knew that if we were to present a clear and up-to-date analysis of the theories, issues, and practices, it would be necessary to involve the leading individuals in our field. We established a procedure through which the first author of each chapter could share his or her work with colleagues who represented the same theoretical position. The goal of this exchange of ideas was to insure accuracy and clarity of material. After the author team was formed and all chapters drafted, the manuscript was submitted to colleagues outside the author team. We wish to express our appreciation to Wesley Brown, East Tennessee State; Albert Fink, Indiana University; and Luanna Voeltz, University of Minnesota for their significant help on all chapters. Also we thank Victor L. Baldwin, Teaching Research; Herbert S. Boyd, University of South Florida; Lyndal M. Bullock, North Texas State University; Stanley A. Fagen, Montgomery County Public Schools; Patricia A. Gallagher, The University of Kansas Medical Center; Judith K. Grosenick, University of Missouri, Columbus; Charles Heuchert, University of Virginia; and William C. Rhodes, University of Michigan for reading and commenting on selected chapters. We believe that these efforts have resulted in a text that will be quite useful to all concerned with the education of emotionally disturbed children and youth.

We would like to recognize the assistance of Melissa Russell, Charlie Lakin, Patricia Silverstein, Meave Stevens, Nora Ryan, Michael Moffett, and John Porec during the initial phases of this project. A special note of thanks must go to Ellen Klein for continuing input and assistance in the editorial process. We also would like to thank DeeAnn Quintana of the Department of Special Education, University of New Mexico for her assistance throughout the preparation of the manuscript. Lastly, we wish to express our appreciation to Sue Warne at Little, Brown for her efforts throughout the book production process.

R.L.M.
G.W.A.
F.H.W.

Brief Contents

Contents

ix

Teaching Emotionally
Disturbed Children

Prologue

Richard L. McDowell
University of New Mexico

Recorded history is replete with examples of human behavior that was perceived as being different from an expected norm. Behavior of this sort has been described as atypical, abnormal, and deviant. The people who exhibited these behaviors have sometimes been treated with kindness, as in ancient Greece, and sometimes with great cruelty, as in the Middle Ages. With the exception of ancient Greece, history records only a few instances of persons concerned with the humane treatment of the emotionally disturbed. Two of the better known were the Frenchman Philippe Pinel during the latter half of the eighteenth century and Dorothea Dix in the United States during the middle of the nineteenth century. Pinel removed the chains of asylum patients and worked for more humane treatment. Dix worked for the overall improvement of conditions for the mentally ill. Unfortunately, for almost all of recorded history, the emotionally disturbed have been treated harshly. Historical accounts of the care and treatment of emotionally disturbed children indicate that they were treated very cruelly (Despert, 1965; Lewis, 1974; Kauffman, 1977; Newcomer, 1980).

Treatment has always reflected the perceived cause of the disturbed behavior. Until the nineteenth century, the most frequent explanation of the cause was possession by devils or demons. No distinctions were made between children and adults. Treatment for possession by demons involved removing the demon and freeing the person's soul with methods ranging from confession to whippings, dunking, and burning at the stake. In many instances the victim did not survive the treatment.

By the early nineteenth century, demon possession as an explanation of cause had given way to the notion that mental disorders were the result of masturbation (Rie, 1971; Kauffman, 1977). This interpretation of causality led to the use of cruel and drastic methods to discourage masturbation, including castration. Fortunately, some people questioned these practices and promoted the idea that humane and nonpunitive care should be the goal of treatment. Although only applied to adults at first, this philosophy eventually influenced the care and treatment of emotionally disturbed children. Schools were established in institutions or asylums. Education was perceived as a positive factor contributing to good mental health. In the later 1800s, professionals began to seriously study mental disorders in children.

Although we continue to profess humane treatment, our methods still reflect our notion of cause. The emotionally disturbed patient has continued to be the beneficiary (or victim) of theories involving such treatments as lobotomies, hydrotherapy, insulin shock therapy, and electro-convulsive shock therapy. A recent treatment currently widely practiced is the use of various drugs — primarily tranquilizers — to change or control behavior. In addition, a variety of talk therapies and behavioral therapies have been developed and enjoy wide use today. Almost all of our major advances in treatment have been made since 1900, and even today it is rather frightening to realize how primitive an art it is.

DEFINITION

Emotionally disturbed children may exhibit a multitude of deviant behaviors. Some children are overly aggressive, others are withdrawn. Whatever the behavior, it tends to create discomfort in the people around them, particularly adults. Emotionally disturbed children tend to have difficulty getting along with others. They often exhibit behavior that does not match the situation they find themselves in. The problem appears to be multifaceted. It may involve (1) the inability to identify quickly and correctly the environmental expectations being placed on the child; (2) not knowing what behaviors are appropriate to respond successfully to a situation and to people's expectations; (3) a timing problem in which the child's response is delayed to the extent that when it is given the situation has changed to the degree that the response is no longer appropriate; (4) knowing the appropriate response to an expectation, but deliberately choosing an inappropriate response to elicit a desired positive or negative response from the environment; and (5) having learned or been taught an inappropriate response to a given situation. Regardless of how the disturbed behavior manifests itself, it reflects the stress felt by the emotionally disturbed child, which is generally felt by everyone around him or her.

Correctly identifying the children who would best be served by programs designed for the emotionally disturbed child is a major problem. It goes beyond the technology of measurement. The decision to place a child in a special program is based on such factors as judicial rulings pertaining to the rights of children and their parents, personal judgments made by professionals and parents regarding the child's behavior, and the child's performance (or lack of performance) on assigned tasks.

The rights of children are defined by legislation and judicial rulings. All handicapped children, including the emotionally disturbed child, stand to benefit from two major laws, the Vocational Rehabilitation Act of 1973 (PL 93-112) and the Education for All Handicapped Children Act of 1975 (PL 94-142). Section 504 of the Vocational Rehabilitation Act states that public facilities and services must be available to the handicapped. The Education for All Handicapped Children Act states that an education based on individual needs must be provided for all handicapped children. Since the law states that we must provide an appropriate education, it is crucial that we do all we can to correctly identify and diagnose the emotionally disturbed child.

The teacher responsible for teaching a group of children has little difficulty identifying the child with emotional problems. Most of us are sensitive to those around us and can recognize the source of any discomfort we feel. This ability is generally based on subjective judgments of the child's behavior relative to the behavior we expect and the behavior of the other children in the group.

Any perception you might have of a child's behavior should be understood in the context of the situation in which it occurs and the community or environment from which the child comes. The expectations of the teacher, along with the personal values of the teacher which determine or influence those expectations, may be in conflict with those in the child's environment. We must consider what the accepted behavior variance is for a specific behavior in a given situation. Karl Menninger, in his book *The Vital Balance* (1963), discusses the concept that behavior may be perceived as a continuum between two extremes. Acceptable behavior is viewed, not as a fixed point somewhere between the two extremes, but as a range of behavior falling within the two extremes. The limits of this accepted range are determined primarily by situational, cultural, and environmental factors. As long as a person's behavior remains within these limits, the behavior is considered acceptable. Only when the behavior becomes fixed or exceeds the accepted limits is it viewed as deviant. If we are to accept this view of behavior variance and use it to identify deviant behavior, there are four factors we should consider before labeling a behavior as deviant. First, what kind of behavior is being considered deviant? Second, to what degree is the behavior considered deviant, that is, to what extent does the behavior exceed the accepted limits? Third, in what situation does the deviation occur? Under what conditions does the deviation appear? Fourth, which person concludes that a deviation actually exists? These considerations do not necessarily identify a child as emotionally disturbed, nor do they allow us to label the child as such. However, they do provide us with a framework within which we can assess individual behavior. This framework is important because observation is the primary diagnostic tool for identifying emotional disturbance.

No definition of emotional disturbance is universally accepted. The definition included in PL 94-142 is as close as we come. Since it is a federal law, it effectively supersedes other definitions that occur in state regulations. Its power, however, is limited to those agencies receiving federal funds. Clinical facilities which operate independently from the public schools need not adhere to that definition.

Before presenting specific definitions, I would like to mention some general characteristics of definitions. First, a definition should help to identify the population with which it is concerned. Second, a definition should help us determine the prevalence of the disorder. Third, a definition should provide us with clues for designing intervention strategies. Fourth, a definition should help us to establish the need for services through child counts, which may guide the development of legislation providing the necessary resources, including financial assistance, for program development and maintenance as well as teacher training.

It is not possible here to present a single definition and suggest that it is sufficient for all the purposes of this text. Three definitions will be presented to illustrate the similarities found in most definitions presently being used. The first, the definition for the seriously emotionally disturbed, is included in the regulations for PL 94-142. This definition was developed by Bower (1960). He stated that to be considered emotionally disturbed, a child must exhibit one or more of the following characteristics, either to a marked extent or over a period of time:

1. An inability to learn which cannot be explained by intellectual, sensory, or health factors . . .
2. An inability to build or maintain satisfactory interpersonal relationships with peers and teachers . . .
3. Inappropriate types of behavior or feelings under normal conditions . . .
4. A general, pervasive mood of unhappiness or depression . . .
5. A tendency to develop physical symptoms, pains or fears associated with personal or school problems. *(pp. 9–10)*

The second definition, by McDowell (1975), stressed the situational aspect of disturbed behavior.

> The behaviorally disordered child is defined as a child whose behavior within the educational situation may be discordant in his relationships with others and/or whose academic achievement may be impaired due to an inability to learn utilizing the presented teaching techniques. The child's current behavior manifests either an extreme or a persistent failure to adapt and function intellectually, emotionally, or socially at a level commensurate with his or her chronological age. *(p. 2)*

The third definition, by Kauffman (1977), recognized not only the level of severity, but also the implications for educational programming.

Children with behavior disorders are those who chronically and markedly respond to their environment in socially unacceptable and/or personally unsatisfying ways but who can be taught more socially acceptable and personally gratifying behavior. Children with mild and moderate behavior disorders can be taught effectively with their normal peers (if their teachers receive appropriate consultative help) or in special resource or self-contained classes with reasonable hope of quick reintegration with their normal peers. Children with severe and profound behavior disorders require intensive and prolonged intervention and must be taught at home or in special classes, special schools, or residential institutions. *(p. 23)*

The similarities between these definitions, as well as others (by Pate, 1963; Graubard, 1973; Ross, 1974; Hewett, 1980; Newcomer, 1980) become quite clear once you cut through their semantic differences. The similarities involve two major points: (1) the inability to establish appropriate satisfactory relationships with others; and (2) the demonstration of behavior which either fails to meet or exceeds the expectations of those with whom the person comes in contact. These two points, along with the concept of behavior variance, can be used to begin formulating a working definition of emotional disturbance. It is unlikely that a universally acceptable definition of emotional disturbance will be developed soon. Educators may as a result have to use the above considerations to identify and define the population they intend to work with.

PREVALENCE

Estimates of the number of emotionally disturbed children vary, depending on where they were made. Reliable figures simply do not exist. Now that PL 94-142 has specified a definition in its regulations, more accurate data may be forthcoming. Existing studies reflect the use of multiple definitions to describe the children being counted. When a variety of definitions are used by different investigators in the identification process, children identified by one investigator may not be identified by another. As a result of this inconsistency, some eligible children may not be identified by some researchers.

One method that we use to determine numbers is to review programs serving emotionally disturbed children and record the number of children presently receiving help. The major weakness of this approach is that those who are disturbed but do not have contact with a service are not counted. A second method is to survey a sample population for emotional disorders, use inferential statistics to analyze the data, and then generalize the findings to the larger population. At present this method provides us with most of our data on the prevalence of emotional disturbance. However, this method has also introduced some inconsistencies in the figures. Studies have reported prevalence figures ranging from .05 to 15 percent (Schultz et al.,

1971). The most widely used figure is an estimate made by the U.S. Office of Education (1979), which estimated that 2 percent of the school-aged population is emotionally disturbed at a level severe enough to require some type of special service.

Several studies indicate that the 2 percent figure is not evenly distributed within the school-aged population but varies according to age, sex, and socioeconomic levels. Graubard (1973) reported that the lower socioeconomic groups produce more aggressive, acting-out children than would be expected. Studies by Peterson (1961), Quay (1972) and Schultz et al. (1974) indicate that boys act out more than girls. Kauffman (1977) states that as children grow older, boys continue to demonstrate acting-out behavior, while girls tend to exhibit personality and neurotic problems. A study by Miller et al. (1971) reports that boys outnumber girls three to one in programs for the emotionally disturbed. There are a number of possible explanations for this uneven distribution. I would suggest, for example, that in our society some boys are taught to be active and aggressive, but in some circumstances this behavior is considered inappropriate and deviant. These boys are behaving as they were taught, but the expectations for their behavior in a particular situation call for a different behavior. The discrepancy between the behavior and the expectation identifies the child as being different. It will be interesting to see if research continues to support this ratio as the women's rights movement continues to exert an influence.

CLASSIFICATION

Throughout history man has felt a need to order or classify the things around him. Every area of science has its division concerned with classifying relevant phenomena; the study of human behavior is no exception. Basic to any training program in clinical psychology is a course in abnormal psychology, in which the various types of deviant behavior are described and compared. The ability to classify deviant behavior clarifies the characteristics of the behavior, which should facilitate its diagnosis and treatment. Classification also helps professionals communicate effectively.

DSM-III

The primary classification system used by mental health professionals today is known as the Diagnostic and Statistical Manual of Mental Disorders prepared by the American Psychiatric Association. This system was established with the publication in 1952 of DSM-I, which contained descriptions of the identified diagnostic categories. DSM-II, a revision made to bring the system into agreement with the International Classification of Diseases (1968), was made in 1968. Unlike DSM-I, DSM-II included a specific category pertaining to children and youth. This category was labeled "Behavior Disorders of Childhood and Adolescence." It consisted of seven subcategories: (1) hyperkinetic reaction, (2) withdrawing reaction, (3) overanxious reaction, (4) runaway reaction, (5) unsocialized aggressive reaction, (6) group delinquent reaction, and (7) other reactions. The strength of this category was that the labels reflected the use of behavior descriptions, rather than the use of terms representing a particular philosophical position.

In 1979, a new and heavily revised classification scheme, DSM-III, was released; the official manual was published in 1980. DSM-III goes beyond preceding editions by specifying more precise criteria for clinical judgment. It contains a vast and detailed network of categories of psychological disturbance. Whereas DSM-I had 60 and DSM-II had 145, DSM-III has 230 separate categories. Unlike earlier classification manuals, which emphasized interpreting clinical problems or speculating on their causes, DSM-III focused on naming the disorders and describing them as clearly as possible. Because of the more precise language in the classification system, the increased coverage of the manual itself, and the use of more examples of various problems, DSM-III represents an advance in clinical classification.

A second important change in DSM-III over previous editions is that it requires much more information about the person being diagnosed. DSM-III instructs the diagnostician to evaluate the person on five different axes or areas of functioning (see Table 1). This multiaxial classification system means that instead of simply placing a person in one category, each case is evaluated in terms of a number of important factors. Axis 1 describes abnormal behavior patterns such as anxiety or depression. Axis 2 covers two areas: personality disorders in adults or specific developmental disorders in children and adolescents. Axis 3 refers to any medical or physical disorders that may be relevant to the psychological problem. Axis 4 assesses psychosocial factors such as divorce that may have been causing the person stress. Examples for both adults and children are included. Axis 5 is the highest level of adaptive functioning attained by the person during the previous year. A rating of the person's adjustment in such areas as occupation or social relationships is used.

Axes 4 and 5 are especially significant. Knowing what demands the person has been trying to meet is necessary to understand the problem behavior that has developed. Moreover, knowing the person's general level of success in meeting the demands of adjustment can help in formulating an appropriate, realistic treatment plan.

The DSM classification system is fairly standard in this country, but DSM-III does not have unanimous professional support. Some object to the whole notion of defining anyone's behavior as abnormal, or to assigning diagnostic labels. DSM-III has also evoked criticism (Garmezy, 1978) because it classifies many problems in childhood behavior as mental disorders. The whole system of classification also implies acceptance of the medical model for explaining abnormal behavior, which states that, like physical diseases, emotional disorders have their underlying causes, etiology, and resultant

TABLE 1
DSM-III CLASSIFICATION: AXES I AND II
CATEGORIES AND CODES

All official DSM-III codes and terms are included in ICD-9-CM. However, in order to differentiate those DSM-III categories that use the same ICD-9-CM codes, unofficial non-ICD-9-CM codes are provided in parentheses for use when greater specificity is necessary. The long dashes indicate the need for a fifth-digit subtype or other qualifying term.

Disorders Usually First Evident in Infancy, Childhood, or Adolescence

Mental retardation
(Code in fifth digit: 1 = with other behavioral symptoms [requiring attention or
treatment and that are not part of another
disorder], 0 = without other behavioral
symptoms.)
317.0(x)   Mild mental retardation, _____
318.0(x)   Moderate mental retardation,

_____
318.1(x)   Severe mental retardation,

_____
318.2(x)   Profound mental retardation,

_____
319.0(x)   Unspecified mental retardation,

_____

Attention deficit disorder
314.01   With hyperactivity
314.00   Without hyperactivity
314.80   Residual type

Conduct disorder
312.00   Undersocialized, aggressive
312.10   Undersocialized, nonaggressive
312.23   Socialized, aggressive
312.21   Socialized, nonaggressive
312.90   Atypical

*Anxiety disorders of childhood or
adolescence*
309.21   Separation anxiety disorder
313.21   Avoidant disorder of childhood
or adolescence
313.00   Overanxious disorder

*Other disorders of infancy, childhood,
or adolescence*
313.89   Reactive attachment disorder
of infancy
313.22   Schizoid disorder of childhood
or adolescence
313.23   Elective mutism
313.81   Oppositional disorder
313.82   Identity disorder

Eating disorders
307.10   Anorexia nervosa
307.51   Bulimia
307.52   Pica
307.53   Rumination disorder of infancy
307.50   Atypical eating disorder

Stereotyped movement disorders
307.21   Transient tic disorder
307.22   Chronic motor tic disorder
307.23   Tourette's disorder
307.20   Atypical tic disorder
307.30   Atypical stereotyped movement
disorder

*Other disorders with physical
manifestations*
307.00   Stuttering
307.60   Functional enuresis
307.70   Functional encopresis
307.46   Sleepwalking disorder
307.46   Sleep terror disorder (307.49)

Pervasive developmental disorders
Code in fifth digit: 0 = full syndrome
present, 1 = residual state.
299.0x   Infantile autism, _____
299.9x   Childhood onset pervasive
developmental disorder, _____
299.8x   Atypical, _____

Specific developmental disorders
Note: These are coded on Axis II.
315.00   Developmental reading disorder
315.10   Developmental arithmetic
disorder
315.31   Developmental language disorder
315.39   Developmental articulation
disorder
315.50   Mixed specific developmental
disorder
315.90   Atypical specific developmental
disorder

Source: Diagnostic and Statistical Manual of Mental Disorders (3rd ed.). Washington, D.C.: American Psychiatric Association, 1980, p. 15. Used by permission.

observable symptoms. Another major concern is that DSM-III uses the same multiaxial framework for both adults and children. The only category that refers specifically to disorders in children is the one labeled "Disorders Usually First Evident in Infancy, Childhood, or Adolescence." In actual practice, adults may be classified under categories listed for children, and children may be listed under categories for adults. DSM-III appears to be extremely limited with regard to what role developmental factors play in the disorders of children.

Factor Analytic Approach

Erickson (1978) describes a factor analytic approach to the classification of deviant behavior. Such an approach is based upon the collection of data pertaining to the characteristics of the population being studied. These data are treated by factor analytic methods to determine the correlations between characteristics. This process identifies those characteristics which seem to represent certain groups or disorders. Quay (1964) used this technique to identify certain types or dimensions of delinquency. Following this approach conceptually, Kauffman (1977) has listed four categories of disturbed behavior which he believes will have more meaning to educators. Those four categories are (1) hyperactivity, distractibility, and impulsivity; (2) aggression; (3) withdrawal, immaturity, and inadequacy; and (4) deficiencies in moral development.

Any form of classification should focus upon the disorder rather than the child. Its primary uses are to communicate information between professionals and to guide us in our efforts to develop appropriate intervention strategies.

ROLE OF EDUCATION

When you consider the various environments that children spend their time in, school stands out as a major influence upon the child's life. Whether children succeed or fail in school has a continuing effect upon how they perceive themselves and their ability to function on various tasks. Generally, our society equates school failure with being a failure in adult life. Glasser (1969), in his book *Schools Without Failure,* addressed the issue of the possible effects of school failure on personal life. Based upon his personal experience working with black children in the public schools in the Watts district of Los Angeles, Glasser developed a system to help children avoid failure situations. A primary goal of this program is to help children feel worthwhile to themselves and others. The school is definitely in a position to help children feel good about themselves. If appropriate, the very nature of the learning experience is to help the child acquire a new skill. The ability to demonstrate a newly acquired competency brings feelings of accomplishment. Appropriately designed school programs can emphasize the success aspects of learning and provide experiences that help the child gain feelings of self-worth.

School programs for the emotionally disturbed have three primary goals. The first is to teach the child relevant academic skills. The second is to teach children appropriate social skills to facilitate their interactions with others. A third purpose is to arrange experiences from which the child can gain feelings of self-worth. I am sure you can see how these goals are interrelated. All programs strive to accomplish these goals to varying degrees. The relative emphases of these goals depend largely upon the philosophical basis of the program. The philosophical stance may also determine the order in which they are to be accomplished. Regardless of program philosophy, the result should be children with reasonable academic skills who are able to demonstrate appropriate self-control and who feel good about themselves.

For children to be successful, their assets and deficits must be identified, reasonable goals must be established, and appropriate curricular materials and intervention strategies must be selected. The teacher enhances these components by reinforcing the child's efforts. Children gain positive feelings towards themselves through accomplishing meaningful tasks.

Educational programs for emotionally disturbed children are relatively new. Although some educational programs in institutions existed previously, valid attempts to provide assistance in the public schools did not occur until 1918, when compulsory education laws were enacted in all states. By 1930, sixteen states had passed legislation that allowed school districts to receive additional financial assistance to support the education of handicapped children (Kauffman, 1977). For the most part, however, the disturbed child was excluded from these programs. By the mid 1940s, a few concerted efforts were being made to design therapeutic programs for the emotionally disturbed. In 1944, Dr. Bruno Bettelheim began his work at the Sonja Shankman Orthogenic School at the University of Chicago. Bettelheim used the concept of the "therapeutic milieu" in conjunction with psychoanalytic theory to develop educational methods to use with severely disturbed children.

In 1946, Dr. Fritz Redl and Dr. David Wineman established Pioneer House in Detroit to demonstrate the hygienic management of delinquent children. They extended the concept of the therapeutic milieu and laid the foundations for the management and treatment technique known as "life space interviewing." In the same year, the New York City Board of Education established the "600" schools to serve emotionally disturbed and delinquent children. These schools were an alternative to excluding children from school and represented one of the first public school programs designed specifically for the emotionally disturbed child.

Dr. Carl Fenichel established the League School in Brooklyn, New

York, in 1953. It was the first private day school for the severely emotionally disturbed in the United States. In the same year, the American Orthopsychiatric Association conducted a symposium entitled "The Education of Emotionally Disturbed Children." From this symposium evolved the rationale for including education as an integral part of the treatment process for emotionally disturbed children.

Dr. Nicholas Hobbs was instrumental in establishing the Project Reeducation Schools in 1961. The Re-ED Schools reflected an ecological approach to the treatment of disturbed children. They emphasized changing the child's total environment, rather than just changing the child. In 1962, Dr. Norris Haring and Dr. E. Lakin Phillips published the results of their research, creating a classroom intervention model which became known as the "structured approach." This research, referred to as the Arlington Study, was one of the first pieces of research to test the efficacy of a specific classroom intervention model. The structured approach, which incorporated behavioral theory, was based upon the work of Strauss and Lehtinen (1947) and Cruickshank et al. (1961) in the control of environmental stimuli. The program design and operating procedures described by Haring and Phillips (1962) served as a model for the establishment of many public school programs for the emotionally disturbed throughout the United States.

In 1964, the Council for Children with Behavioral Disorders became a division of the Council for Exceptional Children. It remains the primary advocacy organization promoting the treatment of emotionally disturbed children.

Dr. Frank Hewett published the results of the Santa Monica project in 1968. The program design for this project became known as the "engineered classroom." It was based upon behavioral theory and emphasized the importance of environmental design, special curriculum, token reinforcement, and a hierarchy of educational tasks.

If the time prior to the 1970s saw much program development, the time since then has seen much application. Fewer major new advancements were made in the 1970s. Dr. William Rhodes and Dr. Michael Tracy conducted the "Conceptual Project in Emotional Disturbance" during the first half of the decade. This project brought together in published form a summary of theory, research, and intervention in the field. The other major event of the 1970s was the passage of Public Law 94-142, The Education for All Handicapped Children Act, in 1975. This law mandated an appropriate education for all handicapped children, including the seriously emotionally disturbed. The other notable events of the 1970s concerned application. The implementation of the concept of the "least restrictive environment" as supported by PL 94-142 opened the door to additional public school programs and other classroom models for the seriously emotionally disturbed. Much work was done to validate a number of behavioral techniques in the classroom. Applied behavior analysis became an integral part of many classroom programs. PL 94-142, requiring an Individual Education Plan, made parents members of the educational team. Parent involvement and parent training programs became commonplace.

Many of the trends and issues of the 1970s have been carried into the 1980s. Issues pertaining to labeling and definitions continue to be forum topics. Trends such as the evolution of alternative program models also continue to come to our attention. These issues and trends remind us that the field is still in its infancy.

PURPOSE

The purpose of this text is to present the major theories and educational intervention strategies in use today. These strategies have been developed to assist the emotionally disturbed child in the classroom. The term *emotionally disturbed* will be used to refer to these children throughout the text. The term will be assumed to subsume labels such as emotionally handicapped, emotionally impaired, emotionally maladjusted, behaviorally disordered, and behaviorally handicapped. In recent years, the term *behaviorally disordered* has become more popular due to the negative connotations fairly or unfairly associated with the term emotionally disturbed. However, PL 94-142 has identified this population as seriously emotionally disturbed.

The remainder of the text is divided into four sections. Part I presents the theory and research relevant to the behavioral model, the psychoeducational model, and the ecological model. Part II presents techniques for managing behavior and measuring behavior change from both the behavioral perspective and the psychoeducational perspective. Part III presents the curriculum considerations that would be made from the behavioral and psychoeducational perspectives. Part IV concerns new applications of theory to classroom intervention. These applications are social learning theory, developmental therapy, and parent involvement.

Part I

THEORETICAL FOUNDATIONS

Attempts to understand and explain human behavior have resulted in the development of many divergent theories. The originators of these theories were concerned with both the developmental sequence of behavior acquisition and the etiology of deviant behavior. Theories, which cover developmental concepts as well as causal factors, provide a basis for planning intervention or corrective strategies. The vast majority of educational programs for emotionally disturbed children and youth are variations of either psychodynamic theory or behavioral theory.

In Chapter 1, Cullinan, Epstein, and Kauffman present the precepts of behavioral theory as influenced by the principles of operant conditioning. They emphasize arranging environmental consequences to influence behavior and using data collection to monitor its effects. Disturbed or disordered behavior is viewed as the result of faulty learning. It is believed that more effective or efficient behaviors can be taught by systematically applying consequences.

In Chapter 2, Rezmeirski, Knoblock, and Bloom address the theoretical bases of the psychoeducational model. This model interprets behavior in relation to its internal and external dynamics, and states that important contributions can be made to the child's mental health outside the therapy hour. The theory emphasizes helping children correct their perceptions of situations and recognize the contributing role they may have played. Another important aspect is helping disturbed children recognize and deal with their feelings effectively. The reader is cautioned that familiar names commonly associated with this approach may not be found in the discussion of theory. Many of the people identified with the psychoeducational approach identify themselves as practitioners rather than theorists.

Chapter 3, by Swap, Prieto, and Harth, discusses the ecological approach. This approach had its origin in the psychoeducational approach. It stresses that emotional disturbance is not necessarily something within the child; it may result from the interface between the child and his environment. The resulting strategies emphasize working with both the child and his or her environment to effect change. The ecological approach represents an evolving alternative to both the behavioral and psychoeducational approaches.

Chapter 1

The Behavioral Model and Children's Behavior Disorders: Foundations and Evaluations

Douglas Cullinan
Northern Illinois University

Michael H. Epstein
Northern Illinois University

James M. Kauffman
University of Virginia

Human development, functioning, and deviance are open to diverse interpretations, each emphasizing selected phenomena over others. The behavioral model concentrates on the interaction of specific behaviors and specific aspects of the immediate environment, especially with respect to how each changes the other across time. Intervention efforts are directed toward particular environmental factors which frequently can be changed to improve the individual's functioning. Through its highly practical emphasis on changing the environment so that deviant behavior will be modified, the behavioral model has, in the past two decades, revolutionized the helping professions — education, school counseling, psychotherapy, social casework, psychiatric nursing, medicine, and numerous other professions and arenas for intervention. The model has widespread and growing applicability in special education, in part because behavioral interventions are readily usable by teachers and paraprofessionals. The behavioral model has pervasively influenced professional training programs for teachers of pupils with behavior disorders (Fink, Glass, and Guskin, 1975). The goals of this chapter are to describe the behavioral model for understanding and intervening with behavior disorders of children and to indicate how evaluations of behavioral interventions can benefit the continuing effort to improve education for pupils with behavior disorders.

THE BEHAVIORAL MODEL AND BEHAVIOR DISORDERS

The behavioral model currently encompasses a variety of positions about the nature of behavior, methods of intervention, and strategies for experimental evaluation of intervention efforts. Respondent conditioning, operant conditioning, social learning theory, behavioral approaches to self-control, cognitive behavior modification, and several other theories, positions, and topical areas should be included in the behavioral model. There is a certain amount of disagreement and controversy among these viewpoints, but it is still possible to specify certain points of commonality among them which can help to define the behavioral model. Two of its most salient basic assumptions are (1) its view that human behavior, including deviant behavior, is acquired and regulated by certain experimentally determined learning principles, and (2) its commitment to scientific methods of investigating behavior and behavior change.

Respondent Conditioning

Respondents are behavior patterns, especially those involving the autonomic nervous system and the glands and muscles which it controls, that are almost invariably produced by certain environmental events (*unconditioned stimuli*). Unconditioned stimuli are said to *elicit* respondents. For example, bright light can elicit contraction of the pupils; food on the tongue can elicit salivation; noxious sensations arising from intense environmental events (such as loud sounds or physical blows) can elicit respiratory, circulatory, hormonal, skeletal-muscular, and other organismic respondents corresponding to a perceived state of arousal.

Some respondents are subject to learning in that previously neutral events can come to elicit them. This occurs when the neutral event is present as the unconditioned stimulus elicits the respondent; subsequently, the formerly neutral event can elicit the respondent in the absence of the unconditioned stimulus (the neutral event has become a *conditioned stimulus*). For example, neutral events associated with unconditioned stimuli for "arousal" respondents can become capable of eliciting the arousal states even in the absence of the unconditioned stimuli, as has been illustrated repeatedly with animals and occasionally with humans. In a famous case report, Watson and Rayner (1920) described how fearful emotional responses could be established through respondent conditioning. An eleven-month-old child originally played freely with a white rat. Then a loud, startling noise was presented when the child attempted to play with the animal; this pairing of an unconditioned stimulus (noise) for emotional respondents together with a neutral stimulus (white rat) took place only a few times over several days. Subsequently, the mere presence of the animal elicited emotional respondents similar to those produced by the noise. Additionally, other stimuli similar to the white rat could produce the fearful reaction, indicating stimulus generalization of the fear. Incidentally, informative as the Watson and Rayner (1920) demonstration may be, current ethical and legal constraints would almost certainly preclude replications of such a study.

Respondent Conditioning and Behavior Disorders.   The application of respondent conditioning to the understanding and treatment of emotional disturbances was pioneered by Eysenck (1960), Salter (1949), Wolpe (1958), and others. All were influenced to some extent by Pavlov's work on respondent conditioning (1927). In general, the respondent conditioning viewpoint holds that various unconditioned or conditioned stimuli elicit observable and covert respondents, especially those associated with autonomic arousal corresponding to the experience of anxiety. When such anxiety is experienced, the person behaves in ways that either avoid the anxiety-provoking stimulus or otherwise function to temporarily reduce autonomic arousal. If such behavior is disturbing to the person or to others around him, it is designated "neurotic."

Operant Conditioning

Most important human behaviors are not automatically elicited, as in respondent conditioning; they are *emitted* by the individual in response to circumstances. The likelihood that these behaviors (called *operants*) will be emitted again under similar circumstances is largely controlled by the effect they have on the environment. Principles of operant conditioning describe this kind of interaction between behavior and environment.

Operants are behaviors that can be controlled by environmental events which follow them (*consequences*). A consequence may either strengthen (increase the future likelihood of) or weaken (decrease the future likelihood of) the operant that it follows. The vast majority of human behaviors are operants. It has recently become clear that even some respondents are also operants: For example, heart rate, blood pressure, and other responses elicited by unconditioned stimuli can also be modified by consequences. Certainly, the vast majority of responses that teachers of children with behavior disorders wish to change are operants; that is, responses regulated by consequent environmental events.

Principles of Operant Conditioning.   Operant conditioning involves principles that describe the relationship between operants and specific environmental events that affect the operants. These principles are surprisingly few in number, especially in view of the fact that they are based on and verified by an incredibly large body of basic and applied research. Because most professional educators are at least slightly familiar with operant conditioning, only a brief, nontechnical description of principles of operant conditioning will be presented here. (For details see Ferster, Culbertson, and Boren, 1975; Reynolds, 1968.)

Consequences.   Most of the principles of operant conditioning are concerned with consequences. A consequence is a change in the environment after an operant occurs. For a consequence to strengthen or weaken the operant behavior it follows, it must be either *dependent* or *contingent* upon the occurrence of that behavior. When a behavior invariably produces a change in the environment (as pushing a swinging door will cause it to open), the consequence is dependent upon the behavior. Many behaviors, of course, do not invariably produce a consequence; when environmental changes follow these operants, a contingency is said to exist. Noncontingent consequences, that is, consequences occurring independent of a person's response, do not ordinarily affect behavior. Contingent consequences — those occurring only after a particular response is performed — are capable of altering behavior.

Reinforcement.   Reinforcement is the process whereby a behavior becomes more likely to occur in the future as a function of its currently resulting in contingent consequences. Contingent consequences which strengthen behavior are termed *reinforcers*. It should be emphasized that the defining characteristics of reinforcement include (1) a contingency between a response and its consequences, and (2) a strengthening of the response; reinforcers are not necessarily perceived as subjectively pleasant, and pleasant environmental events do not invariably reinforce behavior.

   Two variations of reinforcement are positive reinforcement and negative reinforcement. In positive reinforcement, the consequence for a strengthened behavior involves the addition of something (a "positive reinforcer") to the environment. In negative reinforcement, the consequence for a strengthened behavior involves the removal of something (a "negative reinforcer") from the environment.

Response Classes.   Careful observation of most human responses would reveal that the physical aspects of a response are virtually never identical from occurrence to occurrence. There are innumerable different ways for a student to raise his or her hand, for instance. Reinforcement for a particular instance of hand-raising is likely to strengthen some other ways of raising one's hand as well. The various ways of raising one's hand would constitute a *functional response class*. A functional response class includes all behaviors that produce the same change in the environment; reinforcement of a particular behavior can strengthen similar behaviors, a phenomenon known as *response generalization*. The other behaviors may be slight physical variations of the reinforced response, or they may be physically dissimilar, having in common only that they achieve the same effect on the environment.

Schedules.   A schedule specifies the details of the relationship between a response and its consequences. Schedules of reinforcement have been studied in detail (Ferster and Skinner, 1957) and are of great importance in determining how consequences affect operants. Well-controlled laboratory research has consistently shown that investigators can predict and control response changes quite consistently by imposing different reinforcement schedules. In applied settings, however, most reinforcement schedules are difficult to impose on behavior. From the point of view of the behaver, two broad categories of schedule are discernible: predictable reinforcement and unpredictable reinforcement. Reinforcement for every occurrence of a particular response (continuous schedule), every nth occurrence of a particular response (fixed ratio schedule), the first occurrence of the response after a known period of time (fixed interval schedule), and no reinforcement for any instance of the response (extinction schedule) are contingencies that usually can be readily discerned by behavers. On the other hand, people are unable to predict which instance of a reinforceable behavior will actually be reinforced if a variable number of appropriate responses must occur before reinforcement (variable ratio schedule) or if variable intervals of time must elapse before an appropriate response is reinforced (variable interval schedule).

Reinforcement schedules can be important in determining how durable behavior changes will be after an intervention is withdrawn. For example, if reinforcement for appropriate responses has occurred on an unpredictable basis before intervention is terminated, the person is less likely to determine that new conditions are in effect. Other features of an intervention program, such as making certain that, following withdrawal of formal intervention, behavior changes can be maintained by reinforcement naturally available in the environment, can be even more important in efforts to promote durable behavior changes.

Punishment.   Operant conditioning principles also describe procedures for weakening behavior. Punishment is the process wherein a particular response is followed by a consequence and subsequently is less likely to occur. Like reinforcement, punishment is defined by the effect of a contingency on the future strength of behavior. Admonitions, penalties, and chastisements do not necessarily function as punishment, and punishment of behavior is often without pain or physical coercion. In one variety of punishment, positive punishment, the consequence for a weakened behavior involves the addition of something to the environment. In negative punishment, the consequence for a weakened behavior involves the removal of something from the environment.

It is clear that human behavior can be reliably decreased through punishment, but less is known about (1) how punishment of one response produces generalized reduction of similar or related responses, (2) the production and limitation of functional response classes dependent on punishment, and (3) schedules of punishment.

One way to summarize the types of punishment and reinforcement is represented by Figure 1.1. Reinforcement and punishment processes labeled within the boxes are determined by what effect the contingency has on the post-response environment and by the future likelihood of recurrence of that response.

Extinction.   Another operant conditioning process is extinction, which takes place when a behavior that has formerly been on a reinforcement contingency is no longer reinforced. Extinction occurs if the future likelihood of behavior is decreased.

Antecedents.   Operant conditioning principles also deal with changes in the environment preceding a response, or *antecedents*. Behavior always takes place in the context of some situation, and any situation includes a large number of stimulus events. A stimulus event which reliably precedes a reinforced response becomes a signal ("discriminative stimulus") for reinforcement. Because a discriminative stimulus indicates that previously reinforced responses will probably be reinforced again, it increases the likelihood that the previously reinforced response will be emitted.

Discriminative stimuli, because they indicate that reinforcers are avail-

FIGURE 1.1
OPERANT CONDITIONING PROCESSES AS DETERMINED BY FUTURE LIKELIHOOD OF OPERANT AND CONTINGENT ENVIRONMENTAL CHANGE

	Present	Withdraw
Positive	positive reinforcement (strengthen behavior)	punishment (weaken behavior)
Negative	punishment (weaken behavior)	negative reinforcement (strengthen behavior)

able, can acquire the power to reinforce operants that produce them. Suppose that in a sequence of two responses, response 1 produces an environmental change which signals that response 2 will be reinforced, thus increasing the probability of response 2. Subsequently response 2 is performed and another environmental change occurs, this time a reinforcing consequence for response 2. Responses 1 and 2 then make up a simple "chain" of operants. Various complex human behaviors appear to be chains of many operants, all but the last of which are reinforced by the environmental changes they produce. These environmental changes are discriminative stimuli, each signaling that the next operant in the chain has become reinforceable. The last response in the chain then produces an established reinforcing consequence. Each discriminative stimulus for the next response in the chain also serves as a *conditioned reinforcer* for the prior response. Conditioned reinforcers, then, are originally neutral environmental events which acquire reinforcing properties because they indicate that some further response is reinforceable. (Analogously, neutral events can acquire punishing capability.) It is apparent that much human behavior is regulated by conditioned reinforcing or punishing stimuli.

Stimulus Generalization. Responses made more likely to occur by one antecedent may also be facilitated by other stimuli, especially those that resemble the original discriminative stimulus. Stimulus generalization refers to the development of a class of discriminative stimuli, that is, a set of antecedents which all increase the probability that a particular behavior will occur. Thus, behaviors reinforced in one situation may be performed in other appropriate situations even though reinforcers are not provided.

Discrimination. Of course, there is a limit to the number of settings in which any particular behavior is appropriate. When a behavior is not appropriate, there frequently are antecedents that can indicate that a response will not be reinforced. Such a discriminative stimulus for nonreinforcement is referred to as an S^Δ; the likelihood that a behavior will be performed is decreased in the presence of S^Δ. When an operant behavior is reliably performed in the presence of its discriminative stimulus (or stimuli) but not performed in the presence of its S^Δ (or S^Δs), the behaver has made a discrimination.

Operant Conditioning and Behavior Disorders. Various aggressive, immature, bizarre, disruptive, or other disturbing child behaviors naturally draw attention in classrooms or other social settings. Research (Walker and Buckley, 1972b) and informal observation indicate that teachers, for example, commonly give much of their attention to undesirable behavior, whereas pupils behaving productively and prosocially are often ignored. Teacher attention to deviant behavior may take a variety of forms, including reprimands, rule reminders, dialogues about the situation, physical approach or contact, and the like, all of which provide attention as a consequence for the disordered behavior. Typically, these strategies produce temporary relief from the problem; thus the teacher may mistakenly believe his or her actions to be effective. It has been clearly shown, however, that teacher attention, even disapproving attention, can strengthen and maintain the very behavior it is designed to reduce (Becker et al., 1967).

Patterson (1975) has described the development of a class of disruptive behaviors, including whining, threatening, crying, screaming, hitting, and pushing. Each member of this functional response class can coerce others to comply with the child's demands. If a teacher or other adult initially refuses a demand, the child may escalate the level of coercion, making compliance more likely. If compliance is eventually achieved, the coercive behavior is reinforced, and the child also learns that higher levels of coercion are more likely to succeed. Compliance also stops the child's undesired behavior, which teaches the teacher to give in. The coercion analysis of disturbing behavior also applies to child-child and adult-adult interactions.

Other Applications of the Behavioral Model

Social learning theory is a comprehensive approach to understanding human functioning, closely associated with the research and writing of Albert Bandura (1969, 1973, 1977a, 1977b, 1978). Although it is not primarily a model of remediation or rehabilitation, selected aspects of social learning theory have been used to improve the functioning of deviant children and adults. Chapter 8 of this volume addresses the implications of social learning theory on children's emotional disturbances. Most obviously, social learning theory details the role of modeling in a child's acquisition and performance of deviant behavior.

There are numerous other developments associated with the behavioral model for understanding and intervening with human deviance. Some of these represent variations and extensions of existing models. Some accounts of self-control, for instance, are closely related to operant conditioning, such as analysis of thoughts as covert events obeying principles of operant conditioning (Homme, 1965), or a person's manipulation of antecedents and consequences to change his own behavior (Ferster, Nurnberger, and Levitt, 1962; Kazdin, 1975; Thoresen and Mahoney, 1974). Other lines of thought, such as rational-emotive therapy (Ellis, 1962), cognitive therapy (Beck, 1976), and self-verbalization therapy (Meichenbaum, 1977) have evolved from theories, research, and clinical experiences that were originally (and to many behaviorists, remain) outside the realm of the behavioral model. In general, behaviorists remain highly skeptical of new developments — however logical, and whether offered by proponents of the behavioral model or some other — until enough scientific evidence has been obtained to justify confidence.

Behavioral View of Behavior Disorders

The behavioral position on the nature of deviance follows from its view of human behavior. Disordered behaviors are believed to be developed and regulated by the same kinds of environmental influences and principles of learning that govern nondisordered behavior — the chief difference being that the former have been labeled deviant, either informally or by persons officially designated to make such decisions. This position is reflected in behavioral definitions of children's behavior disorders. For instance, Ross (1974) stated that a behavior disorder is indicated "when a child emits behavior that deviates from a discretionary and relative social norm in that it occurs with a frequency or intensity that authoritative adults in the child's environment judge, under the circumstances, to be either too high or too low" (p. 14).

Many theories look to past events to explain how behavior disorders are caused. Most often these past events relate to the child's personal history (e.g., inherited characteristics, prenatal injuries, or early childhood experiences) or to broad cultural forces (e.g., socioeconomic status or belonging to a particular subculture). But because past personal or cultural influences are difficult to experiment with, theories that say they cause a child's behavior disorders are just guesses — thought-provoking but as yet unverified. Besides, interpretations of past behavior are not nearly as valuable to practitioners as the ability to predict and change behavior in the future. Scientific evaluations have shown applications of the behavioral model to be relatively accurate in predicting and changing behavior by altering specific aspects of the environment in which the behavior takes place. This is the chief meaning of "cause" in the behavioral model: a behavior is explained — in a very important and practical way — when environmental alterations that can predict and control that behavior are identified. Not surprisingly the majority of the behavioral literature on behavior disorders consists of scientific evaluations of procedures to change deviant behavior. The main behavioral technology for changing deviant behavior and evaluating these behavior changes is called *applied behavior analysis* (described later in this chapter).

Growth of the Behavioral Approach to Children with Behavior Disorders

When thinking about the history of behaviorism or any other theoretical model, it is important to remember that the model is merely an attempt to explain certain natural phenomena. The model itself does not represent a new way to deal with behavior, but rather a coherent and pragmatic way to explain relationships among events, an ostensible discovery of natural laws that have always operated and that may have been the basis for successful manipulation of behavior before the laws were clearly described. The laws themselves are *discovered;* their descriptions and their systematic application are *invented*. Thus, one can find in the literature of our profession, as well as in the literature of medicine and psychology, examples of the unwitting (but sometimes systematic) use of behavioral interventions long before the basic principles of behaviorism were explicated (Kauffman, 1976, 1977). "Moral therapists" of the early nineteenth century and the progenitors of special education, for example, used strategies that were probably successful because they employed behavioral principles, although those principles had not yet been described (Itard, 1962; Seguin, 1866). Systems of token reinforcement were invented long ago, although their technical description occurred only recently. Kazdin (1978) reports on a token system established in a British penal colony in 1787, and Repp (1977) notes that Seguin used tokens in the mid nineteenth century.

It is also apparent more recently that behavioral principles have been applied in the absence of relevant theoretical explanation. In the 1940s, Strauss and Lehtinen (1947) described a highly structured educational program for brain-injured children, many of whom exhibited behavior disorders. Although their program emphasized making events in the child's environment highly predictable and consistent, Strauss and Lehtinen did not appeal to learning theory as a rationale for their methods. In the late 1950s, Cruickshank et al. (1961) conducted a research project in Montgomery County, Maryland, in which the structured program of Strauss and Lehtinen was elaborated and extended to include work with hyperactive children. Part of the rationale for their methods was derived from the learning theory. Also in the late 1950s, Haring and Phillips (1962) operated a highly structured special class for emotionally disturbed children as part of a research project in Arlington, Virginia. Predictability or consistency of the child's everyday home and school environment, including the arrangement of explicit and consistent consequences for behavior, was the principal strategy recommended by Haring and Phillips. Although the arrangement of consistent consequences is, assuredly, a strategy associated with the behavioral model, Haring and Phillips did not refer to principles of operant and respondent conditioning.

In the early 1960s, however, other studies were published in which highly structured special education environments were employed with behavior principles clearly providing the theoretical backdrop. These studies followed a great deal of basic experimentation with animals in operant conditioning laboratories. They were preceded also by applied behavioral research with adults, mainly severely handicapped adults in institutional settings. In the late 1960s, Hewett (1968) described his Santa Monica Project, an experiment involving special classes for behavior disordered children which made explicit use of behavioral principles. Thus, one can see a gradual emergence of special education programs based on the behavioral model during the decade from the late 1950s to the late 1960s.

It is difficult, if not impossible, to determine just where the behavioral model was first applied with behaviorally disordered children in special education settings. Not only must one consider that the theoretical underpinnings of some early, structured programs were not clearly and explicitly behavioral, but one must also note that (1) many of the intervention agents in early studies were not clearly "special educators" (many or most were trained as psychologists), although they taught exceptional children, and (2) that many of the seminal studies dealt with children not labeled emotionally disturbed or behavior disordered although they exhibited maladaptive behavior. Many were labeled mentally retarded or brain-injured. Suffice it to say that by the early 1960s, a small but significant number of professionals working with exceptional children began to demonstrate not only the utility of a highly structured approach to teaching and managing children with behavior disorders — an approach focusing on the consistent arrangement of antecedent and consequent events for specific behaviors that could be measured directly and reliably — but also the parsimony of behavioral principles in explaining the outcome of such interventions.

From the early 1960s on, persons espousing the behavioral model have sought to teach adaptive responses, to eliminate maladaptive behaviors, and to analyze the controlling variables for the target behaviors. Some of the early studies were anecdotal reports, containing no direct measurement of behavior and no experimental design that would allow analysis of controlling variables (Zimmerman and Zimmerman, 1962). By the late 1960s, applications of behavior principles had become considerably more sophisticated and technological, as evidenced by the *Journal of Applied Behavior Analysis,* which was launched in 1968. Direct measurement and experimental analysis of behavior are now considered indispensable in any study intended to contribute significantly to the behavioral model.

Early studies included intervention with both severely disordered (autistic and schizophrenic) behavior (Ferster and DeMyer, 1962; Hewett, 1964, 1965; Lovaas, 1966) and mild or moderate behavior disorders (Allen et al., 1964; Patterson, 1965a, 1965b). In the years since the early studies were reported, the literature has expanded to include behavioral experiments with disorders in nearly every conceivable category. The scope and variety of intervention techniques have been widened, and intervention agents of nearly every description — including teachers, teacher aides, parents, siblings, community volunteers, classmates, and even behavior disordered children themselves — have been trained to carry out behavior modification procedures.

In reviewing the history of behavioral intervention in special education since the early 1960s, one can see several stages of development. First, sound behavior management practices were described anecdotally using the technical terminology of behavior principles (Haring and Whelan, 1965). Second, direct daily measurement of behavior in the natural environment was instituted to allow more precise assessment of outcome (Bijou et al., 1969; Lindsley, 1964), and behavioral intervention was applied to a wide variety of problems by a wide variety of change agents (Becker, 1971;

Ullmann and Krasner, 1965). Third, intervention techniques that had been demonstrated repeatedly to be effective were recommended to teachers (Becker, Engelmann, and Thomas, 1971; Wallace and Kauffman, 1973; Worell and Nelson, 1974). Fourth, increased emphasis was placed on issues involving measurement and experimental analysis (Gentile, Roden, and Klein, 1972; Hersen and Barlow, 1976). Fifth, the proliferation of behavior modification programs in schools led to the accusation that children were often being taught mindless conformity to arbitrary standards (Winett and Winkler, 1972). Finally, there has been a developing concern for issues involving social responsibility, relative efficacy of interventions, and integration of behavior principles with some aspects of other theoretical models (Kauffman and Hallahan, 1979; Mahoney, 1974; Meichenbaum, 1977). These stages are not clearly demarcated in time. They are to a large extent overlapping and complementary themes in the refinement and application of the behavioral model.

There is today, in short, a very considerable body of empirical evidence indicating that behavioral principles provide the conceptual framework for a multitude of effective interventions for an extremely wide range of behavior problems. Yet many proponents of the behavioral view are not satisfied that these interventions are sufficiently effective and socially relevant. As we state elsewhere in this chapter, there are concerns that (1) interventions should produce positive behavioral change that is more enduring and that generalizes to a wider range of settings and responses, (2) interventions should involve the target subject's cognitions and be designed to replace external manipulation with self-control, and (3) interventions should be designed to induce behavioral change consistent with a sociocultural consensus regarding norms for appropriate behavior.

In a sense, the behavioral model has come of age. It is no longer of special significance to demonstrate that behavior can be defined and measured reliably, that behavior can be changed by arranging consistent environmental responses to it, or that behavior can be experimentally analyzed as a function of environmental events. The critical issues now confronting proponents of the behavioral model are matters of social validation and social policy, and the integration of some of the features of other conceptual models (e.g., cognitive psychology) with behavior principles.

We wish to emphasize a final point regarding the history of the behavioral model in special education. As noted elsewhere (Hallahan and Kauffman, 1978; Kauffman, 1977), the origins of special education are found primarily in the histories of medicine and psychology. The great majority of persons responsible for the development of the behavioral model, and even of those pioneering the application of the model to the education of children with behavior disorders, have been trained as psychologists, not as special educators. Special education as a profession has been at best a consumer of conceptual models, not a synthesizer of them. Those of us who have been trained as special educators face the challenge of contributing new insights into the causes and cures of disordered behavior.

APPLIED BEHAVIOR ANALYSIS

Applied behavior analysis is the application and experimental evaluation of procedures for changing important human behaviors in practical situations. The procedures used in applied behavior analysis involve changing and rearranging specific aspects of the environment in which the important behaviors occur. These applied behavior analysis procedures chiefly, but not exclusively, involve controlling the consequences of behavior.

Early behavior modification applications were typically directed towards the inappropriate and incompetent behavior of severely handicapped people in institutional or other restrictive settings. Recently, however, applied behavior analysis has been used with a very wide range of important behaviors in institutions, educational settings, communities, homes, and many other situations. The experimental evaluation requirement of applied behavior analysis calls for very frequent recording of reliably measurable overt behavior or products of behavior; the effect of behavior change procedures on the overt behaviors are studied through the use of single case experimental designs.

Although some applied behavior analysis interventions are rather direct translations of operant conditioning principles into practice, most procedures are more complex in that they involve simultaneous operations of several operant conditioning principles and may not obviously resemble behavior change procedures derived from animal research. The abundant texts, reviews, and reference works on applied behavior analysis have organized and classified applied behavior analysis procedures in several ways. The following material represents our brief treatment of four principal foci of applied behavior analysis: observable phenomena, target assessment, intervention procedures, and experimental evaluation of intervention effects.

Observable Phenomena

Like other empirical scientific activities, applied behavior analysis focuses on measurable phenomena. Further, the concern is chiefly with observable behavior or behavior functions (products of behavior) rather than indices of human performance such as test scores, attitudinal scales, and the like. In practice, then, the behavior to be changed (target behavior) is precisely defined so that a minimum of inference is called for in judgments about its occurrence. Alternatively, easily measurable products of behavior can be used as data. Behavior disorders of children are frequently encountered in the form of general problem statements that must be translated into directly observable target behaviors. For example, "hyperactivity" might be restated in terms of seat-leaving, limb movement, entrance into various sectors of a delimited space, etc.; "poor self-image" might be restated as failure to engage in a task a second time after the child's first attempt was unsuccessful, statements about one's own incompetence, etc. The use of observable behaviors and behavior products as targets not only greatly increases the likelihood of reliable assessment, it frequently suggests the general nature of intervention attempts, in that some targets obviously must be increased while others should be decreased.

In addition to a careful specification of targets, applied behavior analysis requires that the independent variable (the intervention procedure) be clearly specified. This not only helps others make use of published accounts of successful treatments, but permits direct or systematic replication by other researchers, which contributes to development of the applied science of behavior.

Target Assessment

Once the problems of a behaviorally disordered child have been stated in terms of observable behaviors, consistent observation and recording of targeted behaviors are begun. Compared to informal judgments, intuitive impressions, or clinical estimates of pupil functioning, which may be available only occasionally and are likely to reflect changes in judgmental standards as much as actual changes in pupil functioning, data from target assessment provide a closer approximation of continuous monitoring of behavior levels and changes and are more likely to provide objective information. To reduce and guard against changes in measurement standards even when target behavior has been carefully specified, simultaneous recording of target behaviors by independent observers takes place occasionally throughout an applied behavior analysis effort. Procedures for carrying out and enhancing interobserver agreement ("reliability") are available from numerous sources (Hall, 1971; Hersen and Barlow, 1976). Potential instrumentation problems in applied behavior analysis research have been reviewed by several authorities (Hersen and Barlow, 1976; O'Leary and O'Leary, 1976).

Intervention Procedures

The vast majority of applied behavior analysis intervention procedures involve at least the contingent allocation of interpersonal attention to target behaviors. Applied behavior analysis generally involves specific human efforts to modify specific human problems. Thus, even when an intervention such as the use of "token reinforcement" for targeted behaviors is identified, interpersonal attention is required to deliver the token. The relatively rare exceptions to this dictum might include pupil interaction with teaching machines, computer assisted instruction, and self-administered consequences for self-monitored behaviors. As a corollary, contingent attention to desirable behaviors implies that undesirable behaviors are not to be attended to, which leads to their extinction. Examination of the components of applied behavior analysis interventions is an important type of evaluation and will be addressed later. For the following discussion, it should be kept in mind that most behavioral interventions represent more than one principle of operant conditioning.

Positive Reinforcement. A wide range of behavior disorders have been improved through procedures in which various kinds of positive reinforcers have been made contingent on the occurrence of adaptive behavior. These positive consequences have included *consumables* (Risley and Wolf, 1968), such as candy, gum, parts of a meal, refreshing drinks, and so on; high *probability activities* (Hart and Risley, 1968), such as classroom privileges, extra recreation time, and other opportunities to engage in preferred behavior; *tokens* (O'Leary et al., 1969) including checkmarks, "funny money," stars, points, and other conditioned reinforcers redeemable later for other reinforcing items or activities; and *social attention* (Kazdin, 1975).

One widely used positive reinforcement procedure may be termed *differential attention,* which refers to allocating favorable forms of interpersonal attention (e.g., eye contact, praise, recognition, physical approach or contact) contingent upon desirable target behavior, while refraining from paying attention to undesired or other behavior is avoided. This is probably the most widely used and researched applied behavior analysis intervention.

A series of experiments by Hall, Lund, and Jackson (1968) investigated the effect of teacher attention on study behavior of disruptive children. In one case, a student occupied his time during spelling period by snapping rubber bands, talking or laughing with peers, or playing with milk cartons. His behavior typically brought urgings by the teacher to study. For intervention, teacher praise was delivered contingent on study behavior (as carefully defined and recorded) while other behavior was ignored. This differential attention was shown to improve the percentage of time spent studying from 25 percent to over 70 percent.

Differential attention has become an impressive intervention because it so frequently has improved a range of child behaviors, including behavior problems such as oppositional behavior (Wahler et al., 1965), uncooperative play (Hart et al., 1968), lack of motivation (Cormier, 1969), thumbsucking (Skiba, Pettigrew, and Alden, 1971), and poor academic performance (Kirby and Shields, 1972). These changes were accomplished in such diverse settings as homes (Wahler, 1969), special education classes (Broden et al., 1970), and other classrooms (Madsen, Becker, and Thomas, 1968). It has been implemented by teachers (Thomas, Becker, and Armstrong, 1968), parents (Wahler, 1969), peers (Solomon and Wahler, 1973), and other people frequently found in the environments of children with behavior disorders (Tharp and Wetzel, 1969).

Negative Reinforcement. Although many human behaviors are strengthened by negative reinforcement in real life (e.g., taking pills to reduce headache, speaking loudly to quiet a noisy classroom, closing a window to stop a cold draft, fastening a seatbelt to avoid a buzzer, watching dull television programs to avoid doing other work), there are very few applied behavior analysis interventions based on negative reinforcement. In one application, Lovaas, Schaeffer, and Simmons (1965) developed positive interpersonal behaviors (approaching and interacting with adults) in withdrawn profoundly disturbed young children through negative reinforcement. In this technique, the socially unresponsive youngsters were given a harmless but painful electric shock, which was immediately terminated when they showed social behavior toward an adult. Initially, a child had merely to make eye contact with the adult; in subsequent stages, facing the adult, moving in the direction of the adult, and similar closer approximations of social interaction were required before the shock was terminated.

Punishment. A number of disordered behavior patterns have been weakened through interventions featuring contingencies intended to punish behavior. For instance, McAllister et al. (1969) reduced verbal and motoric disruption of pupils in a high school classroom through an intervention in which teacher reprimands were carefully and consistently applied as consequences for the undesired behaviors, along with praise for appropriate behavior. Applied behavior analysis punishment interventions have more frequently taken the form of time-out from reinforcement and response cost.

When it is suspected that undesirable behavior is maintained by peer attention and other social reinforcers difficult for a teacher to control, reductions in an undesired behavior can often be produced by making a period of "time-out from reinforcement" contingent on the behavior. Time-out requires briefly blocking the behaver's access to positive reinforcers, especially pervasive social reinforcers. During time-out, the person does not have access to the common social reinforcers. Typically, time-out involves removing the pupil from the class or otherwise providing brief social isolation.

In one study of time-out, a classroom teacher reduced verbal obscenities of an elementary student (Lahey, McNees, and McNees, 1973). Following limited success with other intervention procedures, time-out was instituted. The student was immediately placed in a room adjacent to the classroom for about five minutes contingent on any obscene statement. By the end of the experiment, the frequency of obscenities was nearly zero. Time-out, alone or in conjunction with other behavioral interventions, has been used by parents (Zeilberger, Sampen, and Sloane, 1968) and teachers (Clark et al., 1973) to modify various behavior disorders including aggression (Bostow and Bailey, 1969) and negativism (Nordquist, 1971).

When a student has access to desirable resources such as recess, free time, or tokens, disordered behaviors can be reduced by a response cost procedure, in which a target behavior is punished by the contingent removal of a positive reinforcer. In one application, Phillips et al. (1971) improved awareness of current news events among predelinquent youths. Each evening, the youths watched a television news program, after which they were quizzed about the show's contents. Initially, few questions were answered correctly. Only a slight increase was noted when points were awarded contingent on correct answers. But when the experimenters made points contingent on a minimum correct criterion and removed previously earned points for failure to meet the criterion, performance dramatically improved. The inclusion of the response cost procedure appeared to be the critical component for improving news awareness. Response cost has been used to modify the aggressive verbalizations of delinquents (Phillips, 1968), off-task behavior of students (Iwata and Bailey, 1974), and, in general, as an integral part of many token economy interventions (Kazdin and Bootzin, 1972).

Behavioral Self-control. One rapidly developing area of applied behavior analysis is self-control (Bandura, 1978; Catania, 1975; Jones, Nelson, and Kazdin, 1977). It is clear that people can apply various behavior modification techniques to strengthen or weaken behaviors of their own that are specified by themselves or others as targets (Meichenbaum, 1977; Thoresen and Mahoney, 1974). Behavioral self-control may take many forms, including self-observation, self-reward, self-punishment, and covert self-control. For example, in self-observation procedures, a person may observe and record data on his or her own overt behavior to increase or decrease it.

Broden, Hall, and Mitts (1971), for example, had a junior high school girl self-record whether or not she studied and paid attention in a history class. Following a baseline period in which independent observers recorded her level of study behavior at about 30 percent, the self-recording intervention was applied. Self-recording consisted of the student's noting plus or minus marks every few minutes depending upon whether she was or was not studying according to her own judgment. This procedure increased the student's study behavior to almost 80 percent. In a second experiment, the authors found self-recording to have a similar effect on reducing talk-outs of another junior high student.

Behavioral self-control interventions have favorably affected a number of child behaviors of importance to special educators. For example, self-recording has improved academic proficiency (Fink and Carnine, 1975; Johns, Trap, and Cooper, 1977); self-reinforcement has reduced disruptive behaviors (Bolstad and Johnson, 1972) and increased story writing skills and on-task behaviors (Ballard and Glynn, 1975).

Composite Behavioral Interventions. Some behavioral interventions involve the simultaneous and/or sequential application of numerous behavior modification techniques. The *token economy* (Kazdin, 1977a) has been used to modify a wide range of socially important behaviors, such as classroom and home conduct, decision-making skills, speech disorders, and self-governance of young delinquents in a group foster home (Fixsen, Phillips, and Wolf, 1973; Phillips et al., 1972; Fixsen, Phillips, and Wolf, 1972). *Behavioral contracting* involves written specifications of the relationships between desired behaviors and the consequences for performing such behaviors (DeRisi and Butz, 1974; Dinoff and Rickard, 1969; Jesness and DeRisi, 1973; Stuart and Lott, 1972; Tharp and Wetzel, 1969). The technique has been used therapeutically with delinquents (Stuart, 1971; Stuart and Lott, 1972), emotionally disturbed children (Dinoff and Rickard, 1969), and other pupils (Homme et al., 1969). *Group-oriented contingencies* (Litow and Pumroy, 1975) are applied behavior analysis procedures modified for use in the classroom or with other groups of behavers to more efficiently utilize teacher time and effort and the social influence capabilities of a group of children. *Reinforced modeling* (Bandura, 1973; Sarason and Ganzer, 1969, 1973) features demonstration, practice, and feedback for each major response component of a complex behavior chain. This procedure has been used to teach coping responses to deviant adolescents (Kifer et al., 1974; Sarason and Ganzer, 1973). These and other composite interventions illustrate the flexibility and potential complexity of behavioral treatments.

Experimental Evaluation of Intervention

As previously stated, applied behavior analysis requires that the target of change be stated carefully in measurable terms and regularly recorded using reliable procedures. If such considerations are adequately attended to, it is possible to determine the extent of behavior change over time, regardless of the intervention strategy employed. However, such behavior changes could not be attributed to the effects of an intervention procedure unless the behavior changes were evaluated through the use of some sort of experimental design. In this section, the experimental designs most compatible with applied behavior analysis are briefly described and illustrated.

The importance of experimental evaluation of treatment effects cannot be overstated. Only through this process can the effects of an intervention upon target behavior be determined in detail. This process allows us to (1) determine which interventions are ineffective in particular situations; (2) ascertain the relative effectiveness of different interventions for a particular problem; (3) determine the most powerful aspects of an effective treatment package for the purpose of streamlining interventions; (4) compare behavioral interventions to nonbehavioral procedures for remediation of a particular problem; (5) determine the potential generalization of treatment effectiveness to untreated settings and to untreated responses, and the long-term maintenance of immediately apparent behavior improvements; and (6) evaluate social validation objectives.

Single Subject Design.   Single subject research designs (Hersen and Barlow, 1976) are preferred for behavioral research. Their requirement for repetitive, regular recording of behavior appeals to researchers and educators alike. Both behavioral researchers and teachers of handicapped children are interested in questions such as "Will giving Carol token reinforcers for correctly printing letters produce an increased rate of letters printed correctly?" and "Will subtracting five minutes of Sam's access to free time for each verbal outburst produce fewer verbal outbursts?" Regular measurement of the target behavior, together with application of an intervention evaluated within a single subject research design permits practitioners and researchers to react immediately to data. Because single subject research can be performed in applied situations with one child, special education teachers can and frequently do carry out applied behavior analysis research.

In the succeeding sections *reversal* and *multiple baseline* designs are discussed in some detail, and two others, *changing criterion* and *simultaneous treatment,* are mentioned. Each of these designs utilizes one or more "baseline" conditions of measurement. The baseline phase of a design is used to portray the record of behavior in the absence of an intervention which is to be evaluated (to establish the operant level of the target behavior). Baseline measurement does not indicate level of behavior under "no treatment," because a "no treatment" condition does not exist. Behavior always occurs in the context of some collection of environmental events, including physical stimuli and the behavior of others. Baseline phases may portray levels of behavior (1) under "typical" teaching conditions, or (2) under treatment X if treatment Y is the intervention to be implemented and evaluated. Consumers of research need to be attentive to the descriptions of baseline conditions in published reports to more intelligently evaluate what a successful intervention was better than.

In descriptions of single subject designs, baseline "stability" is frequently identified as a prerequisite to implementation of an intervention. Baseline stability generally refers to the emergence of a predictable pattern of data based on recordings of behavior under baseline conditions. For instance, when all data points are of about the same magnitude, or when data variability falls within a predictable range, baseline stability is indicated.

Although the designs to be described are referred to as "single subject designs," occasionally the target behaviors of two or more persons are added to produce data points. These data points are then presented as if the behavior of a single person were involved. This is a logical procedure in some cases, as when the dependent variable of interest is the total number of fights taking place in a classroom per day. The collection of pupils in the classroom is treated as an individual, because a reduction in classroom fights (regardless of which children are fighting) is what interests the educator or researcher. At any rate, the research design considerations are essentially the same in single subject designs whether obtained data points represent behavior generated by a single person or by several.

Reversal Design.   The reversal, or ABAB, design evaluates the effect of an intervention procedure on behavior by alternating the presentation and removal of the procedure. A "functional" (cause-effect) relationship is established between intervention and behavior change if changes in behavior co-vary with the presentation and removal of the intervention.

In the first phase (baseline), the target behavior is measured until it is either stable or moving in a countertherapeutic (nondesired) direction. The baseline level of behavior serves two purposes: (1) as an estimate of behavior if no intervention were to be introduced, and (2) as a standard for judging the magnitude of behavior improvement. Following baseline$_1$ the intervention is introduced and continued until a noticeable, stable change occurs in the target behavior. Once this is evident, the intervention procedure is discontinued and the environmental conditions characterizing the baseline are reinstituted (baseline$_2$ phase). If the intervention was responsible for the observed change in the target behavior, its removal should result in a return to the baseline level of behavior. If so, a functional relationship between intervention and behavior is more credible than alternative explanations for behavior change, such as the action of uncontrolled independent variables. Further phases in which the intervention is applied and withdrawn, and in which predictable behavior changes are noted, increase the researcher's confidence that a functional relationship does exist between the behavior and the intervention. In the last phase, the demonstrably effective intervention is reintroduced to close the evaluation with the pupil functioning at the improved level.

The reversal design was used by Hall et al. (1971) to evaluate an intervention for excessive talk-outs of a thirteen-year-old emotionally disturbed boy assigned to a self-contained special classroom. Following an initial baseline period, the experimental condition was introduced: the teacher praised the student for low rates of talk-out behavior. Once a stable decrease in the talk-outs occurred, baseline conditions were briefly reinstated. When a countertherapeutic change in behavior was observed, the contingent praise treatment was reintroduced. As shown in Figure 1.2, the changes in the number of talk-outs covaried systematically with the presentation and removal of treatment conditions, demonstrating that the behavior change was a function of the treatment.

The reversal design is frequently used in applied behavior analysis research, and is capable of demonstrating the effects of an intervention program very clearly. When a target behavior changes only with the presentation and removal of the treatment variable, control over the behavior has been demonstrated, and competing explanations of the observed behavior change become difficult to accept.

There are certain disadvantages associated with the reversal design. Its

FIGURE 1.2
REVERSAL DESIGN

A record of talking-out behavior for a junior high emotionally disturbed student. Baseline: before experimental procedures. Feedback, Attention to Low Rates₁: feedback and teacher attention to low rates of talking out. B₂ return to baseline conditions of attention to low rates of talking out.

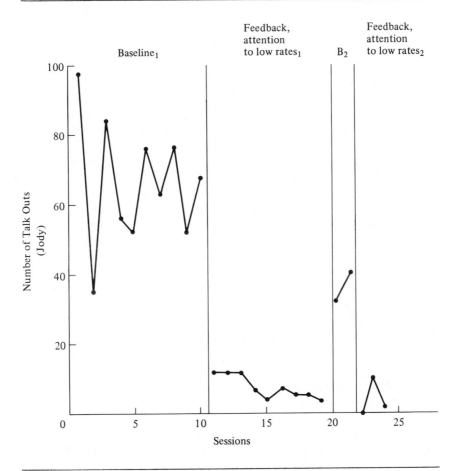

Source: R. V. Hall et al. The teacher as observer and experimenter in the modification of disrupting and talking-out behaviors. *Journal of Applied Behavior Analysis,* 1971, *4,* 144. Copyright 1971 by the Society for the Experimental Analysis of Behavior, Inc. Used by permission.

logic requires a reversal of the level of behavior during baseline₂. If such a reversal is not obtained, confident cause-effect statements cannot be made. A reversal design is inappropriate when (1) the intervention may have originally produced behavior change, but such changes are subsequently maintained by variables other than the intervention; (2) behavior levels logically would not be expected to reverse; or (3) a reversal in behavior would be unethical. Interventions sometimes produce behavioral improvements that are maintained by reinforcement available naturally, as when more acceptable behavior brings spontaneous praise from peers or others. Additionally, there are behavior patterns involving skills which may be trained by a particular intervention but are unlikely to be lost when intervention is withdrawn. Examples of such behaviors include many important educational skills such as reading, arithmetic, and problem-solving skills, which may not be reversible. Finally, there are instances in which a reversal would be possible but unethical. For example, when a teacher is able to significantly reduce the rate of self-destructive acts of a severely emotionally disturbed child, a return to the baseline level of behavior is usually undesirable. For these reasons and others, researchers and practitioners may decide that the reversal design is not appropriate for some evaluations.

Multiple-baseline Design.   The multiple-baseline design does not rely on a removal of intervention to demonstrate a functional relationship. Baer, Wolf, and Risley (1968), who first described the design, stated that "in the multiple-baseline technique, a number of responses are identified and measured over time to provide baselines against which changes can be evaluated. With these baselines established, the experimenter then applies an experimental variable to one of the behaviors, produces a change in it, and perhaps notes little or no change in the other baselines" (p. 94). A functional relationship is established if change in a target behavior is apparent when and only when the intervention is applied. Variations of the multiple-baseline design, include multiple-baseline (1) across settings, (2) across individuals, and (3) across behaviors (see Kazdin, 1980).

In the across-settings variation, data on one target behavior of an individual are recorded in two or more different settings. Once stable baselines are obtained, the intervention to be evaluated is applied within the first setting only, while baseline (no-intervention) conditions remain in effect for all other settings. When behavior improvement is noted in the first setting, the same intervention is extended to the second setting as well. This process is repeated until intervention is extended to all settings. A functional relationship is demonstrated if behavior in each setting changes when intervention is applied, but not before.

Allen (1973) used this design to evaluate the effects of praise and ignoring on the bizarre verbalizations of an eight-year-old brain-damaged boy attending a summer camp. The child's bizarre verbalizations were recorded in four settings: in the dining hall, cabin, classroom, and walking on the trail. After several days, the ignoring procedure (inattention to bizarre language plus attention to appropriate statements) was implemented in one of the settings; eventually the treatment was applied in all settings. Figure 1.3 shows that changes occurred in each setting only when treatment was introduced in that setting.

In the across-individuals variation of the multiple-baseline design, data are recorded on one behavior that is performed by two or more persons (for an example, see Schumaker, Hovell, and Sherman, 1977). In the across-behaviors variation, data are recorded on two or more separate behaviors exhibited by one person (see Bornstein, Bellack, and Hersen, 1977). Regardless of variation, the procedures for using the multiple-baseline design are similar.

In the multiple-baseline design, if behavioral changes occur only after the treatment is implemented, a functional relationship between the dependent and independent variables is more credible than alternative explanations. This design has some advantages for applied behavior analysis research. Unlike a reversal design, there is no alternation of phases; thus it is unnecessary to lose behavioral gains made during the treatment condition. This advantage should appeal especially to teachers of children with behavior disorders, who are naturally reluctant to permit even temporary losses of behavioral improvements as required in a reversal design. Also, because the multiple-baseline design requires simultaneous observation of several target behaviors, persons, or settings, the very nature of this design allows the researcher to study some generalized effects of the treatment program (Hersen and Barlow, 1976).

Along with these advantages, the use of a multiple-baseline design offers some problems. The need for extended baselines may delay treatment of all but the first-treated behavior problem, person, or relevant setting for a significant amount of time. Thus, if the delay of intervention is not in the therapeutic interest of the student, an alternative design must be sought. Another potential problem of the multiple-baseline design rests with the assumption that the behaviors, persons, or settings recorded are independent of one another, because a treatment is expected to change a behavior only after the treatment is applied to the behavior. If, however, the behaviors are interrelated, successful intervention for one behavior may produce other behavior changes before intervention is extended to them (Kazdin, 1975). Although the problem of generalized effects has not arisen much in the behavioral literature (Kazdin, 1975; Leitenberg, 1973), the potential for such problems calls for great care in planning research. Recently, Kazdin and Kopel (1975) presented a number of specific recommendations to strengthen the multiple-baseline design, including (1) the use of independent, topographically distinct behaviors, (2) measurement of at least four baselines, and (3) use of a reversal phase within the multiple-baseline design.

Other Designs.   The *changing criterion* design (Hartman and Hall, 1976) is appropriate in situations where behavior is expected to improve in a step-wise manner. The essential components of this design include (1) an initial baseline phase, (2) determination of the criterion behavior level for which consequences will be delivered, (3) application of the treatment program,

FIGURE 1.3
MULTIPLE-BASELINE ACROSS SETTINGS DESIGN
Daily number of bizarre verbalizations in specific camp settings.

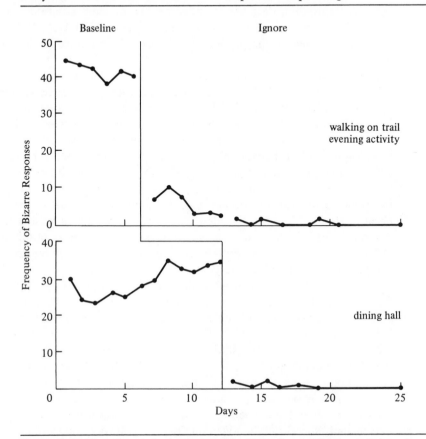

Source: G. J. Allen. Case study: implementation of behavior modification techniques in summer camp settings. *Behavior Therapy,* 1973, *4,* 573. Used by permission.

and (4) systematic, stepwise changes in criterion until the desired level of target behavior is reached. When the behavior improves only as each stepwise criterion change is imposed, experimental control is demonstrated. For examples and further discussion of this design see Dietz and Repp (1973), Epstein, Repp, and Cullinan (1978), and Hartmann and Hall (1976).

The *simultaneous-treatment* design (Kazdin and Hartmann, 1978) permits a comparison of two or more interventions for a target behavior. The interventions are applied in alternating fashion, with other variables — different time periods, teachers, settings, and so on — counterbalanced to equalize their influence on the target behavior. In this design, it can become apparent relatively quickly which intervention produces the greatest behavior change, enabling the researcher or practitioner to determine which of

FIGURE 1.3 (*Continued*)

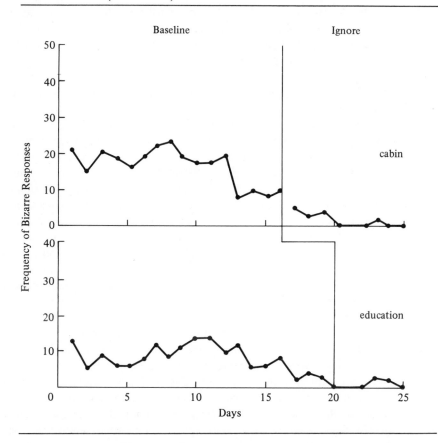

several techniques is preferable. For examples and further discussion of this design see Browning and Stover (1971), Kazdin and Geesey (1977), and Kazdin and Hartman (1978).

Single Subject and Group Experimental Research. Single subject research designs such as those described are strongly preferred in the experimental evaluation of applied behavior analysis. There are several major reasons for this preference over traditional group experimental research strategies, in which group performance averages, variability, or both are used to determine whether differential group outcomes can be confidently attributed to the power of treatment procedures as opposed to chance effects. Group experimental studies, for example, typically produce data based on brief measurement samples taken on one or, at most, a few occasions. Such data are more likely to be subject to weak effects of treatments or uncontrolled variables than data arising from multiple, regularly repeated observations of a particular dependent variable. In the latter case, which characterizes applied behavior analysis, weak or transient effects will be unable to produce the dramatic and consistent changes in behavior of interest to single subject research. Additionally, group experimental research relies on statistical probabilities indicating the confidence with which results can be attributed to treatments. Thus, potentially important results which approach but do not achieve statistical significance may be unjustifiably ignored; conversely, results that are highly significant statistically may reflect very small absolute changes or treatment effects that nevertheless achieve significance due to large sample size. For instance, given large enough groups, an advantage in favor of a treatment group over a control group of .1 reading grade level may be statistically significant, but if the study ran for one year, such results would have little practical importance.

Further, group designs may mask individual variations of great importance in effective treatment, because individual performances are pooled to produce group statistics. Although individual differences are accepted as a "given" in group research, experimental control of individual variation in behavior through single subject methodology has frequently shown that many so-called "individual differences" are actually reducible through the manipulation of treatment variables. This point may be especially important to researchers and practitioners involved with children with behavior disorders, whose behavioral functioning is widely thought to be especially variable. More detailed reviews of single subject and group experimental research are available (Hersen and Barlow, 1976; Kazdin and Wilson, 1978).

Group experimental research has some potential advantages under certain conditions. In some cases, for example, simultaneous contrast of more than one treatment variable and the interaction among treatments is more readily studied through group experimental designs than single subject designs. Also, when subjects for a group experimental research design are sampled representatively from a particular population, experimental results are more likely to have generalized applicability. In practice, of course, group experimental designs do not typically derive their subject pools on the basis of representative sampling from a population.

COMPONENT ANALYSIS OF APPLIED BEHAVIOR ANALYSIS PROCEDURES

Behavior analysis interventions typically contain several components; that is, a particular treatment is frequently a package of two or more independent variables. (The same is true of nonbehavioral treatments, of course.) Even after a single subject evaluation design has determined that the treatment package is better than nonspecific teaching practices or another type of applied behavior analysis intervention, it is not known whether the strength of the effective package requires that all of its components be applied or whether some may be deleted with no loss of effectiveness. If some of the components are relatively expensive, difficult, distasteful to implement, or time-consuming, it may be important to determine the effectiveness of components individually or a few at a time, with an eye toward streamlining the intervention. Component analysis of treatments through single subject research has not been widely practiced in applied settings, although there are several studies which can illustrate the potential benefits of this strategy. The "good behavior game," for example, is a behavior change procedure for groups of pupils that typically includes the following components: (1) class rules are listed; (2) pupils are divided into classroom teams; (3) criteria are set for winning the game; (4) the teacher provides feedback on rule violations; and (5) desirable resources are awarded to members of the winning team (or all students if each team meets or surpasses preset criteria) (Barrish, Saunders, and Wolf, 1969). Harris and Sherman (1973) examined components of the good behavior game as applied in two classrooms. They found that the most important components of a good behavior game designed to reduce classroom disruption were dividing the class into teams, setting criteria for team performance, and providing consequences for achieving the behavioral criteria.

Component analysis research not only provides treatment improvements for the benefit of practitioners, it indicates that applied behavior analysis is moving beyond demonstrations that particular intervention procedures can be effective. Important as such demonstrations are (and as far advanced as applied behavior analysis is on this first level of evaluation compared to most recommended interventions for children's behavior disorders) component analysis research is a welcome advance which will almost certainly lead to improvements in behavioral treatment of children.

SOCIAL VALIDATION

The concern for social validation in behavioral research can be traced to the classic paper by Baer et al. (1968) in which the parameters for evaluating applied behavioral research were defined. Baer et al. set the stage for later efforts at social validation by emphasizing two key concepts of applied behavior analysis: *applied* and *effective*. "Applied" pertains to the importance society places on problems under study. In applied research with behaviorally disordered children, target behaviors and intervention techniques must be selected on the basis of their importance to the children involved and to society. "Effective" requires that the magnitude of behavior changes be great enough to have practical, and usually immediate, value. This requirement has at least two implications. First, interventions which produce small effects have little applied value (even if effects are statistically significant), although there may be theoretical value. Second, the judgment of whether a behavior change has practical value may be made by (1) consulting data-based norms that indicate how the target behavior is performed by peers whose behavior is considered adaptive, competent, and appropriate (the *social comparison* method), and/or (2) having knowledgeable persons in the treated child's social milieu (parents, peers, teachers, or others) indicate their level of satisfaction with the behavior change (*subjective evaluation* method). Social comparison and subjective evaluation methods are becoming widely used by behaviorists for *social validation of interventions* (Kazdin, 1977a).

Social Comparison

In the social comparison approach, untreated persons are appropriately selected and assessed with respect to the behavior for which the target individual is to be treated. For example, persons selected for social comparison of a highly aggressive elementary school girl referred for special education might include a random sample of classmates, all girls, or whatever other children the girl might be appropriately compared to.

Behavior assessment of a pupil with behavior disorders and his or her social comparison group can serve important purposes. First, it can help responsible persons determine (1) whether the referred child's behaviors are discrepant from those of the comparison group, (2) which particular behaviors are involved, and (3) to what extent they are discrepant. Second, assessment of nonreferred peers can suggest objective exit criteria from special education. When the treated child's behavior again falls within the range established by social comparison, the pupil would seem to be ready in some important way to experience a reduction in special services. Further, social comparisons after a child leaves special education can help estimate the durability of intervention efforts or give early warning of the need for preventative "booster" treatment.

Walker has utilized normative peer data to socially validate intervention programs (Walker and Hops, 1973; Walker, Hops, and Johnson, 1975; Walker, Mattson, and Buckley, 1971). Walker and Hops (1976) reported on a treatment program for three groups of students displaying low rates of appropriate classroom behavior (e.g., following instructions, attending to task). Target students were observed first in the regular classroom, then in an experimental classroom, and finally in a regular classroom during follow-up. Throughout each phase of the study, data were collected on appropriate behavior of each target student's classroom peers. Following baseline conditions in the regular and experimental classrooms, intervention consisting of token and social reinforcement for appropriate academic and social functioning was introduced. Data on the percent of appropriate behavior for one group of children are presented in Figure 1.4. These results indicate that the behavior of target children, markedly different from classroom peers at referral, was brought and maintained within normal limits.

FIGURE 1.4
UTILIZING SOCIAL COMPARISON FOR SOCIAL VALIDATION

Behavioral observation data for Group III subjects during successive treatment phases.

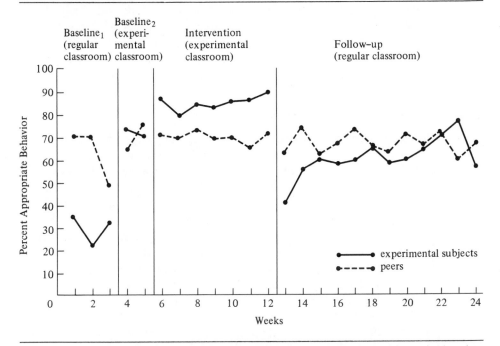

Source: H. M. Walker and H. Hops. Use of normative peer data as a standard for evaluating class-room treatment effects. *Journal of Applied Behavior Analysis,* 1976, *9,* 165. Copyright 1976 by the Society for the Experimental Analysis of Behavior, Inc. Used by permission.

Subjective Evaluation

Another important standard in social validation is consumer satisfaction with results. This may be gauged by seeking the opinions of qualified individuals in the community on the importance of behavior changes: teachers, community workers, mental health personnel, school administrators, legal professionals, parents, etc. Such judges are chosen because they either interact with the person or possess specific expertise with regard to the treated behavior. Generally, the judges are requested to determine the social significance of the target behavior, then assess the performance of the treated person. Behavioral researchers have recently incorporated this type of measure into evaluations of applied behavior analysis programs.

Brigham, Graubard, and Stans (1972) modified the composition writing skills of thirteen behaviorally disordered students assigned to an "adjustment" classroom. Intervention consisted of using tokens to reinforce increases in the total number of words used, the number of different words used, and the number of new words used. Following intervention, the overall quality of the students' compositions was assessed by expert judges on the basis of mechanical aspects (e.g., length, spelling), vocabulary (e.g., variety), number of ideas, development of ideas, and internal consistency of the story; each dimension was scored on a 0–5 scale. Across all the dimensions, the compositions from the treatment phases were rated higher than writing samples from the baseline phase. This use of judges' ratings served as a second source of data and further confirmed the efficacy of the educational procedures to increase the quality of writing skills.

Other Implications of Social Validation

Normative peer data may be useful in developing a consensus definition of behavior disorders. Components of available definitions that are difficult to measure (Epstein, Cullinan, and Sabatino, 1977; Kauffman, 1977) such as deviation from a norm, severity, and chronicity might be made usable through the social comparison procedure. The observation of unreferred children could determine the rates of deviant and nondeviant behavior in the population to which referred children are to be compared. Johnson et al. (1973) have collected data on the deviant behavior (e.g., failure to comply, demands attention) of "normal" children in the home.

Social validation may also be useful in bridging the gap between research and practice. Keogh (1977) and Kazdin (1978) have commented on the hiatus between the two areas, pointing out that the voluminous research conducted has had little influence on how handicapped children are educated. Social validation, with its emphasis on applied social importance, may provide the impetus for a new compatibility between researchers and practitioners. Further, the impact of an effective treatment program may be increased by allowing consumers such as classroom teachers and parents to evaluate its social importance. The input of community and school members in determining treatment goals may increase the acceptability of the program to the consumer (Wolf, 1978).

Finally, the potential for social comparison data to objectify placement, treatment, exit, and follow-up activities for children with behavior disorders may help mainstreaming efforts with these pupils. Not only might reductions in special educational services be programmed and adjusted on the basis of pupil progress toward normative levels of appropriate behavior, assessment of normal pupils in several classrooms into which the handicapped pupil may be mainstreamed could reveal which one is characterized by levels of behavior that might be most conducive to successful reintegration.

Social validation, like any other recent innovation, presents a number of problems. For instance, (1) using normative data as standard criteria presupposes that a norm is available and is an adequate standard; (2) normative peer behavior differs from setting to setting, and many variables account for the rate of behavior in any given environment; and (3) subjective evaluation procedures need to be developed to reliably and validly measure socially important behaviors (Kazdin, 1978). Such problems need to be resolved so that social validation can become a more scientific part of treatment evaluation.

CONCLUSIONS

The behavioral model for dealing with human problems, and especially applied behavior analysis, has grown and diversified to a remarkable extent in the two decades or so since its real beginnings. While this has made the task of describing the behavioral approach more difficult, it also means that the model has achieved a fair degree of maturity in terms of a broad scope of applications, amenability to use by a wide range of helping agents, and expansion of methods and criteria for evaluating treatments. Thus, applied behavior analysis has been successfully employed for such diverse purposes as building language in the severely handicapped (Lovaas and Koegel, 1973), teaching self-governance to delinquents (Phillips et al., 1973), developing intellectually creative behavior (Glover and Gary, 1975), and teaching adaptive vocational and job related skills (Azrin, Flores, and Kaplan, 1975), to mention only a few of the applications relevant to the education of children with behavior disorders. These behavioral techniques have been successfully employed for children's behavior problems by parents and other relatives, attendants in institutions, peers, and other nonprofessionals (Ayllon and Wright, 1972; Tharp and Wetzel, 1969), as well as teachers, psychologists, psychiatrists, and other members of the helping professions. This chapter has suggested the depth and scope of evaluation efforts with applied behavior analysis.

The behavioral model has also expanded in the direction of departures from traditional operant conditioning, as evidenced by the growing number of reports from within the behavioral literature of "cognitive behavior modification," "behavioral self-control" techniques, and other developments. Other models of intervention, such as the psychodynamic model, have also experienced diversification of theories and approaches. However, the evaluation components within the behavioral model serve as a damper on hasty acceptance of new possibilities, which generally must earn acceptability through empirical evaluation and replication.

The behavioral model has had an important influence on education for children with behavior disorders, and holds great promise for the future. Several developments are needed for this promise to be translated into reality. First, many of the behavioral techniques have been clearly shown to be effective for behavior problems relevant to children identified as behaviorally disordered. In many cases, however, the findings have not been replicated with children so identified. Such evaluations with identified children are needed to determine whether and how intervention procedures need to be adapted for use with children served in resource rooms, special classrooms, or other special educational situations.

Interventions that produce beneficial but short-lived results are of limited use to special educators. Virtually all educational interventions, including those arising from the behavioral model, need to be evaluated in terms of the durability of the effects they produce and how behavioral improvements can be maintained. Additionally, it is obviously highly desirable that an intervention which is capable of improving a child's functioning in the treated setting also lead to similar behavioral improvements elsewhere — in other classroom settings, at home, and so on. Thus, the power of behavioral interventions to produce desirable setting generality needs to be studied. Along the same lines, interventions capable of improving target behavior need to be evaluated in terms of how well they promote correlated improvements in other behavior problems (response generalization).

The emerging interest in social validation is a welcome development. While social validation has little meaning for interventions that are ineffective in improving target behavior, effective interventions, especially those in educational settings, can be made more valuable through attention to the peer comparison, consumer satisfaction, and other social validation issues, as previously described.

The material on evaluation was presented in the context of its applicability to behavioral interventions. It should be apparent, though, that evaluation concerns apply to interventions based on any model of human functioning. The single subject research designs used in behavior modification studies could probably be used to evaluate the effectiveness of many nonbehavioral intervention techniques. The responsibility for such research lies with the proponents of a particular intervention.

Finally, the thousands of published reports on "behavior modification," the growing body of positively evaluated behavioral treatments for socially and educationally important behavior problems of children, and the widespread use of behavioral procedures in special education clearly indicate that this mode of educational intervention is efficacious, recommendable, and will continue to grow in use with pupils showing behavior disorders. But additional evaluative research is required to refine available applications and enhance their value to the children served. The needed research and demonstration may be encouraged best by foundations and state and federal government agencies, through policy decisions and the financial support of carefully planned and appropriately evaluated projects. Such projects should translate available research on applied behavior analysis into local programs for educational treatment of children and youth with behavior disorders.

Chapter 2

The Psychoeducational Model: Theory and Historical Perspective

Virginia E. Rezmierski
University of Michigan, Dearborn

with

Peter Knoblock
Syracuse University

Robert B. Bloom
College of William and Mary

The objectives of this chapter are (1) to examine the theoretical basis for the psychoeducational model of education for emotionally disturbed youngsters, and (2) to delineate the historical stages in the development of this type of educational programming. In meeting these objectives we will consider the following questions:

1. What is the focus of this model? What does it emphasize?
2. Is there agreement about the meaning of the terms *psychotherapeutic* and *psychoeducational?*
3. Is the emphasis on the learning style and educational performance of the individual or the therapeutic treatment of the personality?
4. Is the goal education or therapy?
5. Do theoretical constructs exist that can direct the identification of interventions for this model?
6. Does a comprehensive model exist, or are the programs known as psychodynamic and psychotherapeutic only sporadically supported by theory?
7. Can these constructs be confirmed?

Long, Morse, and Newman (1971) suggest that the psychoeducational model uses information from a variety of sources to understand children. These sources range from the study of human growth and development to group dynamics, mental health, academic learning, and so forth. The major assumptions that underlie this approach are: (1) Careful attention must be paid to the student's interaction with the school, staff, peers, and curriculum in order to develop a supportive educational milieu. (2) Emphasis is placed on understanding the teacher-student relationship. (3) Learning gains interest, meaning, and purpose when it is invested with feelings. (4) Learning new ways to understand and to cope with stress can be facilitated by using the conflict generated by the student. (5) Learning style is individual to each student. (6) Returning to earlier levels of behavior temporarily allows relearning to take place. (7) The student's current level of functioning directs teacher effort. (8) Consultive skills enable the teacher to effectively work with other members of the school and community. (9) Music, art, dance, and play are important to learning and should not be removed for misbehavior. (10) A behavior may have many causes, while a single cause may result in different behaviors in different persons. (11) Each member of the group contributes to group behavior.

THE PROBLEM OF TERMINOLOGY AND EMPHASIS

In the past twenty years, many terms have been associated with psychoeducational programs for emotionally disturbed students. The following terms are common: *psychoanalytic treatment, psychotherapeutic education, psychoeducational programming, psychodynamic education,* and even *education programs with psychological emphasis.* To better understand the differences among these terms, we should recognize the emphasis each term places on either therapy or education within the programming effort.

Figure 2.1 illustrates the range in therapeutic and educational emphases in these programs. Note that the terms *psychoeducational* and *psychodynamic* are nearly synonymous. The first refers primarily to the educational program, the latter to the approach that focuses upon the psychological dynamics of the person within the program.

Interestingly, changes in the terminology associated with this model parallel the changes in emphasis that have taken place in the programs themselves. Early programming efforts were primarily associated with analytic treatment. More recent educational efforts have emphasized educational aspects of the programs rather than therapy. We will elaborate on this parallel as we examine the evolution of programming.

Much of the terminology and several of the concepts associated with the psychoeducational model have been poorly understood. In early psychoeducational programs, the importance placed upon the expression of feelings and the need to understand the child's perceptions was often misinterpreted. Many persons felt that the psychoeducational model basically promoted free

FIGURE 2.1

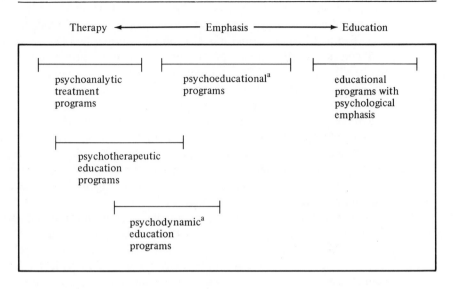

a The terms *psychodynamic* and *psychoeducational* are sometimes used interchangeably. In this chapter the slight difference in emphasis which is noted on Figure 2.1 will be observed.

expression of feelings coupled with an absence of adult control over behavior. Psychoeducators do rely heavily on the expression and understanding of feelings in designing an educational program, but these feelings help educators understand the unique needs of each child and design an education program that will restore individual growth and improve social, academic, and emotional functioning. We should emphasize that the continuous, uncontrolled, undirected expression of feelings is contrary to the purpose of the psychoeducational model. In some cases, it is more destructive than therapeutic. A variety of management techniques to promote acceptable expression of feelings have been developed (Redl 1966a, 1976a, 1976b; Redl and Wineman 1951, 1952; Morse 1971, 1976a; Long and Newman 1976). (These techniques and others are further described in Chapters 5 and 7).

Whelan (1978) emphasizes the importance of talking about feelings when he states that

> teachers, by building trust and being supportive of children's efforts, gradually become valued sources of expectations and corrective feedback. Whenever possible, teachers should encourage children to talk about their feelings, an appropriate mode as contrasted to destructive acting out of feelings and impulses. Talking leads to insight and often leads to changes in behaviors: "Yes, there is a better way to express anger than tearing up a book. Here are some alternatives." This is analogous to the "light bulb" over a cartoon character's head: "Now I understand. I see it all now." *(p. 347)*

Learning to understand and cope with one's feelings is a basic part of the psychoeducational approach. This model dynamically associates the process of education with the psychological process of therapeutic support.

The psychoeducational model is an educational model — it represents and guides the educational programming efforts of professionals in their work with emotionally disturbed youth. In this sense the educational setting and tools are an integral part of the application of the approach.

Understandably, many of the most significant names associated with this model are outstanding educators rather than theorists or therapists. Although the model stems from psychoanalytic theory, educators such as Morse, Redl, Long, Fenichel, and Newman have contributed both psychological depth and educational guidelines to the model, helping to define it. Their contributions associated with behavior management are discussed in Chapter 5, with curriculum, in Chapter 7.

Although the psychoeducator uses the tools of education and works in the educational setting, these aspects of the approach are not used solely to promote the education or achievement of children. In the psychoeducational model, the educational component is also used to achieve other therapeutic results for the child. An understanding of the basic needs of the child is the basis the educator uses to determine how the educational process should be pursued. The basic intent of this model is to use this specially designed and executed educational process to narrow the gap between the child's needs and the environment's ability to meet those needs. The educational program uses the events of the child's life and occurrences in the educational setting to promote a healthier personality development. Although the main emphasis of the model is education rather than therapy, the psychoeducational program and its techniques result in treatment of the emotional disturbance. Cheney and Morse (1976) refer to the psychoeducational approach as a "restorative curriculum which capitalizes on the latent self-corrective capacities of the disturbed child to enhance emotional growth and mental health" (p. 318).

This model is prescriptive in nature, designed to meet a child's unique and changing emotional needs. Results are achieved primarily through the prescribed use of the interpersonal and physical educational environment to provide maximum emotional support for the child. Although Lawrence Peter did not specifically refer to a psychoeducational model in the statement below, his conceptualization of the use of structure in education is excellent regarding one aspect of psychoeducational programming. Peter (1965) states that

> in order to restore the child's learning capacity and mental health through the educational processes, we know what educational modifications to make. Prescriptive teaching makes educational modifications upon the principle that where a child has been unable to organize his perceptions or centralize his concepts, the solution lies in organization of the environmental stimuli. The only way we change a child's thought processes, values and behavior is by changing the stimuli.

The more disturbed the child is, the more order or structure is needed in his environment. The more his perception is distorted, the more he needs structuring of his stimuli. *(p. 35)*

This statement is in marked contrast to the earlier Berkowitz and Rothman (1960) position supporting a more permissive classroom environment. However, Berkowitz and Rothman later joined Fenichel in acknowledging the importance of structuring the educational environment. Fenichel (1966) states, "there is a need for a highly organized program of education and training that can bring order, stability, and direction to minds that are disorganized, unstable, and unpredictable" (p. 9).

Competent management of stimulation requires planning. A task which seems simple, such as calmly walking down a long empty school hall with highly polished floors, can be a taxing and difficult duty for some emotionally disturbed youngsters. One new teacher reported an incident that illustrates this difficulty. To her chagrin, and to the surprise of the principal (who happened to be watching), her entire class of ten disturbed boys ran and then slid the entire length of the hallway, some on their stomachs. The importance of anticipating such effects of environmental stimulation with adequate prescriptive management within the school setting is an important part of the psychoeducational model. We should again emphasize, however, that human interactions are managed as well as the environmental stimuli that Peter describes.

As we have noted, the educational model is not represented adequately by the term *psychoanalytic treatment* or the program of education generally associated with that term. Historically, the emphasis of psychoanalytic treatment programs has been on the treatment aspect of the program, the therapy. The adjunct educational programs were usually regarded as remedial and secondary in nature. They were viewed as the arena in which children's conflicts were to be identified, from which the therapists pursued treatment goals.

At the other extreme, the term *education programs with psychological emphasis* also misrepresents the model. In most cases, the education component has extended only very slightly into the affective area. In such programs, the therapeutic effects and responsibilities have generally been underplayed. Although the use of diverse terminology has led to much misinterpretation in the past, a fundamental precept of the psychoeducational model is the balance and dynamic interplay between education and therapy.

HISTORICAL EVOLUTION OF PSYCHOEDUCATIONAL PROGRAMS

Educational programs for emotionally disturbed children have been evolving since the early 1950s. In the past twenty years, an increasing number of classrooms for emotionally disturbed youngsters have been established in clinics, hospitals, and public school buildings. This increase reflects a change in the responsibility educators have felt toward this special population of children. A recent indication of this change is the passage of PL 94-142. We have presented the development of program changes first through reference to the changes in terminology discussed previously. Next we address the design and emphasis of the psychoeducational programs themselves.

Early 1950s

The first classrooms for emotionally disturbed students were associated with inpatient psychiatric services for children. These classes were often located in hospitals, clinics, and state institutions, and were usually run by psychiatrists. The emphasis was on the psychiatric treatment of the child. Educational programs were regarded as a remedial service to the children intended to improve their academic skills and occupy the children's time between therapy appointments. The school periods were often continuously interrupted by therapists taking children to therapy and then returning them to the classroom.

Teachers in residential treatment centers eventually recognized special educational programs as a more central component of a child's treatment. They began to see the restorative power of prescriptive curriculum and educational support. In some settings, treaties were negotiated between the educational and medical personnel so that therapy hours did not disrupt the school sessions. As a result, school time began to be prescribed by psychiatrists. Although the educators were not yet recognized as significant forces in the treatment of the children in these settings, remediation of academic problems was definitely considered valuable. Educators were often invited to observe and sometimes participated in theoretical discussions or teaching sessions held by medical personnel. Fritz Redl (1964) described this situation as the process of "throwing crumbs from the table of the rich" (p. 2). The goal was for educators to better understand the psychodynamics and psychopathology of their students, but they were only privy to the more general medical and psychiatric information.

In some cases, the setting provided a fine exposure to analytic theory, especially if the inpatient service was a site for the training of psychologists and psychiatrists. During this period, teacher-training institutions began to increase the amount of theoretical work in their degree requirements to help educators understand the therapeutic process. Nevertheless, the prevailing attitude of early classrooms for the emotionally disturbed was that education was separate from the main objective of therapy.

Perhaps the most significant influences upon the design of psychoeducational programs during this period (and in later periods) were the work of Bruno Bettelheim (1950, 1955) and the work of Fritz Redl and David Wineman (1954). They provided leadership for those interested in designing therapeutic environments and applying psychodynamic intervention. The work of these men was based largely on psychoanalytic theory. Bettel-

heim worked with children and youth placed in the Sonja Shankman Orthogenic School, a residential treatment center for children labeled severely
emotionally disturbed.

Redl and Wineman described in *The Aggressive Child* (1954) the
approach to intervention they used with the acting-out behaviors of the disturbed youth in Pioneer House, a group home they established in Detroit.
They credit Aichhorn, Bettelheim, and Anna Freud with inspiring their creation of the Pioneer House therapeutic environment, and also with contributing theoretical information important to their approach and interventions. Of Aichhorn, they wrote:

> His was the first large attempt to apply what had been learned
> through the medium of psychoanalysis of neurotic children and adults
> to the youngsters with whom the usual channels and resources of
> treatment somehow didn't seem to work. *(p. 11)*

Redl and Wineman's book is still considered a basic source of information
for those who seek to apply psychodynamic interventions in work with
emotionally disturbed children.

While inspiring work was being accomplished by Bettelheim and Redl
and Wineman, the number of children who could be served in inpatient settings remained small. The cost of such residential treatment centers became
prohibitive. In the public schools, special classes for mentally retarded
youngsters had existed for many years. Regular classroom teachers began
to request relief from some of the students who were viewed as behavioral
problems in their classrooms. Professionals came to believe that they had
an educational responsibility to the less severely disturbed students in the
schools as well as those who needed intense inpatient hospitalization. These
needs were addressed in the years that followed.

Late 1950s to Mid 1960s

In the late 1950s and early 1960s, special educational classes for emotionally disturbed children began to develop in the public schools in response
to the need and increased feeling of responsibility. During early efforts to
serve this population, considerable attention was devoted to providing a
team of service personnel who could interrelate the educational and therapeutic processes. The teachers in these programs generally received training
in the area of mental retardation or in the area of emotional disturbance.
The latter training not only helped teachers understand psychotherapy and
psychopathology, it encouraged them to extrapolate from theory to the educational process itself — to determine prescriptive psychodynamic interventions.

In school programs, the service team frequently included a psychiatric
social worker, a clinical psychologist, and a part- or full-time psychiatrist,

in addition to the educator. The entire team was exposed to interdisciplinary information regarding the student's needs. The programs developed from these collaborative efforts stressed interplay between therapy and education in a particular milieu. The relationships in this setting often reflected significant interpersonal dynamics. It was not uncommon for the teacher as well as the children to receive symbolically loaded emotional outbursts. For example, we recall an anecdote of an exasperated second year teacher who reported her fury when, after several periods of difficulty in the classroom, she called the psychologist to remove a disruptive student, Sammy, from the classroom. She was drawn aside by the psychologist and told that observations indicated that the problem was more hers than Sammy's. He would be glad to remove Sammy, however, until she could regain her composure and continue teaching. Although the psychologist momentarily became the target for the teacher's frustration, which she expressed in no uncertain terms, his interpretation was correct. It helped her regain perspective on her classroom goals. Clarifying classroom dynamics helps to keep disruption in the proper perspective.

During this period of development, education played a major role in therapy. Eventually, therapy and the educational process became reciprocally supportive. The educator was expected to help the child learn through a sound understanding of both affective and cognitive development. While the educator's training experiences in both the affective and cognitive domains were far from adequate during this period, the period represents the typical interplay between theory and educational practice within the psychoeducational model.

As Redl and Wineman applied individual therapeutic notions in an extended treatment milieu, Morse (1965) and Long (1974) applied such principles in the classroom. They helped classroom teachers understand children's behavior and designed specific interventions to promote child mental health and reduce deviant classroom behavior. Fenichel, one of the first practitioners to develop a day treatment program for severely disturbed children, brought this group to the attention of the community with a report published in 1965.

Late 1960s and Early 1970s

By the late 1960s, increasing numbers of students were being identified as needing services unavailable in regular classrooms. Classes in hospitals and special schools for the emotionally disturbed continued to meet this demand. Expansion of programs in the public schools also began. More special classes were developed, but they often lacked clear operational guidelines. During the previous stage, certain issues and events had caused significant concern about the intervention programs in use. These issues had important effects on the planning and implementation of programming during the 1970s. We have outlined these issues below.

1. School building administrators often felt uncomfortable with what they saw as a division of administrative power in their buildings. For example, the program planning for special education children was determined almost totally by a team of itinerant personnel — most of whom were not housed in their buildings and some of whom were only remotely connected with the school system.

2. The issue of therapy being provided within public schools also caused much concern. It was difficult for most educators to accept having a child meet with a psychologist for play therapy during school hours. Most significantly, however, regular educators were alarmed to discover that special education teachers tolerated an unusually wide range of behaviors in their classrooms. They often allowed students to work on the floor, and were observed using such techniques as life-space interviewing in the school hallways to calm angry and distraught students. General education teachers were frequently heard to ask special educators, "What do you do with these children all day?" or to comment to their own class of students when passing an open special education doorway, "Well, those children really do work at their desks!" The appropriateness of psychodynamic techniques in education was not established at this time and threatened the normal order of things.

3. There was a high attrition rate among special education personnel in these self-contained classes. The demands upon the teacher's emotions, patience, time, and even interpersonal status within the building were heavy. Often special education teachers were not accepted or were only marginally accepted by the other staff.

We recall one year in a special program in Syracuse, New York, when a special education teacher decided to increase the contact that he and his students had with the general education students and teachers. The teacher and his students prepared a large fish tank which was empty except for water, pebbles, and grasses. The students painted a sign which read, "Come see our Japanese invisible fighting fish." The word spread throughout the building. Before the week was over, every teacher and class within the building had visited his room. For nearly all of them it was the first visit they had made to the special education class in the history of the program. For many of the teachers it was one of the very few times they had interacted with the special education teacher.

The special education class size was another area of conflict. Teachers with classes of twenty-eight envied those who had classes of only ten. It was felt that special education teachers were not carrying their fair share of the educational load in the building.

4. The cost of team treatment for a small number of students was another concern. Financial constraints began to cause administrators to question the efficacy of such educational team programs. These concerns resulted in the establishment of more special education classes, but without adequate support personnel.

After this school-based programming, the emphasis on psychoeducation gave way to an emphasis on education. More attention was given to academic achievement than to the total functioning of the child. Teachers of emotionally disturbed children often lacked specialized supervision, therapeutic supports, and even teaching peers. Special education classes were established in separate buildings, without provisions for the special education teachers to exchange information.

To cope with this transformation, special program teachers began to depend more completely upon their general education peers for support, ideas, and teaching techniques. It soon became obvious that the emphasis in school systems was on the *containment* of emotionally disturbed youngsters. At best, special education teachers were able to maintain a therapeutic approach in their management of the student's behavior — a carry-over from previous training. At worst, they began to blur the qualitative distinctions between managing behavior, building ego, restoring growth, suppressing behavior, and continuing pathology.

The changes we have described were taking place very rapidly during the 1960s and early 1970s. As training programs for teachers of emotionally disturbed children developed to meet growing demands, their effects on school guidelines for the operation of programs for the emotionally disturbed became evident. Because rapid results had not been forthcoming from the therapeutic programming of previous periods, pressures developed in school systems to focus primarily on the more disruptive behavior. Emphasis was thus put on reducing behavioral problems and managing surface behavior of the students rather than addressing the broader personality issues involved.

Quay, Morse, and Cutler (1966) were among those involved in developing future training programs. Knoblock and Goldstein (1971) and Knoblock (1973) stressed the importance of a teacher's personal growth and the teacher-pupil relationships in settings using a psychoeducational model. It also became clear during this period that simply increasing the number of programs for disturbed children was not sufficient to meet the needs of the growing number of children being identified for special services.

Another trend of this period was the growing discontinuity between educational practices and psychoanalytic theory. Educational personnel were hampered in pursuing this theoretical tie by their decreasing interaction with the milieu-therapy setting. Behavior modification techniques began to provide special educators with a structured approach that explained more generalizable intervention methods, which were perceived to be unavailable from psychodynamic theory.

The mainstreaming concept also began during this period. Initial efforts, however, were only partially successful. When teachers of the emotionally disturbed thought a student could function in a regular class for even one period, they often met with resistance. It was often suggested that they in return take the three or four lowest readers from the class back to the special education room for remediation. General educators typically withdrew from responsibility for their students once they were taken from the regular classes by the special education teacher.

This difficulty in reintegrating the students for continued growth and normal stimulation was a significant problem for psychoeducational programs. About this dilemma, Knoblock and Johnson (1967) wrote:

> We have learned to feel less smug regarding the issue of integration or segregation of programs for emotionally disturbed children in the public schools. Many program planners have begun to recoil at the organizational problems confronted in designing such programs and the rush toward integrated programming has not materialized. It is clear that the broad area of education of emotionally disturbed children is simulating the educational provisions, i.e., the special class, previously adopted by other areas of special education. (p. 3)

This recognition of the need for integration and coordinated services to promote the growth of the child has continued until the present.

Mid 1970s to the Present

Around 1975, the evolutionary process of educational programming entered a fourth stage of development. Programs and services for emotionally disturbed youngsters became plentiful. Services now available include contained special classes for those who need special education for the entire school day or most of it, and support services for those who are mainstreamed in regular classes for varying lengths of time during the day. While current programming encourages the integration of emotionally disturbed children, the emotional handicaps defined in legislation refer only to the more severe disorders, those students considered most difficult to integrate. The Education of All Handicapped Children Act, PL 94-142 (1975), only provides services for students considered seriously emotionally disturbed. The definition reads, in part,

> a condition exhibiting one or more of the following characteristics over a long period of time and to a marked degree, which adversely affects educational performance. . . . an inability to learn which cannot be explained by intellectual, sensory, or health factors, inability to build or maintain satisfactory interpersonal relationships with peers and teachers. (p. 42,478)

The important phrases are *marked degree* and *over a long period of time*.

Another irony is that the definition in PL 94-142 was originally designed to identify the mildly handicapped. As a result of this definition and law, however, some school personnel are concerning themselves less with the mildly impaired and more with those who have severe emotional impairments. Others resist this definition because the disturbed child continues to demand an inordinate amount of programming attention and effort. State departments of mental health and education have failed to agree on spheres of mutual and exclusive responsibility. This legislation will certainly affect the design and nature of programs in the 1980s.

The following issues will significantly influence the service design in the 1980s:

1. *Labeling.* Many educators resist labeling children to obtain services. The benefits and disadvantages of the labeling process have been thoroughly explored in the professional literature. One reason for the resistance that is rarely discussed is the fact that most school personnel lack confidence when using diagnostic procedures.

2. *Parent involvement.* In the early stages of psychoeducational programming, work with parents was seen as an instrumental part of the educational/therapeutic process. The intent of PL 94-142 is to establish a partnership between educators and parents in planning and programming for handicapped children. There is a growing trend to hire parents as co-workers in special education programs. In the area of the emotionally disturbed, however, there has been a recognized reluctance to discuss the emotional problems of students with their parents. Other disabilities are much easier to discuss with parents and ultimately to accept. This resistance to dealing openly with the problems of emotionally disturbed children often begins with a search for more desirable labels before identifying the problem as emotional, labels that might otherwise explain the observed discrepancy between performance and potential. The label of *learning disabled* is most popular at present. Undoubtedly, many students currently identified as learning disabled are struggling with an emotional disturbance which is misdiagnosed or avoided by professionals and parents alike.

3. *Support personnel.* The failure to provide sufficient supportive and adjunct therapeutic personnel for programs for the emotionally disturbed has changed the nature of these programs dramatically. The ties between cognition and healthy affective functioning have apparently never been established sufficiently to satisfy educators. Very little attention is paid to these ties in practice. Education has seemingly stepped away from the responsibility of restoration or remediation of affective growth and only marginally addresses the issue of promoting mental health in students.

Many special educators feel that the preceding issues have produced a rather bleak educational picture for most of the children who have emotional problems in public schools. Many are concerned that children are being identified for special services without sufficient diagnostic information to support and direct specific programming and intervention. Psychoeducators feel the need to establish effective guidelines for programs that do more than contain student behavior. Present guidelines appear to be more determined by financial and service definitions than by theoretical information or by the needs of the children. There is great professional and parental concern that students known to have emotional problems in their early developmental years simply continue through the educational system without receiving the services they need. Their condition is sometimes worse when they leave. We are inclined to believe this is the result of the movement of educational programming away from its original theoretical base in the search for more specific interventions, to a programming effort overly concerned with behavior containment. Perhaps today's emphasis on programming for the seriously emotionally disturbed will encourage a return to a theoretical base and a search within psychoeducational theory for concomitant educational direction. An attempt must be made by the proponents of this model to provide definitive guidelines for the extrapolation of theory to educational practice.

THE PSYCHOEDUCATIONAL THEORY

Of the theoretical models considered in this book, the psychoeducational model has the oldest roots. Most special educators associate the psychoeducational model with the psychoanalytic movement and Sigmund Freud. As Cheney and Morse (1976) wrote, however, "the psychodynamic position owes much to Freud and the analytic school, but this psychological approach is not owned or circumscribed by them; many other psychologists have been concerned with the inner life" (p. 259).

The association of the psychoeducational model with psychoanalytic theory has both positive and negative ramifications. Many of the major concepts of personality development and the dynamic nature of behavior have come from psychoanalytic theory. At the same time, many of the criticisms of the psychoanalytic approach are automatically leveled at the psychoeducational model. Models, if they are to be effective, must be based on theory. It is theory that provides organization and consistency. The psychoeducational model has established its foundation on psychoanalytic theory.

Cheney and Morse (1972) identified two basic constructs they felt to be "critical to the psychodynamic explanation of the nature of the child and his development" (p. 262). These constructs were (1) the evolution of the self around biologically determined predispositions and (2) the interactive nature of the personality with the environment. These constructs also represent the two basic groups of theorists who have contributed to the body of psychodynamic theory. The most important theorists in the first group, who suggested the biological predispositions of the individual personality, included Sigmund Freud, Anna Freud, and Heinz Hartmann. In the discussion which follows, we will examine some of the contributions of these theorists.

According to Rezmierski and Kotre (1974), Hartmann considered six constructs basic to Freud's early formulations:

1. The *topographic* point of view emphasized the existence of "areas" of the mind and insisted that unconscious as well as conscious processes were at work in people.
2. The *dynamic* point of view emphasized that behavior was motivated, that all behavior was purposeful and meaningful.
3. The *structural* point of view posited the existence of id, ego, and superego and implied that "conflict is implicit in all behavior and there are mental structures for mediating conflicts" (p. 191).
4. The *genetic* point of view emphasized that the "past persists into the present" (p. 191).
5. The *economic* point of view, probably the most controversial of the underlying constructs, postulated a quantitative relationship between drives and resistances.
6. The *adaptive* point of view regarded the environment or real world as a determining factor of behavior.

The least significant construct for this educational model is the *economic* point of view, which will not be discussed further.

The ideas that behaviors are meaningful, that they reflect both conscious and unconscious motivations, and that past persists into present are central to the psychoeducational approach to children. Psychoeducators search for patterns in observable behavior. They believe that each behavior reflects needs, but they don't hope to understand the meanings of the behaviors until the patterns are obvious. Efforts are made to understand the needs which the behaviors represent and to assist the child in meeting those needs so that development can continue without excessive conflict. The role of the unconscious in determining behavior is considered significant, but the emphasis upon the id, Freud's structural construct, is less important in the psychoeducational model than in psychoanalytic theory.

The construct of structuralism was decidedly changed by the contributions of Anna Freud. She emphasized the functions of the ego rather than those of the id, which are so significant in Sigmund Freud's conceptualizations. The ego is described as the intermediary between a person's needs and impulses and the ability to meet them. The purpose of the ego as a psychological mechanism is to channel impulses to sources of gratification to reduce the tension of the organism. Anna Freud theorizes that this is an orderly process whereby defensive postures protect the organism from excessive tension and the needs of the individual are met in the most economical fashion possible. Anna Freud describes the relationship between the person's needs and the ego's maneuvers to reduce tension as passing through definite stages of development. Rezmierski and Kotre (1974) reinforced the existence of this relationship.

> The functions of the ego and the relation between id and ego are not seen as static, but rather as constantly changing. The changes occur most predictably at various developmental stages. Anna Freud

points out that, because of the dynamic nature of the ego, a particular ego reaction to stimuli cannot be termed pathological or normal without extensive examination of the stage of development which is being reflected at the particular time. *(p. 212)*

This work relates to the psychoeducational model in that it theoretically brought the internal determinants of behavior into the arena of systematic study. If the maneuvers of the ego to reduce tension and channel the organism towards the gratification of needs, or to defend against the tension, are identifiable in observation of behaviors, and if the conflicts are predictably greatest at given stages of development, then the development of the personality might be monitored or even assisted by interventions or support at those critical points.

Heinz Hartmann extends this conception of the ego in his hypothesis concerning its basic precursors, which both biologically determine, and develop to become, an organization of the ego. He calls these precursors the *ego apparatuses.* They include perception, motility, memory, and stimulus screen. Rezmierski and Kotre (1974) state that

the apparatuses develop in response to stimulation and learning from the environment and in line with the maturational laws of their biology. They become integrated into a pattern of interdependent functions and become the ego. *(p. 213)*

These potential structures develop in response to stimulation and learning and become increasingly complex. As development proceeds, these structures become increasingly well-organized. The ego grows ever more able to manage the process of adaptation to the environment with the cohesive strength of these interdependent functions, which constitute its strength.

Recognition of the important role of the ego, through such functions as memory, perception, and the screening of stimulation in adapting to the environment, is credited to Hartmann, although others were involved in elaborating the concept. These extensions of the structural and adaptation constructs of psychoanalytic theory bring the development of personality further into the arena of educational endeavors. At least theoretically, the possibility exists that the environment plays a role in promoting ego growth through adequate stimulation and structure.

While Hartmann seems to have opened the door to better understanding of the adaptive function of the ego and the interactive nature of the person with the environment, the second group of theorists we review in this chapter has vastly extended this concept. Maslow (1972) once wrote regarding his conceptual relationship to Freudian doctrine:

I am carrying on the spirit of Freud — not the psychoanalysts, who are merely pious and loyal. I try to tell them that I can take it all for granted. I have eaten it all and digested it and have made it into my flesh, which it now is. But I am eager for the next meal. I am not content to regurgitate and chew and rechew on the same cud. I've already gotten the nourishment out of it, discarded the non-nutritious parts, and then gone on to building something myself. *(p. 72)*

Each of the following theorists has gone on to build unique conceptual models. Erik Erikson, who will be discussed in the most detail, has made significant contributions to the psychoeducational model. Abraham Maslow, an existentialist, is included because he conceptualized motivation not as a conflictual struggle between id and ego, but as a self-perpetuating flow towards health. Like Erikson, Kurt Lewin, another eminent pioneer, has extended our focus beyond intrapsychic inquiry through his conceptualization of the importance of the individual's *life space*. Carl Rogers could also have been included in this group. Instead, we have chosen to discuss the work of Lawrence Kohlberg, a cognitive theorist following Piaget's work, because of the educational implications of his theory and its potential relationship to the psychoeducational model. Erikson's work provides the most support for the psychoeducational model, so his work will be discussed first.

Erikson's work incorporates all of the constructs of the Freudian theory previously discussed, but he also built something for himself. The concept of development as an orderly progression from stage to stage is extended by Erikson's model. Like previous theorists, he emphasizes that the stages of development are more visible due to the crises which occur at each psychosocial state. He sees these crises, however, as highly significant signs, moments for decision between growth and regression.

Erikson incorporates the important concept of adaptation to the social environment at each stage of psychosexual development. He describes eight distinct stages of psychosocial development through which every person can potentially and progressively pass as he or she matures. He characterizes each stage according to the antagonistic forces that cause its central conflict within that stage — conflict which must be resolved for development to continue. At each stage the conflict exists because the needs and the impulses of the person must be met in harmony with the social resources of the environment. The ego's maneuvers to adapt and match needs to resources are most visible during these crisis periods. Successful matching and the resultant reduction of tension free the person for continued development and interaction with the environment. Unsuccessful matching and adaptation cause the binding of energy and the continuation of conflict or the regression to earlier forms of need gratification. The eight states which Erikson delineated in *Childhood and Society* (1950) are:

1. basic trust versus basic mistrust
2. autonomy versus shame and doubt
3. initiative versus guilt
4. industry versus inferiority
5. identity versus identity diffusion
6. intimacy versus isolation
7. generativity versus stagnation
8. ego integrity versus despair

According to Erikson's scheme, growth is the successful resolution of conflicts at each stage of development. This leaves the person as fully responsive to the social and environmental influences and as free from stress as possible. In such a case, needs are fulfilled in harmony with environmental and social gratifications. It should be noted that although Erikson identifies stages in a person's growth as characterized by certain conflicts, he does not consider the developmental process to be laden with conflict. Rather, he regards these stages as more visible because of the critical nature of the ego's struggle at these stages. In Erikson's words, the conflicts are the ego's attempt to accommodate the needs, the "timetable of the organism," with the acceptable modes of adjustment, the "structure of social institutions."

It is important also to note the nature of these stages. Erikson describes these stages as a hierarchy through which each person passes in invariable order. The speed with which a person accomplishes this journey is determined in part by biological endowments, accomplishments at previous stages, and interaction with the environment. The accomplishment or the resolution of conflict at each stage frees energy and causes a need to progress on to higher stages of development. The motivation is inherent in the successful resolution of conflict by adapting internal needs to the external sources of gratifications.

The contributions of Erikson's theory to the psychoeducational model are (1) that it identifies the distinct stages of development, (2) that it claims a common sequence of development through which each person may potentially pass, and (3) that it speaks directly to the aspects of struggle that the environment affects and indicates ways in which environmental resources might assist in the successful resolution of conflict at each stage. Promotion or restoration of development may be a direct result of the environment's responsiveness.

Maslow is cited in this discussion because his conceptualization resembles that of Erikson. Erikson's stages nearly parallel the needs system of Maslow. The progression from one set of needs to another higher one, said to be the motivation for growth, is similarly explained by Maslow (1970) who states that "the most basic consequence of satisfaction of any need is that this need is submerged and a new and higher need emerges" (p. 60).

Two of the more important aspects of Maslow's theory are (1) that people's needs are satisfied in a progression, one step at a time; and (2) that all human needs are arranged in a hierarchy of potency. The first concept is basic to his theory. As each set of needs is satisfied, a new set emerges and the person strives for that set to be satisfied. The second concept is identical to the hierarchical stage conception of Erikson; however, instead of emphasizing antagonistic forces, Maslow identifies the sets of needs which characterize steps on his hierarchy. The basic needs identified in *Motivation and Personality* (1970) are: (1) physiological needs, such as the need to satisfy hunger, thirst, etc.; (2) the safety needs, for security, stability, dependency, protection, freedom from fear; (3) belongingness and love needs, which include the need for togetherness with someone else, for belonging and rootedness; (4) the esteem needs — the desire for strength, achievement, adequacy, mastery, and competence; and (5) the need for self-actualization, which is the need for harmony between what is realized in self-fulfillment and one's potential.

Maslow's theory provides an added dimension not only to the hierarchical schema of development but also to a more comprehensive understanding of human motivation, which is certainly a critical aspect of any educational model. Erikson and Maslow have both illustrated the importance of interpersonal and environmental experiences on individual development and growth.

Perhaps no theorist, however, has emphasized the importance of the human and physical environment as extensively as Kurt Lewin. For Lewin, the space around a person, the environment in which a person finds himself or herself, is important both because it represents the pattern of forces that interact with the person and also because it illustrates a completely individual momentary interaction, the "momentary situation of the child." Lewin (1935) writes:

> The actual behavior of the child depends in every case upon his individual characteristics and upon the momentary structure of the existing situations. It is not possible, however, as is increasingly obvious, simply to single out one part to be attributed to the environment and another to be ascribed to the individual.

Lewin's work combines dynamic information regarding the stages of development of the person with an examination of factors in the environment. It is through an analysis of the patterns of a person's interactions with that environment that one comes to understand the person's behaviors. In this conceptualization, the environment is not simply an arena in which the person's needs are evident, or the cause of a conflict, or simply the source of fulfillment of needs, but rather the determinant of behaviors, the determinant of which needs will be displayed. According to Lewin (1935),

> To understand or predict the psychological behavior (B) one has to determine for every kind of psychological event (actions, emotions, expression, etc.) the momentary whole situation, that is, the momentary structure and the state of the person (P) and of the psychological environment (E). $B = f(PE)$. Every fact that exists psychobiologically must have a position in this field and only facts that have such position have dynamic effects (are causes of events). The environment is for all of its properties (directions, distances, etc.) to be defined not physically but psychobiologically, that is, according to its quasi-physical, quasi-social, and quasi-mental structure. *(p. 79)*

This theory has special importance for the psychoeducational model. With its delineation of a potential field of influences on the child, a more comprehensive assessment is made possible for the educator. The child need not be seen as responsive solely to an internal set of drives and needs. The school and classroom environment must be considered as having a variety of influences on the behavior of the child, and as such a more global setting within which the educator may truly effect the growth and restoration of the child's functioning. Morse (1965) states:

> The life space theory, as we use it, holds that the distillates of one's life history constitute the present self-concept. Thus dynamics are incorporated, but the emphasis is in terms of their impact on the current field. . . . Historical material is not eliminated in favor of the circumstantial or the sociological, but it is jelled in the present self-concept and self-esteem of the child. *(p. 281)*

Lewin's theoretical premises have affected the way psychoeducators view the environment and many of the techniques they have developed. Similarly, cognitive theorists will probably affect the way psychoeducators view learning and cognitive development.

Cognitive psychologists, while relying on the metaphor of thought rather than affect, can be regarded as further differentiating the parameters of the psychoeducational model. They endorse several constructs identical to those of psychoeducators. Those we feel are most relevant are:

1. Development proceeds undirectionally in an orderly manner.
2. There are distinct organizational differences between children's and adults' behavior in all areas of human functioning.
3. Previous life experience persists by becoming structurally integrated with present experience.
4. Human behavior is the result of an interplay of conflicting forces.
5. Early development is basic to later development.

The final theorist included for discussion in this review, Lawrence Kohlberg, builds on the work of Piaget. His work can be viewed as explicating the development of the superego from the simplistic punishing parental introject of the analytic theorists to a highly complex cognitive structure. We include Kohlberg, not because his work has contributed to the psychoeducational model as it currently exists, but because of its potential for having a significant influence on this model in future years.

Kohlberg has delineated six different stages in three major levels of cognitive functioning. His work is designed to show how a person's moral decision-making reflects progression through these stages. The three levels are termed *preconventional, conventional,* and *postconventional.* While most persons consider his theoretical work cognitive in nature, it is the authors' opinion that the major levels he describes can be viewed as cognitive reflections of total personality development at different psychosocial

TABLE 2.1
PARALLELS AMONG THREE THEORISTS

Erikson	Maslow	Kohlberg
Ego integrity versus despair	Self-actualization	
Generativity versus stagnation	Esteem needs	Postconventional level
Intimacy versus isolation		
Identity versus identity diffusion		Conventional level
Industry versus inferiority	Belongingness and love needs	
Initiative versus guilt	Safety needs	Preconventional level
Autonomy versus shame and doubt		
Basic trust versus basic mistrust	Physiological needs	

stages. According to Galbraith and Jones (1975), at the preconventional level,

> an individual's moral reasoning results from the consequences of actions (punishment, reward, exchange of favor) and from the physical power of those in positions of authority. At the conventional level an individual's moral reasoning involves consideration of the interest of others (family and peers) and desire to maintain respect, support, and justify the existing social order. At the postconventional level an individual's moral reasoning incorporates moral values and principles that have validity and application beyond the authority of groups. Moral reasoning becomes more comprehensive and reflects universal principles. *(p. 17)*

These states reflect different organizations of the personality and the cognitive processes. A careful study of the two stages for each of Kohlberg's three levels reveals striking parallels to the Erikson and Maslow stages (see Table 2.1).

Edwin Fenton (1976) has summarized the generalizations drawn from research involving Kohlberg's theory:

1. People think about moral issues in six qualitatively different stages arranged in three levels of two stages each.
2. The most reliable way to determine a stage of moral thought is through a moral interview.
3. A stage is an organized system of thought.
4. An individual reasons predominantly at one stage of thought and uses contiguous stages as a secondary thinking pattern.
5. These stages are natural steps in ethical development, not something artificial or invented.
6. All people move through those stages in invariant sequences, although any individual may stop at any particular stage.
7. People can understand moral arguments at their own stage, at all stages beneath their own and usually at one stage higher than their own.
8. Higher moral stages are better than lower ones.

9. Stage transition takes place primarily because encountering real life or hypothetical moral dilemmas sets up cognitive conflict in a person's mind and makes the person uncomfortable.

10. Deliberate attempts to facilitate change in schools through educational programs have been successful.

11. Moral judgments are a necessary but not sufficient condition for moral action. *(pp. 189–190)*

The similarity of these generalizations to the theories previously discussed is striking. One should not miss: (1) the emphasis on crisis as an indicator of stage transition; (2) the hierarchical conceptualization of developmental stages; (3) the organization of the system (in this case the cognitive structure) around one level at a time; and (4) the invariant progression through the stages and the potential for stalled growth.

Perhaps the aspect of Kohlberg's work most important to the psychoeducator is that, while it is cognitive in nature, it has been directly applied in educational settings. Kohlberg's group has attempted to show that it is possible to identify a person's present stage in terms of his or her moral reasoning. They have also shown that growth can be promoted by teaching, using the moral discussion method and exposing the person to higher levels of reasoning.

The psychoeducator assesses the organization of the personality by the way a person responds to the environment and by the needs he or she demonstrates. The stages identified by Kohlberg can be an important cognitive component of these observations. We anticipate that assessment practices in areas such as moral judgment will prove helpful in identifying the stages of individual growth and facilitate the selection of appropriate curricula. Kohlberg's group has applied its findings to the selection and prescription of curricula in the same manner as psychoeducators. The ties between Kohlberg's work and that of the other theorists discussed deserve the attention of students of the psychoeducational model. These theorists provide the basis for the model. Yet the student may rightfully ask why, with so much theoretical support, this model has not been defined more specifically.

Problems with the Psychoeducational Model

In the final section of this chapter, we address the alleged lack of specificity of the psychoeducational model. We also discuss several related issues that have influenced and continue to influence the model's design.

Although the theoretical basis for the psychoeducational model seems to consist of bits and pieces, much theory reflects its well-integrated, cohesive structure. Yet practitioners who subscribe to this model continue to be haunted by major concerns. They ask why the psychoeducational model for educating emotionally disturbed children remains an enigma. Why can't this model develop a more carefully defined prescriptive technology to confirm its premises and assist its practitioners? Three issues should be examined to answer these questions.

First, there seems to be a need among psychoeducators to maintain a nonspecific design. Perhaps the task of extracting the applicable educational principles and techniques in this theory is simply impossible. Perhaps empirical study of the area is not yet possible. Perhaps we have determined that there are no benefits to extrapolating such principles for education. Most probably, however, the answer is simply that no one in any of the academic disciplines has considered it his or her responsibility to translate the theory into educational goals or objectives. Educators are rarely sufficiently trained in the theory to undertake such academic pursuits. Researchers typically pursue other endeavors. Additionally, much of psychoeducational theory pertains to concepts such as ego development and the expression and resolution of feelings. It is not easy to quantify such ephemeral dynamics as personality change and growth. They are not parceled into easily measurable bits like *out-of-seat* and *talk-out* types of behaviors. Nevertheless, a critical gap seems to exist; there is a kind of no-man's-land where neither the theorist nor the educator wants to work or feels qualified to work. The result is an approach with nonspecific practices, disconnected from fundamental theory.

Second, there is much emotional resistance to expending the effort necessary to bring the appropriate practices and prescribed interventions into use. Perhaps this is a residual attitude in education, in which it has long been felt that teachers are born, not made, and in which the process of teaching is proudly referred to as an art rather than a science. The rationale often heard is that children are not machines and that the teaching process is not easily made objective. This is an argument scientists are quick to use as evidence of the psychoeducator's lack of desire to discipline students. Practitioners must begin to ask how this motive has contributed to the persistent vagueness of the psychoeducational model. At present, a project entitled "Intervention by Prescription," under the direction of Rezmierski, is contributing to work in this area. A goal of this project is to develop and demonstrate a system for working with emotionally disturbed youth that derives psychoeducational interventions directly from developmental theory via an extended diagnostic and ecological search process. Perhaps this project will render the model more specific.

The third major concern for psychoeducators is why the parameters of the model continue to shift and change and seem to incorporate aspects of each new model that is introduced. Is the model defined or is it still evolving by absorbing pieces of other models as they become popular? The concept that the total environment must be examined to understand an emotional disturbance, for example, is being rapidly adopted by psychoeducators, although it is the foundation of the ecological model. Since Redl's work in the 1950s, and Lewin's work in the 1930s, the importance of the milieu has been a significant part of the psychoeducational approach.

The locus of disturbance was still viewed as within the person, however. The emphasis has now changed. The person remains an integral part of the model even though the ecological perspective claims no such singular locus. Perhaps some constructs have always been recognized as part of the psychoeducational model but are now being elaborated upon in other models. The concern of psychoeducators for milieu consistency and predictability, for example, is very similar to that of the behaviorists who have embellished these concepts with exquisite systems of contingent punishments and rewards. Perhaps, too, in response to the accumulated clinical knowledge and the need to be responsive to an ever-changing world, psychoeducators adopt as their own what they perceive to be the best of each model. Do these characteristics of the psychoeducational model make it less viable, less meaningful, less useful? Or are these, rather, significant issues that must be dealt with as this model is further developed and refined?

Long, Morse, and Newman (1976) have identified eighteen principles which they consider basic to the psychoeducational approach. These principles distinguish the psychoeducational model from the others: the dynamic interaction between affect and cognition and between the educational process and a child's unique needs; the important role of human and physical structure in meeting needs; the importance of understanding needs to plan educational or behavioral programs; the changing nature of needs; the potential for restoring growth through prescriptive and timely interventions; and the role of curriculum in their prescription.

SUMMARY

In this chapter we have identified the trends in the development of the psychoeducational model, the theoretical constructs that form its fundamental base, and the current significant — albeit troublesome — issues which influence it. In the chapters that follow on curriculum and management techniques, the methods associated with this model of educating emotionally disturbed children will be discussed. It is incumbent on those of us who wish to further develop and refine this model to create the concert, to conscientiously implement and document our efforts and extrapolate the practical information we need from the theory.

Chapter 3

Ecological Perspectives of the Emotionally Disturbed Child

Susan M. Swap
Wheelock College

Alfonso G. Prieto
Arizona State University

with

Robert Harth
University of Missouri, Columbia

Proponents of the ecological perspective believe that emotional disturbances are the result of the interaction between a child and a particular environment. They do not assume that a problem resides in the child exclusively. As a result, ecological research and theoretical formulations focus on understanding the physical and social properties of environments, the characteristics of children, and the interactions among them.

Ray's experiences demonstrate how a child's environment can influence his performance. Ray came from a small town in North Carolina. His parents were wealthy, and he was enrolled in a demanding school where most children performed one to two years above national achievement levels. Ray was a serious behavior problem in this school, and he also had major academic difficulties.

He was placed in a special school for disturbed children, where he made considerable progress in social behavior and academics. At the end of treatment he returned to his former school. Despite the progress he had made, he was still a marginal student. His teachers questioned whether he could manage there and continued to express concern about his behavior.

Consequently, he was assigned to another school, where the achievement level was considerably lower and the staff was more relaxed about behavior. In this school, Ray blossomed. He advanced to the top of the class and became an acknowledged leader.

Ray's experiences are not unique. Many children who exhibit behavioral and academic problems in one classroom succeed when they are placed in a different program with different expectations and a new teacher. Some children who seem lost and inadequate in a regular class flourish when individually tutored or placed in a special class (Pastor and Swap, 1978). Mercer (1971) has found that mildly retarded children in regular classes are less likely to be referred for special class placement if they have a friend in the regular classroom. Children's behavior at home may vary considerably depending on the situation. Aggressive, highly active behavior in a three-year-old between 4:00 and 7:00 P.M. can sometimes be alleviated by an early dinner at 5:00 P.M. or exaggerated by a visit from a friend or by the expectation that the child amuse himself or herself quietly during this period.

In each of these examples, disturbing behavior is influenced by the environment. You may wonder whether the inappropriate behaviors of these children are the result of problems in the child, in the setting, or in the interaction between the child and the setting. The answer to this question is determined by one's assumptions about the nature and causes of disturbance.

The first section of this chapter explains the assumptions about disturbance that characterize the ecological perspective. Because the evaluation of environments is essential to this model, we present a framework for categorizing environments into levels of increasing complexity.

In the second section, we explore the historical roots of the ecological model. Many disciplines share an interest in ecology and provide information related to an understanding of deviance. We discuss the contributions of ecological psychology to the ecological perspective on disturbance. These two approaches are different, but the ecological perspective has borrowed many methods, concepts, and findings from ecological psychology.

In later sections we present examples of assessment tools and intervention approaches based on the hierarchy of levels developed in the first section. We also weigh the value and limitations of the assessment tools and intervention strategies offered by this relatively new perspective on disturbance.

ASSUMPTIONS OF THE ECOLOGICAL MODEL

The ecological model of disturbance is based on several assumptions about the interaction between a child and the environment.

Assumption 1: The Child Is Not Disturbed

According to the ecological model, emotional disturbance is not the exclusive property of the child (Rhodes, 1970). Rather, disturbance results from an interaction between the child and his or her environment. The ecological system or environment contributes to the interaction in two ways. First, the environment may present conditions that elicit disturbing behaviors in the child. A series of assignments that are too difficult for a child may encourage him or her to behave badly. A group of children teasing or bullying a child may make the child spit at them. Second, people in the setting must identify or label specific behaviors as disturbed. Rhodes (1967) maintains that disturbance does not exist without a reactor group to register the condition. He contends further that whether a given behavior, once identified, is seen as disturbed depends on "which societal institution at a particular period of time in a particular culture is allowed to make the judgment and provide the enjoining response" (p. 450). According to Rhodes and Paul (1978), the same act of physical assault might be labeled and dealt with differently by different social institutions. The act may be seen as a crime by the legal system, a sin by religious institutions, a symptom of physical illness by a neurologist, or of mental illness by a mental health professional. Treatment would vary accordingly.

This view of disturbance is in sharp contrast to the psychodynamic and medical models, which do locate disturbance in the child. According to these approaches, the *child* is schizophrenic or neurotic — the disease defines the child. The child is disturbed whether or not the disease is diagnosed properly. The environment is regarded as having a more limited influence on the production of disturbance. The medical model focuses on the physiochemical "environment" — nutrition, oxygen shortage at birth, etc. — that may lead to disturbance by damaging the child's brain (Rimland, 1969). The psychodynamic model emphasizes the "social" environment, particularly the role of the parents in increasing the child's internal conflict. From this perspective, although a stressful environment may contribute to the development of disturbance, no environment or event is stressful unless it is interpreted as such by the child (Freud, 1954).

The ecological model, then, represents a significant shift from the way disturbance has been viewed through the psychodynamic and medical models. The ecological model transforms the ways we evaluate the causes and treatment of emotional disturbance in children and the ways we define and study the environment and the interactions between the child and the environment.

Environment and Ecological System: Definitions.   These two terms are often used interchangeably by ecologists seeking to understand emotional disturbance in children. They may be narrowly or broadly defined. Swap (1978) identified three uses of these terms, which vary in inclusiveness and complexity. The narrowest definition of environment or ecological system states that it consists of a child in a single behavior setting. According to Gump (1975), a behavior setting consists of a physical milieu, a program of activities, inhabitants, and a location in time and space. Examples include a drug store and a classroom (the latter includes several subsettings, such as reading groups or art lessons). We will consider this use of the terms *environment* or *ecological system* Level 1.

At Level 2, these terms refer to the behavior of a child in more than one behavior setting. The ecological system might include the child's behavior both at home and at school, or in the homeroom and the lunchroom at school.

Environment or *ecological system* is still more broadly defined at Level 3. At this level, investigators search for patterns of behavior settings in the community or culture. Ecologists would regard the fact that residential institutions and public schools across our country have many similarities in physical milieu, programs of activities, inhabitants, and schedules as a reflection of the values and priorities of our culture.

Patterns of Disturbing Interactions.　Although the fundamental assumption of this model is that a disturbance never exists in the child exclusively, different patterns of faulty adaptation between the child and the environment (or precipitants of disturbance) can be identified. Sometimes a child elicits disturbing responses in many different settings. This pattern is relatively rare. In such a case, extensive adaptations must be made in each setting inhabited by the child to prevent disturbance. For example, an autistic child might cause consternation by hand flapping or spinning objects in the supermarket, in a normal classroom, or at the family dinner table. This behavior might be reduced and replaced by appropriate behavior in a quiet, familiar, unstimulating setting in which demands on the child are minimal, appropriate to the child's capacity, and presented by a single, affectionate caregiver (Park, 1967).

More frequently, a disturbance is the result of a faulty interaction between a particular child and a particular setting. In the second pattern, a disjunction between a person's characteristics and the expectations of the setting creates a disturbance. Trouble might be expected from a child with dyslexia in a class of highly verbal children with an academically demanding teacher; from a highly active, intense child in a chaotic open classroom with a teacher who dislikes setting limits; or from an uncoordinated son playing catch with a father whose own ambition was to be a major league ball player. These children might not be disturbing in a different setting; these settings may be quite supportive to a child with different characteristics.

A third pattern of faulty encounter occurs when a child learns a pattern of behavior that is adaptive in one setting but creates problems in another. In a case reported by Thomas, Chess, and Birch (1968, pp. 144–

146), a four-year-old boy was ridiculed and attacked by other children because of his formal politeness, pedantic language, and disorganized apprehension (crying, confusion) when hit by other children. His parents modeled and encouraged Hal's pedantic, formal language, but they grew concerned when it became clear that this behavior led to ridicule by other children. Guidance provided to the parents emphasized a formula that would help Hal deal with both the home and outside environments and reduce the dissonance between them. The parents encouraged Hal to hit back and refrain from crying when he was hit, to restrain his use of pedantic language, and to consider the wishes of other children. The parents were able to modify their behavior, which led to a decrease in the deviant patterns and the establishment of good relationships between Hal and other children.

Finally, there is a pattern in which the characteristics of the setting are so demanding that disturbance in some of its inhabitants is common. The characteristics of these settings are often dictated by a cultural blueprint: young children are expected to learn to read by spending long hours seated quietly at a desk; single mothers with little education raise children in poverty and isolation; minority children who are slow in school and who exhibit behavior problems are sent to classes for the retarded; adolescents who fail in school are not given an opportunity for responsible employment. Community or cultural patterns affect how classrooms are organized, who provides services to children, how such services are delivered, how abnormal behavior is defined, and which children are funneled into which services.

One child experiencing stress in a given setting may act out and become the target for intervention, but other children in the setting may also be experiencing difficulties. Settings with very limited choices and very demanding expectations seem to compel disturbing interactions from some of their members. An interaction between the child and the setting is still required to produce disturbance, but in this pattern, alternatives for one target child are usually easily found.

At the opposite end of the spectrum are settings that do not reflect a cultural pattern and contain bizarre and destructive elements. A child kept in a locked attic might be an example. Studies of "invulnerable children" (Garmezy, 1976) remind us, however, that interaction with the characteristics of the child is always required to produce disturbance, since some children appear to thrive even amidst extreme environmental stress.

In conclusion, faulty interactions are sometimes prompted by unusual characteristics in a given child or a given setting. More frequently, disturbance is caused by a lack of mutual adaptation between child and setting or an inconsistency of expectations across settings. Some faulty interactions patterns are commonplace in particular cultures and seem to be dictated by shared values or historical precedents.

Assumption 2: Interventions Must Alter the Ecological System

According to the ecological model, interventions designed to eliminate disturbance must focus on altering the system in which disturbing behavior occurs. As Hobbs (1975) explains, "the objective is not merely to change or improve the child but to make the total system work" (p. 114).

To understand how the total system works, one would need to assess the characteristics of the child, the setting, and the points of discord between them. Interventions would be designed to alter the discord. The child would not be the sole focus of the intervention strategies. In fact, proponents of the ecological model consider it inappropriate and unethical to exclude children from the setting in which disturbance is occurring, treat them in isolation, and then return them to an unchanged environment. The chosen treatment might not satisfy the requirements of the child's natural environment, and it might be impossible for the child to demonstrate or maintain treatment gains in a different setting.

Consider the interventions chosen for Michael, who was enrolled in a laboratory preschool at age five. Although he had participated in the program for three months, he still could not locate his cubby and called his teacher only "Teacher." The psychologist suspected emotional problems because of Michael's disorientation and lack of relationship skills and wondered whether he should be placed in a program for disturbed children.

Michael's assessment by the psychologist involved considerable discussion with Michael's mother. It emerged that Michael's home environment was quite impoverished: a few small rooms, a television and a Sears catalogue for the child's amusement. In contrast, the lab school class was a large room with many complex units, such as a climbing structure. Behind one wall was a screened observation booth through which shadowy forms and subdued voices could be heard. Another side of the classroom was bounded by a window which looked out on a busy outdoor play area. There were four adults supervising the class of sixteen children.

It became clear that Michael was overwhelmed by this environment. In addition to the lack of experience with the materials and arrangement of the environment, diagnostic tests revealed that he had difficulties in visual perception and visual association.

Several adaptations in the classroom were made for Michael. The teacher greeted him at the beginning of the day, oriented him to the environment, and offered him two choices for the first activity. She spent twenty minutes a day with him in a small room next to the classroom, exposing him to materials used in class. A tutor also worked individually with Michael every day for half an hour, focusing on enjoyable activities that trained visual skills. After a month, another child was included in the tutoring sessions.

Michael improved significantly under this program. He learned his teacher's name, approached every day's activities with enthusiasm, and began to initiate activities with other children. Emotional disturbance was no longer suspected.

It was crucial in this case to conduct an assessment which evaluated Michael's characteristics, setting characteristics, adult expectations, and the relationships among them. Labeling Michael "disturbed" and removing him to a special class was unnecessary and probably would not have helped Michael adapt and learn from the challenges that this setting presented.

Three implications follow from the assumption that interventions should alter the total system. First, we must devote serious attention to the taxonomy of ecological systems; that is, to discovering, identifying, and classifying the personal and environmental variables that contribute to disturbance. Both child and adult behaviors are normalized — the child is seen, not as disturbed, but as reacting to the disjunction between his or her characteristics and the expectations for behavior in the setting. The adult is not regarded as inadequate or pathological either, but as temporarily unable to structure the setting so that the child can respond appropriately.

Adherents of this model de-emphasize individual deficits. In fact, some ecologists (for example, Rhodes and Paul, 1978) advocate not simply an increased tolerance of difference in children, but the celebration of individual differences in children and adults.

Ecologists are generally active and optimistic about creating changes in ecological systems. Since they emphasize changing specific discordant interactions in particular settings rather than altering personalities or a person's perception of reality, they assume that success will be more easily attained. Adults in the setting (and sometimes children as well) are considered competent partners in a problem-solving effort.

A final implication of assumption 2 is that interventions can occur at several levels, including the community-cultural (Level 3). David's story is an example of an ecological intervention at the community-cultural level.

David had been placed in a self-contained class for emotionally disturbed children when he entered public school. In November, 1975, PL 94-142 was passed, which made placement of children in the least restrictive environment mandatory by 1978. It also specified, among other things, that every child's program be evaluated annually, that an individual educational plan be provided for each child, and that evaluation and placement decisions be agreed to by a child's parents or surrogates.

These federal guidelines had an immediate impact on David's school experience. An evaluation meeting was held in October, 1978, which included his parents, the teacher in his self-contained class, the regular teacher at his grade level, the special education director for the system, and the consulting psychiatrist. It was determined that he would spend 25 percent of his time in the regular class, and specific objectives were developed for his performance over the next year. The regular teacher was well prepared for his entrance into her class and was very receptive. David flourished under the new arrangement and plans were developed to place him in a regular class for 70 percent of the time during the next year.

The changes in David's school environment and experience did not stem from any changes in David's behavior or any initiative by those who knew David, but from a blueprint for action developed by Congress and guided by intensive lobbying for protection of the rights of the handicapped. The impetus for the evaluation, the goals and processes of the evaluation, the roles of those in attendance at the evaluation, and even the percentages of time spent in the regular classroom were suggested by the federal blueprint.

Assumption 3: Ecological Interventions Are Eclectic

Ecologists borrow from many disciplines when designing interventions to alter a disturbing interaction. In a given system, it may be most appropriate to provide the child with psychotherapy and the mother of the child with a home care provider. In another system, key people in the ecosystem might be trained to use a behavior modification system and helped to clarify and simplify their expectations for the child's behavior. Hobbs (1975) suggests several possible intervention strategies appropriate to the ecological model: helping the child gain competency, change his or her priorities, or acquire needed resources; helping key individuals in the system revise their perceptions, gain new competencies, change their priorities or expectations, or acquire needed resources; restructuring the ways the child and others interact, or temporarily removing the child from the discordant situation (p. 120). Effective planning and implementation of an ecological intervention might also require coordinating resource persons from various disciplines and "someone who can move freely among and communicate with diverse disciplines in the performance of a liaison function" (Hobbs, 1975, p. 120). Teachers, medical personnel, and social workers have obvious roles in developing a program for a child in a school setting. Effective intervention at the community-cultural level might require the participion of people from even more diverse disciplines: lawyers, economists, politicians, and media experts.

Assumption 4: Interventions in a Complex System May Have Unanticipated Consequences

Willems (1971, 1977) emphasizes the interdependence of the ecological network and the inevitable emergence of additional effects, both intended and unintended, of an intervention designed to change one element in the system. An example of this principle is provided by Ann's treatment.

Ann was a seriously disturbed twelve-year-old in a residential school for disturbed children. At the time of referral, the public school was more concerned with her behavior and adjustment than her family was. In fact, her family was not particularly upset at Ann's behavior. They had a low income, little education, and minimal expectations for Ann's academic and social development.

In the residential school, Ann made considerable progress. Besides the changes in adjustment, however, the school inadvertently fostered other changes that subsequently proved disruptive. In particular, the school encouraged such behaviors as bathing every night, appropriate verbal manners, and eating with correct utensils. When Ann returned home after treatment she immediately began attacking her family for such things as not bathing every evening. In fact, it was impossible for them to do so because there was no running water in the home.

Needless to say, the family was quite upset with Ann; they were more upset with Ann at the end of treatment than at the beginning. Thus, because the ecology of Ann's home was not taken into consideration in treatment, the actual program tended to make Ann dysfunctional in that setting.

Assumption 5: Each Interaction Between Child and Setting Is Unique

No two children, no two settings are the same; any part of the system may change from week to week. No culture is like another; similar settings in a given culture may affect children differently. This assumption underscores both the power and the limitation of the ecological model. The need to treat each episode of disturbance as unique makes it inappropriate to try to predict what variables should be assessed in each case or to evaluate interventions and generalize the results to additional settings. On the other hand, this assumption provides freedom to assess system variables objectively, without a preconceived (and perhaps also limited or inappropriate) notion about what to look for and what to do when one finds "it." The ecological model provides a framework for assessment and intervention, but no characteristic and predictable strategies for action across systems or cultures.

ROOTS OF THE ECOLOGICAL PERSPECTIVE

Contributions from Other Disciplines

The ecological perspective emphasizes the interactions and interdependencies between organisms and environments. According to Holman (1977), "human ecology" has developed from three main sources: (1) plant and animal ecology, (2) geography, and (3) studies of the spatial distribution of social phenomena. She claims that there is little agreement, cohesiveness, or homogeneity about basic tenets and principles of the ecological approach among ecologists, primarily because of the different methods and interests pursued by ecologists from different disciplines.

A kinder view, presented by Rogers-Warren and Warren (1977) is that "the meaning of ecology is still evolving" (p. 4) and that the varied contributions of psychologists, educators, and sociologists who share the term *ecology* have elucidated different aspects of the connections between behavior and environments.

Rhodes and Paul (1978), for example, cite studies from many disciplines to support their argument that environments contribute to the development and expression of deviant behavior. To oversimplify, they cite sociological literature that related emotional disturbance to low socioeconomic status and area of residence, and medical literature that linked ulcers to the frequency and seriousness of illnesses. They argue that it is the community that defines deviance and present anthropological studies which illustrate that what is considered inappropriate in one culture (having hallucinations, being stingy) may be highly valued in another. Some of these studies focus on the individual and his or her particular response to environmental variables; others focus on the tendency of environments to compel behavior in any person. The aspects of environment that are studied also vary from discipline to discipline: residence patterns, availability of human and physical resources, and behaviors of peers are among the different variables examined.

It is not possible to derive a single definition of environment or ecology from these studies or to select a particular level of individual-environment interaction for attention. Nonetheless, hypotheses are generated from each of these ecological studies that may be useful in studying emotional disturbance in children.

A concept derived from ethology and sociology is that of the "ecological niche." An ecological niche is the role an organism plays in any of the various ecosystems available to it (Feagans, 1972). Rhodes and Paul (1978) suggest that a person who is emotionally disturbed occupies an "alien" niche or "a nonviable life pattern" that is "isolated and socially without function" (pp. 194–195). A person is shunted into this place by the community through a series of "ecological traps." The authors cite Mercer's study (1973) in which she discovered that a child placed in the alien niche called "mentally retarded" in Riverside, California went through a predictable series of traps. Enrollment in a public school (rather than a Catholic school) was crucial, since the Catholic school had no self-contained classes. The child had to fail; to perform unsatisfactorily after failing; to be perceived by the teacher as having low academic competence, poor adjustment, poor work habits, low competence in English, and few friends; to be referred to a psychologist, be given an intelligence test, and do poorly on it; and to have parents willing to agree to the label. Rhodes and Paul (1978) conclude:

> Thus, it can be seen in this set of studies that a child may be shunted through a variety of binds into a superfluous or specially contrived alien niche. It is also apparent that the way in which the teacher, the psychologist, the parent, and peers respond to the child plays a part in ascribing deviation and in processing the child into a spurious niche outside the mainstream of life of the larger ecosystem. *(p. 197)*

Contributions from Ecological Psychology

Distinctions Between Ecological Psychology and the Ecological Model of Disturbance. The discipline labeled *ecological psychology* has often been confused with the ecological perspective of emotional disturbance. Although the perspective presented in this chapter has borrowed many concepts and findings from the ecological psychologists, there are some important differences between the two approaches. As we have seen, the ecological perspective of disturbance provides guidelines for intervention in disturbing interactions. Ecological psychologists (typified by Barker, 1968, or Gump, 1975) are not interested in interventions, but in learning how humans ordinarily behave. They have developed elegant methodologies for exploring what happens in natural human environments. Ecological psychologists are not expected to alter the natural stream of behavior or to intervene or manipulate the environment or its inhabitants in any way. They examine objectively the multiple effects of others' (or nature's) interventions over short and long time spans.

A second distinction is that ecological psychologists have not been preoccupied with children and disturbing interactions, although such investigators as Kounin (1970) and Gump (1975) have provided considerable information about how disturbing interactions originate for normal and "disturbed" children in a variety of settings.

Another difference is that ecological psychologists have not systematically explored the fit or match between an individual child (including his level of development, temperament, motivation, and intelligence) and a given behavior setting (including aspects of teacher expectation, physical environment, and programming). As we have seen, this is a significant pattern for study in the ecological model of disturbance. Rather, their emphasis has been on describing what an individual child ordinarily *does* or on extracting from the behaviors of many children the patterns compelled by behavior settings and clusters of behavior settings. The insights borrowed from the ecological psychologists will now be more fully presented.

During a conference of behavior analysts and ecological psychologists, Gump (1977) summarized what behavior analysts might be able to learn from the concepts, methods, and findings of the ecological psychologists. Since behavior analysts are also interested in disturbance and intervention strategies, his summary is equally applicable to this chapter.

Learning to Observe in Natural Settings. First, Gump highlighted studies that have helped us learn to observe children's behavior in natural settings in meaningful ways. He cited Wright's work (1967), which emphasizes the importance of identifying what level of behavior one is observing (a raised eyebrow, making a collage) and provides a schema for classifying levels of behaviors. He mentions the contributions of Barker and Wright (1954) and Wright (1967) in developing a method for describing meaningful episodes of behavior as they occur in the natural stream of events and which include natural beginnings and endings. This system avoids collecting isolated "pieces" of behavior such as those generated by behavior-sampling or time-sampling observation systems, which frequently lose much data about the structure and interrelationships of behaviors. Gump also emphasizes Schoggen's (1963) method of recording how a child is influenced by others in a natural setting and breaking the information into units.

Measuring the Effects of Environments on Behavior. Even more extensive insights have been provided by the ecological psychologists in helping us conceptualize and measure behavior-environment interdependencies. Barker (1968) was struck by the power of our environments to elicit behavior. He explained, "We found, in short, that we could predict some aspects of children's behaviors more adequately from knowledge of the behavior characteristics of the drugstore, arithmetic classes, and basketball games they inhabited than from knowledge of the behavior tendencies of particular children . . ." (p. 4). Yet he also identified difficulties inherent in studying environments. Three problems were especially knotty: studying the characteristics of environments independent from the persons who inhabit them; determining which of the "infinite number of discriminable phenomena external to any individual's behavior" (p. 14) have important effects on that individual's behavior; and determining the boundaries and interrelationships among the different environments inhabited by people.

Barker and his associates (1963, 1968) originated the concept of the "behavior setting" as an appropriate ecological unit for studying interactions between people and environments. They suggested that a behavior setting (such as a baseball game) consists of one or more standing patterns of behavior and milieu (e.g., fielders catching fly balls, teams taking turns at bat). The milieu encompasses the behavior (the baseball field is the site for the baseball game); a fit, or *synomorphy,* exists between the milieu and the behavior (fielders all face the same direction, all members of the team at bat except the batter and base runners stay off the field); and there is a specified degree of interdependence among synomorphs or behavior-milieu parts (pitching, batting, and catching batted balls are all interdependent behaviors fundamental to the completion of a game). Gump (1975) summarized these sophisticated concepts in his definition, presented earlier, which stated that behavior settings encompass a physical milieu, a program of activities, inhabitants, and a location in time and space.

Studying Educational Environments. Ecological psychologists have used the concept of the behavior setting to study how naturally occurring educational environments affect children's behavior. Gump (1974) studied such aspects of the behavior settings of open and traditional classrooms as group size, external stimulation and guidance, and amount of time spent by pupils in moving, waiting, and getting organized. He found, among other things, that in the most open classroom, on-task behaviors of the children were significantly lower than in more traditional environments. He felt it was a mistake to judge only the individual motivation of students in explaining his results, since he discovered that the involvement of students in activities was consistently related to differences in setting characteristics.

In another study that used behavior settings as an important level of analysis, Kounin (1970) studied the influence of environmental variables in classrooms on the production of deviant behavior. He found that teachers' skill in managing transitions and in programming to relieve boredom was related to low deviancy rates in both disturbed and nondisturbed children. Kounin's emphasis was not on individual differences in pupils and teachers, but on the predictability of the influence of certain setting patterns on pupil behaviors. An extension of his work in preschool settings (Kounin and Sherman, 1979) led to the conclusion that preschool children's "length of stay in an activity setting is more reasonably attributable to an activity's holding power than to a child's attention span" (p. 146).

According to Gump (1977), ecological psychologists have also demonstrated that clusters of behavior settings such as those found in schools and communities condition our behaviors, expectations, and roles. Willems (1967) found that size of high schools was an important determinant of students' satisfaction with themselves, their sense of being valued, and their sense of obligation to the school. Students in the smaller schools were apparently needed more to sustain ongoing environmental operations, to occupy central roles, to work hard, and to take responsibility.

Ecological psychologists' investigations of environment-environment interdependencies focus on the relationships between behavior setting units and unit clusters. Gump (1977) illustrates the importance of the relations between units by emphasizing their relative location in time and space. Krantz (1974), for example, found that preschoolers' attention to stories was affected by their preceding activity. If recess preceded story time, they were less attentive than if rest time was presented first. Gump also emphasizes the discovery of the necessity for support settings and appropriate supportive relationships between settings in creating and maintaining beneficial environments. Libraries or learning centers are essential support settings for open classrooms — a two-way flow of teachers and students is essential for the supportive relationship to work.

ECOLOGICAL ASSESSMENT STRATEGIES

Purpose of Ecological Assessment Techniques

The purpose of ecological assessment is to identify the nature and cause of the faulty adaptation between the child and environment which has resulted in disturbance. It is an extraordinarily complex task, since as we have seen it requires assessing the child, the setting (or settings) the child inhabits, and the interaction between them. Baer (1977) states the problem succinctly: "Assessment of phenomenal reality is an infinite task, like defending against 'enemies.' We can spend any amount of our resources on it, we will never finish, we will never solve the problem, and if we fail eventually, we will not care much afterward anyway" (p. 116).

There is no single assessment tool that could be used to evaluate each relevant child-setting-system variable in a faulty encounter. Each instrument selects certain variables for attention; different assessment tools are generally used in combination to create as complete a picture of the interaction as possible. The striking new development in the literature is the recognition that setting variables must be assessed to clarify and correct a child's "problem" in behavior or learning. Many instruments are being introduced that require assessment of environmental variables. A highly selective review of some of these instruments follows.

Assessment of Children in Single Settings

Prieto and Rutherford (1977) devised a screening procedure for behaviorally disordered and learning disabled children based on ecological theory. It focuses on Level 1, the single behavior setting. This screening procedure focuses on a child's behavior in the classroom. The classroom is viewed as an ecosystem, and the classroom teacher is responsible for assessing a child's ecological niche, or role, in each classroom interaction. The breadth of the child's niche, or the range of roles that the child plays in the ecosystem, can also be assessed. The procedure has three distinct steps. The teacher first hypothesizes whether a child's niche in each encounter or interaction is positive or negative. A Niche Breadth Assessment Card is then used to determine how many positive and negative roles the child is playing in the ecosystem. If it is found that a child has one or more negative niches, as stated in the original hypothesis, then an Ecological Baseline Assessment Card is used. This card is used by the teacher to state the problem objectively and to begin to collect data related to the stated problem. Antecedent and consequent variables related to the production and maintenance of the child's behavior are also recorded on the card. With the information gained using this systematic technique, the teacher is better able to analyze the problem and devise appropriate intervention strategies. Examples of both the Niche Breadth Assessment Card and the Ecological Baseline Card are presented in Figures 3.1 and 3.2.

It should be emphasized that this screening procedure is used to analyze the child's interaction within the ecosystem. The purpose is to allow the teacher to assess the milieu or setting and the interactions that take place within it. With this information the teacher can restructure the behavior settings to expand the child's niche breadth and provide for an expansion of the roles available to the child. Although the child's behavior is the initial

FIGURE 3.1
NICHE BREADTH ASSESSMENT CARD

Child's Name _____ Date _____

Interface	Positive	Negative
Teacher Relations		X
Peer Relations		X
Other Adult Relations		X
Math	X	
Science	X	
Social Studies	X	
Reading		X
Language		X

focus, the major concern is assessing the interaction between the child and the reaction in the ecosystem. This provides an opportunity to change the behavior setting as well as the child.

Other ecological assessment techniques directed at Level 1 classroom settings are summarized by Wallace and Larsen (1978). They describe the recent trend toward ecological assessment of children with learning and behavioral problems, which emphasizes "those situational factors that may, in fact, have initiated or, at least, maintained the behavioral patterns that are of concern to the teacher" (p. 101). They suggest that "at a minimal level the teacher should be prepared to assess pupil-teacher interaction, pupil-curriculum 'match,' peer relationships, school and classroom climate, and extraneous variables existing outside the school setting" (p. 102). Several methods, such as systematic observation, teacher-child interaction systems, checklist and rating scales, and sociometric techniques may be used to gather information in these areas.

Carroll (1974) recommends evaluating nine setting characteristics and five learner characteristics to provide the basis for generating goals for the child, hypotheses about the child's learning and emotional characteristics, and a learning plan. The framework for assessing the learning environment includes questions to be answered about classroom facilities, personnel, curriculum, climate, and resources. The selection and presentation of tasks are also studied, as are the formation and use of groups and the collection and analysis of data. How time is spent is also measured.

Laten and Katz (1975) emphasize gathering information on the par-

FIGURE 3.2
ECOLOGICAL BASELINE CARD

Child's Name _____ Date _____

Antecedents to problem: Statement of problem: Consequences of problem:

_____   _____   _____

_____   _____   _____

_____   _____   _____

_____   _____   _____

_____   _____   _____

Time (When does problem occur?):   Frequency (How often or long does
                                          problem occur?):

_____

_____   Day 1 _____   Day 6 _____

                                          Day 2 _____   Day 7 _____

Place (Activities/Location problem   Day 3 _____   Day 8 _____
occurs):
                                          Day 4 _____   Day 9 _____
_____
                                          Day 5 _____   Day 10 _____
_____

ticular settings and personnel involved when children are engaged in successful as well as problematic interactions. Knowledge about the skills required for a child to function successfully in different environments helps develop reasonable expectations for the child and for teachers in areas where the problem is most notable.

A long-term program of research undertaken by Moos (1979) has yielded an assessment tool for evaluating the effects of educational environments on student attitudes and behavior in high school and college settings. He identifies three key dimensions for evaluation: physical and architectural design, organizational factors, and the composition of the group. These factors are related to such variables as student absenteeism and satisfaction, achievement and competition, and student problem behavior. Assessment of educational environments is accomplished by using The University Residence Environmental Scale and The Classroom Environment Scale. The data collected by Moos and his associates with these instruments suggest many provocative changes in educational settings.

Assessment of the Same Child in Different Settings

The second level of assessment compares behavior across settings to determine the effect of different behavior settings on the behavior of the subject. Behavioral pattern differences across behavioral settings have been observed and described by several researchers. Thomas and Chess (1977) developed interview schedules and behavior checklists which enabled observers to compare the perceptions of significant adults concerning the characteristics of a child's behavior at home and school. Their study revealed that the same behaviors were occasionally viewed differently across settings, and behaviors which were perceived as problem behaviors in one setting were sometimes not perceived as problems in another. They concluded that perceptions of behavior as being troublesome or acceptable were a function of the expectations and the value systems held by the person making the observations.

One of the most significant contributions to the assessment of behavior across settings is the recent work by Mercer and Lewis (1978). Their instrument, the System of Multicultural Pluralistic Assessment (SOMPA), draws on several theoretical models: the medical model, the social systems model, and the pluralistic model. The SOMPA uses norm-referenced assessment procedures such as the WISC-R and Bender Gestalt. The scores from these instruments are then converted to scores that reflect the cultural variables that influence the child's performance. This conversion is done through the use of the sociocultural modality of the family. The Adaptive Behavior Inventory for Children (ABIC) and a physical dexterity instrument are also administered in this procedure. The data are then entered into a regression equation which results in an Estimated Learning Potential (ELP). The strengths of this assessment procedure are that it takes into account an array of variables that affect performance and expectations for performance and it uses information from various behavior settings. This assessment method evolved from the concept that the determination of dysfunction cannot be based on information or observations obtained from a single behavior setting.

Wahler, House, and Stambaugh (1976) have developed a procedure called the "Ecological Assessment of Child Problem Behavior." The procedure may be used to evaluate the behavior of a child in a single setting, in multiple settings, or both. The first step in the assessment is an interview with significant adults in the child's natural settings to identify problem behaviors and the specific situations in which these behaviors occur. The interview is used as the basis for data collection by the significant adults about their own behavior as well as the child's. In addition, a clinician or impartial observer collects observational data in thirty-minute samples with an instrument that measures adult and child behaviors and interactions in a natural setting. The clinician and the other participating adults compare their findings, try to decide what the problem is, and use these data to plan appropriate intervention.

Assessing the Effects of Cultural Values on Behavior Settings

Evaluation at the third level of analysis, the effects of community, culture, or both on the design of settings and patterns of behavior is even more complex and difficult than assessment at the other two levels. This level of evaluation must focus on the evaluation of clusters of settings, systems of interaction, and delivery systems through which services are made available to children. The technology of systems evaluation is not well developed.

Apter (1977) presents a model for community education based on ecological theory that might provide a starting point for assessing the effectiveness of a community's educational system. According to his model, learning should be continuous and lifelong; school and community participation in educational decision-making should be maximized; more kinds of educational programs for children and adults should be offered; personnel should realize that education is not owned by any one agency; and research and program development should address the totality of a person's education.

It is perhaps evident from Apter's criteria for community education that assessment of community blueprints cannot be value free. To evaluate the role of the community in creating disturbing interactions, one would need to study which children become labeled, how identification occurs, what service delivery systems are available, and how they affect the patterns and effectiveness of treatment according to multiple criteria. If we are to intervene at the community or culture level, we must establish methods to evaluate the bureaucratic structures and program components imposed on local service units, study the effects of regulations and guidelines related to the funding of programs, and examine methods by which service delivery systems can prevent discordance between the child and his or her ecosystems.

It is unfortunate that the courts have become one of the few effective methods available for assessing the appropriateness of the solutions developed by the community for the treatment of its disturbing children. In the last ten years, stunning decisions have, among other things, prohibited schools from excluding deviant children, required due process for any placement decision, required the participation of parents in evaluation and placement decisions, and required that a child be tested by more than one instrument as the basis for placement.

Gillespie-Silver (1979) developed a very comprehensive and practical format for assessing the community and the school as the basis for creating total programming for a child. Specifically, she created a checklist for assessing local services, which included information about local industries; ethnic groups; medical, legal, and mental health services; and their interactions. A second checklist assessed the types and nature of services provided by the state and region. Questions were asked about centers for community education, universities and colleges, regional mental health centers, regional resource centers, and state and local educational associations. Information was provided about services at the national level, and guidelines were presented for developing coordinated programs of services for the child. She also provided checklists for developing an educational plan for a child which uses community resources, and for developing a problem-solving strategy to implement the plan which attends to system variables such as availability of resources and support systems for the change agent.

ECOLOGICAL INTERVENTIONS

The Link Between Assessment and Intervention

In the ecological model, assessment and intervention are intertwined. As we have seen, the ecological model as applied to disturbance in children emphasizes *altering* faulty interactions as opposed to simply describing them. Wahler, House, and Stambaugh (1976) make this point clearly in introducing the ecological assessment package they have developed:

> The use of any assessment tool is, of course, closely associated with the question of intervention. A statement of assessment, no matter how reliable or valid, is useless unless it allows one to respond to a problem more appropriately than would have been possible without that information. The real value of an assessment instrument is its utility for planning and evaluating a treatment program. *(p. 1)*

The assessment procedures described in the preceding section are presented by their developers as bases for intervention. The intervention strategies discussed in this section are based on ecological assessment procedures. The authors mentioned here could also have been included in the assessment section — the differences in emphasis are generally very slight.

Interventions in Single Settings

Many articles have presented models for adapting single settings to optimize appropriate interactions. Swap (1974) presents a model for reducing disturbance in a classroom by adapting to developmental and temperamental differences in children. She mentions ways for the teacher to alter programming, expectations, and physical setting characteristics for children at different developmental levels. She emphasizes the need for teachers to evaluate their own values and expectations and to develop specific goals for themselves as well as the children.

Knoblock and Barnes (1979) describe an environment they have created for autistic and nonautistic children which emphasizes individualized programs for children based on a developmental assessment and an attempt to match "a child's needs with a teacher whose style and skills respond directly to those needs" (p. 221). Although the authors do not call their program ecological, their philosophy emphasizes mutual adaptation and tolerance for differences, developing support systems for teachers and parents, an eclectic methodology, and a variety of individual and sociometric assessment techniques that monitor multiple aspects of the environment and child-environment interactions.

Rogers-Warren (1977) proposes a set of guidelines to be used in developing ecobehaviorally based interventions in a classroom. This approach to planned change draws heavily on both ecological and behavioral concepts. The guidelines focus on tailoring change procedures to fit the specific characteristics of the setting and the target behavior. The steps are as follows:

1. *Identify the target behavior.* In addition to identifying the behavior by name and topography, assessment of the function of the behavior for the subject in the target setting is recommended.

2. *Assess the physical setting.* This is accomplished by initially identifying the persons frequently present in the target setting and noting their general functional relation to the target behavior and to the subject. The next step is to identify the important elements of the physical setting (room design, furniture, etc.). The final step of this phase involves identifying physical cues for the target behavior.

3. *Evaluate the contingency environment.* This phase is accomplished by determining what the consequences for the target behavior are and by considering the use of other contingencies to support changes in behavior.

4. *Determine the constraints the environment may place on an intervention.* The author emphasizes examining the feasibility of implementing a change effort. Variables related to feasibility include the amount of staff time required, the level of staff training needed, and the degree of alteration necessary to the physical arrangement.

5. *Determine if there are environmental arrangements that might facilitate the behavioral intervention.* Recommended steps involve, first, selecting reinforcers that are functionally related to the behavior and that are likely to occur in the setting. The second step is to select reinforcers that can be easily managed by the intervention practitioner. The third and final step is to incorporate cues for the behavior into the reinforcer complex whenever possible.

The author provides a hypothetical example with two parallel target behaviors to illustrate how these guidelines could be applied in planning an intervention in a classroom setting. The author emphasizes that the guidelines are intended for the practitioner in the natural setting, who may not have an extensive research repertoire, but who wishes to conscientiously and effectively modify behavior.

Interventions Across Behavior Settings

Intervention programs at Level 2 provide the child with a treatment program designed to reduce the discordance in the child's many environments. Intervention is intended to increase congruence across settings.

Project Re-ED, developed in the 1960s at George Peabody College, is perhaps the best example of this type of intervention. Hobbs (1966) described the project as providing short-term residential treatment (an average of six months) for mildly to moderately disturbed preadolescents. Several basic assumptions are defined according to the ecological perspective. Cure is abandoned as a goal. The emphasis is placed on making the system work, not simply adjusting something inside the child's head. The child is viewed as an inseparable part of a social system, which is an ecological unit made up of the child and his or her family and neighborhood. The goal is to get each component of the system functioning effectively with respect to the requirements of the other components. Ideally, the Re-ED school becomes a part of the ecological unit for only a brief time, withdrawing when the probability that the system will function appears to exceed the probability that it will not.

In an overview of the program, Lewis (1967) presents an essential premise of the Re-ED treatment plan: traditional child-rearing practices in our culture are effective for a child's development. A disruption of child-rearing functions is looked upon as a disturbance in the system influencing the child rather than in the child himself. The Re-ED approach, therefore, is thought of as a social rather than a psychiatric treatment. The general Re-ED strategy involves looking at the effects of a child's overt behavior and determining how this behavior creates conflicts in the child's social systems. Sequences of learning experiences are developed for the child to directly influence the area of concern in the child's behavior. Four staff roles are defined in a Re-ED school: teacher-counselor, social worker, liaison teacher, and consultant. After a child is referred to the Re-ED school, these professionals collaborate to influence the behavior of the child and the primary socializing system to which the child returns. The Re-ED staff tries to provide an engaging, goal-oriented educational climate during all of the child's waking hours and to keep the child related to his or her natural settings. The latter is accomplished through planned weekends at home and careful liaison work that prepares the child for his or her return after a brief stay at the Re-ED school.

Lewis (1970) reports that the most significant contribution of Project Re-ED to other children's programs was the employment of ecological strategies in working with children identified as emotionally disturbed. Direct teaching is seen as a constructive response to children's problems. Problem behavior is not regarded as reflective of a deeper emotional problem. Along with this direct teaching, important changes must be made in the child's ecological unit, his or her natural behavior settings. Lewis uses the term *discordance* rather than *emotional disturbance* to emphasize the interaction between a child's behavior and judgments about that behavior by important people in his or her life. This discordance can be reduced in two ways. One could increase the child's competence in highly valued areas of behavior so that he or she meets more expectations. A second way would be to modify those expectations to help the child function more effectively in his or her ecological unit. An ecological analysis considers both sources of discordance as targets for intervention.

Another program, similar to Project Re-ED, is Project CASA — Community and School Adjustment (Harth and Grosenick, 1973). This program is patterned after Project Re-ED but is different in several important ways. First, the program is held in a day-school rather than the residential setting of Project Re-ED. Second, the techniques of behavior modification are more prominent in Project CASA. Third, Project CASA is operated under the auspices of the public schools (in Columbia, Missouri). Project Re-ED is operated by the Tennessee Department of Mental Health.

Another program which attempts to alter a child's interaction across settings is Project ACE (Lloyd, 1973). Project ACE (Adjustment via Community Ecology) was designed to remedy what was seen as a serious programmatic problem by the Therapeutic Education Department at St. Joseph State Hospital in Missouri. The first year recidivism rate was too high: adolescents discharged from the Therapeutic Education Department and the hospital were returning at a rate of 35 percent in the first year after discharge. Project ACE was instituted to facilitate more successful community functioning of youths returning to their homes from the hospital.

In this program, a youth discharged from the hospital was assigned a community worker (ecological resource investigator), who defined appropriate goals with the youth and the family. Some of the youths went back to school, some to jobs, some to job training programs. The ecological resource investigator also arranged for other community social services that could support the youth. Eighty percent of the ecological resource investigators' time was spent in contact with the youths in their community. Twenty percent of the time was devoted to developing new community resources for these youths.

In an evaluation of the program carried out during its first year of operation (Harth and Lloyd, 1975), a treatment group was compared to a matched control group. There were eighteen subjects in each group. The return rate for the control group was about 34 percent, similar to what it had been before. The recidivism rate for the group receiving the services of the ecological resource investigator was about 17 percent, half of what it had been.

Harth (1975) developed an "ecological service model" that emphasizes providing remedial services both to the child in school and to other people who might maintain a child's negative behavior or contribute to the disruption of the ecosystem. He specified strategies for influencing these people, including: (1) helping parents set up behavior modification programs in the home to encourage more careful observation of the child and consistency in the environment; (2) helping the family achieve more financial security; (3) consulting with the regular classroom teacher to facilitate the child's transition to public school; and (4) helping the family get help from other service agencies.

In Harth's model, teaching the child and those who influence him or her to acquire new strategies and providing support for the system in maintaining these behaviors are emphasized equally. The responsibility for working closely with the child and his or her "community" is assumed by the liaison teacher.

Altering Cultural Blueprints

Interventions at Level 3 attempt to alter the blueprints for the identification and treatment of disturbance that are created by communities, sustained by them, or both. Recently, some of the most successful interventions have been instigated by the judicial and legislative branches of government. PL 94-142 has led to many changes, including mainstreaming; the requirement to "show cause" if a child is to be placed in a more restrictive environment; prohibition of unfair testing leading to labeling and placement; the requirement for regular evaluation of a child with special needs; and due process guidelines. These are all fundamental alterations in established patterns of dealing with the disturbed child. Deinstitutionalization and child advocacy were also encouraged by the courts.

EVALUATION OF THE ECOLOGICAL PERSPECTIVE

The Value of the Model

The ecological perspective emerged partly as a reaction to perceived limitations of other models of disturbance. The fact that traditional psychotherapy, for example, was conducted away from the child's natural settings led to two problems. Beneficial changes developed and sustained in therapy were not necessarily maintained at home or school. Even if such changes were maintained, they might not have been relevant to the skills required of the child or to the values, expectations, and priorities of influential adults. Concerns about the behavioral model involved the narrow focus of therapy and doubts about whether gains could be generalized. Unintended consequences were not evaluated, and behaviors changed might not be important or sufficient to alter negative patterns of interaction at home or school.

In addition to concerns about the ineffectiveness of existing models, it was considered unfair to regard the child as the locus of disturbance. The ecological perspective gained strength during the 1960s when the war in Vietnam caused many people to challenge standard conceptions about what was normal, what was deviant, which behaviors and persons were good and evil, and who was in the minority or majority. The intensity of disagreement generated by the issues of those years led many to the conclusion that judgments about deviance depended on the values of the persons making the judgment and the perspective from which they viewed behaviors.

Regarding the child as disturbed raised questions about whether we were "blaming the victim" and whether traditional models of education or child-rearing practices should be the targets for intervention rather than the child. In this climate, many professionals working with children became convinced that disturbance was created by and evaluated in specific contexts, and that effective and ethical treatment required altering that context. The ecological perspective was developed to address the perceived limitations of the other models by clarifying these principles.

It is important to emphasize that these cornerstones of the ecological model do not constitute a theory. They are, rather, a philosophical orientation or perspective. The work of defining and developing the model is still under way. Many questions need to be answered more fully. What environmental variables are related to the production of disturbance? How do these variables interact with individual characteristics? What treatments are most effective for particular interactions or in particular settings? These questions are particularly important because of the eclectic nature of the model: assessment and intervention techniques may be borrowed from other models as long as the child *alone* is not the focus for assessment and intervention.

Under these circumstances, the danger is that anything and everything could be defined as ecological. Without principles for assessment and intervention and a developed theory for analysis of interactions, the power of this approach could be lost in sloppy, undisciplined thinking and action. Potentially, however, we may learn a great deal more about how and why disturbance occurs, develop a more sophisticated technology for analysis, and achieve solutions that modify settings as well as children.

Evaluation of Assessment Strategies

Contributions to the assessment of disturbing interactions between children and influential others are being made in two areas. The first area is the development of instruments designed to measure the context in which disturbance occurs. As we have seen, Mercer and Lewis (1977), Wahler, House, and Stambaugh (1976), and Moos (1979) have made significant progress in distinguishing significant variables in the school or family setting and in finding reliable ways to measure them. Their work is receiving national attention and has been quite widely used.

The second contribution made by investigators within an ecological perspective is the identification of frameworks for collecting assessment data that will provide rich descriptions of the context of disturbance. These frameworks provide for the use of multiple measures and formal and informal procedures. Wallace and Larsen (1978), Carroll (1974), and Laten and Katz (1975) are among those who have identified the variables that should be measured in an ecologically based assessment and who have developed instruments and procedures for doing so.

At this point, there is no consensus about which variables tend to be crucial in measuring across settings in order to gain a sufficiently complete perspective about the causes of disturbing interactions. The lack of consensus is due in part to differences among settings. Different variables assume importance in a family or a school setting, in a preschool or high school, in a behaviorally oriented or developmentally oriented program. The amount and type of data collected in various areas also depend on the goals identified for children's growth. A preschool program that emphasizes language development may need several informal and formal instruments for increasing children's progress in this area, whereas a program that stresses play and social development may seek a variety of instruments that measure growth in this dimension.

Another reason for the lack of consensus stems from the philosophical perspective that generalization about causes of disturbance across settings is inappropriate. Thomas and Chess (1977) have expressed this position very clearly:

> An interactionist view does not assume any *a priori* hierarchy in which different variables are then assigned greater or lesser positions of importance. In this approach, consequently, no variable has any absolute reified significance. Each must at all times be considered in relationship to the simultaneous operation of other influential variables. For temperament, a variable which reflects the organism's own behavioral traits, this means that its significance must at all times be considered in the context of other characteristics of the organism and environment. The importance of temperament for the developmental process can, therefore, be estimated only if the other attributes of the individual and the nature of the environment are delineated as comprehensively as are the details of the temperamental traits. This is why we insist at all times that temperament can be defined only in the context within which the behavior occurs. . . . *(pp. 206–207)*

What we seem to need are: (1) an initial screening procedure that provides a list of variables that have proven to be essential in assessing disturbing interactions in particular contexts; (2) instructions for using such a screening procedure to identify variables that might be salient in the setting or settings to be assessed; (3) instruments or methods for providing an in-depth evaluation of selected variables *in context,* such as the questionnaires and interview schedules developed by Thomas and Chess (1977) to evaluate temperament; and (4) a technology for assessing the interaction of the selected variables.

The advantage of the ecological approach is a much richer, fuller, and more usable description of behaviors in the context they occur in, which can then be fairly easily translated into intervention strategies. There are two major disadvantages of the ecological approach to assessment. The first is that this kind of assessment procedure is complex. The demands of this approach are much more time-consuming and challenging than using a single, streamlined checklist to identify which children in the classroom are causing trouble, or even collecting baseline data on one or two child behaviors. The second disadvantage is that even if one doggedly pursues an ecological assessment strategy, one's understanding of the environment is still bound by the variables selected for study. One would still need to pick targets for intervention from the "chaos, babble, and rubble" as Willems puts it (1977, p. 27), and this selection would affect what was seen and how it was seen. We need to strike a balance between collecting more data and descriptions than we can use or understand, and collecting enough data to allow us to intervene successfully and efficiently.

Evaluation of Interventions

Ecologically based interventions have been successfully implemented at each of the three levels. Strain and Wiegerink (1976) report an intervention in a single setting which significantly increased levels of peer interaction in a group of behaviorally disordered preschoolers. They persuaded the teacher to alter her usual schedule of activities by providing opportunities for the children to act out stories such as *Goldilocks and the Three Bears* following story time. These structured sociodramatic experiences led to a significantly higher rate of peer interactions, which were maintained over time. This intervention concentrated on a single environmental manipulation and used one outcome measure. Although this procedure reduced the complexity of the multiple interactions in this preschool setting, it could be used to evaluate the impact of environmental variables (in this case, an alteration in program design) on children's behavior.

Project Re-ED, an intervention program which attempts to alter a child's total ecosystem (Level 2), has been systematically evaluated. In a recent article (Montgomery and Van Fleet, 1978) academic and behavioral gains of 138 children enrolled in this program from 1974 to 1977 were documented. The average rate of improvement of inappropriate behaviors was 95 percent. Ninety-five percent of the children also improved in peer and adult interaction skills as indicated by Re-ED staff responses to weekly questionnaires. Parents also provided an index of improvement at home and in the neighborhood. Weekly ratings yielded an average 95 percent improvement rate in home behaviors by termination and an average 90 percent improvement rate in neighborhood interaction. Academic gains were noted as well. The limited longitudinal data available to date demonstrate that both academic and behavioral gains are maintained.

The Re-ED staff also offers support to the children's parents through biweekly meetings with teachers, an eight-session parent-training course, and follow-up contact after the child leaves the program (Reed, 1978). Since the goal of the program is to alter the child's ecosystem, the parent program is a significant aspect of the total therapeutic effort. Reed concludes that "Re-ED's greatest benefits to the child occur in direct proportion to parental involvement" (p. 94) and provides examples of changes in parents' behaviors, attitudes, and experiences with the target child and voluntary involvement in the Re-ED classes to document the positive effects of the parent program.

Re-ED provides multiple interventions for target groups of children, parents, and teachers. A wide variety of data collection methods and outcome measures are used to measure the effectiveness of the program. The staff has not elected to evaluate which elements of treatment might be most important for particular children or how different aspects of the treatment program interact to produce positive effects. An assessment of unintended effects is made by maintaining contact with the parents until two years after the child's termination.

Public Law 94-142 is, according to Rhodes and Paul (1978), an example of an ecological intervention (Level 3). Since the law went into effect in 1978, published data on its effects on school systems are limited. A report commissioned by the U.S. Department of Health, Education, and Welfare (1979), as well as observation and interview data, already make it clear that this law has altered the process by which children are identified, diagnosed, and treated and has compelled important alterations in public school settings.

The three examples of successful intervention programs presented illustrate diverse approaches to evaluation, in part because of the progressively enlarging scope of intervention at each level. One of the most significant challenges to adherents of the ecological model is to develop evaluation approaches that adequately measure the success of complex intervention strategies. At Level 1 this might involve developing more sophisticated unobtrusive measures for evaluating the impact of furniture arrangement on children's behaviors. At Level 3 this might require new techniques for evaluating planned change strategies. Ecological interventions do not typically lend themselves to evaluation by standard statistical procedures. Interventions are often undertaken with a single subject in a single setting who functions as his or her own control. There are many uncontrolled setting variables which affect results. The conditions that suggest the intervention and the intervention itself may not be replicable in a different setting.

Consequently, the study of ecologically based interventions faces three challenges. First, relatively few intervention studies are available in the literature. This is due in part to the newness of the perspective as applied to emotional problems.

Second, the technology for evaluating interventions based on a naturalistic single-case approach is available (see for example Bryk, Meisels, and Markowitz, 1979; Hein, 1979; Kratochwill, 1978). These evaluations yield a rich data base for assessing a child's growth and practices that optimize growth. But it is difficult for a program to implement an evaluation effort based on this approach. Collecting, interpreting, and using the enormous amount of data generated is very time consuming for practitioners and requires considerable administrative support. Methods for streamlining the data collection and evaluation procedures need to be developed.

Third, the emphasis on the uniqueness of each pattern of individual-setting interaction makes it difficult and inappropriate to expect replications of particular individual-setting interventions. This may lead practitioners to the discouraging conclusion that the "wheel must be re-invented" for each child in each program. We all search for a simple, consistent method to "cure" disturbance. The ecological model does not present simple solutions, but interventions that vary by child and setting. Defining and disseminating the ecological approach to intervention is therefore quite a challenge.

Nonetheless, we have seen that the process of individually based naturalistic assessment and intervention can be successfully used. We have seen that programs built on these models (like Project Re-ED) have led to significant growth in the target children and in the behavior and attitudes of others in the ecosystem. The processes a program develops to select interventions and evaluate their effectiveness may certainly be generalized across settings. These are vital contributions that have significantly altered the lives of children and their caretakers and advanced our understanding of disturbance and the interactions between children and environments.

SUMMARY

The ecological model provides a new perspective for understanding and evaluating emotional disturbance. Disturbance is not located in the child; rather disturbance emerges from the interaction between a child and a particular context. The context may be a single setting, several settings, a neighborhood, community, or a culture. To understand and alter a disturbing encounter, we must evaluate the characteristics of the child, the context in which problems are occurring, and the interaction between them.

This perspective represents a significant shift in the way in which we view disturbance. Once having viewed disturbance in this way it becomes difficult to return to the previous conceptualization. Because the ecological model is eclectic, other models and the insights they provide can be incorporated. But if one adheres to the ecological perspective it no longer seems possible to avoid such questions as "What role do the teacher's expectations play in this crisis?," "Why does a child have tantrums in the social studies class but not in mathematics?," or "How did the child's difficult temperament affect her parents' confidence and consistency?" The model requires further elaboration and refinement, but it has proved to be a fruitful approach.

Ecological assessment procedures collect data which describe variables contributing to disturbing interactions in natural settings. As we have seen, environmental variables such as school size, the schedule of a school day, or the arrangement of equipment and materials in a nursery school may have powerful effects on behavior. Elucidating how such variables influence particular children is the goal of ecological assessment. In this chapter we reviewed several models for assessing single variables as well as some approaches to conceptualizing the groups of variables which need to be evaluated in school or home settings. These approaches appear to be sophisticated and useful. However, several challenges continue to confront the development of a comprehensive assessment package: identifying the range of variables that need to be studied, improving the methodology for assessing these variables and the interactions among them, and integrating the results into a coherent framework.

Ecological intervention strategies focus on the points of discordance between a child (or children) and their natural environments. This strategy should be both efficient and effective. We have seen that projects based on the ecological model (such as those developed by Hobbs, 1966 and Lloyd, 1973) have been efficient and effective in altering disturbing interactions and maintaining a low rate of disturbance.

There are two secondary advantages of ecological intervention strategies. The emphasis on promoting competence and growth in system members helps them to avoid the trap of being placed in a "sick" or "disturbed" role. Therefore the potentially significant consequences of a negative label and its role requirements can be avoided. A second advantage is that interventions which alter an ecological system can often benefit not just the target child but many other children as well. As interventions are applied to increasingly complex or large ecological systems (particularly those at the community-culture level) this advantage becomes increasingly important.

The wider application of ecological intervention strategies would be aided by three factors. We need to provide more examples of ecological intervention programs in the literature. The technology for evaluating these programs needs to be improved and streamlined. Finally, we need to find ways of articulating and disseminating the *processes* by which programs develop appropriate approaches to individual-setting disturbances. Rising to these challenges would further enhance the exciting potential of this perspective for helping disturbed children, their families, and the professionals who serve them.

Part II

BEHAVIOR MANAGEMENT

To help emotionally disturbed children gain self-control, we must be able to manage their behavior. The control of disruptive behavior enables us to create a climate in which disturbed children and their classmates can attend to the tasks at hand.

In Chapter 4, Neel, McDowell, Whelan, and Wagonseller discuss a framework for developing a management plan using behavioral principles. Environmental organization is stressed as a prerequisite to the use of management procedures such as positive reinforcement. The authors also discuss data collection and charting as methods of measuring behavior change.

In Chapter 5, Rich, Beck, and Coleman present the psychoeducational perspective on managing classroom behavior. They describe many of the techniques identified by Redl and Wineman, Newman, Long, and others for intervention with behavior. Also included is a discussion of techniques for evaluating behavior change.

Chapter 4

The Management of Behavior and the Measurement of Behavior Change

Richard S. Neel
University of Washington

with

Richard L. McDowell
University of New Mexico

Richard J. Whelan
University of Kansas

Bill R. Wagonseller
University of Nevada, Las Vegas

When asked to identify the single most disconcerting problem they face, teachers usually mention the general topic of behavior management. Their concerns range from problems with destructive physical violence to motivating children to complete their work. Unfortunately, the term "behavior management" often conjures up associations of unilateral control, mechanistic procedures, and abusive interactions, to list only a few. But behavior management need not involve such characteristics.

Children identified as emotionally disturbed are unable to manage their own behavior. They have not acquired the self-control necessary to make success a more frequent event in their lives than failure. The disordered behavior of children is often a signal that they need external assistance from the environment, particularly from the people in it.

A behavioral approach, properly implemented, can help emotionally disturbed children acquire the self-control they so desperately want and need. This approach emphasizes positive rather than negative child-adult interpersonal relationships. It requires the systematic use of positive values for children. Unless adults acquire these values, the approach will not work.

Two fundamental principles underlie the behavioral approach.

1. Apply the approach only when it is determined that a child needs an organized program of external support. A rule of thumb is, the more severely involved the child, the more systematic the approach.
2. Withdraw the external support when the child demonstrates self-management of behaviors that lead to pleasurable rather than aversive consequences.

In addition, a person using a behavioral approach must always recognize that "the child knows best." This means that the child's behavior is the only indication of the success or failure of the approach.

The behavioral approach is deceptively simple to understand at a cognitive level. Its application to children, however, is exceedingly complex. It requires adult knowledge, skill, compassion, and understanding if it is to benefit children. It is especially important that emotionally disturbed children be beneficiaries, not victims, of this useful and powerful approach.

MANAGEMENT OF BEHAVIOR

The behavioral approach to managing emotionally disturbed children is a combination of principles of learning and the systematic measurement of behavioral change. Principles of learning are used in designing programs to change behavior. Measurement techniques are then developed to determine whether the desired change has occurred. To fully understand the system, one must know the assumptions that underlie it. A behavioral approach to teaching emotionally disturbed children is based upon five assumptions:

1. Nearly all behavior is learned. The word "behavior" is comprehensive. As used in this chapter, it includes all conduct usually associated with both social and academic behaviors. This is true for both good (accepted) and bad (disturbing) behaviors. Behaviorists contend that even the most bizarre behaviors are to a great extent learned, and that they operate under the same laws and principles that affect normal behavior. The implication for education is obvious: if a behavior is learned, it can be unlearned, and a new behavior can be learned in its place.

2. The principles of behavior can be used to change disordered behavior. This is an outgrowth of the first assumption, and on the surface it seems elementary. After a few minutes of observation, however, the casual observer would notice that many children labeled "emotionally disturbed" are not being taught because their caregivers feel their behavior excludes them

from the school. These people feel that education must wait until the child's condition has been treated and cured. Behaviorists reject this notion.

3. The focus of a behavioral educational program is on current rather than past situations. This does not imply that a person's past is unimportant. Quite the contrary. A person's past history can be very helpful in determining what reinforcing events have strengthened the disturbing behavior. The solution to modifying the problem behavior, however, must occur in the present. It is the reinforcement a person receives in the current environment that maintains the disturbing behavior; it is not some unresolved conflict from the past.

4. The behavioral approach focuses on observable phenomena rather than internal states. This principle is often misunderstood. A focus on observable behavior does not deny the existence of emotions or thoughts. All of us have thoughts that are never translated into any observable behavior. The behaviorist does not deny these thoughts. A problem arises, however, when we try to infer thoughts, feelings, or intentions from observable behavior. We are all familiar with the wide variety of interpretations that can be given a single act. Each interpretation is really a hypothesis about an internal state based on a behavioral observation. Validation of the inference can only be based on additional observations. The behaviorist believes that limiting our initial efforts to observable behaviors will be more effective. It is necessary to observe the problem behavior, plan a program to change it, and then measure the change in that behavior. This allows the teacher to determine if his or her teaching has had the desired effect. Attention to these requirements often prevents teachers from spending large amounts of time and energy trying to identify inferred "causes" of problem behaviors they are responsible for changing.

5. Techniques used in a behavioral approach are subjected to empirical testing (e.g., observed effects) each time they are used. No technique should be accepted solely because it is a logical product of a theoretical approach. Success with one person or population is not assumed to be sufficient evidence that a technique will be successful with everyone. This is not a trivial distinction. Many techniques or approaches have been developed based upon a theory or upon the results of work with a single population. These techniques are then used with others. If the technique is unsuccessful, it is assumed that there is something wrong with the child, not with the technique. The literature is replete with examples of techniques being used with youngsters for long periods of time without any signs of success, and then being defended on theoretical grounds. A technique can gain acceptance and utility through repeated use. Any technique that has been shown to be effective with a large number of children, in a large number of settings, and over an extended period of time, would of course be likely to be the technique of choice for a teacher. The behavioral approach, however, requires collection of data to establish the effectiveness of the technique with the particular persons involved. In other words, if a tech-

nique is not working with a particular child, then it should be modified, regardless of how successful it was with others or how thoroughly steeped it is in theory.

Goals of a Behavioral Program

The goal of any educational program is to make realistic and desirable behavior changes. It is hoped that the changes will allow the child to behave in a way that will make him or her successful in most environments. The problem for the educator is to describe which behaviors to change in a child. Certain behaviors, such as reading or computation, are behaviors that most people would agree should be increased. Other behaviors, such as stealing and physical attacks, should be eliminated. There are, however, a whole host of behaviors that fall between these two extremes that are a focus of concern for teachers of emotionally disturbed children. Agreement about which behaviors should be changed and in which direction is impossible. How, then, should the goals of a behavioral program be chosen?

The goals of a program often reflect the philosophy of a school system, agency, and a teacher. The comprehensive goals described below are the product of a philosophy that attempts to maximize the number of positive behaviors a child emits, so that a child's receiving reinforcement will be the rule instead of the exception.

The first goal of any behavioral program is to increase the number of appropriate behaviors in a child's repertoire. Far too often, the focus of teachers of emotionally disturbed children and others is to reduce some behaviors without strengthening others that will be more successful in the child's environment. It is important to recognize the desired behavior as well as the undesired behavior. Often these two behaviors are found on the same continuum, with each falling at the other's extreme. Such behaviors are referred to as "incompatible." If a teacher identified "out of seat" as the behavior to be reduced, the incompatible or opposite behavior would be "in seat." It is often easier to attend to and increase a desired behavior than it is to decrease an undesired behavior. If the frequency of the desired behavior (in seat) is increased, then the frequency of the undesired behavior (out of seat) is decreased, since it is not possible for both behaviors to occur at the same time. Improving the positive behavior is emphasized.

The second goal is that programs should reduce the behaviors that cause a child to be identified as emotionally disturbed. It is important for children to recognize how people respond to them in their environment. If others are likely to respond negatively or not at all because of the child's set of behaviors, then it is a reasonable goal for a teacher to modify those behaviors. An alternate solution, of course, would be to alter the expectations of the significant others. This strategy works in some instances, but a teacher is more likely to be able to modify the behavior of a child than that of an entire community.

The third goal of a behavioral program is to improve children's timing of their behaviors. Timing is a critical skill for all children. Society is concerned with when and where we do things. Children must be able to discern when it is appropriate to emit a behavior and when it is not. They must also be able to determine what is expected in a wide variety of settings. Consider the command, "Be good, Johnny." We all remember being told to be good and then having to figure out all the different "goods" that were required. This skill of knowing what to do and when to do it is also a necessary component of any behavioral approach to educating emotionally disturbed children.

Finally, the overall goal for the teacher using a behavioral program is to help the child acquire academic skills and learn self-control. Each of these goals helps facilitate the child's ability to function successfully in both academic and social situations.

Behavioral programs for the emotionally disturbed child have borrowed heavily from early research with brain-injured and hyperactive children. The work of Strauss and Lehtinen (1947) and later the work of Cruickshank, Bentzen, Ratzeburg, and Tannhauser (1961) contributed several concepts from which Haring and Phillips (1962) designed the "structured approach" and Hewett (1968) designed the "engineered classroom." Both Haring and Phillips and Hewett believed that the environment could be used to control certain behavior. By arranging the environment and including certain features such as study carrels and interest centers, the type and quantity of certain stimuli could be controlled. Both programs used the concept of a planned day to provide consistency to the disturbed student. Materials were selected for their stimulus value. Task expectations were chosen with the individual needs of the disturbed child in mind. Teachers in both programs emphasized the teaching of behavioral alternatives. Behavioral principles such as reinforcement were used to help the disturbed child recognize the relationship between behavior and its consequences. Each of these concepts is directed toward managing behavior and learning self-control.

Environmental Arrangement

We all rely on the environment to provide us with clues about what behaviors are appropriate in a given situation. We have learned to distinguish between behavior acceptable on the playground and behavior acceptable in the classroom. The playground is designed so we can run and scream, but the classroom is not. Finer discriminations are required in our everyday lives. Students must discriminate not only between areas in the school environment, but also between class periods, class activities, physical areas within the classroom, and so on. Recognizing and being able to respond appropriately to expectations is a valuable skill. Unfortunately, it is one of the skills that emotionally disturbed children seem to have great difficulty mastering. The teacher can help these children acquire this skill by arranging the physical environment of the classroom to support different behaviors under different conditions.

Hewett and Taylor (1980) stress the importance of classroom design in establishing a satisfactory learning climate. They suggest a classroom arranged to include several activity centers. Each center has a purpose for being included — the "mastery center" is the area in which most academic tasks are completed, whereas the "order center" contains activities such as puzzles and dot-to-dot drawings that help the student learn sequencing skills. Hewett and Taylor identified four major centers for the classroom, the order center and mastery center, already mentioned, and the communications center and exploratory center. These centers reflect the concept of a hierarchy of learning tasks proposed by Hewett (1968).

We encourage teachers to arrange the physical environment of the classroom to support the behaviors they wish to see their students exhibit. Structuring the environment in this manner helps provide students with some of the external clues they need to behave appropriately. Many students still need to be taught what behavior is appropriate. The structure allows them to consistently associate the learned behavior with the appropriate aspect of the environment.

However you arrange your classroom, you will need to take five factors into consideration. These five factors relate to physical areas within the classroom.

The first pertains to individual work. Each student should have his own desk or table located in the academic or task area. It should be understood that this area is used for academic work. It is often of value to have private individual study areas such as study carrels available in the classroom for times when distractions must be reduced.

Second, you should identify an area for group work. There are situations in which you will wish to work with a small group or the total group. Two work tables with chairs are adequate for this purpose. When working with a small group, you might need only one table; when working with the total group, you might put both tables together. Although individual work could take place in this area, the focus should be on group interaction — group instruction, group discussion, class meetings, group projects, etc.

Third, a separate area should be arranged as a free-time, or high probability, area. This area contains equipment and materials for various activities that, if given a choice, the student would choose to do — work a puzzle, play a game, read a book or magazine, listen to a record or tape, or build a model. The purpose of this area is to give the student something to do and a place to do it upon completing assigned tasks. Most teachers make the use of the free-time area contingent upon the completion of assigned tasks or upon the accumulation of a certain number of points or tokens. When used this way, it reinforces completed work.

Fourth, if possible, you should designate a small area away from the academic area and free-time area for limited isolation. Not all programs are able to provide a time-out room for use as a consequence to disruptive behavior. In many instances, a time-out room is unnecessary; limited isolation is just as effective a consequence. It is used when a student is disrupting the work of others. You may choose to partition off a corner of the room and put a single desk or chair in that area. Placing a student in this area should be the result of specific behaviors and should be for limited periods of time known to the student. Time in limited isolation should not exceed two to five minutes for a single instance of disruptive behavior. It is enough simply to tell most students that when they are able to control their behavior they may return to the group or to their desks.

Fifth, storage areas should be provided for equipment, materials, and other property belonging to the students and the teacher. You will need to decide which equipment and materials should be visible and which should be stored out of sight, as well as which storage areas the students should have free access to and which they should not. Typical storage equipment includes file cabinets, book shelves, standing cabinets, and possibly built-in shelves or cabinets. When choosing this equipment, you should keep in mind the general operation plan for your classroom. If you want most equipment and materials to be stored out of sight to reduce unwanted stimuli, then choose cabinets and shelves with doors that close. Free-standing storage equipment allows you to create limited barriers between other designated areas in your classroom (see Figure 4.1). Fixed equipment has a tendency to use up valuable wall space. Whatever design you choose for your classroom, organize it around desired student movement patterns. Various types of teacher-approved movement for students are a necessary component in any behavior management plan. Arrange your classroom environment to support this movement.

The additional structure you add to the special classroom for the emotionally disturbed student is one way of helping the student gain self-control. The environment is a prosthetic one when compared to the regular classroom. As a student gains self-control and begins to move back toward placement in the regular classroom, the prosthetic model is gradually changed to simulate that of the regular classroom. This process would be very simple if all of your students achieved these skills at the same rate. Since this is rarely the case, the teacher must be prepared to alter how certain components of the classroom environment are used based upon the individual needs of a specific student. These approximations of the regular classroom environment help the student generalize self-control skills learned in the structured environment to the regular classroom.

Management Strategies

The environmental arrangement of your classroom should be developed in harmony with the day-to-day operational procedures of your program. This will involve making some decisions before the program begins. Planning is a key factor of any behavior management program. We know, for example,

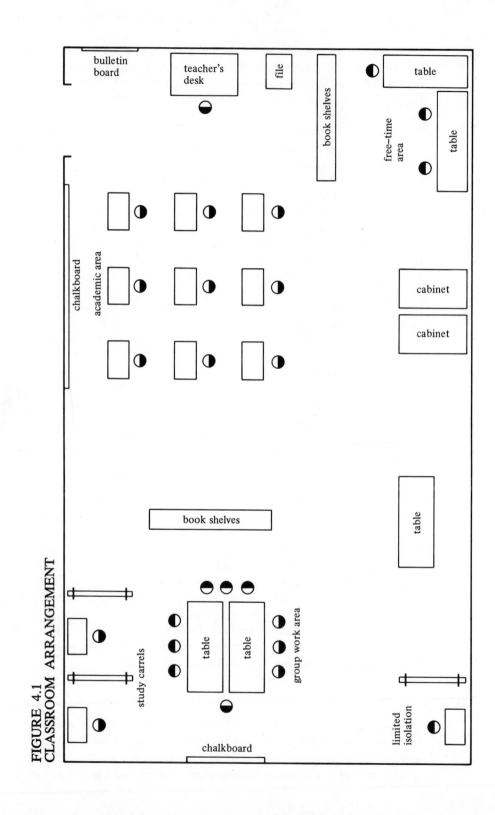

FIGURE 4.1
CLASSROOM ARRANGEMENT

that there are certain behaviors that occur in every classroom every year. A student will take something that belongs to someone else, something will get broken, someone will hit someone else. Each of these situations requires some form of teacher intervention. By recognizing that these behaviors will occur, the teacher can plan how to respond to each before it happens. When we respond to inappropriate behavior spontaneously, without having planned what to do, we have a tendency to respond negatively or in a punishing way. By planning our response prior to the behavior, we respond with consequences much more suitable to the offense and in a manner more supportive of teaching appropriate alternatives.

Many of your decisions should revolve around issues such as the use of consequences, how you will use or administer reinforcement, considerations pertaining to punishment (i.e., time-out), the use of learning stations or areas, the use of study carrels, the use of free time as a consequence, what to do if a situation demands that you physically restrain a student, and how to communicate quickly with another teacher or the principal if you need their assistance. Each of these issues is central to the operation of a behaviorally oriented classroom and should be resolved before you begin working directly with students.

The overall management system is designed to promote the acquisition of academic as well as social skills. It does attend to the resolution of inappropriate behavior. The emphasis of any management program, however, is to teach new appropriate behaviors, not merely to control student behavior. This principle must be kept in mind whether you choose to use a token economy, a point system, contingency contracting, or contingency management as the framework for your program.

Basic Considerations. There are several considerations teachers should keep in mind when working with students. This list should in no way be regarded as complete, but should serve as a guideline for daily interactions with students.

1. Believe that a student wants to do his or her best but needs firm support to do so.
2. Keep verbal directions to a student at a minimum — make them simple, clear, and concise.
3. Check to be sure the student understands what is expected.
4. When possible, demonstrate to the student what he or she is to do.
5. Clearly define any limits you impose on the student and do so without long, drawn-out explanations, which tend to cloud the issue.
6. Avoid head-on clashes with students whenever possible. When you back a student into a corner, he or she has no choice but to fight you.
7. Stress behavior alternatives — show the student a better way or inform the student of the time or situation when his or her chosen behavior would be appropriate.

8. Don't argue with a student — you can't win. Student-teacher interactions should not be win-or-lose situations. When appropriate, allow consequences to resolve the issue.
9. Remove "seductive" objects from view. There are pieces of equipment, games, etc. that almost demand that the student touch or play with them. If you want to accomplish assigned tasks, remove temptations until you are ready for them to be used.
10. Respond to behavior in its most recent episode. Don't play the game of saying, "One more time and I'm going to . . ." Students will one-more-time you to death.

Expectations.   We often have preconceived notions of how students will perform on the various tasks or activities they are involved in. Too often our expectation does not match the student's ability. The discrepancy between our expectation and the student's ability to fulfill it often leads to frustration for both the teacher and the student. This is especially true when the expectation exceeds the student's ability to successfully meet it. The resulting conflict is frequently illustrated by misbehavior on the part of the student in an effort either to escape the situation or to justify his or her performance.

Expectations can be a powerful force in determining outcome behaviors. The extent of this power has been reported in the work of Rosenthal and Jacobson (1968). Most students wish to please the teacher. The reinforcing consequences in a classroom have been arranged to support expectations being met. How realistic or appropriate the expectation is may determine the behavior you get. If you expect a student to act out, he or she probably will. Many students continue to exhibit inappropriate behavior because they believe those are the behaviors they are expected to exhibit. In a sense, they have a reputation to uphold, and for them, reinforcement is associated with the behaviors that make up that reputation. A teacher often hears about a student's inappropriate behavior in other programs. When that student enters that teacher's program, one of the first things said to the student is, "I've heard about you and the things you do." With that statement, an expectation has been set for the behavior to recur. Statements reflecting behavioral expectations should be positive, referring to desired behaviors. The key to using expectations to positively influence either academic or social behaviors is to keep the expectations within the student's ability to successfully fulfill them. Expectations must be based upon the realistic assessment of the student's skill in light of the student's age, sex, intelligence, academic achievement, and development or growth patterns. Make expectations work for you rather than against you.

The Concept of Follow-Through.   Basic to any program which uses reinforcement to support desired behaviors is the concept of "follow-through." It implies that any arrangement between behaviors and their consequences will occur consistently. This consistency is an integral aspect of work with emotionally disturbed students. Consistency supported by follow-through helps the student learn the relationship between a behavior and the consequences that follow the behavior. The ability to see and understand this relationship helps the emotionally disturbed student develop self-control. The implications for the teacher are (1) to give careful attention to the selection of consequences, and (2) to recognize the importance of saying what you mean and meaning what you say. The latter point reflects the importance of identifying appropriate tasks and expectations and, once they have been established, following through with the designated consequences. The general outcome of this is that students come to understand that you are involved in their school program and that you can be trusted. The practice of follow-through is a critical component of the management of behavior.

Rules.　Stated limits are necessary to run any program. When working with emotionally disturbed students, three limits seem to be universally accepted, regardless of the philosophical stance underlying the program. These three limits as stated to the student are (1) you may not harm yourself, (2) you may not harm others, and (3) you may not destroy the property of others. Many classroom programs operate with only these three limits as rules. It is amusing from time to time to walk into a classroom and see the class rules written on the chalkboard or tacked to the bulletin board. All too often you find a long list of rules there to help the students remember what they are not to do.

　　The problem that arises is not the rules themselves, but the number of rules. Rules are necessary, but it is good to have only as many as necessary to accomplish your goals. The more rules you make, the more difficult it is to remember them (that applies to both the teacher and the students).

　　When it becomes necessary to establish a rule, three considerations must be made. First, the rule must be clear. Everyone must understand the expectations associated with the rule. Second, the rule must be reasonable. The expectations must be realistic as well as fair. And third, the rule must be enforceable. Rules that cannot be enforced are of little value to anyone. When establishing rules or limits, let common sense be your guide and ask yourself, "Is this rule really necessary?"

Behavioral Alternatives.　Emotionally disturbed students exhibit many behaviors that adults and other students perceive as noxious. Many of these noxious or irritating behaviors are simply responses a student has learned for a particular situation, or there may be consequences operating that reinforce the occurrence of the behavior. When the behavior is emitted, the student may perceive that behavior as the best or only response to the situation. Helping a student learn appropriate social behaviors requires that the teacher help the student recognize possible behavioral alternatives. The teacher's goal is to help the student learn problem-solving techniques that will help him or her analyze the situation and identify the alternatives available. The mechanics of this process involve the use of a reinforcement system to support the desired or appropriate alternatives. Major gains are not usually obtained overnight, but the consistent emphasizing of alternatives and the use of reinforcement for the selection of appropriate choices does result in the acquisition of desired skills.

Use of Space.   We have already discussed the major uses of space in the classroom in our discussion on arranging the physical environment, but there is one other dimension that warrants mention here. We are referring to the use of empty space between students. When students are in close proximity to each other (within reach), there is a high probability that they will make physical contact. During the early portion of the school year, or when you have students who are active and aggressive, it is prudent to provide enough space between students to serve as a buffer zone. Such a use of space can reduce the frequency of physical contact between your students. A major aspect of behavior management is prevention. Utilizing distance between students can prevent certain behaviors by reducing the chances they have to occur.

Scheduling.   An aspect of behavior management that is frequently overlooked by teachers is the daily schedule, or how the daily tasks are sequenced or arranged. There are three major considerations to be made regarding scheduling.

First, recognize the value of routine. The use of a general routine provides the students with a degree of security by simply knowing what comes next.

Second, recognize the possibility of a carry-over from one task to another. A skill many emotionally disturbed students have difficulty with is knowing when to stop certain behaviors that are appropriate for one task but not for another. A common practice in the primary grades, for example, is to begin the day with a "show and tell" activity. During this activity, the students are encouraged to express themselves verbally. Often this activity is followed by an academic study or work period during which open conversation is not encouraged. Some students have difficulty stopping or controlling their talking after this shift has been made. A common occurrence among emotionally disturbed students is that the tone or mood struck early in the day persists throughout the day. If that initial mood is appropriate, then the day will probably go well. If not, you may have helped set the stage for additional problems. Evaluate the tasks and activities you have planned to determine what effect they will have on each other, and arrange your sequence or schedule accordingly. Allow for transition times or activities to help the student gear down from high activity tasks, whether verbal or physical.

Third, recognize how one task or activity may be used as a consequence to another. The Premack Principle (Premack, 1965), discussed in Chapter 1, establishes the concept that a behavior with a low probability of occurrence, if followed by a behavior with a high probability of occurrence, may increase in its rate of occurrence. If working arithmetic problems is an activity a student would not choose to do if given a choice (low probability behavior), and reading a magazine is an activity that the student would choose (high probability behavior), and we make reading the magazine contingent upon working arithmetic problems, we have a good chance of increasing the likelihood that the arithmetic problems will be worked. This same principle can be used in the schedule to increase the chances that low probability tasks will be completed. Plan your schedule carefully so it will be a positive contributing factor to your management plan.

Reinforcement. The use of reinforcing or rewarding consequences is the primary method of supporting the acquisition of appropriate behavior. Chapter 1 provided an extensive discussion of the principles of reinforcement. To review briefly, reinforcement is the presentation of a pleasing consequence (positive reinforcement) or the withdrawal of an aversive stimulus (negative reinforcement). Reinforcement, whether positive or negative, increases the frequency of the behavior upon which it is contingent.

The emphasis in the behavioral classroom for emotionally disturbed students is on the use of positive reinforcement for appropriate behavior. For reinforcement to be effective, the teacher must apply it systematically and consistently. This is accomplished by first deciding which system you will use to dispense the reinforcement (check marks, points, etc.) and preparing the materials necessary to put it into operation.

Second, determine what the reinforcers will be. If a check mark or point system is used, what reinforcing consequences can this check mark or point be traded for? Remember that what is perceived as reinforcing by one student may not be perceived as reinforcing by another. One method that takes into account these differences is the use of a reinforcement menu. A reinforcement menu is a list of various items (tangibles, activities, etc.) from which the student may choose. There are two basic types of reinforcement menus. The first is the open menu, which is composed of a list of reinforcers of equal value (see Table 4.1). Upon earning reinforcement, the student may choose any one of the items from the menu.

TABLE 4.1
OPEN REINFORCEMENT MENU

Read a magazine	Play computer football
Listen to the record player	Work a puzzle
Use the tape recorder	Choice of art activity
Play a game of cards	Work on a model car or airplane

TABLE 4.2
PRIORITIZED REINFORCEMENT MENU

Item	Points Needed
1. One piece of candy	1
2. One piece of gum	2
3. One pencil	8
4. One eraser	12
5. Free time (ten minutes)	20
6. Bring record and listen to it	25
7. Play a game	28
8. One spiral notebook	35
9. Magazine	50
10. Model	75

The second is a prioritized menu. It consists of items with differing values that have been arranged in a sequential manner, starting with items that have a low value and progressing to items of higher value (see Table 4.2). One advantage it has over the open menu is that it can be helpful in teaching children to delay gratification. The low value items require few points (tokens, check marks), whereas the high value items require many points. Because of the high number of points required to obtain these items, the student will need to save his or her points, thus delaying gratification.

Reinforcement menus are a great help in organizing how reinforcers are awarded.

Third, identify which behaviors you wish to reinforce. Consider both academic and social behaviors. These may include starting a task, completing a task, correct responses on assignments, appropriate behavior on the playground, appropriate behavior in the classroom, and other behaviors you wish to increase or maintain. Reinforcement is a powerful and effective technique. Use it thoughtfully to support the behaviors that will benefit the student.

Time-Out.   Time-out is a procedure in which the sources of reinforcement for a particular behavior are removed for a period of time, contingent upon the emission of the behavior (Sulzer-Azaroff and Mayer, 1977). It is probably the most misinterpreted procedure used in the behavioral approach, yet it is widely used informally. After students misbehave, teachers have often asked them to put their heads down, sit on benches, or leave the room.

The key element in time-out is the teacher's removal of the opportunity for reinforcement. This can be accomplished by either removing the student from the situation or by removing reinforcing events from the environment. Often a teacher can modify a behavior by using limited time-out. This might include action as mild as the teacher's turning away or sending the student back to his or her seat or out in the hall. Sometimes, however, a student cannot remain in the problematic situation. A quiet area or room is then necessary to insure that opportunities of reinforcement are removed. Time-out areas or booths are often used for this purpose. The mention of a time-out booth may bring to mind the image of a dark, closed dungeon, but this is not what a time-out area is. A time-out area should be generally pleasant and free from harm. Its only purpose is to prevent the student from gaining reinforcement for a particular behavior.

Time-out should be used consistently (Zimmerman and Baydan, 1963). It should be applied in a calm, matter-of-fact manner (Sulzer-Azaroff and Mayer, 1977), and the actual time-out period should be relatively short (Zimmerman and Feister, 1963; Clark et al., 1973; Risley and Twardosz, 1974).

Time-out will not be as effective if it is used to allow a student to escape an aversive situation. If a student wants to avoid an unpleasant task, he or she can misbehave and then be sent to time-out. If such a pattern develops, the time-out is reinforcing the misbehavior.

Time-out will also be ineffective if there is too much of a struggle to place a student in a time-out situation. Many students are reinforced by the attention they get when time-out procedures are applied. If the immediate consequence of a disruptive behavior is attention, and attention is reinforcing to a child, then this attention may have a stronger influence than time-out.

It is necessary, unfortunately, to discuss the misuse of seclusion as time-out. Far too many children have been locked up in rooms for extended periods without any evidence that the procedure is effective. Many early studies placed students in seclusion for several hours for disturbing behaviors such as stealing, lighting fires, and bed-wetting (e.g., Burchard and Tyler, 1965). Such abuses have led to several court cases that restrict the use of seclusion (*Morales* v. *Turman,* 1973; *NYARC* v. *Rockefeller,* 1973; *Wyatt* v. *Stickney,* 1972). See Budd and Baer (1976) for a review of court cases affecting seclusion. Any person who decides to use time-out procedures is advised to use good judgment and safeguards to protect the rights of everyone involved. (See Sulzer-Azaroff and Mayer, 1977, or Benoit and Mayer, 1975, for guidelines.)

Token Economies. One of the major problems in applying a behavioral approach to modifying disordered behavior is that the same thing is not reinforcing to all children. One child might be reinforced by ice cream, but another might hate the stuff. Some children require tangible reinforcers, whereas others change their behavior for a smile or a moment of praise. An image may come to mind of a teacher who has a large bag of reinforcers to meet every need. Such a system is obviously impractical, if not impossible. A token economy can simplify this problem. A token economy is a system of reinforcement in which tokens or points are administered as the immediate reinforcer and the tokens are later exchanged for more substantial reinforcers. Each child is presented with a menu of rewards (Homme, 1971) and allowed to select the reward that is motivating to him or her at that moment. Tokens eliminate the need for the teacher to have a bag of rewards to dispense at the appropriate time. Another advantage of a token system is that the teacher can manipulate the rate of exchange. Some children need reinforcement for short intervals of work or time. Others can work for extended periods between rewards. Tokens allow the teacher to make individual modifications in children's programs. Children also have varying needs during a day or week. On Monday, they may feel quite capable of working for five whole days to receive a reward. By Wednesday, however, they may be more interested in immediate gratification of a lesser value. A token system allows them, and the teacher, that flexibility.

A teacher must consider three things when setting up a token economy. First, target behaviors must be identified. These will probably include some behaviors that should be increased and some that should be decreased. Second, the teacher must define the currency to be used with children. Examples include poker chips, stars, ditto money, paper, paper clips, plastic "credit cards," and tickets. No particular currency has been shown to be more effective than another. The third consideration is the rate of exchange. The teacher must devise two rates of exchange. The first is how many tokens a particular effort is worth, and the second is how many tokens will be required to "buy" a certain back-up reward.

A token system is best used when the reward requirements of the children are widely varied. The variation might be in the type of reinforcer needed (food, trinkets, activities) or in the frequency of reward required. One child might require rewards every few minutes, or for a small step in a program, whereas another child might require rewards only occasionally or at the end of a project.

As in any behavioral program, the teacher must have access to the reinforcing stimuli and be able to control dispensing it. If either of these conditions is not met, the program will probably fail. The target behaviors must also be clearly identified and communicated to everyone. It is also necessary to develop competing behaviors to reward if a target behavior needs to be reduced.

Finally, because the program is a system, everyone who works with the children must have a clear understanding of program components and requirements. If someone or several persons are either unaware of or inconsistent in the application of the system, its effectiveness will be greatly reduced. The system is also threatened when the children gain access to the tokens without engaging in the appropriate behaviors. If they acquire currency and can buy rewards without changing their behavior, their behavior will not change. Thus, it is necessary to develop a token system that is easily understood by everyone involved and that has secure currency that can only be acquired through appropriate behaviors, not by other means such as stealing or counterfeiting.

There are, of course, disadvantages to a token system. It does not closely resemble the normal school program to which a child will be returning. This problem has caused many people to abandon such systems. It is true that a child must be able to behave appropriately in a variety of settings to be successful. As a result, any behavior strengthened by the use of a token economy must also be generalized to other reinforcers. It is not true, however, that token systems do not approximate reality. Most of us function on a token economy far more complex than those developed in classrooms. The main difference between a classroom token economy and the real economy is one of timing. The manner of reinforcement and exchange is very similar; only the frequency of reward is different. Thus, if the frequency of reward were lowered, the behaviors emitted in a token economy might very well transfer to the regular classroom. Another reason the transfer of behaviors to the regular classroom has been difficult might be that there are few, if any, rewards in the regular class. This, however, is not a valid argument against the use of token economies, but rather an indication that changes should be made in regular classrooms.

The monitoring and management of a token system can often occupy a large part of a teacher's time. The system can become so elaborate that it is impossible for either the children or the teacher to decipher it. This is especially true if the class has a large number of rules or behaviors that are differentially reinforced. The reader who is contemplating setting up a token system and wants to avoid these and other pitfalls is referred to Kazdin (1977) or Ayllon and Azrin (1968).

Self-Management.   The management of a number of behavioral programs often becomes too much for a teacher. This is especially true when there are several children who require many programs that each involve a great deal of teacher management time. One system that has been developed to solve this problem is called self-management. The procedures are designed to shift the focus of control from the teacher to the pupil. In most instances, this shift must be programmed to be effective. Very few programs used to modify disordered behaviors are truly self-management; a more accurate description would be *shared* management. In either case, the emphasis is on teaching the child to take over more responsibility in managing his or her behavior.

There are two reasons why such an approach has merit. The first and most important is that the ability to plan and monitor one's own activities is a necessary skill. Far too often, children are taught a specific skill rather than the ability to design and monitor programs for themselves. Second, a shared or self-management system increases the number of management skills that children have at their disposal when facing a novel problem or situation.

Many people believe that management strategies are learned spontaneously as part of growing up. This may be true for most children in schools, but it is not true for most emotionally disturbed children. Self-management skills must be taught as systematically as mathematics or reading. This involves identifying the elements of self-management, arranging the components sequentially, and teaching them in sequence (Lovitt, 1973).

Six components of self-management have been identified by various investigators (Glynn, Thomas, and Shee, 1973; Lovitt, 1973). These are (a) self-assessment, (b) self-recording, (c) self-determination, (d) self-administration of reinforcement, (e) self-selection of skills to be learned, and (f) self-selection of time to learn skills. Each of these areas requires a different amount of shift in the focus control. They cannot, however, be considered sequential tasks. Several different arrangements are possible. One teacher might first teach self-assessment, then self-recording, and then shift to reinforcement strategies (e.g., self-administration or self-determination of reinforcement), while another teacher might begin with self-selection of materials, then self-timing of activities. These are only two of the many combinations possible.

Self-assessment is a student's examination of his or her own behavior to decide whether he or she has performed a specific behavior or class of behaviors. This might entail correcting math dittos or deciding whether or not they hit anyone today.

Self-recording requires that the child accurately record the frequency of a specific behavior or class of behaviors. Children often have no trouble describing and recording their behavior, but *accurate* recording is often a problem.

Self-determination of reinforcement usually includes two subcomponents, the nature of the reinforcement and the amount of reinforcement. Children can be taught to negotiate for a specific reward or activity that will be reinforcing to them. The idea of allowing the children to determine the nature of the reward has also been used with token economies. Homme (1971) demonstrated that it is also possible to have a virtually unlimited menu by using a token system. Allowing children to determine the amount of rewards required to reinforce a specific behavior is somewhat more difficult. The requested reward is often too much for the given activity. Glynn (1970) found, however, that ninth-grade girls were actually stingier in rewarding themselves than were their teachers.

Self-administration of reinforcement allows children to dispense their own reinforcement. The reinforcement may or may not be self-determined. When a child has reached a predetermined level of performance, then he or she can get a reward or participate in an activity. An example of this procedure would be the use of free time in a classroom. A teacher would set up an activity center where children could go to engage in a variety of activities following the completion of required tasks. They would not have to ask permission of the teacher. The only requirement would be that tasks be completed satisfactorily. The tasks, amount of time in the free time area, and the activities available in the area could be decided by the student, the teacher, or both.

Selection of skills to be learned is a procedure that allows the child to decide what he or she would like to learn within a certain period of time. This might mean allowing an adolescent the freedom to choose which skill to learn, or it might be something as limited as allowing a child to decide which science project to complete. This procedure capitalizes on children's interest to increase performance. It also provides opportunities for reinforcement.

Selection of skills to be learned is often combined with selection of time to learn a skill. This component is self-explanatory. It requires that the teacher allow a child to schedule his or her own program. Both teacher-selected or child-selected skills can be used with this procedure.

Several studies have shown the effectiveness of self-management procedures with children. Lovitt (1973) reports on seven children using one or more components of self-management. Other exploratory studies have been done by Glynn, Thomas, and Shee (1973) and Drabman, Spitalnik, and O'Leary (1973). The data are impressive. It is possible to teach shared management to many children without sacrificing quality. Although as yet untested, it also seems logical to expect that these management skills would transfer to other environments.

Self-management systems are not effective with all populations. It is necessary to monitor the system to determine whether or not the desired behaviors are being reinforced. A classic example of how self-evaluation programs can work against desired results is reported by Santogrossi et al. (1973). In this study, not only was the self-evaluation phase unsuccessful, but it adversely affected the teacher-directed phases as well.

Group Contingencies.   Group contingencies are used when it is necessary to modify the behavior of several children in one class. Frequently, a large percentage of the children in a class are disruptive. It may be impossible or impractical to isolate one or more children who are so disruptive that they destroy the learning environment. In such cases, group contingency systems should be considered.

There are three types of group contingency systems (Litow and Pumroy, 1975). The first type is independent group contingencies. In this procedure, the same target behaviors and the same consequences are identified for each member of the class. This is a familiar technique that has been used in classrooms for years. Its strongest advantage is the ease of administration. It also seems fair to many pupils. The disadvantage is that it treats all children the same and does not take individual abilities, activities, and rewards into consideration.

A second type of group contingency is the dependent group contingency. In this system, one child's behavior is identified, and the group is rewarded contingent upon a predetermined level of the child's performance. This technique is most effective when a disruptive behavior is being maintained by attention from other children. This program allows all the children to gain from the appropriate behavior of one child and thereby makes them more willing to ignore inappropriate behaviors and reward appropriate ones.

This procedure can also be misused. A child can easily become the target in a class. If the child's behavior does not meet the required standard, the whole class is deprived of a reward. This can lead to hostility and punishment rather than support and assistance. It is essential that the teacher set levels of expectations well within the performance range of the child to increase the probability of reward for both the target child and peers.

Interdependent group contingencies is the third type mentioned by Litow and Pumroy (1975). The same behavior is identified for all members of the class, and then the frequency of the occurrence of the behavior is noted. If the group has less than a certain number of inappropriate behaviors, the group is rewarded. This approach can also be used with teams within a class. This allows the teacher to match children and increase the probability of success.

Group contingencies have been effectively used to modify a variety of behaviors (see, for example, Wolf et al., 1970; Brooks and Snow, 1972; Barrish, Saunders, and Wolf, 1969). All three types have been used successfully. Many teachers find that the use of a group contingency augmented by other individual programs is the best way to manage a class when there are many children with a large number of disruptive behaviors.

MEASUREMENT OF BEHAVIOR CHANGE

A fundamental principle of an applied behavioral approach is that efficacy must be demonstrated. Each technique must be modified to fit the program goals for each child. Teachers must determine frequently if the behavior is changing in the desired way. To make such decisions, some data must be collected.

There's nothing novel about data collection. Everyone, especially teachers, collects and evaluates data constantly to decide what to do. If a car were traveling down a street we wanted to cross, we would collect data on the speed of the car, our walking speed, eye contact with the driver, the road conditions, recollection of past experiences, time requirements for when we had to be somewhere, and maybe even estimates of risk, both in walking and waiting. We would evaluate these data and make a decision. The purpose of measurement, then, is to collect data to make decisions. Correct decisions are based upon two factors, the accuracy of the data we collected and our ability to use data for making decisions.

Quality of Data

The most useful data provide direct descriptions of a specific behavior. This is much better than inferences regarding the behavior. It is easier, for example, to determine a change in the number of verbal outbursts of a child than it is to decide how hostile or angry the child is. This does not mean that children don't get angry or that anger is unimportant; it means, rather, that a measure of "anger" is less likely to lead to good decisions than a measure of the number of verbal outbursts.

Reliability. The data measured must be *reliable*. Every teacher has had the experience of observing a child with another person. If both persons describe the child's behavior, the differences in the descriptions may be so great that it may seem as if two different children were observed. When the behavior measured is defined sufficiently clearly that two or more people reliably "see" the same thing, then the accurate measurement of change is possible. The process of defining behaviors so that they can be reliably observed is often difficult, but it is well worth the effort. The more effort put into describing the behaviors, the clearer the problem becomes, and the solution to the problem often becomes apparent at the same time. Another benefit is that behaviors that evoke an emotional response in the observer are often defused by this process.

When a teacher attempts to describe a behavior, he or she ends up describing a group or chain of behaviors. When a teacher describes a child as hyperactive, it is not really one behavior that is being described, but rather a group of related behaviors — leaves seat, drops pencil, taps ring, talks out, and so on. Hyperactivity can be more accurately measured by describing the *specific behaviors* that make up the group or chain of behaviors. This is not always feasible. If this is the case, you should measure the critical effect of the chain of behaviors. In the case of hyperactivity, a critical effect might be assignments completed. The measurement of changes in assignments completed would allow a teacher to determine whether or not a program to reduce hyperactivity was successful. (See White and Haring [1976] for a more detailed discussion of critical effect.)

Validity. The data observed should also be *valid*. This requires that the teacher specifically identify the behaviors of primary concern. This is often the most difficult task required in measuring behavioral change. Often our efforts to specify behaviors precisely enough that they can be reliably measured produce data that do not apply to the real problem. We can measure changes in a child's word calling, but is that reading? We can count positive statements made to others, but is that an accurate reflection of self-confidence or self-esteem? We can measure proximity to peers in a play setting, but are they friends? The difficulty of the task, however, should not dissuade teachers from trying to collect valid data. Measuring change is a fundamental part of all behavioral programs. Without the measurement, the efficacy of a treatment can not be determined.

Measurement Techniques

When trying to determine change in a behavior, several aspects of the behavior may reflect the change. The choice of which measure to use is based upon decisions about which will provide the best information. Several options or alternatives may be used.

Frequency is the number of times a behavior occurs over a specified period of time. Frequency measures can be taken on a wide variety of behaviors — heartbeats, talk-outs, arithmetic answers, cars crossing an intersection: the list is endless. Frequency is a very sensitive measure; it can readily be used to determine whether a change has occurred. Frequencies can also be used for comparison after they are converted to a standard unit — talk-outs per hour, heartbeats per minute, or similar measures.

Some behaviors do not lend themselves to frequency measures. A child might have three one-hour tantrums on Monday and five five-minute tantrums on Tuesday. Is the child improving? According to the frequency data, no, but most teachers would say yes. Duration data would probably lead to better decisions. Duration data concern how long a behavior is emitted. Having tantrums, screaming, studying, playing, and similar behaviors lend themselves to duration data. This is especially true when one is interested in detecting an increase or decrease in behaviors that occur frequently but last a relatively long time during each occurrence.

Another way to determine if change has occurred is to observe the accuracy of responses. The rate of responding may not change, but the accuracy might. This measure is especially useful in measuring success on academic tasks. Consider a child who can finish eighty problems in a minute, but who misses seventy-eight of them. A program to increase this child's rate of responding or the duration of the program would not change the results. What is needed is a program to improve the percentage of accurate responses.

Latency is a measure of the time between stimulus and response. Some children specialize in receiving cues and then doing nothing. This usually causes the teacher to repeat the cue, repeat the cue, repeat the cue — and then blow up. Latency measures can be used to plan programs to increase compliance and to assess the effectiveness of many types of program.

The use of latency measures in planning a program allows the teacher to predetermine when to provide a consequence for a response. If the teacher asks Johnny to stand up and Johnny argues that he doesn't want to, a latency period could be part of the teacher's plan. He or she could wait fifteen seconds after the command and then, depending upon Johnny's response, choose the appropriate consequence.

Latency can also be used to assess other programs. Since latency measures the interval of time between the occurrence of the stimulus and the behavior controlled by the stimulus, many attention-to-task or on-task programs can be assessed with a latency measure. Program changes that reduce the delay between stimulus and response can be evaluated by latency measures.

Behavior Observation Alternatives.   Data are collected to make decisions. When a single measure is taken, inferences about the measure are used to make decisions about performance. The inferences are often wrong. To reduce this error, behaviorists usually measure data frequently over time. Most applied behavior analysis programs rely on daily measurement. The purpose of measurement of this frequency is to provide a more representative or average sample of performance and to be able to determine quickly the extent of change.

These data provide the information on which to base program decisions. When considering what data to collect and how often to collect them, teachers must ask themselves which procedure will yield the best information for making decisions. The data must, of course, be valid and reliable. These two factors often dictate the other considerations. The type of change to be measured — frequency, duration, accuracy, or latency — must also be determined. A final consideration is how often to collect data, how to collect data, and how to display the data so that they can be used to make decisions.

Continuous measurement is just what the name implies. Every occurrence of a behavior is observed or measured. This measure gives the most information, but it is often impossible as a practical matter. Continuous measurement is especially beneficial for programs in which the total number of responses emitted is small, where a behavior only occurs in a particular setting, or when a behavior occurs sporadically. Academic tasks also lend themselves to continuous measurement, because they yield products that remain intact after completion.

More often, however, a sampling procedure is used to collect data. Few classroom teachers have time to collect continuous data. The teacher relies on representative samples to provide an estimate of the behavior. There are two types of sampling — time sampling and interval sampling.

In time sampling, the teacher selects a period or series of periods during the day to record responses. During this period, all target behaviors are recorded. Teachers often use observation periods of five minutes or more out of an hour or even a morning. The assumption, of course, is that these samples approximate the whole time period of interest. Time sampling must be used carefully. It would be unwise for a teacher interested in disruptive behavior to sample this behavior for five minutes at the start and end of the day and five minutes after each recess. This selection of observation periods would bias the information and lead to inaccurate decisions.

In interval sampling, the period of interest is divided into equal intervals. An hour might be divided into sixty one-minute samples. If the target behavior occurs one or more times during the interval, a yes is recorded; if the behavior does not occur, a no is recorded. The result is that the teacher records the number of intervals in which a behavior occurred during a day, a math period, or other period of interest. This sampling technique is especially useful for recording behaviors that occur often.

It is sometimes useful or necessary to combine the two sampling techniques. When there are too few people in the room to observe and record a behavior, the teacher can sample many intervals. This technique requires that the teacher choose intervals that represent the entire period, and also that the behavior occur at a high enough rate that counting each behavior or measuring its duration would be impossible.

Sampling techniques are never as accurate as continuous measurement, but if they are carefully done, the results obtained can be quite useful. Whenever data are collected, the question of how often to collect always arises. No hard-and-fast rule can be given. The answer depends upon two factors: (1) the quality of decision to be made, and (2) the risk in making an error. When a teacher carefully designs a sampling technique to reflect the whole period and also analyzes the relationship between the sample and the whole when making decisions, the quality of decisions is rarely impaired.

Data-Based Decisions

The worth of the data a teacher collects is determined by the decisions they enable the teacher to make. Careful collection and recording of elaborate data is of little value if it does not lead to good program decisions. Some program decisions must be made without specific data. These decisions fall into the category of broad educational goals. For example, what skills will be necessary in 1999? How should children behave? Is reading more important than wood shop for a seventeen-year-old? Societal values decide many of the broad goals in education. Other goals are decided by the staff members of schools. These decisions are based on a mixture of experiences, expectations, and values. Books have been written about the success or failure of the goals of schools. Once goals have been established, it is still necessary to determine whether or not the teaching activities provided for a child produce the desired result. This is the function of decision-making rules based on direct data.

Behavioral analysis programs have developed many techniques to help the teacher determine the effectiveness of a teaching program. A thorough description of those techniques is beyond the scope of this chapter. The reader is referred to either *Exceptional Teaching,* by White and Haring (1976), or *Applied Behavior Analysis with Children and Youth,* by Sulzer-Azaroff and Mayer (1977) for complete descriptions of how to use data analysis in making decisions.

Any data analysis system must include both tools of data analysis and descriptions of how and when to make decisions regarding the analysis. Most behavioral analysis programs use data display techniques that monitor the behavior of a child and simultaneously direct progress toward a specific aim or goal. Data may be displayed by using a wide variety of lists, charts, and graphs.

Deciding what decisions to make is a difficult task. Research on decision-making rules based upon differing patterns of data is in its infancy. White and Haring report the preliminary results of their research in *Exceptional Teaching* (1976). In their program, they stress that skills are learned in phases and that the teacher needs to determine what phase of learning the child is in before making a program change. They also identify behavioral patterns that seem to suggest various program changes. White and others have extended this preliminary work to include prediction of future performances and analysis of trends and patterns in the data. Their recent findings indicate promising results (White and Haring, 1976; White, Billingsley, and Munson, 1978).

Rules for decision-making and data analysis will never replace qualified teachers. Applied behavior analysis programs are designed not to mechanize the art of teaching but to increase the skill of the practicing teacher by allowing him or her to monitor the behavior of children and simultaneously evaluate progress toward the goals of the program. Future analysis of data on how and when children learn will yield rules that will allow the teacher to select the program changes that have the highest probability of being successful. Without behavior analysis data systems, teachers and children frequently learn that a program is ineffective only when it is too late to change it. Evaluation once or twice a quarter simply does not yield enough information to modify programs so that they will provide the best opportunity for learning. Data analysis and decision-making rules are improving the level of instruction success, and should improve it even more in the future.

Data Display

Data are displayed to increase the ability of the teacher to make accurate decisions. Data may be displayed on many different types of lists, graphs, and charts.

Lists of data can be used to provide an accurate description of some behaviors. They can also be used to determine an average or typical response for a specified period of time. It is difficult, however, to detect trends or shifts in data from a list. The tendency to attend to extremes makes lists poor instruments for evaluating change or predicting future performance.

Graphs or charts are better instruments for determining progress or change over time. They can be designed to show changes in frequency, duration, or accuracy. Several procedures have been derived to allow a teacher to display current progress in terms of a predetermined goal, and also to predict future performance (White and Haring, 1976). The reader is referred to *Exceptional Teaching* (White and Haring, 1976) or *Applied Behavior Analysis Procedures with Children and Youth* (Sulzer-Azaroff and Mayer, 1977) for a more detailed discussion of how to use graphs and charts.

The use of graphs and charts improves the decision-making ability of the teacher. It allows the teacher to interpret data to determine whether a program change is required. Graphs provide the teacher with information about typical performances when making decisions, so he or she need not rely on high or low scores or the most recent results. The use of charts and graphs also increases the accuracy of predictions regarding future performance (White, 1978).

The Behavioral Analysis Approach: An Example

A simple example of the use of behavioral analysis is displayed in Figure 4.2. It was selected because it shows a simple application of the basic aspects of a behavior analysis approach. This example is a systematic replication of a case study reported by Kroth, Whelan, and Stables (1970). It comes from a public school classroom and indicates that a teacher functioning independently can use the approach successfully.

The teacher was concerned about a third grade child who was not attending to assigned arithmetic tasks. Instead, the child was gazing about the room, opening and closing the desk top, and generally distracting the other students. The teacher had to make several decisions. Should the behavior analysis program focus on decreasing gazing about the room and playing with the desk top, or on increasing the accuracy and number completed of assigned arithmetic problems? The teacher decided to change the child's academic behavior, for two reasons. First, it would increase the needed academic skill. Second, completing arithmetic problems was incompatible with gazing about and fiddling with a desk top. In this instance, the desired academic behavior happened to be incompatible with the undesired social behavior, but this is not always the case. What if the child were swearing in addition to not completing arithmetic problems? The teacher would probably have to devise one management program to reduce swearing and another to increase arithmetic problem completion. As any student who has labored over a complex algebra problem knows, it is possible to swear and do work at the same time.

After deciding to change the child's academic task performance, the teacher had to make another decision. Was the work too difficult for the child? If so, the materials (antecedent event) should be changed. The teacher decided that the work was at an appropriate instructional level and that motivation appeared to be the most important problem. The teacher then had to determine how to initiate a behavior analysis approach.

FIGURE 4.2
EFFECTS OF A CHILD-TEACHER CONTRACT FOR COMPLETION
OF ARITHMETIC SKILL PROBLEMS
The contract specified that the child could earn time to play with a puppet if twenty
assigned problems were completed at 80 percent or better accuracy within thirty minutes.

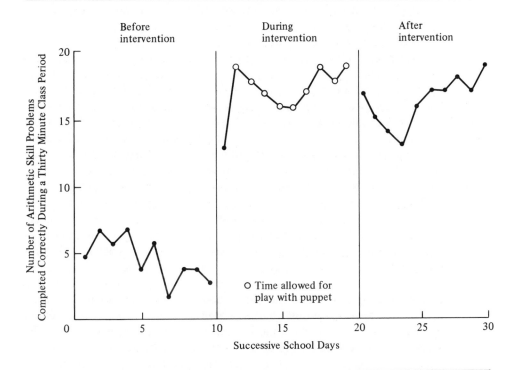

The teacher knew from his observations that the child enjoyed playing
with a puppet during free time periods. Would contingent puppet play increase the number of arithmetic skill problems the child completed correctly? The teacher decided to test the power of the puppet as an external
motivation factor to help the child be more successful in academic tasks.

Ten days before intervention, the number of problems completed and
the number correct were observed and recorded. At that point, the teacher
and child made a contract which stipulated that if the child completed the
twenty assigned problems within thirty minutes and got at least 80 percent
of them right, time for puppet play would be allowed.

How did the child respond to the program? On day 11, the first day
of contingent puppet play, the child did not reach 80 percent accuracy, so
time for puppet play was withheld. Was the child testing the teacher to see
if he would do what he said? Probably, since only two problems less than

the required 80 percent accuracy were completed. However, this is an inference, and it may not be correct. Perhaps the problems assigned were especially difficult that day. In any event, the only statement we can make is derived from the data — the child obtained a 70 percent score and did not receive time to play with the puppet. For the other nine days of the intervention, the child scored above 80 percent accuracy, and was allowed time to play with the puppet, as indicated by the open circles in Figure 4.2.

Did the intervention program account for the change? Did allowing time for puppet play have an effect on the child's problem completion and accuracy? These questions could not be answered unless the opportunity for puppet play was withdrawn. On day 21 the teacher informed the child that time for playing with the puppet would not be available after the arithmetic skill problems were completed. For the first three days of the after-intervention period, the child scored at 80 percent or above. On day 24, however, his accuracy dropped to 70 percent. More importantly, the first four days (21 through 25) showed a sharp decline in accuracy. Was the contingent puppet play withdrawn too soon? The teacher had used praise in conjunction with improved task completion throughout the intervention, but was it strong enough to sustain the child's efforts? What about the child's internal feeling of satisfaction for completing the assignment — would these feelings be enough to motivate continued acceptable task completion? The teacher was faced with a decision about whether to wait a few more days or to institute contingent puppet play again. The teacher decided to wait, but he did talk to the child about the declining accuracy scores, pointing out how pleased the child had been with improved task completion. As the chart indicates, the child's accuracy began to increase again. The teacher terminated the formal behavior analysis program on day 30, but he continued to monitor the child's behaviors periodically to determine if progress was being maintained.

Even though the behavior analysis intervention approach was apparently successful, certain problems associated with the data display and the effects of the intervention program on social behavior should be noted. It is not known, for example, how many problems the child actually completed, except for the days indicated by the open circles during the intervention phase of the program. The teacher had these data available in the form of the child's written computations. They could have been displayed for the entire thirty-day program to provide a comparison of problems correct and incorrect. In addition, there is no indication that gazing about and desk-top opening and closing were decreased. One can speculate that the undesired social behaviors declined, and in fact the teacher reported that they did, but they are not displayed. Would it have been possible to observe, record, and display the social behaviors? Probably, if the teacher had the services of an extra observer. Remember, though, that this program was carried out in a classroom setting, not as a part of an experimental project.

The teacher used the most efficient and effective means available to help the child begin to enjoy the rewards of successful social and academic behaviors.

There are other issues associated with how the data are displayed. The teacher could have decided to record and display percentage correct rather than number correct, or a percentage and frequency measure could have been displayed. On day 14, for example, the child was 90 percent correct, had a frequency of .60 per minute correct (18/30 minutes). If frequency and percentage done accurately were the issues, the teacher might have used contingent puppet play to increase both. In any event, the teacher decided a numerical accuracy display was sufficient to determine if the behavior analysis approach worked, and it did.

Several other aspects of data display deserve mention. Data are displayed for communication purposes. A figure can be used by the teacher for determining if an intervention program worked and as a record to share with colleagues, a supervisor, or a child's parents. In fact, showing children a display or record of their academic and social behavior may be enough to bring about desired changes. Having children record and display their own behavior can also elicit positive, directional changes. But data display should never be confused with the intervention program itself. The program is often too complex to communicate on a simple two-dimensional figure. Figure 4.2 does not capture the essence of the child-teacher relationship, nor does it indicate the effects of the child-teacher conversation that occurred on day 25 during the after-intervention phase. A data display is just a simple, often incomplete, summary of what the program did or did not accomplish, not the essence of the program itself. What transpires between a teacher and child is far more important than a visual summary of those transactions. Attention to this consideration about display will help those who use behavior analysis programs to maintain a realistic perspective on the power and limitations of such programs.

SUMMARY

This brief chapter has only scratched the surface of a deep and complex approach to helping children learn to cope successfully in school, home, and community. We tried to include a description and examples of the major components of a behavior analysis approach, but we did not include detailed information regarding specific application. Thus, the future practitioner of behavior analysis should not stop after reading this chapter, but should seek the additional study and practice necessary before the approach can be used with children. As indicated previously, children must be beneficiaries, rather than the victims, of this or any other intervention approach. Used wisely, this approach can be of great benefit, but used unwisely it can lead to debilitating encounters between children and adults. We must use the approach wisely if we hope to meet the immense obligation of helping children learn and grow through their school years. But the child knows best and can say it best. As one child said to a teacher, "I like being in your class, because you're there when I need you, and I learn a lot." After all, this is what teaching is all about. Who could ask for a better data-based evaluation?

Chapter 5

Behavior Management: The Psychoeducational Model

H. Lyndall Rich
Memphis State University

with

Mitchell A. Beck
University of Wisconsin at Oshkosh

Thomas W. Coleman, Jr.
Wayne State University

The fundamental characteristic of the psychoeducational model is its emphasis on an intervention process that stresses intrapersonal development in emotionally disturbed students. The interpersonal dimension is also important, but not to the extent that it overshadows the intrapersonal.

The management techniques we describe in this chapter reflect the eclectic nature of this model. These techniques are not to be considered a potpourri of disconnected strategies, however. They are a group of complementary interventions derived from various interrelated social and psychodynamic theories, which were described in Chapter 2. Neither the theory nor the techniques described are meant to include all possible considerations. Rather, as the psychoeducational model emphasizes attention to the idiosyncratic emotional needs of the individual student, intervention requires a certain specificity, regardless of its theoretical base. Along with this theoretical flexibility, however, there must be an internally consistent program to insure that intervention is effective. Beginning with the following elaboration of terminology, we emphasize the importance of maintaining a sense of coherency in program development.

DEFINITIONS

Intrapersonal means "within the person." The psychoeducational approach to behavior management is based on this definition, being concerned primarily with the mental health of students, and emphasizing the inner psychological processes. This emphasis is expressed in terms of two primary objectives: (1) helping students understand their emotions, resolve internal crises, and reduce psychological pain; and (2) facilitating the development of personal and social skills that will enable students to be more self-directed in the appropriate expression of feelings, emotions, and needs. The accomplishment of these intrapersonal objectives among disturbed students often requires intensive, well-designed managerial techniques. These objectives are considered so vital to the mental health of disturbed students that intrapersonal curricular experiences have been incorporated into many school programs (see Chapter 7). We believe it is important to recognize that intrapersonal development is a long-term objective, requiring more than a casual or superficial intervention program. Consequently, we conceptualize behavior management as an intrapersonal learning process by which disturbed students deal with their intrapersonal emotions and develop appropriate self-directed social behaviors.

Intervention is not always such a lengthy process, however. Short-term techniques are also necessary, especially if behavior is physically or psychologically threatening to self and others. Because of the need to manage spontaneous behaviors, the psychoeducational model also uses immediate management techniques. Whenever possible, such techniques should be consistent with the student's intrapersonal needs by managing the present inappropriate behavior in a way that provides some progress toward intrapersonal understanding and self-direction. On occasion, however, because of strong, spontaneous emotions, disturbed students may lose control so that something must be done immediately, "on the firing line" (Redl, 1966b).

A very important precondition for the use of intrapersonal techniques, whether they be short- or long-term in nature, is the teacher's knowledge of individual students and their optimal learning environment needs. Even though this chapter will subsequently discuss a variety of psychoeducational management techniques, they will be of limited use unless the teacher has substantial knowledge of individual students. Although a "trial and error" strategy may be appropriate in some circumstances, management is most effective when the techniques used are appropriate for the individual student. Choosing the appropriate intrapersonal technique for a student requires that the teacher be aware of individual academic, psychological, and physical characteristics, and also of the effects of environmental space and classroom social structure on the student.

An even more critical condition for the classroom is the teacher's sensitivity in developing a meaningful teacher-student relationship. The psychoeducational model emphasizes that the teacher plays an active role not only as an educator, but as a counselor, a group worker, and an advocate for the student. Thus, a basic teacher goal should be to establish a positive, productive relationship based on empathy, understanding, and a genuine sense of caring. Such a relationship does not mean that the teacher is necessarily "soft" or easily manipulated, however; quite the opposite is true. A teacher who is easily manipulated has not developed the relationship necessary to effectively help emotionally disturbed students. A relationship based on empathy, understanding, and caring is one in which the teacher will use the most appropriate intrapersonal techniques available to manage behavior.

Eclectic is a term meaning "selecting the best from what is available." Even though the psychoeducational model emphasizes the intrapersonal needs and characteristics of disturbed students, no management technique, whether based on biological, behavioral, psychodynamic, sociological, or ecological theory (Rhodes and Tracy, 1972b) will be rejected if it might help disturbed students. Although the psychoeducational model places heaviest emphasis upon psychodynamic and social theories for the development of managerial techniques, procedures such as environmental manipulation, reinforcement, and stimuli reduction — all of which grew out of theories often considered incompatible with the psychoeducational model — are also employed. Thus, it is not the theoretical origin of the technique *per se* that is critical to the psychoeducational model, but the technique's consideration of intrapersonal needs and the development of more acceptable, self-directed behavior.

There are, however, some specific management techniques that are used with the psychoeducational model almost exclusively. Techniques that emphasize the therapeutic management of emotions, behaviors, or both through the use of support, insight, and value reorganization are typically psychoeducational in nature. Techniques such as "emotional first aid" (Redl and Wineman, 1957), "life space interviewing" (Redl, 1976a), and "crisis intervention" (Morse, 1976b) are commonly applied with this model.

The term *therapeutic,* used in connection with management, should not be confused with the common medical-analytic meaning related to the treatment of disease. Rather, the psychoeducational model stresses the more generic definition: "helping." In this context, the difference between education and therapy is largely semantic. Any process used to help disturbed students develop greater self-understanding and self-directed behaviors is both educational and therapeutic.

We have presented these introductory remarks to provide the reader with basic information about the psychoeducational approach to managing behavior. Several concepts inherent to this model were discussed to help the reader begin to sense the form and function of this approach. The psychoeducational model stresses "controls from within" (Redl and Wineman, 1957) as a long-term objective. External control, used only during dangerous crises, is considered to be a temporary measure. Behavior management, then, is based upon the belief that disturbed students need to better understand their feelings, emotions, and needs to develop appropriate self-directed behaviors.

APPROACH TO EMOTIONAL DISTURBANCE

The labels "emotional disturbance" and "behavioral disorder" are often used synonymously in the professional literature. For psychoeducators, the label "emotional disturbance" is preferable to "behavioral disorders." "Emotional disturbance" conveys the belief that the student has intrapersonal problems, whereas "behavior disorders" focuses on the external manifestation of such problems. To the psychoeducator, behavior is not an isolated occurrence, but rather an event motivated by past experience, the present situation, and the future expectations of the student. Unless a behavior is immediately threatening, the intervention process requires more than simple surface-level management. Instead, psychoeducators attempt to help students clarify their emotional reactions and develop appropriate self-directed behavior. Successful self-management depends on the extent to which students can internalize coping skills, social awareness, and values consistent with environmental expectations and individual goals.

As a point of clarification, we have used the term "student" throughout this chapter in lieu of "children" or "youth." Although the terms are synonymous in most cases, we chose "student" because it best reflects the age spectrum typically associated with "children" and "youth," and because it conveys the belief that emotionally disturbed persons are primarily viewed as learners rather than patients or clients.

Rationale for the Management of Behavior

Among teachers of the emotionally disturbed, the management of inappropriate behavior has consumed more energy, created more frustration, and resulted in more discussion than any other school-related topic. Even though the issue of "discipline" is a national concern (Gallup, 1979), the frequency and intensity of inappropriate behaviors are especially high among emotionally disturbed students.

To a great extent, the current crisis in behavior management is a consequence of educational practices and expectations that have remained relatively stable in the presence of scientific, technological, and social change. Historically, teachers have been well trained to transmit academic information to large groups of rather homogeneous students. Such an academic, teacher-centered approach usually required an orderly, passive, and controlled learning environment. Classroom control was primarily dependent on students' willingness to submit to teacher demands and expectations. Students who failed to comply with the established standards were reprimanded, punished, or otherwise "disciplined." Thus, the classroom has historically represented a model based on external control in which student conformity to standards of conduct was rewarded and disruptive interference was categorically punished through adult intervention.

Disruptive behavior is not the only source of interfering behavior, however. Some students have inner sources of interference manifested by feelings of fear, loneliness, and apprehension. Teachers have a responsibility to reorient these students to the reality of classroom learning, even when such behaviors are not directly interfering with the learning of other students. We have included this precautionary note to emphasize the marked contrast between a debilitating intrapersonal state and the more highly visible and disruptive acting-out state. Consequently, teachers tend to avoid therapeutic interaction with the more behaviorally compliant emotionally disturbed students, because the demands of overt disruption engage more teacher time.

Clearly, both acting-out and negative intrapersonal behaviors interfere with the learning process and must be managed if individual students and the classroom group are to master the cognitive skills necessary to successfully complete an educational program and develop effective interpersonal skills. Psychoeducators maintain that temporary external control by the adult intervention agent rarely leads to internalization of control with any significant longevity. In contrast, the psychoeducational model includes immediate management techniques and an added emphasis on internalizing control processes and enhancing student self-awareness.

The Classroom Environment

The psychoeducational model also stresses the importance of the classroom environment in managing behavior. Included in our conceptualization of the classroom environment are not only the physical space of the classroom but the interaction of teacher and student within a confined space. In the past, many different terms have been used to describe classroom design, terms such as *environmental psychology, therapeutic milieu, social climate,* and *learning atmosphere,* among others. Although not entirely synonymous, there is a common thread among these labels: they refer to the classroom environment as all "the surrounding conditions and influences that affect personal development" (Dale, 1972, p. 16). Although the classroom is composed of innumerable "conditions and influences" affecting behavior, the most relevant features are the teacher, the peer group, and the physical space. Because of their special importance, we elaborate on each of these components in the following sections.

The Teacher. There is general agreement among educators that the teacher is the most critical influence in shaping the classroom environment

(Smith, Neisworth, and Greer, 1978). The teacher occupies a commanding position in most classrooms. According to Mehrabian (1976), an obvious feature of most school environments is that "a small number of people occupy positions of great dominance — persons who command resources enabling them to reward greatly or punish severely" (p. 153).

Thus, the character of the classroom environment is strongly shaped by the teacher's use of personal, professional, and legal influence on the students in the classroom. How a teacher exercises this influence, then, becomes a critical factor in promoting either a positive or negative environment.

Several studies have demonstrated that teachers' leadership behaviors have a significant influence on the environment, behavior, and academic performance of students. The clearest evidence of leadership effects comes from the classic study by Lewin, Lippitt, and White (1939), who compared three distinctively different leadership styles: authoritarian, laissez-faire, and democratic. Brophy and Good (1974) provide an excellent summary of this study:

> Laissez-faire leadership tends to create chaos and confusion. Authoritarian leadership achieves efficient productivity but at the cost of frustration and a general negative group atmosphere, leading to outbreaks of aggression when the leader is absent. In contrast to both of the above, democratic leadership appears to be successful in enabling groups to reach productive goals but without the cost of frustration and aggression. In fact, it seems to have the advantage of teaching the group to function more maturely, cooperatively and independently in the leader's absence as well as in his presence. *(p. 245)*

In general, psychoeducators seek to build their teaching styles on the strength of the democratic approach. Since the intrapersonal needs of some students may be facilitated best by a style other than the democratic approach, however, no specific teaching style is prescribed. Rather, the eclectic orientation of the psychoeducational model suggests that the style be consistent with the needs of the individual disturbed student. The accomplishment of the most basic personal objectives, such as early stage development crises involving trust and psychological safety, may require a more structured, protective environment, implemented by a more authoritarian leadership style. A similar method and style may be required for disturbed students whose behavior is characterized as impulsive, unsocialized, or fearful. Students functioning on these basic personal developmental levels lack "important basic skills, [and] need direction or protection until they can acquire them" (Joyce and Harootunian, 1967, p. 95). Students functioning on the higher developmental levels require a different teaching style. Students attempting to meet higher-level personal objectives such as "belongingness" and "identity" may be more comfortable with a more "open" environment with a democratic teaching style (Rich, 1978).

In all probability, no single teaching style will be preferable for all disturbed students in a classroom. The teachers' ability to determine the most appropriate style based on the intrapersonal needs of the individual disturbed student will best facilitate the development of a productive environment.

The Peer Group.   Although the interaction between the teacher and the individual student is important in the psychoeducational model, the behavior of individuals cannot be disconnected easily from the classroom as a group. According to Morse (1960), "the teacher can ill afford to ignore alignments when they operate to influence learning behavior of the pupil members" (p. 230). In many classrooms, teachers demonstrate competent management of both group and individual student learning without incident. Even in the most skillfully led classroom groups, however, student behaviors may develop that are counterproductive to effective learning if teachers ignore the more subtle expressions of student conflict. Under such circumstances, the teacher's influence may erode as control is usurped by student disruption; a preventable situation then becomes an out-of-control "power struggle." A delicate balance between classroom goals and individual student needs is necessary in this type of setting. Negative classroom climates can be minimized only if teachers recognize critical group characteristics and their effect upon the individual student and then provide appropriate management techniques.

Group Norms.   In varying degrees, teachers and disturbed students alike are subject to pressures to conform to the group. Although some people may behave in certain ways intentionally to gain peer approval, most people are not consciously aware of the tremendous psychological pressure exerted by their peer group to insure conformity to group standards and expectations of behavior. What one wears, how one behaves, one's expressed motivation for school, and one's choice of teachers and friends are all shaped to some extent by group norms (Jackson, 1960). Often this pressure comes in the form of statements or gestures that convey approval or disapproval of an individual student's behavior, regardless of a teacher's sanction.

Considering this influence, teachers must be sensitive to the norms of the classroom and the school. In most circumstances, teachers who encourage students to violate peer norms are subjecting their charges to potential ridicule and abuse. For example, expectations about how often a student may speak out in class vary from classroom to classroom. Students who speak out more often than is accepted, particularly to the teacher, may be socially rejected and labeled "teacher's pet" or "Miss Know-it-all." Similarly, students who speak out less than the norm requires are often pressured by the peer group into verbalizing, even if their responses are inappropriate. Of course, the acceptable norm for speaking varies from class to class and student to student. In some classes, particularly if the teacher is disliked by the most popular and powerful students, the norm may be very low. Efforts by the teacher to encourage verbal interaction result in blank stares, shrugging shoulders, or barely audible grunts. In any of these exemplary cases, teachers who demand that interaction conform to their expectations without understanding peer group norms are inviting confrontation. Such confrontations have no winners, only losers, and the classroom environment grows steadily more negative.

Although younger children are greatly influenced by adult behaviors and expectations, with increasing age the peer group gradually becomes a stronger force. In fact, it is well documented that older children, especially adolescents, may intentionally violate school rules or teacher expectations to gain or maintain peer approval (Vorrath and Brendtro, 1974). Typically, classroom groups that demonstrate high rates of work output frequently ask the teacher for guidance and show a low tolerance for peer distractions, which are often the result of group norms. Similarly, such behaviors as aggression, defiance, and academic failure may reflect a classroom norm, albeit one contradictory to the expectations of the teacher and the education enterprise in general.

Group Cohesiveness. Group cohesiveness, or peer group attraction and unity, also has critical implications for the classroom environment and the management of behavior. Some groups function as a single unit, moving smoothly from one activity to another, displaying little deviant behavior, and freely cooperating and sharing. In other classrooms it is difficult to shift activities without noise and the frequent use of physical intimidation. In the first type of class, the group structure may reflect a balanced sociometric structure that is attractive to the individual members. In the second example, less cohesion may indicate a group represented by an established hierarchy of power — a "pecking order." A study by Schmuck (1966) found that classroom "groups characterized by a nearly equal distribution of popularity and influence choices in contrast to those more distinctly hierarchical had both more cohesiveness and more positive norms concerning the goals of school" (p. 62).

This balanced peer group social structure, represented by an equal distribution of social choices within the classroom, provides one of the clearest indicators of cohesiveness. Socially balanced classroom groups have a greater capacity to attract new members, function more harmoniously as a unit, and create a positive learning environment. By comparison, groups that are polarized into subgroups are repeatedly plagued by personal conflict among their members. Subgroups may take one of the following orientations: racial (blacks versus whites); economic (rich versus poor); the academic (bright versus slow); and the social (popular versus isolates). This competition for social-psychological superiority rarely results in a positive learning environment. Teachers may unwittingly contribute to classroom polarization by positively interacting with members of one subgroup and punishing or ignoring members of another. Consequently, teachers must be conscious of the distribution of grades, privileges, and responsibilities so that they do not routinely favor one subgroup over another.

The first step in managing behavior in groups is to understand the influence of group norms and cohesiveness on the behavior of disturbed students. The second step is to use management techniques that enlist group support or at least neutralize negative group influence. There are no simple solutions, however. An extensive knowledge of group behaviors and sensitivity to the subtle influences of classroom design and atmosphere are crucial to maintaining some semblance of order.

Whenever deviant behavior occurs in the classroom, the teacher must decide whether to intervene with individual students or the entire group. Of the two choices, the literature more frequently emphasizes managing behavior demonstrated by individual students.

The management of individuals, however, has two primary limitations. First, individual management may have a negative "ripple effect," resulting in unpleasant distractions for nondeviant students (Kounin, 1970). Highly visible or noticeable teacher management techniques tend to reduce the task-appropriate behavior of students witnessing the intervention, thereby shifting the classroom emphasis from learning to management. Second, individual deviant behavior may be a function of group norms rather than individual norms. Thus, deviance may be a "role" behavior, acquired by an individual student but expected and supported by the group as a whole.

The maintenance of deviant roles by the teacher and the group, although potentially productive for group status, is counterproductive in terms of healthy social and emotional development and academic achievement. If deviant behaviors are a function of the group, then management that considers the group in its entirety must be implemented. Competent group management requires a teacher willing to involve the group in open communication and to share in the decision-making process typically allocated to teachers. In short, teachers must develop an atmosphere of understanding and cooperation, rather than one of control and competition (Vorrath and Brendtro, 1974).

The psychoeducational model supports the following specific group management processes:

1. Guiding the group toward examining behavior;
2. Developing problem identification skills;
3. Helping the group clarify problem situations with greater specificity;
4. Guiding the group in diagnosing problems;
5. Helping the group establish goals;
6. Helping the group improve techniques for resolving conflicts.
   (p. 106)*

Effective group management is based on the teacher's awareness of the group's psychosocial structure, an accurate assessment of individual behaviors in the group, and a willingness to involve the group in understanding and resolving problems. In summary, group management is helping the group identify problems and issues that have negative influence on personal adjustment and classroom performance; helping the group decide on solutions and strategies for resolving problems; and helping the group solve their own problems. This approach requires that the teacher be open, communicative, and democratic within the context of a problem-solving orientation.

The Physical Space.   Physical classroom space characteristics are a dimension of behavior management that has often been overlooked. Teachers are aware that factors such as room size, temperature variations, and general decor are related to learning and behavior (Drew, 1971). Research, however, has not established which physical factors predict a greater probability for the expression of inappropriate, deviant behavior. As a result, our comments on the physical space issue will be based on the contention that "physical settings have their own properties which place constraints on some behavior and facilitate, if not require, others" (Proshansky, 1974, p. 553). A listing of all significant classroom physical factors is impossible. There are, however, critical relationships between physical *instructional* space and *learning* space that have important implications for behavior and behavior management.

Even though teachers should be able to justify the physical arrangement of the classroom, many teachers do not recognize "which aspects of learning and social behavior should be expected to change as a function of the particular environmental design" (Cruickshank and Quay, 1970, p. 265). One way of studying the environmental design is to consider both the symbolic meaning and the pragmatic function of the physical classroom arrangement and what that arrangement communicates to students and teachers (Proshansky and Wolfe, 1974). "Symbolic meaning" refers to the psychological expectation of behavior, whereas the pragmatic function refers to the actual effectiveness of the environment in supporting or reducing specific behaviors.

In discussing both the symbolic and pragmatic implications of environmental management, two examples of classroom physical arrangements will be considered—"traditional" and "informal" (Figure 5.1).

The traditional classroom is a formal design, often referred to as a teacher-centered environment. It has been the basic model of classroom arrangement for several centuries. The typical arrangement consists of several rows of student seat-desks, one behind the other, facing the front of the room where the teacher's desk, classroom entrance, and chalkboard are located. The teacher's primary station, near the desk, enables the teacher

FIGURE 5.1
PHYSICAL POSITIONS OF STUDENTS AND TEACHERS
IN TRADITIONAL AND INFORMAL CLASSROOMS

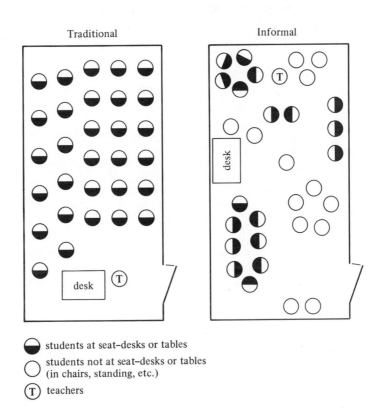

students at seat–desks or tables

students not at seat–desks or tables
(in chairs, standing, etc.)

teachers

to control the flow of traffic in and out of the classroom, to speak directly to students, and to supervise the entire group visually.

Symbolically, the frequent duplication of this standardized classroom design emphasizes expected patterns of behavior on the part of teachers and students alike. These expectations include the exercise of authoritative control, a lecture method of instruction, the passive use of space, and the presumed homogeneity of students. "The location of the teacher's desk in the traditional room not only communicate[s] the isolated role of the teacher; it also physically place[s] that space off limits for use by the children" (Proshansky and Wolfe, 1974, p. 559).

The uniformity and position of the students' seating arrangement suggest educational conformity, passive learning, and an orderly standard of behavior. The lack of variety in student work space implies that all students require the same spatial area regardless of the task, the students' perceptual-motor abilities, or their psychological needs. Because students face the teacher and not each other, the instructional format is predetermined to consist primarily of teacher lecturing, directing, and questioning. The physical arrangement does not encourage student communication with anyone but the teacher.

A student poem reflects one student attitude regarding this traditional classroom arrangement (Schultz, Heuchert, and Stampf, 1973, p. iv):

> ... It was funny about school.
> He sat in a square brown desk
> like all the other square brown desks
> and he thought it would be red.
> And his room was a square brown room like all the other rooms.
> And it was tight and close. And stiff.
> He hated to hold the pencil and chalk,
> with his arm stiff and his feet flat on the floor, stiff,
> with the teacher watching and watching. ...

In summary, the symbolic meaning of the traditional classroom emphasizes controlled behavior and unilateral communication directed and supervised by the teacher. The physical and visible separation of teacher and students reinforces the authoritative role of the teacher and increases the social distance, precluding interpersonal management. The confined, standard student seating arrangement requires passive, isolated learning within the context of reduced motor activity, limited exploratory behavior, and restricted student interaction.

The informal classroom arrangement, which approximates an "open space" or child-centered environment, conveys a different symbolic meaning than the traditional classroom. A visual overview of the informal classroom reveals a nonuniform arrangement of student work areas, a variety of work surfaces of different sizes, and both individual and small group settings. The teacher's physical position in the classroom is not well defined, nor does the teacher's desk constitute a physical or psychological barrier.

This informal arrangement discourages the use of a lecture method of instruction since the teacher does not occupy a commanding position directly visible to all students. Similarly, many students are out of the visual range of the teacher. The lack of reciprocal face-to-face contact requires that task objectives and activities be different for individuals and small groups. Thus, the teacher functions in the role of facilitator rather than director.

Noise, movement, and general activity are expected behaviors since the physical arrangement is predicated on the assumptions of involvement, flexibility, interaction, and individualized programming. Different work surfaces, spatial allowances, and activity settings symbolically suggest that individual differences are accommodated, at least in terms of the physical task requirements and motor needs.

In summary, the informal classroom "is not a single homogeneous space cube; rather, it is a network of interconnected and varied micro-environments" (Sommer, 1977, p. 175). Individualized activities, teacher movement and interaction, and the variety of spatial arrangements add up to a classroom with a great amount of noise, verbalization, and physical mobility. The informal classroom is based in part on the assumption that an individualized physical environment will reduce environmental constraints that impede student performance.

The psychoeducational model clearly encourages the use of informal physical space, but it does not reject the traditional classroom. Pragmatically, neither classroom arrangement is universally preferable — the best arrangement is one that is effective for the people involved. Both the traditional and informal classrooms have managerial advantages and disadvantages.

The traditional arrangement was designed as an orderly, lecture-type environment. If the teacher's style is one of maintaining control and lecturing, then the straight rows of desks are preferable to random clusters of students (Sommer, 1977). The informal arrangement is designed to facilitate more individualized, self-directed learning activities. A personal, facilitating teacher style, favored by the psychoeducational model, is more consistent with this environmental arrangement.

Physical arrangements are also determined by considerations other than teacher's style and preference. Any decision to use a particular arrangement must also take into account the needs of the disturbed students who occupy the classroom. The relationship between teacher style and student needs should determine which classroom arrangement is most appropriate. It is generally assumed, for example, that the hyperactive child should be in close proximity to the teacher and work under conditions relatively free of unnecessary stimulation (Fairchild, 1975). Such management procedures could best be accomplished in the traditional classroom, since teacher mobility and environmental stimulation are critical to the informal class.

The informal arrangement, accompanied by high teacher mobility, has the advantage of permitting management of individual student behavior without drawing attention to the student in question. Certainly it is easier to tolerate a variety of behaviors when students are not expected to conform to an established pattern of passive behavior. Ignoring behavior, spontaneous proximity control, and individual tutoring are similarly consistent with both the symbolic and pragmatic functions of the informal class. Individual student management can thus be conducted in the classroom directly rather than at a later time and place, as one might expect in the traditional classroom.

Certainly no single classroom arrangement will adequately deal with every managerial concern. Each classroom is designed with specific objectives, styles, and behaviors in mind; those inconsistent with the environmental design will be less than successful, however. It is possible to use both arrangements in a single classroom. One segment of the class can be assigned to individual seat desks while the rest of the class works independently or in small groups. Whatever classroom arrangement is used, it should be based on group and individual physical, academic, and psychological needs and reflect the instructional-managerial philosophy of the teacher.

Even though the psychoeducational model supports the use of both physical arrangements, we feel that certain limitations should be pointed out to avoid overgeneralizing this position. Specifically, the traditional classroom lends itself mostly to short-term solutions to student problems. For teachers to respond successfully to intrapersonal conflict and for students to develop greater self-understanding and self-direction, the informal organization is the preferable model.

We have emphasized thus far that, in the psychoeducational model, an effective educational environment results from the complementary mixing of the teacher, peer group, and physical space. Although much is still unknown about these variables, recognition of this synergistic interaction is crucial to subsequent implementation. The fact that democratic or child-centered teaching styles, group utilization, and informal classrooms are preferred over their counterparts is a further indication that the ultimate objectives in management are to encourage "controls from within."

MANAGEMENT TECHNIQUES

Management techniques are teachers' actions designed (1) to prevent or appropriately change student behaviors or emotions that are considered incompatible with human potential development, and (2) to accomplish educational objectives. The management techniques discussed in this section are not based on a single theoretical approach, but drawn from a number of theories. Nevertheless, the combination of eclectic techniques discussed here, which is designed to contain immediate crises and effect long-term intrapersonal changes, is psychoeducational in nature. In addition to the influence of teacher, peer group, and environment, there are many specific management techniques included in the psychoeducational model. For discussion purposes, the managerial techniques have been grouped into the following categories: (1) general principles of management, (2) surface management, (3) interpersonal management, and (4) instructional management. These four categories do not include all of the available management techniques, nor do they guarantee success unless they are individually and appropriately employed.

General Principles of Management

The successful use of psychoeducational techniques requires that we recognize certain guiding principles. Although these principles do not represent all of the possible concerns and conditions, they are frequently reported as prerequisites to behavior management in the literature and by experienced teachers (Long, Morse, and Newman, 1976).

Tolerating Selected Behaviors.   Teachers of the emotionally disturbed should not respond to every "deviant" behavior in the classroom. In fact, some "deviant" behaviors are not maladaptive at all, but constitute acceptable individual responses to various characteristics of the learning environment. According to Long and Newman (1961), tolerating behavior involves such individualized concepts as "learner's leeway," "behavior that reflects a developmental state," and "behavior that is symptomatic of a disease." To use these three concepts, however, teachers must recognize the variability of human behavior.

"Learner's leeway" simply reflects the teacher's belief that students perform in accordance with their individual characteristics. Certainly no group of students will all complete the same number of math problems in the same time or drink the same amount of water from the hall fountain. Similarly, teachers should not expect equivalent physical expression under the varying demands of seat-work immobilization and other taxing situations. Providing for a "learner's leeway" recognizes individual differences and at the same time reduces the need for superfluous management of behavior.

Although most children and adolescents go through the same developmental stages, they do not meet developmental milestones at the same time or the same rate. High levels of motor activity, for example, are more evident among primary-aged students, and show a steady decrease as students get older (Rich, 1978). Similarly, boys are more motor active than girls. Impulsiveness, "lying," "tattling," and grooming habits are other behaviors that may simply reflect transitions in development and not pathological states. Nonthreatening behaviors that are not under the conscious control of the student should be tolerated. Tolerance does not imply a lack of programming, however; it reflects a decision not to attempt management of innocuous expressions of behavior.

Dealing with the Present.   Reminders of past problems serve no purpose other than to kindle feelings of failure and resentment. Teachers' statements such as *This is the third time you've been late, You did the same thing last week,* or *How many times have I had to tell you?* are direct signals to the student that the teacher will continue to use reminders of past problem behaviors to evaluate current performance. Problems should be dealt with as they occur, and past problems should not be brought into the discussion. Certainly, all problems cannot be managed successfully, but current behavior can be successfully changed. Past behavior, on the other hand, is beyond alteration.

Preventing Rather than Interfering.   Most teachers know under what situations a student is likely to demonstrate strong emotional behavior and become a management problem. It is pointless to subject a student to conditions that predictably provoke outbursts of inappropriate behavior that require teacher intervention. The therapeutic procedure would be to prevent the problem by moving to the student, providing an interesting activity, restructuring the environment, or using other techniques suggested in this chapter. Once a deviant behavior has developed, the energy and resources necessary to effectively manage it are much greater than those that would have been necessary to prevent the behavior.

When to Manage.   Classroom teachers obviously have a wide variety of expectations about the appropriateness of student behaviors. Whereas some teachers encourage student movement, verbalization, and exploration, other teachers intervene with the same behaviors. Some teachers interfere more frequently if the principal is near the classroom, when the classroom temperature is uncomfortable, or during the middle of the week. Certainly management is conducted by human teachers with human feelings that will always reflect a degree of idiosyncratic behavior. Nevertheless, the choice of whether to manage behavior should not be totally dependent on the personal or spontaneous whim of the teacher.

Redl and Wineman (1957) developed a set of intervention criteria to guide teachers in making the decision to manage behavior:

1. Reality dangers: Adults are usually more reality-oriented than children and have had more practice predicting the consequences of certain acts. If children are playing with matches so that it looks as if they might injure themselves, then the teacher moves in and stops the behavior.
2. Psychological protection: Just as the adult protects the child from being physically hurt, he also should protect the child from psychological injury. If a group of boys is ganging up on a child, or scapegoating him, or using derogatory racial nicknames, then the teacher should intervene. The teacher does not support or condone this behavior and the values it reflects.
3. Protection against too much excitement: Sometimes a teacher intervenes in order to avoid the development of too much excitement, anxiety, and guilt in children. For example, if a game is getting out of hand and continues another ten minutes, the children may lose control, mess up, and feel very unhappy about their behavior later. Once again, the teacher should intervene to stop this cycle from developing.
4. Protection of property: This is almost too obvious to list but sometimes it is easy to overlook. Children are not allowed to destroy or damage the school property, equipment, or building. When the teacher sees this, he moves quickly and stops it. But at no time does he give the impression so common in our society that property is more important than people. Protecting property protects people.
5. Protection of an on-going program: Once a class is motivated in a particular task and the children have an investment in its outcome, it is not fair to have it ruined by one child who is having some difficulty. In this case, the teacher intervenes and asks this

child to leave or to move next to him in order to insure that the enjoyment, satisfaction, and learning of the group is unimpaired.

6. Protection against negative contagion: When a teacher is aware that tension is mounting in the classroom and a child with high social power begins tapping his desk with his pencil, the teacher might ask him to stop in order to prevent this behavior from spreading to the other students and disrupting the entire lesson.

7. Highlighting a value area of school policy: There are times when a teacher interferes in some behavior not because it is dangerous or disturbing but because he wishes to illustrate a school policy or rule. For example, he might want to illustrate why it is impossible for everyone to be first in line, or to point out how a misunderstanding develops when there is no intent to lie or to distort a situation. The focus is on poor communication.

8. Avoiding conflict with the outside world: The outside world in school can mean neighboring classrooms or the public. It is certainly justifiable to expect more control on the part of your children when they are attending an assembly or are on a trip than when they are in their classroom.

9. Protecting a teacher's inner comfort: Inner comfort is not the first thing to be considered by a teacher. If it is, he is in the wrong profession. For example, if a certain type of behavior makes a teacher feel exceptionally uncomfortable, the behavior may not need to be totally inhibited, but the teacher may have to learn to be more comfortable with it, like it or not. *(Long and Newman, 1961, pp. 51–52)**

These principles of behavior management have been presented as prerequisites to the effective management of disturbed students. The understanding and application of these general principles should help the teacher focus on critical behaviors and emotions of emotionally disturbed children, thereby reducing the time and energy normally devoted to managing incidental, transient behaviors.

We describe a number of specific management techniques in the following sections. These techniques are considered in two basic categories: (1) surface management, and (2) interpersonal management. The surface management techniques, or techniques designed to control or alter overt behavior, are eclectic in nature, borrowing from other theoretical constructs. The psychoeducational model is dependent on other theories because some behaviors must be dealt with immediately, without regard to cause. Even in the use of surface management techniques, however, the psychoeducational philosophy emphasizes those that will produce behavioral change without increasing the level of personal crisis for the disturbed student. Interpersonal management techniques, on the other hand, are more exclusively psychoeducational, with an emphasis on dealing with strong personal feelings, emotions, and need in a way that reduces negative psychological intensity and facilitates development of more appropriate social and psychological skills.

* Used by permission of the School of Education, Indiana University.

Surface Management

"Surface management may be defined as dealing with overt behavior that needs to be regulated immediately without regard to underlying causes or motives" (Fagen and Hill, 1977, p. 209). Surface techniques, thus, are only temporary or stopgap methods designed to eliminate infrequent deviant behavior and restore learning. When teachers are responsible for large groups of students, it is not always possible to look for underlying causes — immediate action is required. Fights, destruction of property, loss of behavioral control, and violent disruption of the learning environment are behaviors that require immediate teacher management. If such behaviors continue to occur, however, more permanent and well-designed solutions are required.

One reason that surface management is often ineffective is that teachers tend to depend on only a few management techniques, even if the techniques are not successful. Sending students to the principal, raising one's voice, telling students to sit down or be quiet, and giving them the "evil eye" are techniques used routinely in most classrooms. With some students such obvious procedures are effective, but for most they have become so commonplace that they don't work. When teachers rely on such stereotypic methods, they convey to the students doubt about their management competence. Students may know that a particular teacher will not manage behavior until she is standing, until her voice reaches a certain decibel level, or until a verbal challenge is made to her authority. Students usually know when, where, how, and with whom teachers will intervene, and they, too, develop stereotypic responses to neutralize anticipated patterns of teacher behavior.

The surface techniques we describe in this section are a synthesis of those reported in the literature (Redl and Wineman, 1957; Gnagey, 1965; and Long, Morse, and Newman, 1976). Teachers will recognize many of the techniques from their own personal repertoire of skills. Other teachers may have used the techniques without any conscious awareness of their effects on students. At any rate, the list of surface management techniques is presented to help teachers enlarge the variety of techniques available to them and to increase their awareness of the techniques' purposes and potential effects.

Ignoring Behavior. Many deviant behaviors are spontaneous and occur infrequently, usually motivated by some extraordinary classroom event. The cancellation of a field trip, a fire drill, and the introduction of a new pet animal to the classroom are examples of incidents that produce an excitement that is contagious. Students typically calm down after a brief period, however. The best interference technique under such circumstances is not to interfere but to ignore the behavior.

On other occasions, however, student behavior may be more purposeful, designed to test the teacher or solicit attention, even if negative in nature. If the purpose of the disruptive behavior is teacher attention, which makes the teacher the rewarding agent, planned ignoring may be the only response necessary to change the behavior. Teachers must be careful in the use of planned ignoring, however. Before employing this technique, the teacher must be certain it is appropriate. If peer group attention is reinforcing the behavior, for example, the teacher's ignoring may produce no change in behavior. This technique does have several advantages, however. It is unobtrusive, limiting, and permits the teacher to continue with the instructional activity in progress.

Signal Interference. This is the most frequent form of interference currently used by teachers. A variety of body postures, hand movements, and facial expressions are routinely used to convey approval and disapproval of student behavior. Smiles, winks, and a pat on the back are used to convey approval, whereas frowns, throat clearing, and finger snapping are used to deter behavior. Although signals can be effective during the initial stage of deviance, their usefulness is limited after deviance has moved into advanced stages of volatile behavior and outbursts of emotion.

The frequent use of signals among teachers is partially responsible for their limited effectiveness. Unfortunately, signals are used indiscriminately in situations where other forms of management would be more appropriate. Because signal interference is quick and effortless, however, it remains a routine management technique.

If signal management is to retain its usefulness, more creative uses need to be developed. Special individualized signals can be designed to communicate with selected students. The signals can be as obtuse and subtle as tugging the ear, touching the nose, or pulling out a handkerchief. These personal signals are successful only if the student knows they are unique messages between teacher and student. Such a technique also has the advantage of remaining a "secret" and does not identify the student in the presence of peers, thereby eliminating a potential confrontation.

Entire classrooms can also participate in the development of signals whereby students become managers of deviant behavior. For example, the class may decide to use the "peace sign" if the noise in the classroom becomes so loud that it is distracting. Any student or the teacher could raise the "peace sign"; when observed, every individual in the class would imitate the initiator's behavior until the class was quiet. We have actually witnessed this technique in a class of emotionally disturbed students and the results were dramatic — contagion in a positive direction.

Closeness Control. Many students, particularly younger elementary-aged students, need the physical presence of an adult to help them control impulsive, anxious, and even "forgetful" feelings and emotions. Without this physical assurance, negative feelings and emotions stimulate behaviors that may be unacceptable in the classroom. If a teacher notices significant behavioral expressions and moves toward the student, the behavior is typically reduced. However, such movement must be interpreted by the student as concern and reassurance and not as inevitable punishment.

Older students also respond favorably to teacher movement in the classroom. Again, the movement must be considered a form of positive concern, academically or emotionally, and not a spying technique to catch students doing something which violates classroom rules. Often teacher movement does little more than remind students that they are off task, which is sufficient to reduce deviance in many situations.

Teachers who stay in a small area of the classroom — behind a desk, in front of the chalkboard, or near a relatively few students — tend to have the highest rates of deviance among those students who are the greatest distance from the teacher. Consequently, management usually takes the form of verbal directions or reprimands shouted across the classroom. Such techniques often do more to disrupt the classroom learning environment than to stem the deviant behavior of students. Classroom movement, or closeness control, can also be used to reduce the frequency of disruptive behavior.

Hurdle Help. This technique combines well with closeness control since it requires individual tutoring to help a student overcome an academic roadblock. Individual "hurdle help" can be an effective management technique when students need only minimal information to begin functioning appropriately. A student may not have understood the teacher's directions, for example, and as a result may not be involved in the lesson. "Instead of asking for help and exposing himself to the teacher's wrath for not paying attention . . . , the child is likely to establish contact with neighbors, find some interesting trinket in his pocket, or draw on his desk" (Long and Newman, 1961, p. 56). Providing the student with directions could get the student back on task, eliminating a source of deviant behavior. The concept of hurdle help as a management technique is thus designed to help the student "hurdle" frustrating obstacles within an academic setting.

Teacher Interest. Student performance on various academic tasks often wanes because of a lack of motivation or interest in the particular activity. Typically, this lack of motivation is accompanied by nonperformance followed by boredom and restlessness. It is at this latter stage that students begin to engage in behaviors that disrupt the classroom.

Before the boredom and restlessness develop into behaviors that are difficult to manage, the teacher should demonstrate interest in the student's assignment. Verbal cues such as *That's an important assignment you are doing* or *You have a difficult assignment, but I'm sure you can do it* can be helpful. Teacher interest is a particularly effective technique for students who have a tendency to seek approval from adults.

Removing Temptations. Classrooms are usually filled with objects designed to enhance learning: globes, bulletin boards, games, and the like. Most students can handle the variety of stimuli that bombard them in the classroom, even though most of the stimuli may be totally unrelated to the current lesson. The globe may be more seductive than the math problems; the baseball on the teacher's desk may be more enticing than the reading assignment; the student's new lunch box may be more visually alluring than the spelling words. In each case, an environmental stimulus unrelated to the lesson is a visual temptation unrelated to the task at hand.

Teacher management in the form of stimuli reduction is needed by students inclined to be distracted by irrelevant visual or verbal stimuli because of their inability to consistently differentiate the relevant from the irrelevant. An effective procedure is to simply remove the irrelevant or distracting stimuli — place the globe, the ball, and the lunch box out of sight. Of course, it may not be possible, or even desirable, to remove all irrelevant stimulation. Observation and analysis of the situation may reveal that some students are more inclined to be distracted by specific objects, in which case removing the temptation would help the student focus his or her attention and reduce task avoidance behavior.

Altering Instructional Methods. Often students are satiated with a repetitive task or a routine instructional method. Examples of repetitive methods include answering every "question box" in a text, completing a specified number of math problems each day, and receiving information only through lecturing or reading. These stereotypic approaches tend to develop an attitude of indifference toward learning that is associated with negative feelings toward the teacher, disruptive behavior, and academic failure.

Teacher management in this context should involve altering the instructional methods, requirements, or both. Using a variety of input and output procedures may prevent satiation, increase interest, and consequently reduce deviant behavior. Methodological changes related to the previous examples of instructional repetitiveness could include using a blend of verbal and written responses, devising a math program that emphasizes real activities rather than abstractions, and organizing exploratory and discussion sessions as a substitute for lecturing. After all, "the task is not so much to teach children as to provide the conditions under which learning can take place" (Long, Morse, and Newman, 1976, p. 313).

Routine Structure. Although some students are bored with the routine of a classroom, other students thrive with a predictable structure. Students who have failed to develop basic trust in themselves, in others, or in their environment are psychologically threatened by confusion, spontaneity, and unstructured situations. When the classroom setting is unpredictable, these students express their fear and anxiety through withdrawal, hyperactivity, crying, and other behaviors that interfere with their learning.

Unstructured situations are created by numerous classroom conditions: when teachers change their minds or make exceptions to selected rules or behaviors; when free time activities or active games are introduced; or when the class schedule is interrupted by announcements, special events, or even a substitute teacher. A structured environment is best, at least at first when students need the security of predictability. A schedule of sequential activities, accompanied by teacher consistency and punctuality and permanent resources such as a desk and books may reduce student apprehension, thereby diminishing the potential for deviant behavior.

Rule Reminders.   When emotions are high or events in the classroom generate excitement, students are prone to forget classroom rules. A teacher should be aware that escalating confusion may eventually erupt into behavior requiring more direct management. We suggest that the teacher remind individual students or the entire group of rules before they are broken. Statements such as *Remember, you must remain in your seat* or *The rule is "keep your hands to yourself"* should be made as reminders before violations occur. Signal interference or closeness control may serve the same function as verbal reminders.

A rule reminder is a minimal management technique designed to prevent deviance and thereby avoid the need for more dramatic interference. Just as speed limit signs are posted along the highway to remind drivers of the legal speed, rule reminders are announced by the teacher to remind students of behavioral limitations. In fact, teachers should routinely remind students of important classroom rules, even when the students are on task and rule violations are not anticipated. These reminders reinforce acceptable classroom behavior, provide predictable structure, and convey the message that classroom rules are important.

Positive Removal.   There are times when students lose control and become a threat to themselves or others. A frequent disciplinary procedure to control threatening behaviors has been to exclude students from the classroom by sending them to the hall or the principal's office. In less severe cases, some teachers use procedures for isolating students in the classroom in special time-out areas. In both cases, isolation has some merit if it is used as the last available measure to protect other persons and property.

Our concern is with making the removal of a student as positive as possible by avoiding its purely punitive use. The teacher's interpretation of the isolation process can be a positive management technique. The teacher could verbally interpret the action as a helping action: "I'm sending you to the hall, because you are going to hurt someone, maybe yourself. I can't permit that. I don't want anyone hurt. When you can help people, you can come back." Or "People are trying to learn in here and you won't let them, so I'm sending you outside. When you think you can help people learn, I'd like to have you back in the classroom."

In both instances, the teacher is excluding the student, but the verbal messages convey a desire to help rather than punish. Consequently, the student's return to the classroom is based on behaviors or expectations that promote a more positive relationship.

Before concluding our discussion of surface management, we must make two important comments. First, surface management techniques should be as individualized as the academic program. Some students may respond as hoped to a specific management technique, but others may become more deviant. A knowledge of the individual student and knowledge of a variety of interference techniques will increase the probability of successful management.

Second, surface management techniques are only temporary solutions to behavioral problems. If deviant behaviors occur frequently, other management techniques must be considered. In addition, some deviant behaviors require techniques designed to interfere with the precipitating causes of behavior rather than externally manage surface behavior.

Although surface management techniques are appropriate for the management of surface behaviors, they are only temporary solutions to the management of emotionally disturbed students. As a result, teachers implementing the psychoeducational model must know management techniques that go beyond the surface compliance of students.

Interpersonal Management

You will remember that "intrapersonal" means "within a person." "Interpersonal," on the other hand, means "between persons." Interpersonal management refers to the psychological and affective techniques that involve personal interaction between teacher and student. Psychological or affective techniques focus on the phases of classroom experience most directly concerned with feelings, emotions, and social acceptance (Krathwohl, Bloom, and Basia, 1956). It is well known that students' psychological and affective states, including anxiety, frustration, rejection, and helplessness, precipitate deviant or disruptive behaviors. Thus, paying close attention to a student's affective state and responding appropriately can not only improve mental health but also reduce the frequency and intensity of inappropriate classroom behavior.

Even though teachers have long known that students' academic, behavioral, and psychological-affective performances cannot be separated, educators tend to promote academics, to control behavior, and to ignore feelings and emotions. This discrepancy in concern about different types of performance exists in part because of traditional curricular designs, the emphasis of subject matter disciplines, and teachers' being responsible for large instructional groups (Weinstein and Fantini, 1970). Interpersonal management requires some alterations in the traditional patterns and beliefs and emphasizes the need for personal interaction between teacher and student.

The personal characteristics of the teacher, rather than the size of the group, the grade level instructed, or knowledge of the academic discipline, is significant in using interpersonal management techniques successfully. We contend that the teachers who are most concerned with teaching material content and maintaining strict order are less likely to exercise effective interpersonal management. For students who require structure, such teaching procedures may be appropriate, but there are students who need understanding, warmth, and even psychological support from teachers more directly and more often.

Hamachek (1969) has identified five characteristics of teachers that facilitate this interpersonal dimension:

1. They generally have more positive views of others — students, colleagues, and administrators.
2. They are not as prone to view others as critical and not inclined to attack people with ulterior motives; rather, they are seen as potentially friendly and worthy in their own right.
3. They have a more favorable view of democratic classroom procedures.
4. They seem to have the ability and capacity to see things as they seem to others — i.e., the ability to see things from the other person's point of view.
5. They do not perceive students as persons "you do things to," but rather as individuals capable of doing for themselves once they feel trusted, respected, and valued. *(p. 343)*

Given that many teachers possess these five characteristics, there are many interpersonal techniques that may be used to manage behavior. However, the use of interpersonal techniques also depends on the rapport the teacher has established with individual students. In this context, "rapport" refers to a positive teacher-student relationship, based upon the student's perceptions of the teacher as a caring, fair, courteous, friendly, and trustworthy person (Howard, 1972). Initial attempts to use interpersonal techniques may be relatively unsuccessful in reducing deviant behavior if positive rapport does not exist between the teacher and students. The greatest deterrent to interpersonal management occurs when students accurately perceive their teacher as an insensitive task-master or censor of behavior who is only going through the motions of caring.

Everyone, normal or emotionally disturbed, experiences unpleasant and exaggerated feelings that make it difficult to function appropriately in the classroom. Typically, large groups of students assembled in schools and classrooms are vulnerable to crises that precipitate frequent negative interaction. Behavioral incidents, or crises, that can generate strong feelings and emotions include student-student crises (threats, teasing, or separation); student-teacher crises (forgetting homework, "talking back," or violating a rule); and internal crises (disappointment, failure, or feelings of inadequacy). Each of these crises may foster so much anxiety or anger that the student cannot function in the classroom. In turn, these feelings and emotions may precipitate deviant behavior that must be managed to preserve the learning environment and protect the students involved. To interfere effectively with the deviant behavior among students, these volatile emotions should be responded to positively whenever possible. Hamachek (1969) has described the following interpersonal techniques that may be appropriate for individual students.

Listening to Feelings.   This management technique requires two basic ingredients — interest and time. On the simplest level, listening to feelings is being physically available to a student at a time when the student needs to ventilate emotions that are about to explode. Sitting close, leaning forward, providing eye-to-eye contact, and showing understanding by nodding or smiling are examples of the body language necessary to convey a personal interest in the student.

This passive listening technique does not condone or condemn the circumstances that precipitated the feelings, but it does indicate teacher interest in the student's problem. This sympathetic communication can be used to "drain off" the strong feelings, which would otherwise result in more deviant behavior (Redl, 1966b). In times of crisis, many people are comforted by the fact that a sympathetic ear is available and that feelings do not have to be dealt with alone, and disturbed students are no different.

Responding to Feelings.   This technique involves more than just passively listening to statements about feelings; it also requires an appropriate response. To facilitate communication, the teacher must become an active listener, accurately interpret the meaning of the message sent by the student, and respond in a way that reflects the student's feelings.

> In active listening, then, the receiver (teacher) tries to understand what it is the sender (student) is feeling or what the message means. Then, with a personal translation, the teacher feeds it back for the sender's verification. The receiver (teacher) *does not* send a message of his own — such as an evaluation, opinion, advice, logic, analysis, or question. He sends back *only what he feels the sender's message meant* — nothing more, nothing less. *(Gordon, 1970, p. 53)*

The technique of responding to feelings requires that the teacher "discern the overt as well as the covert or disguised behavior of another person" (Gazda et al., 1973, p. 39). This is particularly important since the verbal message may not convey what the student is feeling. A student who has failed an exam may, for example, feel inadequate unless the failure is projected on the teacher by saying, "You said this part of the book wouldn't be required on the exam." Similarly, a student who feels threatened by a peer may want protection but say, "I don't feel well today;

I don't want to go out to recess." A student who is not selected to be on a team may elect to reduce the pain by saying, "I really didn't care about being on the team anyway." Depending on the context, these verbal messages may carry an entirely different meaning than the words have expressed.

Teacher responses to feelings should reflect the feelings, not the overt message. For the three examples, teacher responses should be something like: "You're saying that it hurts when you don't do well on an exam"; "We all need someone to help us when we are afraid"; and "It really hurts when we are left out." These examples are based on the teacher's knowledge of the student, an empathic understanding of the problem, and a desire to help. Although the three responses provide little new information, they are certainly more facilitative than "I specifically said that the entire chapter would be on the exam"; "You weren't ill ten minutes ago"; and "Then why did you try out for the team?"

Effective responding techniques can reduce the probability of deviant behavior by demonstrating teacher understanding of the student's personal crisis. Strong feelings and emotions that are increased by responses that condemn, question, or emphasize the negative, often explode into crises that require extraordinary amounts of time and energy.

Maintaining Communication.   During crises, students often retreat into a solitary world and don't communicate with either peers or the teacher. Attempts to identify the problem or find a solution are unsuccessful because the student is nonverbal and nonresponsive. However, "our attempts to involve the youngster in some form of communication may prevent the next level of retreat from us" (Redl, 1966b, p. 49).

A student accused of theft, cheating, or related behaviors may choose this regressive course of action as the least painful available, particularly if a student lacks the skills necessary for adequate self-protection. The teacher's efforts to grill the student, point out the unacceptable behavior, or even encourage more appropriate behavior typically fall on deaf ears, causing the student to increase the personal-emotional distance from the teacher.

To maintain communication, the teacher should involve the student in conversation completely unrelated to the situation that motivated the crisis; that is, find a psychologically comfortable area in which the student can relax the defenses and engage in appropriate behavior. If the crisis involved peers, then the teacher may want to provide the student with a solitary learning task; if the teacher was the source of the crisis, then peer-group activities may be more appropriate; if stealing or cheating was the accusation, then communication involving baseball, dancing, or hobbies may be areas of renewed communication. Even though the teacher may not be able to deal directly with the issue, it is necessary to maintain contact with the student by involving the student in an area or activity that is psychologically safe. At a later time, when communication has been re-established, the teacher may elect to deal with the original crisis.

Emphasizing Natural Consequences.   Many traditional teacher-student disciplinary interactions are based on threats of punishment for noncompliant student behavior. Failing grades, suspension, moral devaluation, and even corporal punishment are common consequences administered by teachers for failure to respond appropriately to classroom rules or teacher expectations. Although these examples are not natural consequences, they are forms of punishment that may only occur in school-related environments.

Natural consequences, in the context of interpersonal management, are those negative experiences which logically and functionally occur as a result of behavior. If a student does not study, the natural consequence is, not a failing grade, but that the student will not learn the information necessary for a vocation. Similarly, fighting physically hurts; the inability to get along with peers causes loneliness; and resentment of authority leads to limited job opportunities.

Many students do not understand the relationship between their behaviors and the natural consequences. Greater emphasis on life situations and adjustment is more meaningful, particularly for older students who may perceive school as an irrelevant obstacle in the path to adulthood. The motivation to perform more effectively will be increased for students who understand that adult success is partially based on correct behavior and is not necessarily related to teacher expectations.

Increasing Verbal Skills.   Educational institutions tend to be highly verbal settings in which teachers talk a great deal and students are expected to communicate appropriately with both teachers and peers. Many students, however, are more physically oriented and lack the verbal skills necessary to communicate their needs and wishes. This physical orientation is especially common among younger students and students who have experienced restrictive language patterns in their home and community. If a second-grade boy likes a girl, rather than saying "I like you," he may knock her books to the ground, inviting a chase. A friendly tap on the shoulder, a shy glance to the floor, and touching in general are physical expressions of affection. Similarly, unverbalized anger may erupt into fighting, cursing, or hyperactivity. Often these indirect but deviant behaviors are the result of insufficient verbal skills necessary to convey feelings, resolve differences, or obtain needs.

The management of behaviors precipitated by inadequate verbal skills requires attention to language skill development. To successfully implement this management technique, teachers need to provide students with more opportunities to communicate, explore feelings, and identify ways of expressing needs. Such a program of verbal skill development requires that teachers talk less and students more. If teachers tell students what they did wrong, why they did it, and what's going to be done about it, students have limited opportunities to talk about or understand their own feelings and behaviors. Currently, there is an inverse relationship between student talk and chronological age in school settings: as students grow older they talk less and teachers talk more (Karlin and Berger, 1972; Rich, 1978). In terms of teacher-student interaction, this regressive development needs to be reversed. Teachers must become effective listeners.

Although the interpersonal management techniques reported in this section do not constitute an exhaustive list, the techniques are believed to be important in facilitating adjustment in the classroom. Prerequisites to interpersonal management, such as trust, acceptance, and understanding, were not discussed at length since they reflect personal teacher characteristics rather than management techniques *per se*. However, the presence of positive personal characteristics is related to both the desire and effectiveness of interpersonal management techniques.

It is important to remember that interpersonal management is basically a personal learning experience for the student rather than a disciplinary action. The process of teacher-student interaction should emphasize an understanding of feelings and emotions and how they are translated into appropriate behavior. Managing behavior, therefore, involves developing skills necessary to express feelings and emotions in a more acceptable manner.

THE EVALUATION OF PSYCHOEDUCATIONAL MANAGEMENT TECHNIQUES

To evaluate the effectiveness of psychoeducational management techniques, teachers and disturbed students must have a broader concept of "successful" management than is characteristic of the traditional educational approach. Certainly, one indication of effectiveness is the occurrence of appropriate changes in behavior among emotionally disturbed students. Applying the methodology often associated with the behavioral model, teachers can identify and count the frequency of behaviors such as fighting or cursing before and after intervention to determine whether a particular technique has been successful. This procedure is relatively direct and produces quantitative data about the frequency of specific behaviors that the teacher desires to alter.

Although changes in the specific behaviors of students are one measure of effectiveness, the social-psychological and intrapersonal orientation of the psychoeducational model requires more extensive evaluation procedures. This reluctance to rely on specific behavioral changes among students is based on a number of psychoeducational principles related to evaluation:

1. The intrapersonal affect of disturbed students frequently cannot be inferred from overt classroom behavior. Similar behaviors may be caused by quite different emotions or needs, whereas different behaviors may be motivated by a similar affect. One disturbed student who is anxious

about a cognitive test may become physically active, but another student may withdraw into a fantasy world. Changing the motor activity or withdrawal level does not deal with the precipitating cause, test anxiety. Therefore, evaluation must go beyond the surface level of behavior and evaluate the cause of behavior.

2. Behaviors and affect may be a function of classroom environmental conditions and, therefore, may not originate within the student. Classroom environmental conditions can cause interfering behaviors when they do not meet the legitimate needs of students, as when teachers have expectancies that exceed developmental competencies, when peer-group pressure requires that personal values be compromised, or when physical space requirements do not permit individual variation. Evaluation must go beyond the individual student and assess the effects of significant classroom conditions.

3. The effectiveness of behavior management cannot be totally evaluated using a quantitative approach. Since the "whole student" cannot be measured, behaviors are considered only *one* aspect of the "whole student." For those aspects of the student that do not lend themselves to measurement, professional inference and human sensitivity are important ingredients in the evaluation process. Evaluation must go beyond the science of measurement and include the art of human relationships.

Early in this chapter, it was stated that the primary objectives of the psychoeducational behavior management model were (1) to help students understand their emotions, resolve internal crises, and reduce psychological pain; and (2) to facilitate the development of self-directed personal and social skills in expressing feelings, emotions, and needs. The achievement of these objectives requires the evaluation of the behaviors and affect of emotionally disturbed students, the influence of environmental conditions, and the perceptions of the people who interact with the students. To attain these ends, several evaluation tools and procedures are described in the sections that follow.

Since this chapter is devoted to managing behavior among emotionally disturbed students, we feel it is most appropriate to begin by focusing on the individual student. Aside from the projective techniques used by psychologists, the two basic evaluation techniques are students' self-reports and teachers' observations of behavior. Of the two techniques, self-reports are more directly oriented toward evaluating intrapersonal change, whereas observation deals more exclusively with overt behaviors.

Self-Reports

Anything students communicate about themselves can be considered a self-report. In the psychoeducational model, self-reports are critical to the evaluation of a program's effectiveness. The importance of self-reports is based on the belief that "an individual's perception of himself may well be a central factor influencing his behavior. . . . The self is involved in social reactions; it operates in the service of need satisfaction, particularly in the enhancement of the self or in relation to self-esteem; it is a vital force in effective adjustment" (Bledsoe and Garrison, 1962, pp. 1–2). Thus, success of the psychoeducational model is at least partially based on positive intrapersonal changes as perceived by the individual.

The evaluation tools most often associated with self-report information include a variety of structured paper-and-pencil instruments. These range from requests for an autobiographical theme to yes-or-no answers to specific questions. Instruments that assess such qualities as self-concept, self-esteem, locus of control, and "how I see myself" are plentiful in the current literature on assessment, psychology, and affective education.

In addition to the self-report instruments, there are at least two verbal procedures that may be used to obtain intrapersonal information. In general, these may be classified as interviews and role-playing. The interview may be between an individual teacher and a student, as with Redl's (1966) life space interview, or it may involve a large group, as with Glasser's (1969) classroom meeting model. The teacher or students may ask directly or indirectly about attitudes or beliefs to obtain greater insight into the student's perception of self. Role-playing has the advantage of placing the student in "someone else's shoes" so that there is less reluctance and greater personal safety in revealing intrapersonal feelings, emotions, and needs (Chesler and Fox, 1966).

For either the instruments or verbal procedures to yield valid information, the relationship between the teacher and the students must be perceived as a positive, helping relationship by the students. Very little useful information about self will be obtained if students perceive their teacher with suspicion and mistrust. It is also important to note that the validity of self-report information is often difficult to evaluate, requiring that the teacher be sensitive to the distinction between real change and what the student wishes the teacher to see.

Observation

The observation of behavior is undoubtedly the most common source of information for the evaluation of behavior management techniques. However, psychoeducators are reluctant to depend exclusively on this or any other single evaluation method, because of the bias, weakness, and fallibility that are inherent in any single methodological approach. According to Gordon (1966), "no observer (including the teacher) can ever fully overcome his own perceptual orientation. The word 'objective' then, is used as a desired goal, rather than as an undeniable reality. It is possible to record what one sees objectively, but it is a mistake to assume that it is seen objectively" (p. 65).

Observational systems may be divided into two categories, (1) "closed" systems that use frequency counts of selected behaviors, traits, or events; and (2) "open" systems that use narrative descriptions of all available information. Although the closed system is relatively easy to record and interpret, a primary limitation is that it takes behaviors out of context, treating behavior as an isolated factor unrelated to other classroom conditions.

The "open" system, on the other hand, is a more difficult procedure since it requires more time to record and interpret. Cartwright and Cartwright (1974) suggest the use of "anecdotal records," brief narrative accounts of classroom events. "An anecdotal record might be thought of as a 'word picture' . . . [or] factual description of the incidents that have been observed" (p. 131). Redl (1966b) suggests the use of behavioral logs, or anecdotes, that focus on behaviors that reflect attitudes, interests, aversions, strengths, and "thoughts, fantasies, [and] fears." An important strength of anecdotes is that they place behavior in the context of the surrounding environmental conditions.

Wright (1967) has provided a list of "Rules of Reporting" recorded behavior when using the "open" system:

1. Focus upon the behavior and the situation of the subject.
2. Observe and report as fully as possible the situation of the subject.
3. Never make interpretations carry the burden of description.
4. Give the "how" of everything the subject does.
5. Give the "how" of everything done by any person who interacts with the subject.
6. Report in order . . . all the main steps through the course of every action by the subject.
7. Whenever possible, state descriptions of behaviors positively.
8. Describe in detail the scene as it is when each behavior setting is entered.
9. Put no more than one unit of molar behavior in one sentence.
10. Put in one sentence no more than one thing done by a person in the situation of the child. *(pp. 48–53)*

To record that "George hits other students" or that "Harry aggravates others" is not a sufficient record of behavior. The following example is more descriptive:

8:15 George was working math problems at his desk. Harry tore up his own math problems and walked over to George's desk. Harry grabbed George's math paper and threw it across the room. George stood up and hit Harry on the shoulder. Harry ran to me and yelled "George hit me" three or four times.

This more descriptive observational record provides more complete information with which the teacher can evaluate change, given the situation in which the behaviors occurred.

Aside from behavioral and situational descriptors, the open observational system requires that the psychoeducational teacher make inferences about the meaning of behavior. Was George showing a degree of control given his history of aggression? Did Harry provoke the situation because of frustration? Was George's physical reaction the result of anger, the lack of verbal skills, or peer-group expectation? Did Harry create the situation to justify teacher closeness or protection? These are the sort of interpretative questions that the psychoeducational teacher must be able to answer to plan the next level of management.

In addition to other students, other important classroom environmental factors must be evaluated. The rationale for including environmental factors is that individual intrapersonal and behavioral characteristics are not solely a function of the individual, but may result from the teacher, the peer group, or the physical space.

The Teacher

No single teacher or teacher style is appropriate for all disturbed students. Although it is not practical to frequently change teachers or students, teachers should be able to evaluate their effect on different students and, when necessary and possible, alter their style to meet the needs of students.

The evaluation of one's own teaching behavior is rarely a pleasant responsibility, primarily because it is a personally sensitive and potentially threatening process that is apt to produce results contrary to those expected or desired. But if teachers are to realize more fully their potential as teachers and behavior managers, some sort of evaluation process should be implemented.

A first step in this process is increasing self-awareness. "Self-awareness includes attending to those factors that screen your responses: past experiences, feelings, values, beliefs, attitudes, perceptions of your teaching self, goals, aspirations, and outside influences, as they relate to your teaching" (Curwin and Fuhrmann, 1975, p. 8). There are a number of paper-and-pencil instruments designed to measure teaching self-awareness (Wehling and Charters, 1969), but it is generally sufficient for teachers to internally monitor their own feelings, values, and other characteristics. Evaluating one's motivation for teaching (money, love, convenience); one's attitude toward different students (hostile adolescents, cute kids); one's acceptance of behavior (cursing, withdrawal, hyperactivity); and one's feelings and reactions to perceived failure (frustration, anger, apathy) are important personal characteristics for the teacher to acknowledge. No tool or procedure is as effective as teachers' willingness to assess themselves — "to penetrate one's own defenses and stand off and look at oneself" (Gordon, 1966, p. 89).

A second step in evaluating teacher influences is to develop in-class measurement procedures. Observation of teacher behavior is a preferable approach, but routine classroom responsibilities typically make this procedure difficult to employ. Modifications in the use of standard procedures can make data available to teachers. Rather than direct observation, for example, using a tape recorder or student observer can be effective. Using any of the verbal behavior systems reported by Simon and Boyer (1967, 1970a, 1970b), a teacher can determine whether or not planned management occurred. Was praise used after each correct answer? Did controlling teacher behaviors follow disruption? Were students involved in the management process? Was the teacher silent when a student wanted to talk? Students can also provide a wealth of evaluation data. Not only can students maintain charts on the frequency of selected teacher behaviors, such as physical closeness and the use of praise, but they can also provide answers to teacher questions: "How can I help you?" or "What do I do that makes you angry?"

A third step in the evaluation of teacher influence is to determine the extent to which students change as a result of intervention. After all, "assessment of teaching can only be valid if salient characteristics are correlated to each other and to some meaningful measure of competency" (Garfunkel and Blatt, 1977, p. 268). In short, does teacher management reduce negative intrapersonal emotions, crises, and needs, while increasing more appropriate expression of behaviors? Measurement and evaluation can range from extensive counting and charting to mental notations of spontaneous events. Regardless of the type of evaluation procedure, critical management and change relationships should be measured. Do students calm down emotionally if the teacher actively listens? When students make value commitments, do they maintain them? If the physical space is altered, do students function more harmoniously? Are students able to express frustration in more acceptable ways after the student has acquired the necessary verbal skills?

These exemplary questions test the fundamental assumptions of the psychoeducational model. Research that provides strong affirmative answers increases the viability of the model as an option for emotionally disturbed students.

The Peer Group

The assessment of peer group influence can take the form of individual member analysis or group evaluation, although the latter is generally preferable. On an individual level, behaviors are usually shaped by the more powerful group norms, unless an individual holds an extraordinarily high status position. The use of sociograms or the observation of dominant-subordinate group-member behaviors can yield the information necessary to make preliminary decisions regarding status roles. If the management focus is on key persons, then repeated measures with sociograms or through observation should reflect reduced polarization of high and low status roles.

Assessment of the total group may also be accomplished with paper-and-pencil instruments and observation. A number of instruments (Barclay, 1974; Moos and Trickett, 1974) are available for rating the classroom climate, including the degree of involvement, affiliation, and goal orientation within the peer group.

The teacher's sensitive observation of group functioning is also useful. To this end, Johnson and Bany (1970) have provided behavioral descriptors that are symptomatic of negative peer group functions.

> A hostile, aggressive classroom group is one that subtly defies the teacher and often disrupts instructional activities [by]
>
> 1. Murmuring, talking, lack of attention throughout the group when tasks are presented or assigned;
> 2. Constant disruptions which interfere with carrying out assignments;
> 3. Subtle defiance, united resistance, and some evidence of solidarity within the group;
> 4. Overall nonconformity to generally accepted school practices;
> 5. Solidarity in resisting teachers' efforts, poor interpersonal relations.
>
> A class that is dissatisfied with conditions in the classroom and frustrated because of pressure stemming from inappropriate teacher control techniques [may have the following characteristics:]
>
> 1. The group applauds disruptive behavior of one or a few individuals;
> 2. Defiant acts of one or two individuals are approved by group as a whole;
> 3. The group sometimes reacts with imitative behavior;
> 4. The group employs scapegoating;
> 5. The group promotes fights between individuals;
> 6. Apathetic and indifferent attitudes are shown to school tasks;
> 7. Indifference about completing tasks is evident;
> 8. The group is apathetic (but exhibits little problem behavior in the classroom), aggressive, and always in trouble on the playground;
> 9. Members are well-behaved when the teacher is present — unruly and aggressive when the teacher is away or does not constantly supervise the group;
> 10. Some individuals are not tolerated by the group — little attempt is made to be a group member.
>
> An insecure, dependent class that has not developed a good functioning group [may have these characteristics:]
>
> 1. The students are easily distracted when any outsider enters the room;
> 2. They cannot adjust to changes in routine;
> 3. Members are easily upset by rumors;
> 4. Changes in the weather upset the class;
> 5. Newcomers to the class may be resented. *(pp. 410–412)* *

The extent to which psychoeducational group management techniques are effective can be determined by the degree of change from overly aggressive displays of interaction to cooperative, harmonious, and more independent group functions.

The Physical Space

The effects of physical space are especially difficult to measure. Research on this area has yielded questionable results. However, such physical factors as lighting, temperature, noise, and general decor are generally assumed to have properties that facilitate or hinder specific behaviors among children. A more important dimension of physical space may be "spatial behavior effects" (Smith, Neisworth, and Greer, 1978), which include personal space (the distance between children), crowding (group functioning within a specified space), territoriality (the ownership of space), and privacy (provisions to withdraw from interactions).

In keeping with the concept of a "therapeutic milieu" (Redl, 1976b), psychoeducational teachers need to continually monitor the physical space to determine if changes in spatial arrangements are associated with more or less deviant behaviors.

In the final analysis, the evaluation of psychoeducational techniques must be made by the persons involved in the day-to-day interaction with disturbed students. Evaluation decisions should be based on observational data, instrument results, verbal feedback, and personal reactions. No source of information that helps the teacher or students make more appropriate decisions should be overlooked. The essence of evaluation, however, goes beyond empirical data and depends on an active, positive relationship between teacher and student. Without such a relationship, behavior management is little more than physical manipulation devoid of the personal experiences necessary to facilitate intrapersonal change.

SUMMARY

This chapter has been devoted to the psychoeducational model for managing the behavior of disturbed students in the classroom. Throughout the chapter, we have stressed a variety of techniques required for teachers to be successful managers of behavior. As we have described it, success involves maintaining an effective learning environment, helping students understand intrapersonal feelings, and facilitating the development of self-directed social behavior. Whereas some disturbed students may respond appropriately to surface techniques, others may require a more personal approach. Similarly, some students may respond to individual techniques, whereas others may be fulfilling group expectations that require group management. Different instructional styles and environmental designs also have varying effects on different students.

The success of any managerial technique is determined by the teacher's knowledge of the student and his or her use of a technique appropriate to the academic, psychological, and physical characteristics of the student. Management should be as individualized as the academic program — just as no two students learn the exact same thing from the same instruction, no two students respond the same way to the same type of management. The evaluation of psychoeducational techniques follows a similar multifunctional approach, relying not only on empirical data, but on the sensitivity of those involved in the management process.

Part III

CURRICULUM

After the emotionally disturbed child's strengths and weaknesses in such areas as math, reading, spelling, and social studies are assessed, daily tasks and activities are arranged. The term "curriculum" covers the rationale for including such academic subjects as well as the selection of appropriate materials to be used to achieve individual goals.

In Chapter 6, Polsgrove and Nelson use the behavioral approach to establish guidelines for developing a curriculum design to serve the individual needs of disturbed children. They emphasize the ability to identify appropriate tasks and the measurement of daily gain.

In Chapter 7, Dembinski, Schultz, and Walton discuss the design of program curricula from a psychoeducational perspective. The acquisition of academic information is stressed, but not to the exclusion of social behavior. The role of feelings is deemed a major consideration in designing a curriculum.

Chapter 6

Curriculum Intervention According to the Behavioral Model

Lewis Polsgrove
Indiana University

C. Michael Nelson
University of Kentucky

The behavioral approach to intervention with children designated "emotionally disturbed" has offered many innovations in educational and mental health practices. In the past decade, behavioral research has produced a wide array of applied techniques that practitioners can use to manage these children in a variety of settings (see Bandura, 1969; Cartledge and Milburn, 1978; Hanley, 1970; Kazdin and Bootzin, 1972; McLaughlin, 1976; O'Leary and Drabman, 1971; Polsgrove, 1979; Strain, Cook, and Apolloni, 1976). In this chapter, we will discuss the major assumptions and concepts underlying the behavioral approach to academic and social curriculum intervention as well as review methods for improving emotionally disturbed children's functioning in the classroom.

Before launching our discussion, we should clarify some critical issues to provide an appropriate rationale for the material to follow.

First, along with a growing number of other writers (Clarizio and McCoy, 1976; Hallahan and Kauffman, 1977; Newcomer, 1977; Reynolds and Balow, 1972; Salvia and Ysseldyke, 1978), we find it difficult to identify reliable criteria or measures that can be used to accurately identify "emotionally disturbed" children and differentiate them from children in other diagnostic or treatment categories. In most cases, the label "emotionally disturbed" pertains as much to the child's milieu as it does to the individual child. Although children labeled "emotionally disturbed" typically display behavior that deviates from normally expected developmental patterns, so do those labeled "learning disabled" or "educably mentally

169

retarded"; at times, so do normal children. Children in the public schools are often placed in one category or another primarily for administrative convenience, with little consideration given to their educational needs. In short, we believe that labels may be misleading and have little relevance for planning or conducting intervention programs. Such programs must be based on the assets and deficits of the individual child. For purposes of our discussion, however, we will identify emotionally disturbed children as those who persistently display excesses or deficits in social behavior that are measurably discrepant from established cultural, social, legal, or chronological-age norms, from personal expectancies, or both, and who also function academically below their peer group.

Second, most children classified as emotionally disturbed are enrolled in public school classes and display mild to moderate behavioral deviations. Although it is popular practice to differentiate categories of mild to moderately "handicapped" children as though there were educational and psychological treatments specific to these categories, research simply has not identified treatment approaches for a specific "type" of child or disability (Newcomer, Larsen, and Hammill, 1975; Ysseldyke and Salvia, 1974; Lovitt, 1975). For this reason, the behavioral approach emphasizes the use of direct teaching methods; in actual classroom practice teachers using this approach employ the same materials and learning activities with children labeled "emotionally disturbed" as they do with normal children or those classified in other categories. The behavioral curriculum, as we will see, emphasizes the systematic use of instructional technology to increase children's learning and improve their social functioning, with little consideration given to how they are classified.

Third, there are several assumptions made by proponents of the behavioral model that distinguish this approach from others.

1. As most behavior is learned, children become classified as emotionally disturbed because they behave inadequately or inappropriately in various situations due to their previous learning experiences.
2. Intervention involves teaching the child appropriate ways of behaving under various circumstances.
3. Interventions focus on changing the child's present behavior rather than providing interpretive insight into the causes of problems.
4. Interventions are not directed toward correcting defects within the child but rather toward reducing the discrepancy between the child's behavior and cultural, social, legal, or environmental expectations.
5. Because environmental factors largely control behavior, classroom intervention involves altering teacher behavior, instructional practices, and reward systems to improve a child's functioning.
6. Children should receive direct training in specific skills that improve their academic performance rather than being taught information processing, psychomotor, or perceptual-motor skills.

7. Educational goals should be clearly stated in terms of measurable behavioral outcomes.
8. Academic tasks must be broken down into small, sequentially arranged steps. Instruction should be designed so that students can easily master each step.
9. Instruction should be planned and administered in such a way to minimize student error.
10. Student progress should be measured directly and continuously and these measures should be used for evaluating the effectiveness of the instructional program.
11. Measurement of student progress is necessary to develop replicable and reliable teaching procedures.

These assumptions affect many of the academic and social interventions conducted using the behavioral model.

The theoretical base of the behavioral model has been presented in Chapter 1. It underlies many educational and instructional training approaches and has been used to explain such complex human behavior as language acquisition, cognitive functioning, and self-control.

In this chapter, we will discuss procedures for conducting curriculum interventions based on the behavioral model and review studies in which the behavioral approach has proved successful. Most children classified "emotionally disturbed" display excesses or deficits in academic or social areas, or both. We will consider behavioral interventions that address both types of problems. Because the vast majority of behavioral classroom studies have been conducted with normal and mildly to moderately handicapped students, and the literature indicates that behavioral interventions are effective with children in all of these categories, we will present behavioral intervention techniques that have proved effective in regular as well as special educational settings.

This chapter was written to acquaint the reader with the extensive variety of behavioral interventions with children that have been and are currently under development in classrooms and other applied settings. It is impossible to discuss the topic comprehensively in one chapter, however. We refer the interested reader to the excellent textbooks and studies listed in the chapter bibliography for more extensive information.

As we previously mentioned, children who display behavior problems often have academic and social problems as well. Academic difficulties may stem from insufficient emotional control, inadequate self-control, poor motivation, or faulty social adjustment. Behavior problems may arise from lack of learning experiences, ineffective study skills, or lack of academic success. The source of a problem is difficult to determine, since all of these factors may interact. It is primarily for this reason that the behavioral approach focuses on developing interventions that improve both the academic and social functioning of these children. In this section, we will present general intervention procedures under four major headings: assessment, programming, instruction, and measurement.

ASSESSMENT

As with any intervention approach, assessment serves an important function in the behavioral model. Behavioral assessment concentrates on pinpointing academic and social behavioral deficits and performance discrepancies between present and expected levels of functioning. Behavioral assessment also involves an analysis of the controlling environmental variables — antecedent and consequent stimuli — that can be altered to teach appropriate behavior patterns.

Academic Assessment

Formal Tests.   Teachers and other practitioners have traditionally used standardized achievement tests to assess students' academic abilities and group students for instruction. As student performance can be compared to standardized norms, these measures are referred to as "norm-referenced measures" (Popham and Husek, 1969). These measures can be given to groups or individual students before and after an intervention to determine the amount of progress made. Individually administered standardized diagnostic tests may be used to determine specific skills or deficits for educational planning.

In recent years, several criticisms have been made about the use of standardized tests. These criticisms concern the use of single test scores for classification and placement, low reliability and validity, the inappropriate use of tests for certain student populations, and the fact that test performance sometimes varies with the characteristics of the examiner (Wallace and Larsen, 1978; Salvia and Ysseldyke, 1978; Hammill, 1971). The major limitation of standardized tests is that, because of the narrow range of education skills sampled, they provide little information for practitioners to use for planning children's individual educational programs, for placing children appropriately in educational sequences, or for measuring their academic progress (Lovitt, 1975, 1976; Wallace and Larsen, 1978). For these reasons, behaviorally oriented practitioners generally use standardized tests to determine a student's relative standing in a group or for screening purposes, and rely more on the use of informal tests and other direct measures to supply information for educational programming.

Informal Tests.   Informal tests are frequently used to determine whether a student can perform a skill to a criterion, which usually is established by the teacher. They are called criterion-referenced tests (Popham, 1978). Informal test items are developed from representative samples of the actual training materials used with students. Whereas standardized or norm-referenced measures typically yield highly irregular grade-level placement information that may vary with different instructional materials, criterion-referenced measures allow teachers not only to pinpoint students' strengths and weaknesses, but to identify their place in an instructional sequence. They are also used to determine whether a student needs further training on a given instructional objective or whether he or she should advance to a higher level.

Although criterion-referenced measures are usually commercially available as part of a set of instructional materials, they also can be easily constructed by teachers. Using available scope and sequence charts and curriculum guides, teachers can identify the specific instructional objectives appropriate to their students to establish instructional sequences. Once an acceptable sequence is developed, the teacher can select a criterion to determine mastery for a particular objective and then develop criterion test items. A teacher might develop an informal reading measure by selecting several hundred-word reading passages from different sections of books in a basal series. The student's reading behavior could be assessed by having him or her read these passages while the teacher scored the errors and recorded the total reading time. The student might then be asked comprehension questions about the passage. The teacher would calculate correct word rates as well as the percentage of comprehension questions answered correctly. This information could be used to pinpoint the student's placement in the basal series and to evaluate progress. Reading rate and comprehension criteria could then be set and used to determine when the student should advance to the next level in the reading series.

Teachers can also develop informal, criterion-referenced measures for assessing other academic skills. Arithmetic problems can be sequenced from easier to more difficult problems, and tests can be made either by collecting and sequencing individual problems or by using every tenth page or so from a math text as assessment tests. Once a sequence is identified, criteria can be set regarding the percentage of correct problems or the number of digits correct per minute required for a student to advance in an instructional sequence. Procedures for constructing informal criterion assessment measures in various subject areas have been outlined by many authors (see Wallace and Larsen, 1978; Wallace and Kauffman, 1978; Wiederholt, Hammill, and Brown, 1978; Deno and Mirkin, 1977; Popham, 1978).

Classroom Observation. Teachers can also identify children's academic problems by observing their classroom behavior under various conditions and on specific assignments. The teacher could assess a student's reading performance by recording the student's on-task and off-task behavior and by making general observations of the child's behavior in oral and silent reading situations. Data could be kept on a student's reading fluency, use of fingers to follow the text, or ability to state the main idea of a reading passage. The teacher could also note the student's word attack and analytic skills, responsiveness to instruction, level of motivation, reading interests, and assignments completed or rejected. Such observations yield valuable information for designing academic interventions and for selecting appropriate instructional materials; they are especially helpful when the teacher observes systematically and maintains accurate records.

Permanent Products.   Another important source of academic information is the analysis of students' permanent products. Children produce permanent records in the form of written papers, marks on a worksheet, drawings, and audiotapes. In evaluating reading accuracy, for example, a teacher can listen to an audiotape of a child's oral reading and score it for the frequency and type of errors, reading rate, and accuracy. The teacher may also assess reading behavior by analyzing written reports, answers to comprehension questions, and various drill and practice sheets. Arithmetic problems can be analyzed by noting error patterns — digits missed, steps omitted, steps included erroneously, or wrong operations. In the area of spelling, a teacher may note misspelled words or letter sequences from written examples, spelling tests, or words mispronounced in audiotape reading exercises. Teachers can evaluate a student's writing by noting grammatical mistakes, organizational ability, punctuation errors, and the ability to make inferences and generalizations.

Social Assessment

Functional Analysis.   An important aspect of assessing a child's social behavior is performing a functional analysis of behavior. The purpose of this activity is to identify target behaviors and the immediate antecedent and consequent stimuli that may control the behavior (Skinner, 1953). In functionally analyzing a child's behavior, a teacher identifies the child's behavioral excesses and deficits as well as any assets the child might have. Mike may tear up his paper, shout, and curse the teacher when given an assignment he considers himself incapable of doing (behavioral excess). He may be socially withdrawn due to an inability to approach and initiate conversation with his peers (behavioral deficit), but be very adept at modeling social behavior (behavioral asset). A functional analysis based on informal field observations might reveal that Mike's temper tantrums are maintained by teacher attention and the fact that they help him avoid completing an assignment. Because of his deficient social repertoire, Mike's peers may openly reject and tease him, resulting in social withdrawal.

In this case, an initial target behavior might be to increase the amount of time Mike spends working on an assignment or even the number of academic responses completed daily — the percentage of math problems, the rate of words read correctly, or the number of pages completed correctly. Another target behavior might be to reduce the amount of negative behavior in the form of refusal statements, assignments destroyed, or curse words. Another goal might be to increase the number of times that Mike initiates conversation with his peers each day. The controlling stimuli identified in the functional analysis, such as teacher attention, escape from potentially aversive situations, and peer approval, may all be identified as factors that can be manipulated to modify Mike's behavior.

In addition to identifying the specific target behaviors and immediate conducting stimuli, other analyses should be undertaken as part of a behavioral assessment procedure. These include:

1. *Motivational Analysis,* to determine (1) the positive consequences preferred by the child and the conditions under which these are effective, and (2) the consequences that the child perceives as aversive (Kanfer and Saslow, 1969).

2. *Developmental Analysis,* which specifies the biological and physical limitations of change (Kanfer and Saslow, 1969).

3. *Social and Cultural Analysis,* to identify (1) the persons who are most effective in controlling the child, and (2) the child's social and cultural expectations for behavior (Kanfer and Saslow, 1969).

4. *Analysis of Self-Control,* to evaluate (1) the child's ability for self-regulation, (2) the situations in which the child can control his or her behavior, (3) the ability to avoid problem situations, and (4) the persons who affect the child's self-control (Kanfer and Saslow, 1969; Kanfer and Grimm, 1977).

5. *Ecological Analysis,* which describes (1) a child's behavior in various situations and at different times of the day, and (2) the degree of support for change available from adults and the surrounding community (Kanfer and Saslow, 1969; Wahler and Cormier, 1973).

Informal Observation.   Teachers and other practitioners commonly use informal observational methods for collecting initial assessment information on a child's social behavior and for performing functional analyses. Preliminary observation may consist of obtaining continuous records of a child's behavior. These records provide a running account of a child's interaction with his or her environment over a period of time. After several samples of continuously recorded data are taken, these records may be transcribed into a "sequential analysis" by categorizing the data into antecedent-behavior-consequent relationships (Sulzer-Azaroff and Mayer, 1977). Information taken from anecdotal reports and sequential analysis of a child's behavior is then used to identify possible target behaviors and the functional relationships of these behaviors with environmental stimuli.

Behavioral Checklists.   Quay and Werry (1972) and Walker (1970) have developed behavioral checklists that can be used to assess students' social behavior. These consist of a list of behaviors that can be used to identify potential target behaviors. Although checklists do not provide the amount of assessment information yielded by direct observation procedures, they may be useful in initial screening stages of a behavioral intervention and in identifying patterns of inappropriate social behavior.

PROGRAMMING

The second component of the behavioral curriculum involves designing academic and social intervention programs to change students' behavior. Information taken from assessment activities may be used to set academic and social goals. The ultimate purpose of intervention procedures is to get the student functioning academically and socially at levels appropriate for his or her chronological age. The student's capacity to change as well as academic and social normative data taken on peers as a reference should be considered in selecting goals.

Academic Programming

Instructional Objectives.   A major part of the academic programming process is specifying long- and short-term instructional and behavioral objectives. Long-term (yearly and monthly) objectives are set as milestones that the child must reach during a school year. Once teachers have established these objectives, they identify short-term (weekly and daily) objectives necessary to attain these more remote goals. Short-term objectives can be further broken down into smaller subtasks. This process, known as *task analysis,* can be valuable for providing specific instruction to children; its purpose is to minimize their errors.

After long-term objectives are identified, each is translated into a specific instructional objective. This involves, first, describing the observable student outcomes — the behavioral movements required to perform a task. These could be writing digits correctly, achieving a certain oral reading rate, correctly identifying parts of speech, raising a hand when the teacher asks a question, or similar behaviors. Then the conditions and criteria under which the student must perform the behavior should be stated (Mager, 1962). An example of an instructional objective is given in Table 6.1.

TABLE 6.1
AN INSTRUCTIONAL OBJECTIVE

Conditions	Behavior	Criteria
Given examples of columnar addition problems 0–10	Student can supply correct digits to solve problems	Student can perform an average thirty digits per minute correctly for a three-minute period

The above objective has three facets: the conditions under which the behavior is to be given, the specific measurable student behavior desired, and the criteria that will be used to judge mastery of the behavior.

Minimal Objectives. Teachers may not only specify instructional objectives for individual children — objectives can be set for entire schools. Required minimal objectives can be set for each grade level during the school year. The specification of annual minimal objectives avoids the necessity for classification and diagnosis with standardized tests. Under this model, children who are half a year or more behind the minimal objectives for a particular grade level are assumed to need special education services. Moreover, the specification of minimal objectives to be mastered at each grade level establishes a sequence of instruction that facilitates making educational placements of children; it enables the teacher to measure student progress in terms of the objectives to be met during a given time period (Christie and McKenzie, 1974; Deno and Mirkin, 1977; White and Haring, 1976). Establishing minimal objectives for a grade level also allows teachers to compare a student's rate of growth over the course of the school year with minimal acceptable standards.

Social Programming

Targeting Behavior. After initial assessment information is collected, a teacher must select and define the target behavior to be changed. Target behaviors are defined in terms of the observable and measurable movements shown by the child. Social interaction, for example, could be defined as the number of times a child approaches another within a three-foot radius, the number of conversations initiated by the child, or the amount of time spent in cooperative play activities. Aggressive behavior might be measurably defined in terms of the number of times a child hits, bites, pinches, or pushes another child during a given time period. The practice of defining specific target behaviors in terms of observable and measurable units provides a basis for recording and graphing student progress during intervention periods.

After several potential target behaviors have been defined, just one is usually selected for change. Selection of a single behavior to change prevents the student from being overwhelmed by demands to change and enables the change agent to concentrate his or her efforts. Also, selecting a target behavior that the student can change with a minimum of effort enhances the chances for student success and improves his or her motivation for undertaking future change programs.

Another useful procedure in selecting potential target behaviors is to identify and define competing pairs of behaviors (Sulzer-Azaroff and Mayer, 1977) to change. A teacher may decide, for example, to reduce aggressive behavior and at the same time to increase a student's prosocial behaviors — the number of sharing incidents, positive verbal statements toward others, or the amount of time spent playing or working cooperatively with others.

Goal Setting.   Once the teacher has selected and defined a child's target behaviors, he or she may set annual, monthly, or weekly social goals to be met. An annual social goal established for a child might involve bringing the child's aggressive behavior within acceptable limits. To do this, the teacher might arbitrarily identify a reasonable objective. A more valid procedure, described by Walker and Hops (1976), establishes normative behavioral standards for specific classrooms. Walker and Hops observed a student's target behavior in one time frame and then immediately rated that of an appropriately behaving peer nominated by the teacher. These data were then used to set reasonable goals for the target student.

Goal Scaling.   After a long-term social goal has been identified, short-term objectives should also be stated. Kanfer (1978) has referred to the process of breaking down long-term goals into more immediate, sequentially arranged goals as "goal scaling." Adults often make the mistake of expecting immediate and dramatic changes in a child's behavior. Scaling goals so that behavior change is gradual increases the probability of success. This procedure assumes that some baseline data have been taken on the child's behavior that could be used to scale appropriate goals. A teacher could reduce a child's excessively disruptive behavior, for instance, by specifying a percentage of reductions per week. Classroom participation could be increased by stating graduated weekly goals for the entire class for increases in the frequency of volunteering information and asking questions.

Environmental Programming.   A final step in designing social intervention programs with children is to plan strategies for arranging environmental and social stimuli to make appropriate behavior more probable. In planning an intervention based on the assessment data for Mike, who as mentioned earlier had a strong negative reaction to assignments, a teacher would first make certain he could complete the assignment or break the assignment down and give him different parts at different times during the day. The teacher might also arrange immediate positive consequences for him upon completion of the assignment. Negative consequences could also be planned, such as a short time-out or response cost (removal of opportunity to earn valuable tokens) for his tantrums and defiant behavior. To improve Mike's social skills, the teacher could arrange for training in appropriate ways to begin conversations with peers, using modeling, imitation, and rehearsal techniques. Designing effective social intervention programs, of course, requires accurate assessment information and the freedom to modify environmental and social variables to produce appropriate behavior.

INSTRUCTION

The behavioral approach to instruction and training draws heavily on the basic concepts of the behavioral model, which were presented earlier. Academic and social instruction are experimental exercises whereby the teacher manipulates independent variables — antecedent and consequent stimuli — to produce changes in the dependent variables, student behavior.

Academic Instruction

Instructional Procedures. Applying the behavioral model to instruction involves bringing specific student target behaviors under the control of specific antecedent stimuli. Becker, Engelmann, and Thomas (1975) have provided what is perhaps the best example of this approach. Using the techniques they describe, the teacher first presents the instructional or task stimulus and then uses verbal cues to induce an appropriate task response from the child. If a child responds, the teacher reinforces this behavior with positive consequences; incorrect responses are verbally corrected by the teacher. Table 6.2 illustrates this process.

The teacher presents the task cue (antecedent stimulus) to prime the student's response. Once the desired student behavior is well established, the teacher drops, or *fades,* the task cue, "Say four." In some instances, this cue cannot be faded abruptly, so the teacher must first say, "Fo . . ."; next "F . . ."; then nothing. The final objective is for the child to respond with the correct answer when the task stimulus is presented alone. Of course, reinforcing consequences are provided periodically to maintain the behavior.

Instructional Strategies. The preceding example outlines the behavioral approach to teaching a concept in a specific teacher-student interaction. It also illustrates the importance of presenting clear antecedent stimuli — instructions, conditions, rules — for a student's response, and of reinforcing correct responses with immediate consequences. Several other behavioral procedures used by teachers should also be examined. Haring and Eaton (1978) have conceptualized behaviorally oriented instructional procedures in terms of a four-level hierarchy that can be differentiated on the basis of response complexity and instructional emphasis (see Table 6.3).

TABLE 6.2
BEHAVIORAL APPROACH TO INSTRUCTION

Task signal	Task cue	Response	Consequence
Teacher: "How much is 2 + 2?"	T: "Say 4."	Child: "Four."	T: "Good boy!"

Source: Adapted from W. C. Becker, E. Engelmann, and D. R. Thomas. *Teaching: A Course in Applied Psychology.* Chicago: Science Research Associates, 1975.

TABLE 6.3
AN INSTRUCTIONAL HIERARCHY AND APPROPRIATE
TEACHING STRATEGIES

Level	Emphasis	Consequence
1. Acquisition	Accuracy of response	1. Demonstration 2. Models 3. Cues (prompts) 4. Routine drill
2. Fluency or proficiency	Speed	1. Repeated novel drills 2. Reinforcement
3. Generalization	Novel stimulus	1. Discrimination training 2. Differentiation training
4. Adaptation	Adapted response	1. Problem-solving 2. Simulations

Source: N. G. Haring et al. *The Fourth R: Research in the Classroom.* Columbus, Oh.: Charles E. Merrill, 1978, p. 35. Used by permission.

In this hierarchy, a teacher's initial instruction is designed to help students acquire concepts. The emphasis is on the accuracy of the students' responses. Instruction involves demonstrating the appropriate steps of a task. A teacher may also model specific responses and have the students imitate them. Next, the teacher provides cues and feedback — information regarding the correctness of students' responses. Routine drill or practice is the final step.

At the second level in the hierarchy, students are taught task fluency or proficiency. At this level, a teacher may be most interested in the rate of students' responses. He or she may initially provide students with practice requiring them to use their newly acquired skills in novel drill situations. When students have acquired the skills and consistently produce accurate performances on the materials, they may be reinforced for completing tasks more rapidly.

At level three of the hierarchy, the instructional goal is to enhance the students' generalization of acquired skills through arranging application of these skills in novel situations. Once students have learned to add a column of numbers, for example, they may be given problems requiring them to identify the appropriate information to use and the appropriate steps required to solve a problem. This process, referred to in the example as *discrimination training,* entails selecting and using relevant information to differentiate the appropriate set of responses required for solving problems.

The final and most advanced level of the instructional hierarchy involves having students adapt or generalize their learning to new situations. At this level, a teacher may expose students to an actual or simulated problem-solving situation. Students who have previously learned to add money, for example, might be given the problem of making change for customers in a store to train them to adapt their skills to applied situations.

Thus, in applying this approach, teachers may use a number of instructional strategies, including:

1. Modeling the correct responses and requiring the child to imitate them.
2. Providing permanent models of the desired outcomes.
3. Giving the student cues and feedback regarding performance.
4. Arranging for routine drill and practice.
5. Reinforcing correct responses.
6. Providing training in discriminating relevant stimuli and differentiating appropriate responses.
7. Arranging activities that teach students to adapt their skills to novel applied situations (Haring and Gentry, 1976; Haring et al. 1978).

Social Instruction

Rule Structure.   Training children in social competencies using a behavioral approach also involves the use of the antecedent-behavior-consequence model. A good example of this approach is provided in a series of classic studies in which teachers established behavioral rules and contingently reinforced appropriate behavior through the use of praise and tokens. One such study, by Madsen, Becker, and Thomas (1968), predicted that telling children exactly what was expected of them would produce desired changes in their behavior. They asked teachers to make a few short rules and to state them positively (e.g., "Do your work quietly" rather than "No talking"). The teachers were asked to review the rules with the children several times a day. The teachers also praised appropriate behavior and ignored disruptive behavior such as leaving a work station, blurting out answers, or inappropriate talking. Merely stating and reviewing rules produced no changes in children's disruptive behavior; the problem behavior actually increased. Inappropriate behavior, however, was effectively reduced and maintained at low levels when the teachers stated rules, ignored inappropriate behavior, and praised appropriate behavior.

Consequences.   Another method for teaching children appropriate social behavior that is used extensively in the behavioral approach involves providing tokens or points that children can exchange for various privileges, activities, or tangible rewards such as candy, trinkets, or toys. The powerful effects produced by a token system were clearly illustrated in a study by O'Leary and Becker (1967), who were among the first to apply behavioral methods to the improvement of children's deviant behavior. The eight students in this study were all assigned to an adjustment class for children diagnosed as emotionally disturbed for displaying behaviors such as tantrums, aggressiveness, and disruptiveness. After taking baseline data, the teacher provided short classroom rules that the children had to follow to earn points. They could redeem them for a variety of tangible (back-up) reinforcers such as candy, comic books, and toys. The teacher awarded points to each of the students at the end of a lesson period based on her judgment about how well each student followed the rules. As the children became accustomed to earning rewards, teacher rating periods were faded and the time period for exchange of points and the number of points required to purchase a prize were increased to bring the children's appropriate behavior under the control of more naturalistic reinforcers such as teacher praise and attention. Observational data revealed that these procedures were effective in reducing deviant behavior from an average of 76 percent during the baseline period to an average of 10 percent during the token phase. Token systems such as these have been used extensively in the classroom for motivating students and reducing their inappropriate behavior. Although their effectiveness has been well documented (O'Leary and Drabman, 1971; Kazdin and Bootzin, 1972), it should be noted that most behaviorists consider token systems only a *temporary* method of controlling or establishing behavior. The final objective is to replace tokens with more natural classroom procedures such as social reinforcement and antecedent control.

MEASUREMENT

Measurement is an indispensable component of the behavioral approach. Teachers can measure student progress in acquiring behavioral objectives by taking periodic probes of their academic behavior or by direct daily measurement of their regular academic responses. A child's progress on a social intervention program can also be measured and evaluated by a variety of observational approaches.

Measurement of Academic Behavior

Measurement by Objectives.   Continuous measurement is necessary not only to evaluate student progress but to judge the effectiveness of the educational intervention program. Once teachers have identified long-term instructional objectives, developed a curricular sequence, and specified the behavioral objectives, measurement is relatively simple because student behavior is expressed in the easily measurable units of the objectives. Examples of the measurement by objectives approach are provided by Christie and McKenzie (1974), Deno and Mirkin (1977), and White and Haring (1976). Using this procedure, the number of objectives to be met during the school year is compared to the period of time that instruction is given.

FIGURE 6.1
AN EXAMPLE OF A STUDENT MONTHLY PROGRESS
CHART IN ARITHMETIC USING THE MEASUREMENT
BY OBJECTIVES PROCEDURE
The arrow indicates the point at which educational intervention was started.

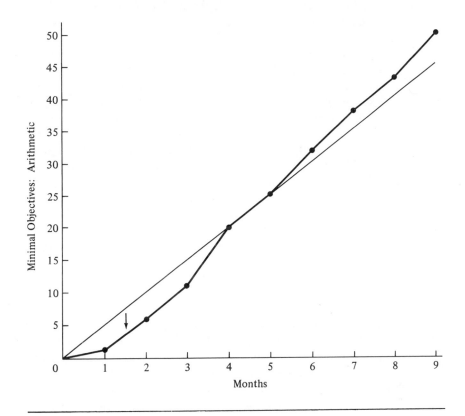

For example, periodic progress charts can be made to display student progress along these dimensions.

Figure 6.1 depicts an example of measurement of student progress by objectives. Minimal objectives for students appear on the vertical axis of the progress chart; the horizontal axis registers time in months. In this case, forty-five minimal objectives have been identified for mastery by students during the academic school year. To make adequate progress, a student must accomplish five objectives each month; a minimum rate of acceptable performance is shown in the line dividing the two axes. We can see that at the end of the first month of school, the student achieved only one objective. Intervention, which started in the sixth week of school, improved performance at a rate approximating that of the desired minimal rate (see arrow) but below the expected performance rate. The student maintained this rate in month three, but by the fourth month she was acquiring arithmetic objectives at the desired rate. In month six, the student's rate of mastering objectives began accelerating, and by the end of the school year she had met over fifty objectives, exceeding the minimum expected for students at her grade level. Although minimal objectives are specified in a particular subject, students can attain as many as they can reasonably manage.

Figure 6.2 displays annual minimal objectives for a group of students in reading. Here we see that the expected academic rate equals approximately ten pages of reading per week. Because the student in this example did not progress at the minimal expected rate, the teacher began an academic intervention at the end of the first month. The intervention appears to have accelerated student performance above that of the expected level during the second month, a gain which he maintained through the fourth month. For the rest of the academic year, the student made adequate progress in terms of the number of pages read. However, student performance dropped between months four and five and between months seven and eight. At these points, the teacher might have investigated the intervention being used at those times to see if it needed modification.

As these examples demonstrate, then, the monthly progress chart may indicate the effectiveness of the educational strategy being used with a particular student. In other instances, the teacher may wish to chart student behavior on either a session, daily, or weekly basis.

Criterion-referenced Measures. Earlier in the chapter we mentioned how criterion-referenced measures could be used to determine where in an instructional sequence of objectives to place a student. After minimal objectives are identified and the specific instructional objectives have been selected, a teacher typically develops criterion-referenced measures (CRMs) to evaluate a student's progress. CRMs are short tests, usually four or five traditional test items requiring a measurable student response. If a teacher, for example, wished to measure whether a student had learned to tell time to the nearest quarter hour, he or she might construct criterion-referenced test items to determine whether the pupil could identify the hands, count the numerals, recognize where the minute hand was at fifteen, thirty, and forty-five minutes after the hour, and also to determine whether the student could tell the correct time to the quarter hour when the hour hand was in various positions.

A CRM for evaluating whether a student could interpret the meaning of a reading passage might include test items that require him or her to respond to multiple-choice, cloze, matching, or true/false items, or to make inferences and generalizations, identify main figures, or describe the plot.

Direct and Daily Measures. Teachers may also gauge student progress through the use of direct and daily measures. Lovitt (1975, 1976) and

FIGURE 6.2
AN EXAMPLE OF A STUDENT MONTHLY PROGRESS CHART
IN READING USING THE MEASUREMENT
BY OBJECTIVES PROCEDURE
The arrow indicates the point at which educational intervention was started.

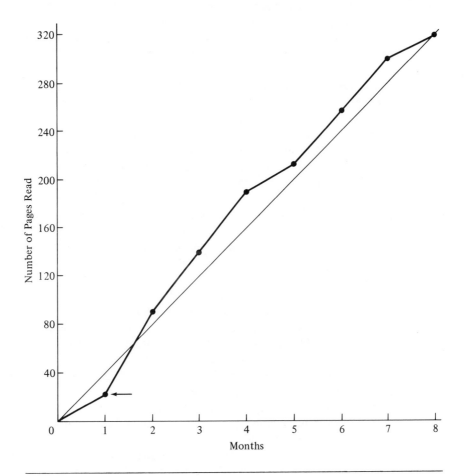

Haring and Gentry (1976) advocate using these measures by taking brief samples of a student's performance from the material on which he is working. These measures are short tests (one to three minutes) about a specific subject. One-minute measures of a student's oral reading, for example, could be taken by having the child read into a tape recorder. This then becomes a permanent product the teacher can refer to when evaluating daily student progress. Similar measures may also be taken in arithmetic.

Another important source of information about students' daily progress in an instructional program is the responses they make. Teachers using a behavioral approach systematically analyze students' academic responses from their permanent products in academic areas such as arithmetic, reading, spelling, and composition. Thus, the percentage of problems worked correctly, of reading comprehension questions answered correctly, of words spelled correctly, or the variety of parts of speech used in a composition could be calculated and graphed daily as measures of student performance. These data could then be used for evaluation and program modification.

Measurement Units.   Whenever possible, units for measuring student performance are expressed in terms of a standardized percentage or rate. The percentage is a ratio of the number of responses correct over the total number of responses possible. In reading, for example, the percentage would be the number of words correct over the total number of words read. Percentages are useful for measuring permanent products, especially when the number of problems, words, or other opportunities to learn varies from assignment to assignment. Rate, however, is a more sensitive and accurate measure of student performance, and behaviorists such as Lovitt (1976) and White and Liberty (1976) have advocated its use because it standardizes frequency in terms of time, thereby making possible comparison across irregular instructional periods or different instructional materials.

The unit of measurement selected by a teacher using a behavioral approach is typically the smallest one possible. In reading, for example, the number of words read correctly per minute is commonly used as a measure of student progress. Reading comprehension can be measured in terms of the percentage of questions correctly answered. In arithmetic, the number of digits correct per minute can be used as a performance measure — this provides a more accurate measure than problems completed correctly because it takes into account the difficulty level of the problems. A two-digit multiplication problem is more difficult and requires more work than a one-digit addition problem.

White and Haring (1976) described a unique way of measuring spelling responses in terms of the number of letter sequences that the student writes correctly. In the word "mother," for example, there are seven sequences capable of being correct of incorrect: $^1M^2\ O^3\ T^4\ H^5\ E^6\ R^7$. If a child spelled $^1M^2\ O^3\ T^4\ H^5\ E^6$, he or she would have six letter sequences correct out of seven, for a score of 86 percent for that one word.

Trap et al. (1978) described a measurement technique for handwriting in which standard templates on transparent overlays were placed over the student's work and deviations from these templates were scored in terms of containment of strokes within the boundaries of the transparency, the length of each stroke touching the boundaries of the template, the closure of loops, the inner-stroke contact, completeness of the letters, as well as the slant of the baseline.

Graphing. Regardless of the procedures used for measuring student performance, data graphing is considered essential in the behavioral approach, for several reasons. Teachers can use charted data to evaluate student progress on specified instructional objectives and also to judge the effectiveness of their educational programs. These data provide feedback to students and teachers alike in the form of a graphic representation of progress.

When charting student behavior, a teacher usually presents the data taken on students in the form of a line graph. In developing this graph, a teacher usually displays the student behavior being measured on the vertical axis and represents the time, preferably in days, on the horizontal axis.

In Figure 6.3, for example, we see that Allen, an eleven-year-old behaviorally disordered student, showed considerable variation in the number of assignments completed daily and in accuracy on his daily

FIGURE 6.3
THE ACCURACY AND NUMBER OF READING ASSIGNMENTS
COMPLETED BY ALLEN, AN ELEVEN-YEAR-OLD STUDENT

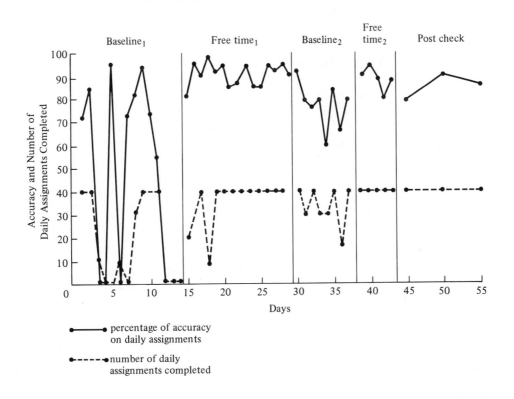

assignments. The teacher continued to chart Allen's behavior throughout the entire intervention period, including periods in which he was allowed free time for completing his assignments accurately. By graphing Allen's daily progress in this manner, the teacher developed a visual record of his progress during an intervention program. Graphs not only enable the teacher to determine the effectiveness of an intervention, they can also be used to motivate students to complete assignments.

Measurement of Social Behavior

As we have seen, the behavioral approach places a heavy emphasis on direct and continuous measurement of student performance. Measurement of a student's social behavior is no exception. Whereas teachers can gauge student academic progress by performance data on stated objectives and permanent products, measurement of social behavior is much more difficult. To avoid subjective inferences and problems arising from the use of standard measures of social behavior ("projective" tests, personality inventories, and "self-concept" surveys), behavioral practitioners rely almost exclusively upon observational procedures and recording procedures. Such behavior sampling techniques as frequency measures (rate, event, or percentage), duration recording, and interval recording allow the teacher to maintain an accurate measure on a variety of student behaviors.

ACADEMIC INTERVENTIONS

Our natural inclination when intervening with children designated emotionally disturbed is to reduce their behavioral excesses. This was the focus of a number of early classroom studies. Some demonstrated that increasing attention and decreasing disruptive, hyperactive, or other deviant behavior produced gains in target children's academic performance.

Studies by Hops and Cobb (1974) and Walker and Hops (1976) comparing direct reinforcement of correct academic responding with "classroom survival skill training" (such as attending to task, volunteering, working, and a combination of these approaches) demonstrated that all three methods may result in significant gains in survival skills as well as academic achievement test results.

Bringing children's problem behavior within manageable limits, however, does not necessarily produce gains in their academic behavior. Weinstein (1969), for example, had to establish a special class to improve the academic performance of children after bringing their severe problem behavior under control. Ferritor et al. (1972) did not increase primary students' accuracy in solving arithmetic problems, although they did improve attending and decrease highly disruptive behavior. It was necessary for teachers to give students tokens for problems correctly solved to increase accuracy. Similarly, Madsen, Becker, and Thomas (1969) observed that although clearly stated classroom rules and teacher praise for task-related behavior reduced the deviant behavior of elementary school children, these procedures did not always produce desirable changes in academic performance. Studies by Harris and Hall (1973) demonstrated that students could be attentive and nondisruptive and still not progress academically.

Although emotionally disturbed children usually require training in social behavior and appropriate classroom behavior, this cannot be the sole objective of a viable intervention program — they must be able to meet the minimal academic performance criteria to succeed in less restrictive educational environments. Although social interventions sometimes take precedence over academic interventions, a major advantage of an emphasis on improving academic proficiency is that it strengthens behavior that competes with problem behavior while building skills that will be valued and reinforced outside the immediate training situation. In general, evidence from classroom studies suggests that academic proficiency cannot be assumed to develop as a consequence of improvements in a child's social behavior; it must be planned as part of a total intervention program for the child. In the following section, we will present behavioral interventions that have been demonstrated to be potentially successful for improving emotionally disturbed children's academic skills.

READING STUDIES

Reading is an important area in which students who have learning and behavior problems often encounter difficulty. A number of applied studies completed in recent years are relevant to teaching children diagnosed as emotionally disturbed. For purposes of this discussion, "reading" will be assumed to refer to word recognition, oral reading, and comprehension.

One of the main problems facing teachers of children who display behavioral or learning difficulties relates to methods of motivating these children in academic areas. Studies indicate that children's reading behavior can be controlled by simply arranging appropriate consequences for correct reading rates. Staats and Butterfield (1965) used tokens that could be exchanged for prizes to increase the word-acquisition and reading-achievement test scores of an adolescent with a history of delinquency, deviant school behavior, and academic failure. Improvement in reading resulted in a decrease in deviant classroom behavior as well. Eisenstein (1975) produced gains in the reading performance of third graders in an inner city school through the use of guitar lessons. Ayllon and Roberts (1974) used points that could be exchanged for preferred activities to increase reading comprehension and the percentage of vocabulary words used correctly in a fifth-grade classroom. Lahey, McNees, and Brown

(1973) also improved reading comprehension in children who displayed reading deficits through the use of teacher praise and monetary rewards for correct answers. Rieth et al. (1977) increased the word recognition, oral reading accuracy, comprehension scores, and accuracy in reading workbook assignments of three behaviorally disordered boys by arranging free time activities for accurate task performances. These and a host of other studies suggest that teachers can develop inexpensive incentive programs to improve the reading performance of students by arranging consequences for appropriate behavior.

Another approach to improving reading accuracy involves modifying antecedent instructional stimuli. In a series of studies reported by Burdett and Fox (1973), for example, children were required to recognize all words in a story before being allowed to read it. Words were presented to the child on flashcards, with the teacher supplying social praise for each word called correctly. When words were miscalled, teachers modeled the correct response and the student imitated her. Words were considered learned when the student correctly called them in three consecutive presentations. Next, students used the words learned in the word recognition exercise during oral reading activities. They were not allowed to progress to the oral reading exercise until they demonstrated mastery of each of the words they were to read in the reading passage. Oral reading exercises consisted of two-hundred-word passages taken from basal readers. After completing a reading exercise, each student was asked five comprehension questions about the material. If the child did not answer correctly, he or she was prompted until a correct response was made. These procedures proved highly successful for improving the reading rates of students with reading deficits.

A procedure for reducing the amount of instructional time reserved for the teacher involves the use of peer tutors. Fox (1973) trained peers to tutor children with reading deficits by modeling the correct training techniques and then rehearsing the correct procedure. Tutors were instructed to (1) make sure they could read all the words in a passage before tutoring; (2) read one sentence at a time to the learner and have the learner read the sentence; (3) have the learner reread the passage; (4) have the learner sound out mispronounced words; (5) model correct pronunciations, supply words omitted, and then have the learner reread sentences in which an error occurred; and (6) provide praise and encouragement for good reading. Tutors were also instructed to avoid teasing readers, to allow them to make mistakes occasionally without correction, and to avoid frequently interrupting them. Tape recordings of the instructional sessions were checked for errors. Readers who performed at or above mean baseline levels earned free time activities for themselves and their tutors. This approach increased oral reading accuracy and correct rate and decreased the rate of errors.

Lovitt et al. (1971) conducted a series of reading studies that resulted in the development of several successful techniques for teaching children with problem behavior to read. One method involves a preview procedure in which the child is exposed to a reading passage either through listening prior to reading or reading it silently before rereading it orally. These authors demonstrated that just having students read a passage silently reduced their error rates. When silent previews were coupled with the opportunity to earn points for free time, a further reduction in error rates and increased correct rate ensued. Listening to a tape recording of a reading passage before reading it also increased oral reading accuracy. Previews combined with instructions to follow along in a text produced further improvement in performance (Lovitt, Schaff, and Sayre, 1970).

Polsgrove et al. (1980), in teaching remedial reading to high school students, compared the effects of listening to a reading passage, reading it twice (rehearsal), and reading it while receiving corrective instruction. Only corrective instruction produced even moderate gains in students' oral reading accuracy rates. Having students rehearse a passage and giving corrective instruction, however, produced significant gains in comprehension. Corrective instruction combined with the opportunity to evaluate personal performance graphs and receive grade points for improvements in correct rates not only increased correct oral reading rates but improved and maintained comprehension scores. Thus, the use of several treatments may be necessary to produce improvements in academic performances when students have a long history of failure with academic tasks.

ARITHMETIC STUDIES

Increasing student math performance is another concern of applied behavior analysis research. As with other subject areas, studies indicate that providing appropriate contingent reinforcement is an important procedure for improving achievement in this area.

Ayllon, Layman, and Kandel (1975) and Ayllon and Roberts (1974) showed that token reinforcement could be used to reduce disruptive and hyperactive behavior and to increase correct student responses to math workbook exercises. Ferritor et al. (1972), however, obtained different results. In the latter study, merely giving valuable tokens to children for attending to an arithmetic assignment improved student attention, but it did not improve arithmetic computation scores. When children were reinforced for correct responses and not for attending, arithmetic accuracy increased, but disruptive behavior increased also. Only when the children received tokens for both academic responding and attending behavior did the desirable behavior emerge.

Several studies reported by Lovitt (1978) indicate that manipulating antecedent events can improve math performance. In one study (Smith and Lovitt, 1974), a student identified a type of problem that he could not work. The teacher then modeled the correct procedure for solving the problem while describing the steps involved. The solved problem was then left on the student's desk as a permanent model to refer to when solving similar problems. This procedure produced rapid and lasting learning effects with several students.

In another study, Lovitt and Curtiss (1969) had students verbalize the requirements of a math problem of the form __ + 4 = 6, and then give the answer aloud. This procedure immediately reduced error rates and improved the correct rate. When the intervention was withdrawn, rates continued to accelerate while the error rate was maintained at low levels.

Blankenship and Lovitt (1976) found that simply supplying one student with immediate feedback — scoring the correct and incorrect responses on the paper — was enough to induce permanent changes in the accuracy of arithmetic performance. In another study investigating the effects of instructional stimuli on arithmetic performance (Smith and Lovitt, 1974), the teacher simply wrote a note at the top of the student's worksheet: "Work faster." This accelerated the correct rates of several children by an average of 24 percent over baseline. Blankenship and Lovitt (1976) also found that complex wording in story problems reduced students' accuracy. When students were required to correct their errors on these problems either orally or in writing, their performance improved.

The use of peer tutors has also improved students' arithmetic performances. Johnson and Bailey (1974) trained high-achieving fifth-graders to tutor kindergarten children in basic arithmetic skills such as sequential counting, counting objects, number recognition, and naming numbers. The teachers trained tutors by modeling such teaching behaviors as speaking clearly, praising appropriate behavior, ignoring inappropriate behavior, correcting errors, and providing appropriate instructions. The tutors then imitated the teacher's role while receiving corrective feedback from the teacher. Following each twenty-minute tutoring session, the children were allowed to play games for ten minutes. Comparisons of gains of five of the kindergarten tutees with five control students revealed that the tutees demonstrated superior performance. Observational data showed that four of the tutors could demonstrate the appropriate teaching behaviors throughout the study.

Harris and Sherman (1973) evaluated the effects of "unstructured" peer tutoring on fourth- and fifth-grade underachieving students. First, students were placed in groups of two and three to work together in studying problems prior to a twenty-minute math period. In the second phase, students who scored 90 percent or more were allowed to go to recess early. In the third phase, students were instructed to study by themselves. Finally, tutoring was reinstated. Tutoring sessions increased math accuracy far more than individual study sessions, and allowing early recess for response accuracy enhanced the effects of peer tutoring.

SPELLING STUDIES

A few studies have described methods that teachers can use to improve student spelling performance. Axelrod, Whitaker, and Hall (1972) found token reinforcement more effective than social praise for improving accuracy on weekly spelling tests of students labeled "learning disabled" or "emotionally disturbed." Using the opportunity to tutor younger students as contingent reinforcement for improving scores on weekly spelling tests, Hall (1971) produced spelling gains in sixth-grade students. Rieth et al. (1974) showed that providing short drill over a few words several times a week was more effective than massed practice in improving the spelling performance of students assigned to a special class.

Broden, Beasley, and Hall (1978) had mothers call words from a spelling list orally to their children and required the child to spell the word aloud. Children were praised for words spelled correctly. Mothers modeled the correct spelling of misspelled words and required three correct trials before presenting new words. These procedures more than doubled spelling scores.

WRITING STUDIES

Hopkins, Schutte, and Garton (1971) found that when primary school children were allowed to go directly to free play after completing their handwriting assignment, both their average handwriting rate and their accuracy increased. Salzberg et al. (1971) demonstrated that just showing students their scores and requiring them to meet prescribed performance levels before allowing them to engage in free play produced better handwriting than simply giving students feedback on their performance.

Trap et al. (1978) improved handwriting performance in twelve first-grade students by giving them information about the accuracy of their performances. During the baseline period, the instructor modeled the correct procedures for writing cursive letters and had students copy the model. In the first intervention, students watched the instructor score their writing samples using transparent overlays. They received corrective feedback for poorly formed letters and specific praise for well-formed letters. In the second intervention, the students received feedback and praise but also had to rewrite poorly formed letters. In the third intervention phase, students worked toward receiving a merit award for producing 10 percent gains over baseline performances. All three changes produced beneficial effects.

Brigham, Graubard, and Stans (1972) demonstrated that when students in a fifth-grade "adjustment class" received points for the number of words they wrote as well as the number of new words they used, the quality of their compositions (as judged by older peers) increased. Maloney and Hopkins (1973) scored the number of letters, adjectives, adverbs, prepositional phrases, compound sentences, and action verbs used in students' compositions and also had independent judges rate them for creativity. The compositions rated highest in creativity used more action verbs. When children were given the opportunity to earn candy and extra recess time for using action verbs, the creativity of their compositions increased, as did the number of adverbs and adjectives.

SOCIAL CURRICULUM

Some behavioral researchers have argued convincingly that children should be trained in social skills (Winett and Winkler, 1972; Cartledge and Milburn, 1978; Greenwood, Walker, and Hops, 1977; Strain, Cooke, and Apollini, 1976). Johnson and Johnson (1974, 1977) presented persuasive evidence that the competitive environment provided in traditional classrooms and the individualistic approach used in most behaviorally oriented classrooms do not develop the cooperative behavior needed for complex tasks or creative problem-solving. Popular support for specific social curricula has also been reflected in recent national pools in which school administrators, teachers, and parents agreed that a top priority of schools is to provide training in prosocial skills (Hoepfner, Bradley, and Doherty, 1973; Gallup, 1976).

In this section, we will first discuss the various group procedures used in the behavioral approach to train children in social competencies. We will then look at studies that illustrate various methods behavioral practitioners have used to train children in specific social skills such as self-control, classroom survival, and interpersonal skills.

CLASSROOM SKILLS TRAINING

Many of the innumerable studies designed to improve the classroom behavior of emotionally disturbed children have used some form of token system to institute the desired changes. Methods for establishing and maintaining token systems have been detailed elsewhere (Sulzer-Azaroff and Mayer, 1977). In this section, we will describe two of the classic applications of total classroom intervention programs that have successfully used token systems as part of a multiple treatment approach. These programs have been used to teach children appropriate classroom behavior. We will then discuss procedures that have been used to improve children's compliance with general classroom expectancies.

Inappropriate Behavior

There have been many investigations of methods for decreasing emotionally disturbed children's disruptive, antisocial, and other inappropriate behaviors. A series of early studies explored the relationship between the use of explicit classroom rules, social reinforcement for appropriate behavior, and systematically ignored inappropriate behavior. In these studies, students who showed appropriate behavior were praised, and their mildly disruptive and inappropriate behaviors were reduced. When the effects of these procedures were evaluated separately, however, it was evident that stating rules alone had little effect on inappropriate behavior, and that only a combination of rule-setting, ignoring inappropriate behavior, and contingent social praise for appropriate behavior minimized inappropriate behavior (Madsen, Becker, and Thomas, 1968). Other studies showed that for some children, rule setting and structuring classroom time into instructional periods produced little effect on levels of inappropriate classroom behavior; in some cases, praising good behavior and ignoring inappropriate behavior produced noticeable *increases* in disruptive behavior.

Although these and other early studies identified viable methods for managing mildly disruptive behavior and improving motivation, students who display high rates of disruptive or off-task behavior (60 percent or more) require more powerful interventions involving a number of treatment approaches.

Hewett (1968) developed an "engineered classroom" with several learning centers and a token economy for teaching children who showed moderately disturbed behavior. Children who display problem behavior, according to Hewett, have trouble functioning in regular classrooms because they lack skills in attending, responding to tasks, following directions, exploring their environment, and getting along with others. These children must learn readiness skills — attention, response, order, exploratory, and social — before they can master educational tasks and become achievement-oriented. Hewett's learning and intervention hierarchy showing educational procedures is depicted in Figure 6.4.

Although children may work at several levels of the hierarchy during some stages of the training process, they must function adequately at the first five levels before being expected to perform consistently at the mastery and achievement levels. At the *attention* level, the child works individually with the teacher and is immediately reinforced for attention and cooperative behavior. Intervention at the *response* level involves assigning the child simple motor or discrimination tasks on which he or she can succeed — running from one point to another, counting, describing a picture, writing names of friends. *Order* training entails having the child complete simple tasks such as tracing designs, sorting objects, or completing simple worksheets. At the *exploratory* level, the child works on appropriate science, communication, and arts and crafts activities. *Social* level intervention involves having the child engage in cooperative tasks such as role-playing solutions to social problems, listening to others, or completing other tasks involving communications. At the *mastery* level, training is provided to develop proficiency in academic areas. The objective of training at the *achievement* level is to provide an enriched curriculum that will

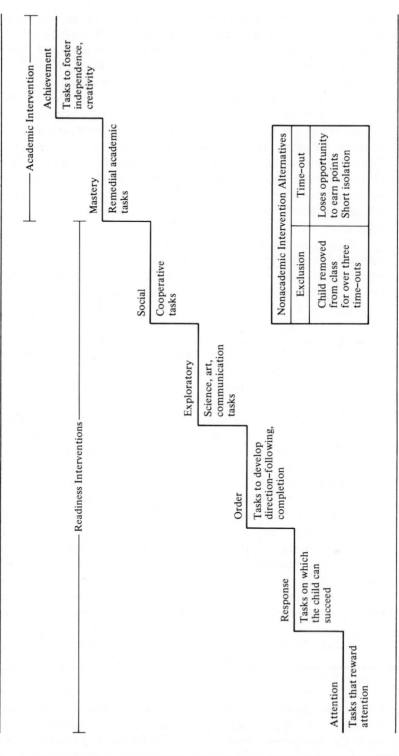

FIGURE 6.4
HIERARCHY OF EDUCATIONAL TASKS

Nonacademic Intervention Alternatives	
Exclusion	Time-out
Child removed from class for over three time-outs	Loses opportunity to earn points Short isolation

Academic Intervention

Achievement — Tasks to foster independence, creativity

Mastery — Remedial academic tasks

Social — Cooperative tasks

Exploratory — Science, art, communication tasks

Order — Tasks to develop direction-following, completion

Response — Tasks on which the child can succeed

Attention — Tasks that reward attention

Readiness Interventions

Source: Adapted from F. M. Hewett. Educational engineering with e. d. children. *Exceptional Children,* 1967, *33,* 459–467; and F. M. Hewett, F. D. Taylor, and A. A. Artuso. The Santa Monica project: evaluation of an engineered classroom design with emotionally disturbed children. *Exceptional Children,* 1969, *35,* 523–529.

develop independence and creativity in students by having them do reports, class projects, or work on their response speed in reading or math.

To train children at the various levels, Hewett advocates providing various learning centers, for order, exploratory, and mastery work, in which children carry out their various assignments. In addition, the teacher dispenses ten points every fifteen minutes: two for starting assignments, three for following through, and five for appropriate student behavior. These can be redeemed for either edible, tangible, or activity reinforcers. Teachers also provide contingent social reinforcement for paying attention and displaying appropriate classroom behavior. Another important aspect of Hewett's program is the use of time-out for brief periods and short-term exclusion from school for persistently disruptive or violent behavior.

Hewett, Taylor, and Artuso (1969), in one of the broadest and most important evaluations of the behavioral curriculum, assessed the effects of this experimental program on fifty-four children diagnosed as emotionally disturbed. Children exposed to the experimental curriculum significantly increased their task attention and their arithmetic scores on a standardized achievement test as compared to children in control classrooms. When the experimental procedures were introduced in two control classes, significant increases in attending and in arithmetic achievement resulted, compared to a control group that received no exposure to the experimental program. Even when the experimental program was withdrawn, the children continued to make gains in task attention.

Walker, Hops, and Fiegenbaum (1976) developed a program for training children with low rates of appropriate behavior that used a combination of procedures: placement in an experimental class and the use of social praise, tokens, and response cost (loss of privileges or reinforcers for inappropriate behavior). Praise and the introduction of a token system produced increases in desired behavior of 59 percent and 78 percent, respectively. The loss of points and use of time-out stabilized and maintained appropriate behavior at an average of 96 percent of the time.

Studies such as these led to the development of the Contingencies for Learning and Social Skills (CLASS) program by Walker and his colleagues (Walker, Mattson, and Buckley, 1971; Walker and Buckley, 1972a; Walker, Hops, and Johnson, 1975; Hops, Fleishman, and Beickel, 1976). The strength of this program was that it could be instituted for managing emotionally disturbed children in regular classrooms without placing them in special self-contained classes. The CLASS program uses consulting teachers to train regular class teachers in the application of praise and tokens, response cost, systematic suspension, parental involvement, and contingent recycling to previous program levels.

At the beginning of the CLASS program, the consultant, teacher, principal, parent, and student sign a contract detailing each person's role and expected level of performance. Consulting teachers initially model for the classroom teacher the procedures for administering points and giving praise to the child for behaviors such as talking quietly, following instructions, remaining in his or her seat, attending, working, and appropriate peer interactions. The target student earns points that can be exchanged for privileges by the entire class; failure to show appropriate behavior during prescribed intervals results in a temporary loss of the opportunity to earn points. When children display potentially harmful, destructive, or continually defiant behaviors, they are briefly placed in a separate room (time-out) or sent home to complete their work for the remainder of the school day (systematic suspension). Parents support the change program by seeing that the children complete their homework on days they are suspended and by giving praise and privileges for acceptable daily behavioral report cards.

The training program is designed such that the point system and group reinforcement activities are eventually faded and the teacher can maintain appropriate behavior through social praise and performance feedback alone. Field test results of the CLASS program conducted at several sites indicate that these procedures are quite powerful in producing desirable changes in problem children's classroom behavior.

Compliance Behavior

Another major direction in behavioral intervention development has been toward increasing complaint behaviors in the classroom. This group of behaviors includes attending, studying, volunteering, asking questions, and reinforcing teacher behavior. An early procedure, developed by Packard (1970), greatly increased attending behavior of disruptive students. It involved starting a visible timer and green light apparatus when all children in the class were working, and stopping the timer and turning on a red light when some students were disruptive. Extra recess time and preferred activities were earned by meeting criteria for the number of minutes the timer advanced.

Adopting Packard's technique in a series of related studies, Cobb (1972), Cobb and Hops (1973), and Hops and Cobb (1973, 1974) explored the relationship of "classroom survival skills" to children's academic progress. Cobb's earlier studies had revealed that attending and volunteering were major predictors of academic achievement. Using these findings as a basis for planning interventions, Cobb and Hops (1973) trained teachers to use a clock and light device to increase students' appropriate behavior. When the entire class was engaged in task-related behavior, the teacher activated the clock and a green light that indicated that the clock was running. The children had to work a specified number of minutes each day to earn access to reinforcers such as free time, additional recess, and toys and games. Teachers also provided the children with contingent social praise and ignored inappropriate behavior. These procedures resulted in a 24 percent increase in the children's survival-skill behaviors; a comparison group, which received no such training, showed no gains. Over the twenty-day intervention, mean reading achievement scores of students in the experimental classroom showed a 28 percent increase, compared to an 11 percent increase by students in a comparison group — gains that were maintained up to six weeks later.

Graubard, Rosenberg, and Miller (1971), in a unique study designed to increase the acceptance of adolescent special education students in regular classes, taught students to make eye contact with teachers, ask for help, react positively to teacher instruction, request extra assignments, and to sit straight at their desks. They were also instructed to break eye contact and otherwise not react to teacher scoldings or provocations. An analysis of the positive and negative teacher contacts with the students revealed a sharp increase in frequency of positive teacher contacts and a reduction in negative teacher contacts when students used these procedures. These effects were clearly reversed when the students withdrew the treatment.

Although these studies demonstrated that rewarding children for paying attention and training them in appropriate behavior resulted in desirable changes in student behavior as well as teachers' reactions to them, in most cases the effects of these procedures on academic behavior were not evaluated. A more recent study (Ayllon and Roberts, 1974) found that when teachers awarded regular class children points redeemable for privileges and activities for answering questions correctly in a reading workbook, not only did correct responses increase, but the students' disruptive behavior decreased. Also, rewarding hyperactive children for making correct math responses reduced their hyperactive behavior during academic periods to levels similar to those observed when the children took medication.

Self-control Training

Although token economy systems have been widely used to change children's social and academic behavior, they have several disadvantages. First, training in a token system does not appear to be maintained across different settings and over time. Second, token programs are time consuming and expensive to operate. Third, some children may manipulate situations in which token economies are employed. Fourth, children may develop a dependence on external reward and fail to learn skills that will allow them to control their own behavior. These concerns have influenced the development of methods for training children in self-control.

Kanfer and Karoly (1972) identified three stages of the self-control process. In the *self-monitoring* stage, a person observes his or her behavior in a particular situation and uses these observations to establish personal performance standards. During stage two, *self-evaluation,* ongoing performance is compared to the standards established in stage one. Favorable self-evaluations may result in positive *self-reinforcement* such as approving self-statements, or access to external rewards for performing a particular behavior pattern; unfavorable self-evaluations lead to withholding self-reinforcement or changing performance standards (Kanfer and Karoly, 1972; Kanfer, 1975; Thoreson and Mahoney, 1974). Several studies have trained children in the use of these processes for developing their self-control.

Self-monitoring

A teacher can train a child to self-monitor by having the child measure a particular target behavior with a wrist counter, abacus, tally card, or stopwatch. The child may also be required to maintain a graph or chart of his or her behavior to evaluate progress in a change program. Gottman and McFall (1972), for example, showed that disruptive adolescents who kept tallies of their class contributions contributed more to class discussions than students who recorded the number of times they felt like speaking out but did not. Bolstad and Johnson (1972) had elementary school students record the frequency of their unauthorized speech, unauthorized seat-leaving, and physical aggression, giving them valuable points for closely matching a classroom observer's and teacher's count. This reduced disruptive behavior more than giving children external reinforcement alone. In another study, Broden, Hall, and Mitts (1971) found that when a pre-adolescent girl recorded her study and nonstudy behaviors and reported them weekly to a school counselor, her classroom attention increased. Five preschoolers who were taught by Reiber, Schilmoeller, and LeBlanc (1976) to count their on-task behaviors during a listening class, and whose teachers showed them a graph of their on-task behaviors from a preceding day, underwent dramatic improvements in attending.

These and other results suggest that self-monitoring may influence behavior most when (1) it occurs early in a behavioral chain; (2) children record both target and competing behaviors; (3) it is used continuously in initial phases; and (4) it is supported by additional procedures such as self-evaluation, self-reinforcement, and intermittent external reinforcement.

Self-evaluation and Self-reinforcement.   Studies in which children are taught behavioral self-control using self-evaluation and self-reinforcement begin by giving subjects valuable tokens for obeying classroom rules or meeting behavioral standards. Typically, children's behaviors are evaluated by a teacher or observer to determine their eligibility for reinforcement. Once appropriate behavior levels are met, the children are allowed to rate themselves; ratings closely matching those of the trainers earn the appropriate number of tokens. After acceptable patterns of self-evaluation and self-reinforcement have stabilized, external control procedures are faded by simply reducing the number of external ratings. Using this approach, Bolstad and Johnson (1972) found that students in two groups using self-evaluation and self-reinforcement showed less disruptive behavior than those assigned to a group that received only external reinforcement. Fredericksen and Fredericksen (1975) demonstrated that with self-management training, preadolescent special education students could improve their task-oriented and prosocial behavior over levels observed during teacher-controlled reinforcement periods. In a similar study by Turkewitz, O'Leary, and Ironsmith (1975), elementary school students' academic performances under self-management conditions were maintained at normal rates, while their disruptive behavior dropped significantly below the level observed during the baseline period.

These studies indicate that when preceded with proper training, self-regulation, self-monitoring, self-evaluation, and self-reinforcement can effectively maintain academic behavior and minimize disruptive behavior. Training children in appropriate self-management methods is, thus, important for maintaining behaviors initially established by token systems or other intervention techniques (Polsgrove, 1979).

Social Skills Training

Although successful academic achievement usually relies on students behaving in ways acceptable to teachers, the importance of training children in social skills must not be overlooked. From a behavioral perspective, training children in prosocial skills involves establishing behavior that can be used when appropriate to secure positive interpersonal consequences and avoid aversive consequences.

Altruism. As with other types of behavior, observational learning experiences have been demonstrated to be effective in encouraging children's altruistic behavior. The procedure typically involves having children observe models contribute rewards they have earned (candy, money, tokens, gift certificates) to needy children while stating why they are sharing. In a classic study, Rosenhan and White (1967) exposed children to an adult model who, after winning gift certificates while playing a game, donated half of his winnings to a charity box for needy children. The model explained what he was doing so the children could hear. Children who were exposed to these procedures showed charitable behavior more frequently than those who did not observe a model. Other modeling studies have shown that powerful models facilitate modeling, whereas warm, friendly, nurturant models decrease this behavior (Grusec, 1971; Grusec and Skubiski, 1966).

Rogers-Warren and Baer (1976) studied the effects of modeling, praise, and direct reinforcement for reports of sharing by observing children's actual sharing and praising in a work group. During each daily work session, two adults modeled sharing and praise behaviors several times. Afterward, in a reporting period, the teacher asked a model to report sharing and praise responses, rewarding the model with praise and food for reporting. Next, each child was asked to report incidents in which he or she had shared or praised during the session. The children received social and edible reinforcement for reporting these incidents. Modeling and reinforcement of all reports of prosocial behavior produced moderate gains. But when children were reinforced for only *true* reports, high, stable sharing and praise rates were established.

These and other studies indicate that children can learn altruistic and sharing responses through modeling, reinforcement, and verbal conditioning. These studies suggest that teachers can increase children's altruistic behaviors by:

1. Designing programs in which children have an opportunity to share items with each other in their work.
2. Making teacher social praise and approval contingent on specific instances of sharing.
3. Modeling altruistic acts while verbalizing the rationale for doing so.
4. Using descriptive praise in publicly identifying peer models who show prosocial behavior.
5. Reserving warmth and affection until they are most appropriate rather than displaying them noncontingently.
6. Using self-praise at intervals following altruistic acts.
7. Having children praise themselves and combine this with external social approval following instances of prosocial behavior.
8. Using examples of prosocial behaviors from the media as models.

Social Interaction.   Several studies have demonstrated the effectiveness of social and tangible reinforcement in increasing children's social interactions. Buell et al. (1968) produced high and stable gains in preschool girls' cooperative play, verbalizations, and touching responses to teachers and peers by having teachers provide social attention for sharing play equipment. Hopkins (1968) significantly increased the frequency of smiling in two retarded children through the use of edible reinforcement. Hart et al. (1968) used peer prompting, contingent social reinforcement, and shaping to increase the helping, cooperative sharing, and proximal behaviors of a preschool child.

Social training can improve the social behavior not only of preschool children with behavior problems, but of their peers as well. Strain and Timm (1974), for example, gave specific verbal praise and positive physical contact to peers for hugging, patting, holding hands, sharing, and other cooperative play with the withdrawn child. This resulted in immediate increases in the withdrawn child's positive social behavior.

Strain, Shores, and Kerr (1976) trained three target children to emit appropriate social behavior through verbal prompts ("Now let's play with the other children"), physical prompts ("leading the subject," "modeling play," "moving body parts"), and specific descriptive verbal praise upon prosocial behavior. These procedures produced increases in the appropriate behavior and decreases in the negative behavior of target children as well as their classroom peers (see Figure 6.5).

In a unique study, Csapo (1972) seated behaviorally disordered students next to socially mature peers and instructed them to observe and imitate their peers' classroom behaviors. Peers were told to model appropriate behavior, and they gave target children valuable tokens for imitating them. These procedures reduced the deviant behavior of these students. Low levels of deviant behavior were maintained after treatment was withdrawn.

Johnson and Johnson (1974, 1977) reported on a series of studies designed to enhance the cooperative behavior of elementary school children. In one study, four student work groups consisting of one or two "normal-progress" males, at least one female, and one learning disabled child were created. Each student was required to share ideas and materials and to help other group members complete assignments. Compared to

FIGURE 6.5
RESPONSE TO SOCIAL TRAINING

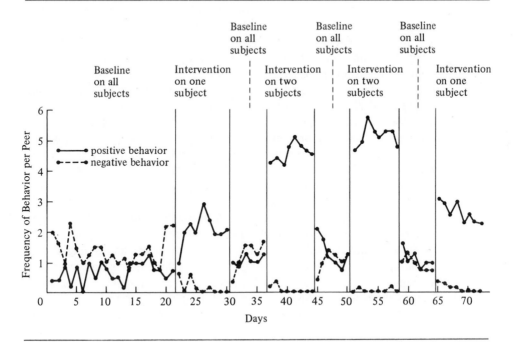

Source: P. S. Strain, R. E. Shores, and M. M. Kerr. An experimental analysis of "spill over" effects of the social interaction of behaviorally handicapped pre-school children. *Journal of Applied Behavior Analysis,* 1976, *9,* 31–40. Copyright 1976 by the Society for the Experimental Analysis of Behavior, Inc. Used by permission.

children who were assigned tasks to complete individually, normal children in cooperative groups rated their learning disabled peers more favorably, selected them as friends more frequently, and rejected them less frequently.

These studies used a variety of techniques to improve the social skills of children classified as behaviorally disturbed. Many of these procedures are still under development, so it is too soon to accurately evaluate their influence on programming for these students. Nevertheless, they seem very promising.

SUMMARY

In this chapter we presented some of the basic assumptions underlying the behavioral curriculum and described the general operating procedures of assessment, programming, instruction, and measurement. We also provided an overview of behavioral interventions teachers have used successfully to instruct and manage children identified as emotionally disturbed.

Applied behavioral research has identified a number of instructional techniques that are effective for teaching academic skills to emotionally disturbed children. In general, studies indicate that the following factors are more important than the materials used in instruction: (1) increasing students' attention to critical and important features of a task, by giving specific and immediate feedback, for example; (2) increasing instructional time through such means as scheduling tutors, systematic drill, or direct instruction; and (3) increasing motivation to learn through providing appropriate reinforcing consequences. Some of the more promising instructional techniques are modeling, rehearsal, corrective feedback, prompting, contingent drill, specific instructions, and graphic display. Undoubtedly, the most effective procedure for intervening with children and youth with learning and behavior problems is providing them with reinforcing consequences when they meet certain criteria. Study after study has shown that, regardless of the instructional procedure employed, teachers who systematically provide contingent reinforcement produce high and stable gains in children's academic behavior.

This chapter also provided a guide through many behavioral studies related to the development of effective social interventions appropriate for use with emotionally disturbed children. These interventions rely heavily on the application of the behavioral model — manipulating antecedent and consequent variables to produce desired effects on children's behavior. Such methods as modeling and rehearsal are also important.

There have been many advances in the development of behavioral intervention in the past decade that can be used to improve children's social behavior. Structured environments such as the behaviorally engineered classroom pioneered in the late 1960s (Hewett, 1968) and the token economy system developed by O'Leary and Becker (1967) gave rise to the development of precision treatment packages designed for early intervention with emotionally disturbed chiildren who may be placed in the educational mainstream.

Social behavioral interventions with emotionally disturbed children, especially those who show behavioral excess, typically involve exposing them initially to some sort of structured environment. Once appropriate behavior has been established, external environmental control is faded and children can receive training in self-control. Studies indicate that teachers using observational and operant procedures can successfully teach children to monitor their own behavior, set realistic goals for themselves, evaluate their own performances, and give themselves appropriate reinforcement for maintaining desirable behavior.

A new direction for the behavioral curriculum is teaching children social skills such as altruism, sharing, appropriate interpersonal interaction, and acceptance of others. Research continues to suggest exciting new intervention possibilities for teaching children designated emotionally disturbed.

Chapter 7

Curriculum Intervention with the Emotionally Disturbed Student: A Psychoeducational Perspective

Raymond J. Dembinski
Northern Illinois University

with

Edward W. Schultz
University of Maine at Farmington

Wilbur T. Walton
Brigham Young University

The purpose of this chapter is to describe the curriculum features of one of the models commonly used in the education of emotionally disturbed children, the psychoeducational approach. We will provide basic information about (1) the conceptual basis of the psychoeducational model; (2) the conceptual attributes of curricula in general, with particular emphasis on how these attributes apply to psychoeducational teaching; (3) representative psychoeducational curricula; (4) implementation and evaluation issues pertaining to psychoeducational curricula; and (5) future challenges in the quest for an understanding of human behavior.

THE PSYCHOEDUCATIONAL PERSPECTIVE

Basic Assumptions and Guidelines

A simple, universally accepted definition of the term "psychoeducational" does not exist. As Long, Morse, and Newman (1976) indicate, "psychoeducation" has been considered a theory, a methodology, and even a general viewpoint. It is not our purpose to delve into the nuances of these various perceptions. A knowledge of the basic assumptions of the model is necessary, however, if one is to understand the psychoeducational perspective.

The following are the fundamental principles of the psychoeducational model (Fagen, Long, and Stevens, 1975):

1. The relationship between the teacher and pupil is central. It must be understood and used effectively.
2. An educational milieu must take into consideration factors that affect pupil interactions with peers, staff, curriculum, and school.
3. Learning becomes interesting, meaningful, and purposive when it is invested with feelings.
4. Emotional conflict can be used productively to teach new ways of understanding and coping with stress.
5. Cognitive, affective, and psychomotor processes interact continuously.
6. Pupils vary in their learning styles and functional levels.
7. One type of behavior may have many causes; one cause may result in many behaviors.
8. Collaboration between the significant adults in a pupil's environment is essential.

To base one's teaching on these assumptions, one must be able to establish and maintain interpersonal relationships with children and other people significant in the environment (numbers 1 and 8), to understand the dynamics of behavior (numbers 2, 4, and 7), and to establish a constructive learning environment (numbers 3, 5, and 6).

Recent work by Fagen and Long (Fagen, 1979; Long and Fagen, 1981) provides a basis for developing instructional guidelines for teachers that reflect a psychoeducational approach. These guidelines may be stated as follows:

1. The school's task is to describe the pupil in terms of functioning skills, emphasizing areas of strength and specifying areas of weakness for remediation.

2. The psychoeducational process involves creating an environment in which each pupil can function successfully at his or her present level.

3. Each pupil should be taught that he or she has the ability and resources to function successfully.

4. Understanding how each pupil perceives, feels, thinks, and behaves facilitates the creation of the educational conditions that will produce optimal behavioral change.

5. Everything that happens to, with, or for the student, or that works against him or her, is important and can have therapeutic value.

6. Emotionally troubled pupils have learned to be less competent in meeting normal developmental expectations such as handling competition, learning to share, learning to trust, and managing closeness. Teachers should recognize such deficiency areas and help children to fill developmental gaps in their behavior constructively.

7. Emotionally disturbed pupils behave immaturely during periods of stress. They will lie, fight, run away, regress, and deny the most obvious realities. Any hope for change depends upon mature behavior from adults.

8. Pupils in conflict often generate similar feelings and behaviors in others. Student aggression, for example, often creates aggressive behaviors in others; hyperactive children can create hyperactivity in others; withdrawn pupils can get other children and adults to ignore them; and passive-aggressive pupils can get others to carry their angry feelings for days. If children succeed in getting adults to act out their feelings and behavior, they perpetuate their self-fulfilling prophecy, which in turn reinforces their defense against change.

9. Emotionally troubled children have learned to associate adult intervention with adult rejection. Teachers must reiterate to pupils that adults are available to protect them from real dangers, contagion, and psychological depreciation.

10. Teachers must learn to listen to what pupils are saying and feeling, whether expressed verbally or nonverbally.

11. Teachers should not only expect a certain amount of hostility and disappointment from pupils and colleagues, they must learn to accept it.

12. A pupil's home and community life make important contributions to the child's health and must be considered in any remedial process. If cooperative efforts with the home are unsuccessful, the school becomes the major source of support for the pupil.

13. Teachers must demonstrate that fairness involves treating children differently. Although group rules are necessary for organizational purposes, individual exceptions may be necessary to promote growth and change.

14. Crises are important opportunities for teachers to teach and for pupils to learn.

15. Behavioral limits can be a form of caring. Physical restraint, for example, can be a therapeutic act of caring for and protecting pupils.

16. Pupils must be taught social and academic skills to enhance their ability to cope with a stressful environment.

17. Pupils learn through a process of unconscious identification with significant adults in their lives. The implication for teachers is that their personal appearance, attitudes, and behavior are factors in teaching.

As you can see, human relationships are an integral aspect of psychoeducational programming. Behavior is extremely complex, and its meaning must be understood by the teacher if the learning environment of the class-room and school are to have a therapeutic influence on the flow and direction of behavior. Furthermore, it is fundamental to the psychoeducational model that a child's thinking (cognition) and feelings (affect) are inseparable; both have a direct influence on how a child behaves. The relationship between these dimensions is evident in the following statement from Krathwohl, Bloom, and Masia (1964): "In the cognitive domain we are concerned that the student shall be able to do a task when requested. In the affective domain we are more concerned that he *does* do it when it is appropriate after he has learned that he *can* do it" (p. 60).

"Cognition," in essence, refers to the activity of the mind. What a person learns and the process by which he or she acquires knowledge are properties of the cognitive domain.

The acquisition of attitudes and values, however, is considered affective learning. Affect, then, refers to the feeling or emotional aspects of experience and learning. The affective domain focuses on how people feel about wanting to learn, how they feel as they learn, and what they feel after they have learned (Brown, 1971). Long et al. (1976) argue that affect involves more than the degree of emotional investment in one's ideas or knowledge. Affect also includes the awareness, acknowledgement, expression, and management of one's feelings. Constructive coping with the pain of one's inner self is as inherent a part of the affective domain as the joyful experience of sharing a loving emotional response. Brown (1971) refers to the integration or melding of the affective and cognitive elements in learning as "confluent education." Others (Allen, 1971; Goodlad, 1966; Hendricks and Gadiman, 1976; Knoblock et al., 1974; Ylvisaker, 1972) have conceptualized this approach as humanistic or transpersonal education.

Regardless of the terminology employed, these investigators agree on one major tenet: Intellectual learning always involves some sort of feeling, and feelings always have an intellectual concomitant. Learning is impeded when students are struggling to resolve unsettling feelings or experiencing strong emotions too complex to be expressed. Teachers aware of this inter-relationship can best facilitate learning by expressing an accepting attitude toward idiosyncratic student reactions to the task at hand, within reason, of course. Consider the example of a class engaged in the study of the brain, who are required to view a human brain preserved in solution and then to dissect the brain of an animal. As the activity approaches, the students have morbid conversations and express revulsion at the thought of seeing and cutting an organ. Comments include "It's dead," "You look like that after you die," "I can't look at it," and "I can't touch it." Some students, in a show of bravado, may tease the more expressive pupils. A sensitive teacher can minimize the disruptive potential of these comments by providing a legitimate opportunity to discuss these feelings. From a psychoeducational standpoint, it is not the students who are avoiding the issue in this situation. A teacher who does not allow for the expression of feelings is guilty of ignoring a vital part of the instructional process.

Fagen, Long, and Stevens (1975) suggest that the relationship between feeling and learning is a function of the following principles:

1. A student who has positive feelings about a subject will be more interested in learning it than one who does not. A student interested in becoming a physician will approach the brain unit in spite of his or her concerns about touching an animal's internal organs.
2. Students will learn a subject more easily if they have positive experiences with similar subject matter. A student who thinks she is good at biology will probably learn that subject best.
3. Learning is enhanced by positive relationships between student and teacher. A student will discuss his feelings about dissecting an organ with his teacher if he knows the teacher will listen and accept his concerns.

In summary, the psychoeducational approach postulates "a circular, interacting relationship between thoughts and feelings such that cognitive experience and emotional experience affect each other simultaneously" (Long, Morse, and Newman, 1976, p. 238).

Relevance to Disturbed Behavior

Fagen and his associates (1975) contend that personal frustration is a natural consequence of interacting with others. To live and work together, we must frequently inhibit our desire for gratification. Unfortunately, there are those who do not learn to manage this frustration adequately. Students may react to demands for control with outbursts of tears, anger, or complete withdrawal. It is not uncommon for teachers to react to these behaviors with criticism and even punishment. Because adults are influenced by unpleasantness, they strive to curb such honest yet sensitive expressions before they erupt, often to protect their self-regard and to avoid discomfort. We feel it is necessary for students and adults to adopt a comfortable attitude toward self-expression of frustration. This results in the acceptance of distress in others. It is a natural inclination to actively avoid unpleasant feelings, but it is also important to learn how to manage these behaviors in a more healthy way. These considerations lead Fagen, Long, and Stevens (1975) to strongly support greater emphasis on affective education curricula for emotionally disturbed students.

Another advocate of the integration of cognitive and affective processes in education is George Brown. Brown (1971) believes that classroom control is almost impossible when a teacher's methods and curriculum ignore the student as a feeling and thinking human being. He associates student acts of aggression, hate, withdrawal, and violence with feelings of isolation, alienation, frustration, impotence, and the loss of identity and purpose. He believes that a gradual integration of affective content in the traditional school curriculum could be accomplished within a decade to form the foundation for a healthier society in the years ahead. We are confident that if this infusion of affective curricula becomes a reality in our schools, the mental health needs of children will be more fully met in both prevention and rehabilitation.

Most proponents of a psychoeducational approach to school curriculum hold some beliefs in common. They believe that some school adjustment problems result from feelings of frustration or impotence. They believe that schools, as currently structured, do not adequately recognize or meet these affective needs. They believe that the integration of affective dimensions into cognitively based curricula can alleviate the feelings of frustration and impotence. They believe that the occurrence of disruptive and disturbing pupils indicates the need for schools to recognize the affective needs of students.

THE CURRICULUM PERSPECTIVE

Traditionally, a dichotomy of responsibility and interest has existed between psychologists and teachers involved in the learning process. Psychologists have emphasized the motivational and emotional aspects of education; teachers have been primarily concerned with the development of intellect and the acquisition of knowledge.

We speculate that the various human rights struggles of the 1960s provided the catalyst for integrating the affective, "inner life" dimension with the cognitive dimension in the educational process. This theme was voiced by a number of educators and psychologists during roughly the same period (Brown, 1971; Combs, 1967; Fantini and Weinstein, 1969; Kelly, 1965; Krathwohl, Bloom, and Masia, 1964). The response to the approach advocated by these theorists was encouraging. A number of innovators developed means by which affective activities could be introduced or integrated into the school curriculum (Borton, 1970; Brown, 1971; Fagen, Long, and Stevens, 1975; Lyon, 1971; Newburg, 1969; Stenhouse, 1971).

The work of these curriculum developers in affective, confluent education is important to the understanding of psychoeducational teaching. The following discussion focuses on how these innovators addressed the affective education issue. Prior to this discussion, however, we will present a more comprehensive definition of curriculum for the sake of clarity.

Webster's Third New International Dictionary (1971) defined *curriculum* as "(a) a set of courses constituting an area of specialization; (b) all planned school activities including, besides courses of study, organized play, athletics, dramatics, clubs, and home room program." It is important to understand the differences between these two definitions. The first definition implies that a course or series of courses will be organized to enable the student to achieve a specific objective. The second implies that the attainment of an objective is a function of everything a student experiences during a school day. This distinction is important, for as we emphasize in the next section, affective educators have used both approaches to integrate affective content into the school curriculum. Several innovators (Chesler and Fox, 1966; Gardner, 1973; Lewis and Streitfeld, 1970; Long, 1974; Schrank, 1972; Shaftel and Shaftel, 1967; Simon, Howe, and Kirschenbaum, 1972; Simon and O'Rourke, 1977) have developed affective programs to be used during specific blocks of time during the school day. Other curriculum developers (Brown, 1971; Fagen, Long, and Stevens, 1975) not only suggest activities to develop affect, but also discuss many opportunities available in cognitive curricula in which affective content could be emphasized.

The important point is related to proportion. It is imperative that equal time be given to content *and* process regardless of which of the following options one chooses: (1) use of individual affective activities; (2) emphasis on affective properties of cognitive content; (3) development of formal affective curriculum units; or (4) use of prepackaged psychoeducational instructional programs.

The early definitive work of Parker and Rubin (1966) is a classic blueprint for those interested in pursuing the teaching and learning process from a psychoeducational standpoint.

Parker and Rubin contend that every process must be founded on a coherent theoretical construct — an underlying schema that provides order and direction. Any assumed contradiction between content and process is related to a difference between passive and active approaches to learning. When the emphasis is on content, the learner usually functions in the passive mode: His or her task is to respond to a higher authority. When the stress is upon process, greater importance is attached to the methods of acquisition and its subsequent utilization. Even so, the assimilation of knowledge is not obstructed. Parker and Rubin argue that attempts to separate process and content are unacceptable. They contend that we know little about the way people learn. We do know that they learn, and that they learn in different ways and at different rates. Consequently, curriculum developers must conceptualize process as the basis of content.

Units of knowledge, however, consist of only content and structure, and attempts at using knowledge as a base for developing curricula are exercises in futility. How does one choose the content that must be included in the curriculum? For Parker and Rubin, approaching curriculum development from this perspective is totally nonproductive. They sought a curriculum design model that took into account the many elements involved in learning. They cite four major requirements of a viable curriculum:

1. Because there are basic processes through which one learns, a curriculum must provide students with the opportunity to develop their capacity for assimilating new information.
2. Because there are processes for making choices and selecting from alternatives, the curriculum must provide experience in confronting issues.
3. Thinking comprises a number of processes. Consequently, the curriculum must provide opportunities for inferring, synthesizing, and apperception.
4. "Valuing" consists of a variety of affective functions, including the procedures involved in assessing, predicting foreseeing, and determining consequences.

There is a real danger in designing a curriculum that treats these points as discrete functions. Although these points have been isolated for the purpose of curriculum planning, in operations they must fuse with one another.

The integrating mechanism in the analysis of content and structure is process. Process is the key to designing a curriculum that incorporates a methodology allowing for the complete range of a student's capacities for assimilating knowledge. The significance of this process in curricula for disturbing students is illustrated in the following vignette*:

> Tom was feeling angry when he came to school today. He couldn't find his tennis shoes, so his mother made him wear his Sunday shoes. He was mad at his mother and his brother. He was convinced that Bill, his kid brother, had hidden them so Tom would get in trouble. Well, Bill was right; Tom had a yelling match with his mother. He could still remember her saying, "If you put things where they belonged, you would have your shoes! It's your own stupid fault! Now get out of here before I give you what you really deserve!" As he left the house, Tom noticed Bill was smiling.
>
> That day, school was a bore. Still thinking about what happened at home, Tom found it difficult to concentrate on his math assignment. He even had difficulty remembering his multiplication tables. After a few minutes he gave up and started poking at his paper until it was filled with pencil holes.
>
> Suddenly Ms. Benson said, "Tom, what are you doing?"
>
> "Nothing," he replied.
>
> "How can you make all that *noise* by doing nothing?" she asked.
>
> Before Tom could answer, Paul said, "He's been tearing up his arithmetic paper."
>
> "I have not," Tom shouted. "Besides, it's none of your business!"
>
> "All right," Ms. Benson said with authority, "you better quiet down before you get yourself into serious trouble! Now, whatever

* Adapted from S. A. Fagen and N. J. Long. Teaching children self-control: a new responsibility for teachers. *Focus on Exceptional Children,* January, 1976. By permission of Love Publishing Company, 1777 South Bellaire, Denver, Colorado.

you were doing, stop it, and get busy with your assignment!"

Tom could feel himself getting angry. He hated Paul and his teacher. He decided he would get Paul after school. He'd either fight him or tease him, telling him that he's a baby, a sissy, and a squealer.

As Tom was entertaining these thoughts, Paul left his desk. Impulsively, Tom stuck out his foot and tripped Paul, who yelled, "You did that on purpose!"

"I did not!" Tom yelled. "It was an accident!"

"It was not," Paul replied.

"Yes, it was!" Tom shouted.

Ms. Benson entered the battle by shouting at both of them to stop. By this time, Tom could not hear, see, or respond rationally. He called Paul a name and hit him. Ms. Benson told Tom to go to the office. He called her a bitch and ran out of the room. He did not report to the principal's office but walked around the halls until another teacher led him to the office.

This incident presents a number of interesting psychological issues. If the principal chose to manage this situation from a content perspective, his actions would probably be designed to solve one or more of the following "problems": running out of a classroom, disobeying a teacher, using profanity, teasing another student, or refusing to complete school work. The principal's actions would probably consist of a reprimand, loss of privileges, or suspension. From the process perspective, Tom will benefit little from these actions. Without an opportunity to explore the effect of prior conflict on his present behavior, Tom will probably have little understanding of how a home problem escalated into a school confrontation. By incorporating Tom in an investigation of the circumstances that led to his inappropriate actions, the principal would involve him in a process that has tremendous transfer value: inductive reasoning, the process of reasoning from the specific to the general. The ability to induce a general principle (When I get angry I have trouble paying attention) could be pieced together with other ideas (I do not like to do what others ask me to do when I am angry; I tease or yell if someone accuses me of things I should not be doing; I curse people if they do not leave me alone) to predict and explain different occurrences (I got yelled at by the principal; I got a detention; I was suspended). According to Parker and Rubin (1966), a learner grows more knowledgeable if he is sent to a laboratory, whether scientific, historical, or social, to learn the process of associating related facts or behaviors to his understanding of a phenomenon (being suspended), and then parlaying this insight into a predictable pattern of controlled activity.

In summary, the requirements of a process-based psychoeducational curriculum are as follows: (1) the identification of worthwhile processes to which students should be exposed; (2) the design of instructional strategies that use the processes effectively; and (3) the realignment of subject matter such that it complements the instructional strategies. The curriculum specialist and the school milieu should provide experiences that reflect a consensual approach to process learning. A child should be exposed to structured experiences in a variety of academic and social contexts to maximize growth potential.

This brief discussion of the unique demands of process-oriented curriculum design provides a framework for understanding and evaluating psychoeducationally oriented curricular strategies. We cannot provide a detailed review of all the relevant curricular approaches, but comprehensive presentations of psychoeducational intervention models are available from several sources (Clarizio and McCoy, 1976; Dembinski, 1978; Dupont, 1975; Long, Morse, and Newman, 1976). Morse and Munger (1975) have developed a comprehensive bibliography of major books, articles, periodicals, organizations, projects, and commercially produced curricula that emphasize affective education.

The curricular models we will describe in this section include strategies for altering student behavior that are based on basic psychoeducational principles. Some of the efforts focus on changing behavior by applying psychoeducational principles to modify academic instruction. Other efforts emphasize direct instruction of affect.

Affective Modification of Academic Instruction

Every teacher is faced with three major problems: what to teach, how to teach it, and how to evaluate the instructional process involved. Teachers of disturbed students who adopt a psychoeducational framework encounter some additional challenges. First, they must understand how learners process the material they receive. Teachers must also be adept at assessing students' individual differences, interests, and abilities. Finally, they must allow for these differences not only in what they teach, but in how they teach it. Since materials and content can be used to improve students' self-concepts, the teacher must be sure that the curriculum is relevant to the learner. The emphasis on these elements differentiates the psychoeducational perspective from most other teaching approaches.

Stiles (1976) provided some insights into the psychoeducational perspective on teaching reading and creative writing. Stiles describes the process by which she engaged Roger, a reluctant reader, in various reading activities (Long, Morse, and Newman, 1976). Her strategy was based on information obtained on a diagnostic reading test, the results of which indicated that Roger knew six initial consonant sounds. Rather than challenging Roger with a reading activity during the tutoring session, Stiles showed him a variety of objects that began with *c,* a consonant he knew. The objects included a cup, a calendar, a can, and a cat. Roger's reaction to this situation was as follows:

> On entering the room he announced, "I'm not gonna read today!"
> "That's right," I quietly assured him, "we aren't going to read today. We are going to do other things." Although this was slightly

reassuring, he was not ready to sit down and start working. As I began to rearrange the objects, he slipped into his chair asking, "Whatta ya doin' with those toys?"

"Well, I'm thinking of something that begins with *c* (giving the hard sound, not the letter name) and you can pour hot chocolate into it," I said.

His face lit up, and with a hint of superiority he said, "Oh, I know that, it's the cup." *(Stiles in Long, Morse, and Newman, 1976, p. 250)*

The remainder of the objects were similarly identified. The letter *c* was traced and then copied on paper. A picture of an object representing the consonant sound was selected from a group of pictures and pasted in a tablet. The activity was then terminated. Roger did not associate this activity with reading. He was introduced to material that he knew, that he could successfully manage, and that he could be successful with. New consonants were gradually added, and a record of his success was kept in a "consonant dictionary," a spiral notebook in which he recorded all the things he knew. Stiles offers a number of suggestions for establishing a learning sequence, for helping the student discriminate between *p, b,* and *d,* and for shared reading. In shared reading, the teacher reads portions of a story to model the appropriate use of expressions, inflections, punctuation, and pacing.

Teaching creative writing to students who have had a series of negative experiences with writing was the challenge for d'Alelio (Long, Morse, and Newman, 1976). He based his approach on the assumption that a class must enjoy literature before it can begin creative writing; that is, a teacher must provide the class with ample opportunity to listen to and discuss different forms of literature before asking the class to write. Fairy tales serve these purposes for younger students — they contain a variety of themes and are of high interest. D'Alelio suggests that discussions of a story focus on the plot, believing that most students respond to the plot of a story more readily than to the theme, character development, or style. Fairy tales also lend themselves to teaching students the progression of a story line. He proposes charting the progression of the story on the board while the students analyze its development by identifying the introduction, development, obstacles, climax, resolution, and solution. Practice at this skill is reinforced until the students need little assistance from the teacher. The use of murals and art work depicting the story line is also suggested to enhance this learning experience.

Once the children understand the plot line, they are introduced to character development. Group discussion is the means of exploring which characters are liked and disliked and how the author describes the characters to make them scary, foolish, mean, or otherwise distinctive. Open-ended discussions focus on such topics as "Are all witches bad?" "What would somebody be doing if he were living happily ever after?" and other questions. When a class becomes proficient in discussing stories, they are ready to explore style and theme. Style is approached through a combination of discussion and listing activities. The teacher may record words used by the children to describe and contrast the good and bad characters in the story. Drawing pictures of the characters is another experience that may help the child appreciate the meaning words convey. The pictures can be displayed in the classroom or can be part of a student's writing folder. It is suggested that initial writing activities be limited to labeling the characters in the picture; at some later time the children can each write a sentence describing the picture. The analysis of writing style is pursued through stories and discussion, with the children using phrases rather than words to describe characters. Discussions should focus on the advantage of using phrases rather than single words to convey meaning. At this point, adjective listing is introduced. Students might be asked to develop phrases to replace adjectives used in a sentence. For example: Theodore is a tiger who is

crafty: always on his guard

huge: big for his age

lazy: usually sleepy

Similar exercises can be adapted for adverbs: "Theodore runs quickly — as fast as the wind." Successful practice in adjective and adverb listing prepares students to grasp the complexities of sentence phrasing. Practice at breaking sentences into phrases is also required. Sentences are placed on the board without punctuation and students are asked to decide where the natural breaks occur. Telegraph messages containing no punctuation serve a similar purpose. Students can also practice reducing the length of sentences and changing the location of phrases in sentences.

The final step in this process is exploring the concept of theme. Through discussion, the children come to understand that writing is simply a way of putting ideas and feelings on paper. Theme can be introduced by comparing several stories the students have read that contain different themes — scary, funny, or sad stories, for example. Discussions focus on why people write these kinds of stories, what heroes are like, why people write about being helpful, doing good, and learning a lesson by making mistakes. The purpose of these discussions is simply to give pupils an opportunity to discover which themes they like best and what kinds of words are most appropriate for describing them. It is only at this point that d'Alelio believes students have enough confidence in themselves to actually begin writing activities.

The approaches taken by Stiles and d'Alelio are designed to make learning attractive to the typically unsuccessful student. They approach this task by recognizing learners' reluctance to engage in activities they have usually failed in. The student's emotional reaction to unsuccessful cognitive activities is as important to Stiles and d'Alelio as the student's verbal or written performance on the same tasks.

Stiles's strategy for teaching reading and d'Alelio's approach to teaching creative writing to disturbed students organize lessons around the following critical instructional steps (Fagen, Long, and Stevens, 1975):

1. Start at or below the functional level.
2. Increase difficulty by small steps.
3. Place teaching tasks in a developmental sequence.
4. Provide positive feedback.
5. Strengthen by repetition.
6. Show appreciation for real effort.
7. Enhance the value of the skill area.
8. Maintain flexibility and enjoyment.
9. Prepare for real life transfer of training.
10. Plan short, frequent, regular training sessions.

Examples of similar approaches in other subjects can be found in Berkowitz and Rothman (1955), reading; Alpher (1976), mathematics; Sprinthall (1974), psychology; and Huber (1976), games. In each case, the learning situation was designed to (1) be appealing to the learner, (2) insure some degree of success for the learner, and (3) introduce a new piece of knowledge that the learner, on the basis of his earlier successful experience, would be interested in trying to master. The key to designing these learning situations is the teacher's awareness that an unsuccessful student will be emotionally reluctant to undertake a learning task that reinforces previous failures.

Direct Affective Instruction

Rather than focus on the affective modification of academic instruction, some curriculum specialists have chosen to investigate the feasibility of direct instruction. Brown (1971) emphasizes the affective content inherent in academic curricula. Simon and O'Rourke (1977), Simon, Howe, and Kirschenbaum (1972), and Casteel and Stahl (1975) present activities for teaching values to exceptional students. Activities for fostering affective development have been developed by Dupont (1977), Glass and Griffin (1973), and Hendrichs and Roberts (1977). These curriculum approaches are of three basic types: (1) incidental instruction, (2) supplemental courses or instructional activities, and (3) teaching units (Kaplan, 1971). We describe the advantages and disadvantages of these approaches in the sections that follow.

Incidental Instruction.   This approach consists of what we call "teachable moments." Instruction occurs when problems are immediate and real, when motivation and interest are at a peak. A good example of this approach was the brain-dissecting activity described earlier. The major drawback to this approach is that the teacher needs to be sensitive to critical incidents and have a sophisticated understanding of the nuances of child development and mental health.

Supplemental Courses or Instructional Activities.   Several developers have chosen to introduce affect into the curriculum via a specific course. The "Getting It Together" series developed by Goldberg and Greenberger (1973) is an excellent example of this approach. "Getting It Together" is a multilevel, high interest, low difficulty reading text. It was designed specifically for adolescents and young adults who have limited reading ability. The purposes of the series are (1) to motivate reluctant readers to read, (2) to strengthen reading comprehension and language arts skills, and (3) to help students develop skills and attitudes useful in coping with problems stemming from peer, family, and community relationships. The series consists of fifty stories developed around the theme of life problems. The story lines revolve around events adolescents are involved and interested in, and the attitudes and feelings of adolescents toward the problems posed are emphasized.

A similar approach for preadolescents is the "Dimensions of Personality" series developed by Limbacher (1969, 1970). In the book called *Here I Am,* Limbacher's objective is to provide the elementary-aged student with insights into his or her behavior. This is accomplished through classroom experiences and the systematic presentation of mental health principles.

In the book *Becoming Myself,* Limbacher presents a series of stories and activities that require the child to examine his or her feelings and the way they influence actions. Limbacher's approach is based on the assumption that children will be more inclined to stop and think before they act if they are aware of how emotion influences their behavior.

Some investigators have chosen to promote affective instruction through supplemental activities. An example of this approach is helping students clarify the conflicts that underlie social interaction problems. These conflicts are explored with a method labeled "values clarification." Values clarification focuses not on the content of people's values, but on the process of valuing. The emphasis is on how people come to hold certain beliefs and establish certain behavior patterns (Raths, Harmin, and Simon, 1966). The goal of the values clarification approach is not to instill a particular set of values; it is to help students clarify their beliefs by acquainting them with the processes involved in making value judgments.

There are many sources for values clarification activities. Casteel and Stahl (1975) provide a primer on values clarification that includes a learning device called a "value sheet," which is used in planning and conducting activities in the classroom. Their primer presents a more formal and structured orientation and description of values activities than is found in Simon, Howe, and Kirschenbaum (1972) and Simon and O'Rourke (1977). Simon and O'Rourke discuss developing values with children who have learning and behavior problems. They supplement the values activities with an overview of the school program and specific examples of implementing a values clarification program in a special education setting.

The integration of values clarification into the school curriculum is discussed by Harmin, Simon, and Kirschenbaum (1973) and by Hawley (1973). Values clarification has been integrated into many specific content areas including science and math (Harmin, Kirschenbaum, and Simon, 1970b), history (Harmin, Kirschenbaum, and Simon, 1969), English (Kirschenbaum and Simon, 1969), writing (Hawley, Simon, and Britton, 1973), and health education (Osman, 1973).

Teaching Units.   Kaplan (1971) regards the use of units to teach mental health principles as a compromise between teaching at specific, relevant moments and offering separate courses. According to Kaplan, units can (1) be built around problems at various stages of child development, (2) become an integral part of courses already in the curriculum, and (3) provide consistent, systematic mental health instruction.

The pioneer of the unit approach is Ralph Ojemann. Ojemann's (1967) curriculum approach to mental health emphasizes a causal orientation to the social environment. His basic assumption is that a person becomes more proficient in coping with stress and crises as he or she becomes more aware and appreciative of the dynamics of human behavior. Ojemann contends that this coping skill can be developed by incorporating behavioral science concepts into a curriculum that emphasizes the causes or motivations of human behavior, as opposed to the surface or behavioral aspects.

The dynamic approach requires an attitude of flexibility and tolerance and an ability to view behavior from another person's perspective. Effective social interaction is seen as requiring greater sensitivity to interpersonal relationships. Table 7.1 contrasts the surface and causal approaches to behavior.

As soon as a child experiences a causal approach to behavior, he or she becomes better prepared to deal with present as well as future crises.

Ojemann suggests the use of stories in which the surface and causal approaches are contrasted. In the primary grades, the teacher reads the stories; in later grades, the students read them. Each story is followed by a discussion focusing on the meaning and causes of the behavior depicted in the narrative. Numerous opportunities to apply this model of behavior analysis occur in the social sciences, English literature, mathematics, and science, at both the elementary and secondary school levels.

A typical application of Ojemann's theory to public school settings is the "Dealing with the Causes of Behavior Series" developed by the Lakewood, Ohio, Public Schools and the Education Research Council of America (1972). The series consists of four books organized by grade

TABLE 7.1
THE SURFACE VERSUS THE CAUSAL APPROACH
OF THE TEACHER TO CHILD BEHAVIOR

Surface	*Causal*
1. The teacher responds to the "what" of the situation in an emotional way.	1. The teacher responds to the "why" of the situation objectively.
2. The teacher does not appear to think of the causes of behavior when he: a. responds to the action rather than to the reason for the action. b. labels behavior as "good," "bad," etc. c. makes generalizations to apply to every situation; e.g., "all boys are like that." d. responds with a stock solution or rule-of-thumb procedure; e.g., lateness is punished by staying in after school.	2. The teacher appears to be thinking of the causes of behavior when he: a. runs over in his mind possible reasons for the action. b. seeks the meaning of the behavior and avoids snap judgments or hasty interpretations. c. searches for specific and concrete clues derived from details of the behavior. d. varies the method; uses a tentative approach; i.e., will try other ways of dealing with a situation if one does not work. In seeking a solution, takes into account motivating forces and particular method used.
3. The teacher does not take into account the multiplicity and complexity of causes.	3. The teacher thinks of alternative explanations for the behavior. The proposition that behavior has many causes may be elaborated as follows: a. The same cause may result in a variety of behaviors. b. A variety of causes may result in similar behavior.
4. The teacher fails to take into account the later effects of the techniques employed and assumes the effects.	4. The teacher checks for the effects of the method he employs and considers its effects before using it.
5. The "surface" approach is characterized by a rigidity of techniques — essentially static.	5. The "causal" approach is characterized by a flexibility, a tentativeness, a trying-out technique, which accommodates new information as it is accumulated — essentially dynamic.

Source: J. D. Lafferty, D. Dennerll, and Peter Rettich. "A Creative School Mental Health Program." *National Elementary Principal* 43 (April 1964): 31. Copyright 1964, National Association of Elementary School Principals. All rights reserved.

level and topic. Teachers' manuals are available, and pre- and post-tests accompany the junior high or middle school program. The series uses several teaching techniques, including small group discussion, buzz groups, small group build-up, fish-bowling, brainstorming, sociometry, role playing, and the use of so-called killer statements.

Additional examples of the unit approach to affective development are found in the work of Dupont (1977) and Fagen, Long, and Stevens (1975). These approaches are based on assumptions somewhat different from those of the approaches described earlier.

Dupont's "Toward Affective Development" (1977) offers a Piagetian approach to affective development. In a review of Piaget's theory, Dupont indicates that these are both cognitive and affective aspects of children's attempts at accommodation. Piaget stated that these parallel transformations of affectivity and intelligence progress through four stages: (1) impersonal-autistic affectivity and sensorimotor intelligence; (2) heteronomous affectivity and preoperational intelligence; (3) interpersonal affectivity and concrete operations; and (4) autonomous affectivity and formal operations. These stages are depicted in Table 7.2.

Affect, objects, and relationships are represented in thought and internalized between stages one and two. At the heteronomous stage, affect is influenced primarily by authority-dependence relationships with the significant adults in the child's life. During the interpersonal stage, the child invests a portion of his or her affective energy in peer relationships. At the autonomous stages, the major investment of affect shifts to abstract self, other persons, ideals, values, and life plans.

Dupont's theory of affective development thus postulates age-related developmental trends in the differentiation and integration of affective responses and the stimuli that elicit them. He believes that affective development implies a structural or organizational component. He also contends that structural transformations in affect have dimensions in common with the structural development of cognition. He conceptualizes affective development as occurring in seven stages, and indicates that he has data

TABLE 7.2
PARALLEL STAGES OF COGNITIVE AND
AFFECTIVE DEVELOPMENT

Typical age period	Cognitive stage	Affective stage
0–18 months	Sensorimotor	Impersonal-autistic
18 months–3 years	Preoperational	Heteronomous-dependent
3–7 years	Preoperational	Heteronomous-opportunistic
7–12 years	Concrete operations	Interpersonal
12–15 years	Formal operations	Personal-autonomous

Source: H. Dupont. Toward affective development: teaching for personal development. Proceedings of a Conference on Preparing Teachers to Foster Personal Growth in Emotionally Disturbed Students. Minneapolis, Mn.: The University of Minnesota, 1977, p. 17.

TABLE 7.3
SEVEN STAGES OF AFFECTIVE DEVELOPMENT

Affective stage	Major referent or object	Cognitive style
Impersonal-autistic	Impersonal (undifferentiated world)	Sensorimotor
Heteronomous-dependent	Parents or mothering one	Preoperational
Heteronomous-opportunistic	Significant adults	Preoperational
Interpersonal	Peers	Concrete operations
Personal-autonomous	Abstract psychological concept of self, ideals, and values	Formal thought
Generative	Persons perceived as needing care, affective	Formal thought
Synergistic	All persons and activities	Formal thought

Source: H. Dupont. Toward affective development: teaching for personal development. Proceedings of a Conference on Preparing Teachers to Foster Personal Growth in Emotionally Disturbed Students. Minneapolis, Mn.: The University of Minnesota, 1977, p. 19.

confirming the first five stages. These stages and their major characteristics are presented in Table 7.3.

Dupont argues that the student's stage of affective development indicates which persons are invested with his or her affection. This knowledge is said to provide important clues about the best source of motivation, the best ways to group students, when to accept their need for support and direction, and when to foster group and independent learning experiences. This knowledge also enhances selection of the most relevant activities for the students.

Dupont believes that some activities contribute to stage development, whereas other activities only assume the existence of a stage. His primary goal is the identification and refinement of activities that stimulate and foster affective and cognitive growth. Dupont has attempted to achieve this goal through two programs: "Toward Affective Development I" (TAD-I) and "Toward Affective Development II" (TAD-II).

TAD-I consists of 191 activities for students between the ages of eight and twelve who are assumed to be either in the heteronomous-opportunistic stage or moving into the interpersonal stage of affective development. The program is organized into basic units. Discussion and role-playing are used in the learning process of each unit.

TAD-II consists of ninety-five activities selected or designed for students between the ages of twelve and fifteen. It is assumed that these students are either in the interpersonal stage or in transition to the personal-autonomous stage of affective development. Activities are introduced that reflect abstract formal thought processes. The abstract concepts introduced include openness and trust, feelings, needs, goals and expectations, and values. The emphasis is on developing communication and problem-solving skills. Dupont is engaged in an extensive field testing program; his work holds promise for advancing the level of affective education by matching activities to a student's level of affective development.

The final example of an affective education model is the work of Fagen, Long, and Stevens (1975). They have developed a process-oriented approach to affective skill development called the "Self-Control Curriculum." The goals of the curriculum are (1) to provide pupils with skills for coping flexibly and realistically with life situations, and (2) to teach children to have better feelings about themselves and an appreciation of the feelings of others. Self-control is defined as "one's capacity to direct and regulate personal action in a given situation flexibly and realistically" (Fagen, Long, and Stevens, 1975, p. 75).

In their model, the capacity for self-control is assumed to consist of eight integrated skill clusters, of which four are cognitive and four affective. The cognitive skills are selection, storage, sequencing and ordering, and anticipating consequences. The affective skills are appreciating feelings, managing frustration, inhibition and delay, and relaxation.

The integration of these skill clusters can be understood in the context of the following classroom incident.

> *Setting:* Math class, twenty-eight kids. Teacher gives the assignment. Students are expected to work quietly and quickly and then put their finished papers in the basket on the teacher's desk. They cannot talk during the work period.

The student gets the materials he'll need for the assignment (selection). He gets to work immediately, despite the talking and noise in the classroom (selection). The first half of the assignment is no problem, but then the word problems become more difficult. He raises his hand (managing frustrations), but the teacher is busy with other students. He'd like to ask his neighbor to help him (managing frustrations), but he wants to follow the "no talking" rule (anticipating consequences, managing frustrations). He raises his hand again (managing frustrations, inhibition and delay). The work period is almost over. If he doesn't get his math done, he'll have to finish it as homework (anticipating consequences). Tonight there is a party at his best friend's house (sequencing and ordering, storage). He won't be able to go if he has homework (anticipating consequences, appreciating feelings, managing frustrations). He raises his hand again (managing frustrations). The teacher is talking with the principal. He asks the girl next to him how to do the problem (managing frustrations, inhibition and delay). The teacher sees him and gives him a disapproving look (appreciating feelings). He tries the problem again. He still can't get it. He raises his hand (managing frustrations, inhibition and delay). The teacher calls on him (relaxation). He says he just doesn't understand how to do the problems (managing frustrations, relaxation). The teacher asks how many are having trouble with the problems. Many hands go up (appreciating feelings). The teacher decides to review the section again tomorrow and make the assignments due the following day.

The self-control skill components are organized into curriculum areas consisting of several units. Table 7.4 presents an overview of the curriculum areas and units.

Rational educational goals and suggested learning tasks are discussed for each curriculum area. Some of the teaching strategies used to enhance the development of the skill clusters are games, role playing, and lessons or discussions.

Like Dupont, Fagen and his associates are field testing their program. A self-control behavior inventory has already been developed to help teachers assess students' self-control skills; a version for students is also available (Fagen and Long, 1976a).

TABLE 7.4
THE SELF-CONTROL CURRICULUM: OVERVIEW OF CURRICULUM AREAS AND UNITS

Curriculum area	Area definition	Curriculum unit
Selection	Perceiving incoming information accurately	1. Focusing and concentration 2. Mastering figure-ground discrimination 3. Mastering distractions and interference 4. Processing complex patterns
Storage	Retaining the information received	1. Developing visual memory 2. Developing auditory memory
Sequencing and ordering	Organizing actions on the basis of a planned order	1. Developing time orientation 2. Developing auditory-visual sequencing 3. Developing sequential planning
Anticipating consequences	Relating actions to expected outcomes	1. Developing alternatives 2. Evaluating consequences
Appreciating feelings	Identifying and constructively using affective experience	1. Identifying feelings 2. Developing positive feelings 3. Managing feelings 4. Reinterpreting feeling events
Managing frustration	Coping with negative feelings resulting from obstacles to goals	1. Accepting feelings of frustration 2. Building coping resources 3. Tolerating frustration
Inhibition and delay	Postponing or restraining action tendencies	1. Controlling action 2. Developing part-goals
Relaxation	Reducing internal tension	1. Developing body relaxation 2. Developing thought relaxation 3. Developing movement relaxation

The approaches we have presented are only a few of the existing psychoeducational curricular interventions, but they are representative of the existing interventions based on psychoeducational principles. Other psychoeducational curricular models are: "The Social Learning Curriculum" (Goldstein, 1969), the "Magic Circle Technique" (Bessell and Palomares, 1973), "Developing Understanding of Self and Others" (Dinkmeyer, 1970), "Child's Series on Psychologically Relevant Themes" (Fassler, 1971), "First Things" (Grannis and Schone, 1970), "Freedom Books" (Martin, 1970), "The Adventures of Lollipop Dragon" (Society for Visual Education, 1970), "Maturity: Growing Up Strong" (Scholastic Book Services, 1972), "Target Behavior" (Kroth, 1973), and the "Coping with Series" (Schwartzrock and Whenn, 1973).

The interest in exploring the relationship between the cognitive and affective dimensions of behavior is reflected in the diverse work of these developers. Each has a slightly different perspective. Some emphasize academic content as the vehicle for exploring affective behaviors; others focus on exploring a variety of developmental and skill components. All of these developers claim the work is exciting and state that it holds great potential for future curricula. But does their enthusiasm match their claims for potential success with these programs? This question is considered in the next section.

EVALUATING PSYCHOEDUCATIONAL CURRICULA

The test of any curricular approach is whether it yields significant results. Student knowledge, performance, behavior, or all three should be improved by a series of learning activities. The success of psychoeducationally oriented curricula in altering student behavior is a function of several factors: the appropriateness and relevance of the learning activities, the teacher's skill in organizing the learning environment, and the degree to which the student applies the new knowledge or skills in his or her everyday problem-solving situations. These factors present many complex evaluation issues.

Student knowledge and behavior can be assessed during a course of study, after it, or both. Assessing the application of knowledge to life experiences is much more difficult. The problem is compounded by the fact that psychoeducational curricula deal with affect, which is a rather ambiguous concept to many people. Krathwohl, Bloom, and Masia (1964) point out that educational objectives in the affective domain tend to be statements of desirable but undefined virtues. They argue for the development of affective objectives to complement the objectives in the cognitive domain, which are much better understood. Based on this position and others, we have identified two critical evaluation issues: (1) How can curriculum implementation be effectively evaluated? and (2) Can an operational definition of "affect" be developed?

Evaluating Implementation

Reports of psychoeducational interventions have typically dealt with either case studies or group research. Each format has its advantages and disadvantages. The case study format enables the investigator to systematically describe in detail the unique facets of the subject, the program, the manner in which the program was presented, changes in the subject's performance, and other significant information. The case study approach also lends itself to the systematic measurement procedures used by proponents of the behavioral model. A major criticism of the case studies reported in the psychoeducational literature is that they rely on perceived change rather than measured behavioral changes in student behavior.

The major advantage of group studies is that they enable the investigator to evaluate changes in many students on a variety of variables. The major disadvantage of the approach is that the data reflect mean changes for the group. Great variations in the effectiveness of the approach with different students may not be evident.

A typical report evaluating the implementation of curricula in group settings includes several components. The rationale of the model is given, and descriptions are provided of the teachers and subjects, the selection of treatment groups, procedures, and the learning materials and experiences used. Comparison data and conclusions are also given. There are many such studies that evaluate changes in student problem-solving behavior or self-concept as a result of some type of curricular intervention (Griggs and Bonney, 1970; Hartshorn and Brantley, 1973; Mantz, 1969; Schulman, Ford, and Busk, 1973; Schulman et al., 1973).

In a comprehensive review of the research on curriculum implementation, Fullen and Pomfret (1977) raise serious questions about current strategies for evaluating the implementation of curricula. They address several points that are directly relevant to the evaluation of psychoeducational curricula. First, they present a rationale for studying implementation. Second, they discuss the problem of defining and measuring implementation. Finally, they identify many specific determinants of the success of implementation.

Implementation is the actual use of a technique. In practice implementation may differ from its intended use and from the initiating decision because circumstances may make some techniques ineffective and require change. The reviewers cite four reasons for examining implementation:

1. To identify what has changed.
2. To understand why educational changes fail to become established when this occurs.
3. To avoid confusing implementation with other aspects of the change process (such as adoption — the decision to use an innovation) or with the determinants of implementation.
4. To more easily interpret learning outcomes and to relate these to possible determinants.

Implementation studies assume one of two major perspectives. One perspective is to determine the extent to which actual use corresponds to intended or planned use. This is called a *fidelity perspective*. The other perspective, the *process perspective,* focuses on analyzing the complexities of how innovations develop or change during the process of implementation.

Fullen and Pomfret (1977) suggest that curriculum change can occur in five areas: (1) subject matter or materials, (2) organizational structure, (3) role or behavior, (4) knowledge and understanding, and (5) value internalization.

Subject matter consists of the content that the teacher is expected to transmit or that the students are expected to acquire, the order in which this content is to be transmitted or acquired, and the medium by which the content is to be transmitted.

Organizational structure refers to formal arrangements and physical design. Changes include different ways of grouping students, alternative space and time arrangements, the presence of new personnel, and the supply of new materials.

Role or *behavior* indices assess changes in teaching style, including alterations in planning and curriculum development roles and new role relationships between teachers and students, teachers and administrators, and teachers and consultants. The essential issue here "is to conceptualize and operationalize teacher behavior in such a way that the effects of change in one role upon another are monitored and not assumed" (Fullen and Pomfret, 1977, p. 363).

The fourth factor in implementation evaluation refers to teachers' knowledge and understanding of the innovation's components: its philosophy, values, assumptions, objectives, organizational components, subject matter, and role relationships.

The fifth factor is valuing. Valuing refers to the teacher's commitment to implementing the curriculum. The reviewers caution that a teacher's valuing an innovation does not mean that the implementation will occur. Teachers may choose not to value an innovation, not because they think its purpose is unimportant, but because they have been frustrated by the process of implementation.

A number of critical evaluation questions were also identified by Fullen and Pomfret as essential to implementing the proposed innovation. How extensive, explicit, and continuous is the training program for the teachers? How much and what types of materials, resources, and time are available to teachers? What kind of feedback, if any, is available to the teachers from consultants and peers? Do teachers participate in the development process, implementation process, or both? Do evaluation criteria differentiate between quality of use and degree of implementation even though the frequency of use is the same between teachers?

A series of questions was also developed to identify units (schools, classes) who might be inclined to adopt innovations. These were: (1) Were the participating teachers volunteers? (2) Were they free to accept or reject the innovation? (3) What were their initial reactions? (4) Were these reactions expressed? (5) What are the demographic characteristics of the adopting units — the social class, level of schooling, and characteristics of individual staff members? (6) Was the unit urban or rural? Are there any design issues? For example, did the experimental group consist of volunteers and the control groups of those who were not? (7) Did incentives play a role in the program's adoption and implementation? For example, was implementation a political decision in which teachers had no input? (8) Was implementation an added responsibility for the participating teachers, or were adjustments made in their usual responsibilities?

It is reasonable to expect curriculum innovators to recognize these evaluation issues and incorporate them into the design of implementation evaluation. Although the questions appear straightforward, they reflect the complexities involved in developing and refining evaluation strategies. How, for example, does one objectively differentiate between a teacher who comprehensively implements a curriculum and a teacher who implements only a limited version of what is expected by the program designer? These two teachers might very well produce different effects.

Evaluating Affect

The second major evaluation issue involves developing an operational definition of affect. The curricular approaches discussed earlier were based on the assumption of a common definition; that is, they proposed that affect is reflected in a series of skills, activities, and issues that the student experiences. Generally, these skills, activities, and issues include such concepts as coping with frustration; understanding aggression, violence, and protest; understanding the real self; assessing personal priorities; understanding interpersonal relationships; decision making; and recognizing and labeling feelings.

The various developers have tried to reflect these considerations in the learning experiences they have designed. The degree to which these concepts have been operationally defined varies widely. It appears that the more recent programs such as Dupont's "Toward Affective Development" and the Fagen, Long, and Stevens's "Self-Control Curriculum" reflect a more sophisticated effort in this respect.

These programs are not without their problems, however. In the Self-Control Behavior Inventory (SCBI) that accompanies the "Self-Control Curriculum," for example, Fagen, Long, and Stevens (1975) use the following referents, among others, to describe appreciating feelings and managing frustration:

Expresses Feelings Through Acceptable Words and Behavior (Appreciating Feelings)

Can use words to describe feelings (e.g., looks sad, happy, angry, etc.).

Can express own feelings in words (e.g., expresses feelings of loneliness, anger, happiness, etc.).

Seeks help or substitute activities when strongly upset rather than displaying gross outbursts or marked withdrawal (e.g., calls for teacher; asks to change task or situation rather than blowing up).

Is not hypersensitive.

Manages External Frustrations While Working on an Assignment (Manages Frustration)

Can accept obstacles placed in way (e.g., persists on task even when faced with outside interference, does not strike back or withdraw quickly when faced with difficulty).

Can accept disappointment (e.g., seems to understand and maintain control when not able to get own way; does not become overly distressed when let down by others).

Can continue working effectively even after interruption or interference (e.g., returns to drawing a picture after others have teased about it). *(Fagen, Long, and Stevens, pp. 254–255)*

In an investigation of the reliability of the SCBI, Dembinski (1979) obtained some interesting responses from regular and special class teachers utilizing this inventory. Although regular class teachers found the descriptors adequate for their rating purposes, special class teachers indicated they were too vague. An attempt was then made to formulate self-control skills in behavioral referents that could be more easily observed and evaluated (Dembinski and Tull, 1977). Two of the affective skills, appreciating feelings and managing frustration, were made operational as follows:

Appreciating Feelings

1. Can label the feelings he or she has with specific words.
2. Can verbally describe the circumstances that precipitate him or her to respond the way he or she does in various situations.
3. Can verbally and tactually express affection, displeasure, and dissatisfaction in an appropriate manner toward another person in a controlled situation such as role playing.
4. Can verbally and tactually express affection, displeasure, or dissatisfaction in an appropriate manner toward others.

Managing Frustration

1. Can verbally describe how he or she feels when not allowed to say or do what he or she wants to.
2. Can label feelings of frustration.
3. Can recognize verbal or physical expressions of frustrations in others.
4. Can identify the frequent sources of his or her frustrations.
5. Can recognize the need to relieve frustration.

6. Can act in such a way to reduce or release frustration.
7. Can verbally describe how he or she feels after acting to relieve or reduce frustration.
8. Can verbally state if others perceive the behavior or response to frustration as appropriate or inappropriate.
9. Can acknowledge that there are alternate responses for relieving or reducing frustrations.
10. Can develop alternate responses for relieving or reducing frustrations.
11. Can list appropriate alternative responses for relieving or reducing frustration in a controlled situation such as role playing.
12. Can act out an appropriate alternative to reduce or relieve frustration in a controlled situation.
13. Can act appropriately to reduce or relieve frustration.
14. Can accept feelings or frustration as normal.

Efforts to determine the efficacy of this particular approach are presently undergoing evaluation. We have identified several problems inherent in this approach, however. The first has to do with the process of assessing skills. For example, can teacher ratings be used, or should independent observers complete the ratings? Affective skills do not lend themselves easily to time-sampling observation systems, because students display these behaviors over an extended period of time and in a variety of situations. Thus, an argument can be made for relying on teacher assessment rather than on independent observers. An alternative would be to design specific tasks for each behavioral referent and have an independent observer present the task and subsequently evaluate the student's response. This approach also has limitations, however; a student may display the behavior in the controlled situation but not in an applied setting. Does this mean the student still has a skill deficit? Disturbed students display appropriate affect at some times and not at others. As you can see, evaluation of affect is quite challenging; curriculum innovators must be able to demonstrate positive change in appropriate affective responses by their students.

Status of Curriculum Implementation

Given the complexity of evaluation issues, an important consideration is the validity of current psychoeducational curricula evaluation efforts. The assessment of validity raises two questions. First, how should one judge the efficacy of integrating affect into academic curricula (the Stiles and d'Alelio approaches)? The second question has to do with the separate course approach versus the unit approach to affective development (the "Getting It Together" series, "Dimension of Personality" series, values clarification, Ojemann's causal orientation, "Dealing with the Causes of Behavior" series, "The New Model — Me," Dupont's "Toward Affective Development," and the "Self-Control Curriculum."

Two research approaches are currently available to demonstrate curriculum efficacy: single subject designs and group designs. Investigators applying psychoeducational interventions have used both. As indicated earlier, case study approaches lend themselves to single-subject design strategies. However, the application of design schema to psychoeducational interventions is a function of the ingenuity of the investigator. It is possible that data from single subject evaluations may enable psychoeducators to generate more efficient models by which they can investigate the complexity of change in affect.

Group-oriented research models are a second evaluation model available to psychoeducational researchers. The purpose of this chapter, however, is not to review group design models; it is, rather, to determine if psychoeducational curricular models satisfy basic evaluation criteria.

Table 7.5 is a model for determining whether the approaches meet the evaluation issues discussed previously. Construction of this table involved listing the fidelity and process issues and the factors identified as the determinants in the discussion on innovation. The curricular approaches were also reviewed to determine if they addressed the appropriate evaluation criteria. A word of caution is in order, however, because only a limited number of psychoeducational approaches were represented. Another important qualification concerns whether a particular curricular approach met the stated criteria as determined by the information contained in the publications available to the authors and the number of publications reviewed; other sources that would alter the evaluation profile of a particular approach may be available in the literature. The evaluation options we have presented are only suggestive of the evaluation issues psychoeducational investigators might consider. Our purpose is two-fold: (1) to present the evaluation procedures available, and (2) to indicate the current status of curriculum programs in relation to the recommended evaluation criteria.

A review of the information in Table 7.5 yields several observations. First, psychoeducational curriculum approaches have emphasized the fidelity and process issues in their evaluation reports. They have either ignored or not reported on the evaluation criteria pertaining to the determinants of innovation. Second, the programs that introduce affective elements into academic instruction appear to satisfy the fidelity and process issues to a greater degree than the direct affective instructional approaches. We attribute this trend to the fact that the academic approaches are highly individual and specific to the developer. The direct affective instruction approaches, by their nature, are controlled more by a manual of instructions than by any particular individual. A third observation is the apparent negligence of most programs in reporting participation, adoption, environment, support, demographic, design, and political complexity issues. We believe these issues are critical to an integrated evaluation process. Curricular models are developed in response to an identified need, and they should

TABLE 7.5
SCHEMA FOR PSYCHOEDUCATIONAL CURRICULUM EVALUATION

Curricular implementation studies / Affect in academics	Fidelity and process issues							Determinants of innovation									
	Subject matter components	Organizational structure	Role-behavior indices	Knowledge and understanding	Valuing and commitment	Explicitness	Complexity	In-service training	Resource support	Feedback mechanisms	Participation	Adoption process	Environmental support	Demographic factors	Design questions	Evaluation	Political complexity
1. Stiles, 1976	X	X	X	X	X	X	X									?	
2. d'Alelio, 1976	X	X	X	X	X	X	X									?	
1. Getting it together / Goldberg and Greenberger, 1973	X	X	?	?	?	?	?										
2. Dimensions of personality / Limbacher, 1969	X	X	?	?	?	?	?										
3. Values clarification / Lockwood, 1978	X	X	?	?	?	X	X	?			?				?	?	
4. Causal approach / Ojemann, 1967	X	X	?	?	?	X	X	?			?				X	X	
5. Dealing with causes of behavior; The new model-Me Series, 1972	X	X	?	?	?	X	?		?								
6. Toward affective development / Dupont, 1977	X	X	?	?	?	X	X	?	?	?					?	?	
7. Self-control curriculum / Fagen and Long, 1975	X	X	?	?	?	X	X	?	?	?					?	?	

X denotes that the criterion is discussed in the curriculum description or in other sources.

? denotes that the criterion is alluded to but not systematically discussed.

A blank space indicates either the criterion was not discussed or information regarding the criterion was not reviewed.

reflect the available resources and idiosyncratic nature of the setting in which they were developed. These are important issues to present to a reviewer considering adoption of a particular curriculum. The efficacy of any program is in part determined by the extent to which the developer meets the objectives of those who adopt the program.

SUMMARY

In this chapter, we have attempted to provide a concise yet comprehensive view of instructional programming for emotionally disturbed children from a psychoeducational perspective. The key elements of our position are as follows:

1. The psychoeducational approach tries to involve the whole child in the educational process.

2. The psychoeducational approach posits a circular interactive process between thinking, feeling, and doing in human behavior.

3. The psychoeducational approach views the quality of the student-teacher relationship as an important part of the effort to change the behavior of disturbed children.

4. The psychoeducational approach views the teacher as a central figure in developing and orchestrating a therapeutic educational environment for disturbed children.

5. The psychoeducational approach suggests that all human behavior is relevant and meaningful. Thus, the purview of education is broadened to include child, teacher, and environmental transactions as potential teaching and learning encounters.

6. The psychoeducational approach tends to stress a process approach to instruction. Thus, it tends to dwell on *how* instruction has occurred as well as *what* instruction has consisted of for a person.

7. The psychoeducational approach makes use of such elements of instruction as affective education, art and music therapy, drama and dance, and therapeutic recreation in developing an individual educational plan. Each of these instructional subjects encourages the intuitive, creative, and imaginative side of the human organism — important considerations in teaching disturbed children who are often too concrete in their cognitive functioning.

It is the interaction of these elements, as expressed through the teacher and the environment of the classroom, that constitutes the "magic" of teaching from a psychoeducational perspective. The interplay of these processes reflects the essence of the model. The search for new ways to refine techniques and evaluate progress with this approach to teaching, curriculum development, and implementation is a viable educational need and a central challenge to those espousing such an orientation to human behavior.

APPLIED STRATEGIES

In Part IV, three strategies relevant to the education of the emotionally disturbed child are described. The strategies are practical applications of established theories. Chapter 8, by Wood, Spence, and Rutherford presents the social learning curriculum. Based on behavioral theory, it is heavily influenced by the work of Bandura.

In Chapter 9, Wood, Swan, and Newman present the developmental therapy model. This model has its foundations in psychodynamic theory. It uses developmental stages to identify appropriate tasks and activities for the disturbed child in the educational program. The strategies are designed to assist the child on a day-to-day basis.

Chapter 10, by Alexander, Kroth, Simpson, and Poppelreiter, discusses the importance of working with the parents of emotionally disturbed children. These authors emphasize the constructive role parents can play through positive involvement with their child. A number of techniques for achieving this involvement are discussed.

Chapter 8

An Intervention Program for Emotionally Disturbed Students Based on Social Learning Principles

Frank H. Wood
University of Minnesota

with

Joyce Spence
Mental Health for Children, Inc.
Eugene, Oregon

Robert B. Rutherford, Jr.
Arizona State University

GUIDING PRINCIPLES

Historical and Theoretical Roots

The intervention program described in this chapter draws its conceptual rationale from the writings of a group of behavioral and cognitive psychologists who have focused on discovering factors important in learning social behavior and using the understanding thus gained to modify disordered social behavior. In establishing a rationale, we have drawn most heavily from the writings of Bandura (1969, 1977b) and Mischel (1973), Mahoney (1974), and Meichenbaum (1977), which have stimulated ideas about the handling of specific issues. Although each of these psychologists has contributed to the development of what we will call "social learning theory," a body of concepts which relates environmental and personal (cognitive) events with behavior, they by no means share a fully unified point of view. For this reason, and because the label "social learning theory" has been used in different ways by various psychologists and educators, we will explain its meaning in some detail in relation to the proposed intervention program. Bandura (1977b) has been seeking to develop a comprehensive general social learning theory which includes cognitive variables but maintains its roots in behavioral psychology. Because of Bandura's more extensive conceptualizing, and because he has been especially concerned with applying his understanding of how social behavior is learned to the problem of disordered behavior, his conceptualizations are particularly useful to special teachers of seriously emotionally disturbed students. The conceptual rationale for the interventions discussed in this chapter comes from our application of the principles put forward by Bandura and the other authors we mention in our own teaching. Thus, this chapter reflects our personal interests and concerns as well as the idiosyncrasies of our personal decoding and encoding processes.

Optimal Personal Development

The social learning theorists we mentioned have a pragmatic, utilitarian attitude toward personal development. The "optimally functioning person" is one whose interactions with the environment produce a satisfying surplus of rewarding or reinforcing[1] consequences over the number of punishing or aversive consequences. The optimal balance will vary for the individual according to the limits set by a particular environment and the person's characteristics. This definition does not presuppose a standard "type" of optimal personal behavior. If anything, it assumes a great variance in the permitted "optimal" behavior of different persons, both in the same setting and across different settings.

Theorists recognize that people's behavior changes as they mature physically and accumulate experiences through interacting with their environments. However, they tend to deny the utility of organizing generalizations about such changes into the "stages" conceptualized by developmental theorists. Bandura (1977b, pp. 43–45), for example, argues strongly against stage theories. Rejecting the common yardstick provided by a stage theory hierarchy with its assumptions of "maturity" and "immaturity" as one basis for evaluating the appropriateness of behavior, social learning theorists typically evaluate behavior through the value judgments of persons in positions of social power or through a person's self-verbalizations of dissatisfaction with his or her own behavior.

Disordered behavior is (1) behavior which is disturbing to another in a position of power over the behaver to such a degree that the disturbed person plans and implements a program of environmental change intended

---

[1] We might note that "reinforcement" is used here in its specific behavioral sense, meaning an event that increases the frequency of occurrence of the behavior it follows. Likewise, a "punishing" or "aversive" consequence is defined empirically as one that decreases the frequency of occurrence of the behavior it follows. Like Bandura (1977b, pp. 17–18), we stress the informative, feedback function of reinforcement rather than its mechanistic, hedonistic function.

to terminate the disturbing behavior; or (2) behavior so disturbing to the individual behaver that he or she makes efforts to change. Social learning theorists speak of self-satisfaction and dissatisfaction, self-management, and self-reinforcement or punishment, but they typically avoid using the term "emotional disturbance" without carefully describing the behavior from which it is inferred. Thus, the goal of social learning theorists in working with disordered behavior is to replace it with behavior that (1) will be reinforced by the environment, including significant other persons in that environment, and (2) will be accompanied by verbal self-reports of satisfaction. For the sake of consistency, the authors of this and most other chapters in this book refer to the group of students served as "emotionally disturbed," but our emphasis will be on the disordered, disturbing behavior that is the basis for inferences about emotional disturbance.

Sequentially ordered lists of behaviors serve a structuring function in a social learning curriculum somewhat analogous to that served by sequences of developmental stages in developmentally based curriculums. The ordering of the sequences is dictated by instructional considerations, the optimal sequence being that which seems to produce the most rapid progress by learners. Behaviors may be clustered by "levels," but these functional groups lack the significance of developmental stages and are not related to chronological age.

Special Education for the Seriously Emotionally Disturbed

According to this social learning conceptualization, students are placed in special education programs and labeled "emotionally disturbed" when their social behavior is so displeasing ("disturbing") to parents, teachers, or others in positions of dominance over them that these others develop and implement plans to suppress the disturbing behavior or replace it with behavior that is more pleasing to them. It is recognized that the social and ethical correctness of this procedure is subject to debate, but we believe it is an accurate description of present practice in American schools. Thus, from the perspective of social learning theory, special education programs have three fundamental objectives: (1) to control or eliminate the student's disapproved behavior; (2) to prompt and reinforce the performance of approved behavior already in the student's repertoire; and (3) to teach approved behavior not yet learned. After discussing some key concepts from social learning theory that can be applied in such a program, we will give examples of various components of a social learning intervention program for emotionally disturbed students.

Some Key Principles of Social Learning Theory

In this section, we will introduce seven key principles from social learning theory to guide the development and implementation of a social learning intervention program for seriously emotionally disturbed students. The principles serve to organize clusters of related social learning concepts.

Principle 1. *Behavior occurs in a continuously interactive system.* Human behavior develops and occurs in a continuously interactive system. The factors interacting together are many and complex, but we shall be guided by Bandura's suggestion that the most important fall into three clusters: "personal factors," "environmental factors," and "behavior" itself (1977b, pp. 9–10). Bandura characterizes the interaction among these clusters as one of "reciprocal determinism," which is to say that any change in one produces changes in the other two. By including the personal characteristics cluster, Bandura's model conceptually accommodates the common observation of a variety of responses to the same or similar environmental settings by different persons more easily than a simple S–R model. Kauffman (1979) has recently discussed the interaction of these three factors in problem behavior from the viewpoint of a special educator.

Both Bandura (1977b) and Mischel (1973) have undertaken detailed discussions of variables hypothesized to make up the personal factors cluster. For the purposes of developing a simplified model to guide us in decision-making in the social learning curriculum, we will limit ourselves to speaking of the "thoughts" and "feelings" that accompany behavior, thus hypothesizing "cognitive" and "affective" aspects of the person. Particularly important as antecedents of behavior are the learner's personal "responsiveness" to a setting, the learner's "expectancy" regarding different options for behaving and the likelihood that they will be rewarded in that setting, and his or her general "plans" for behavior. Also singled out for emphasis are several aspects of personal thoughts and feelings about consequent events: the learner's sensitivity to "vicarious" reinforcement or punishment, that is, the effects of observing another person being reinforced or punished following a behavior of the learner's own future behavior, and the use of self-reinforcement or punishment, rewarding or punishing oneself for one's own behavior. The inclusion of these personal factors in an interactive model provides a conceptual basis for describing and planning to support or change the highly variable and atypical behavior that special educators observe in emotionally disturbed students.

Principle 2. *Cognitive and affective factors are hypothesized to play an important role in human behavior, but observable actions remain our primary data.* This statement reinforces a viewpoint already implicit in our discussion of the first principle. Social learning theorists conceptualize behavior as occurring in relationship to specifiable antecedent conditions and consequent events. Paralleling the familiar behavioral sequence (antecedent conditions → behavior → consequent events), social learning theorists hypothesize a stream of cognitive and affective behavior, previously referred to as "thoughts" and "feelings." The inclusion of such variables, which are not directly observable but must be inferred from the observation of other behavior, including verbal self-reports, has caused these social learning psychologists to be strongly criticized by some other behavioral psychologists. Those interested in pursuing that theoretical debate in greater detail are referred to discussions by Howell (1978, 1979); Mahoney (1977); Wolpe (1978); Bandura (1978); and Deitz (1978). Regardless of one's position on the theoretical issues, we believe the practical utility of attending to such factors has been demonstrated in clinical practice by Bandura (1969), Mahoney (1974), and Meichenbaum (1977), among others.

A knowledge of the existence of this debate does remind us of the difficulty of obtaining valid data on cognitive and affective processes. The behavioral roots of the social learning position should clearly bias us toward using directly observable behavior as our primary data, always seeking to anchor inferences about covert behavior to observable behavior. Put more concretely, we observe a student's behavior and note, as part of the record, his or her verbal explanation of perceptions about and response to the setting, expectancies regarding the adequacy of his or her performance and the probable consequences, and sensitivity to vicarious or self-reinforcement. To the student's verbal commentary, we may wish to add our own inferences about thoughts and feelings, but these comments are secondary to the record of the student's observed behavior. We do not label Bobby "emotionally disturbed" without describing in detail the specific verbal and nonverbal actions on which we base our inferential judgment. Inferences without the accompanying record of observed behavior are an inadequate foundation for a social learning intervention.

Principle 3. *For purposes of analysis and planning, it is useful to speak of fundamental "behavior-contingency units."* Such units are pieces picked from the stream of behavior and "frozen" for analysis. They assist our development of instructional plans by making it easier to conceptualize how behavior may change if projected changes are made in antecedent and consequent events. The term "behavior-contingency units" is borrowed from Mischel (1973). He speaks of focusing on "the individual's cognitive activities and behavior patterns, studied in relation to the specific conditions that evoke, maintain, and modify them and which they, in turn, change" (p. 265). For the purposes of the teacher using a social learning curriculum, the concept of a behavior-contingency unit (BCU) has been diagrammed as shown in Table 8.1. The two dimensions of the figure are the $A \rightarrow B \rightarrow C$ behavioral sequence and the observable and inferred factors related to behavior. The variables included in the six cells were discussed under the first two principles. An example of the application of this figure to the analysis of disturbing behavior will be presented later in this chapter.

Principle 4. *Much social behavior is learned by observing the behavior of real or symbolic models.* Demonstrating this principle and analyzing the effects of varying such contingent events as the reward received by the

TABLE 8.1
A SOCIAL LEARNING BEHAVIOR-CONTINGENCY UNIT

	Antecedent factors	*Behavior*	*Consequent events*
May be known directly through observation	Setting factors	Observable behavior Verbalizations Nonverbal actions	External reinforcement/ punishment
May be known indirectly through inference based on observation	Personal factors Learner "responsive- ness" Learner "expectan- cies" Learner "plans"	Covert Behavior (not observable by ordinary methods) "Thinking" "Feeling"	Vicarious reinforcement/ punishment Self-reinforcement/ punishment

model, the social status or other personal characteristics of the model, and the conditions under which the observer is given a chance to reproduce the model's behavior have been a major focus of Bandura's research (1969, 1975). Since the selection process in our educational system ensures that special educators are better than the average person at learning through written descriptions of real situations, we tend to forget that the most efficient learning conditions for many students involve opportunities to observe directly and imitate the behavior of others. Applying this idea to social learning interventions involves giving students opportunities to observe approved social behavior, directing students' attention to such behavior and the rewards it receives, and permitting students to practice the behaviors in a supported situation before expecting them to produce them in their usual environment. Cognitive processing of abstract verbal material plays an important supportive role in this learning for students who are competent in its use (McLeskey, Rieth, and Polsgrove, 1980), but it does not receive the primary emphasis it receives in intervention programs that stress cognitive interventions like the "life space interview" (Redl, 1959; Morse, 1963).

Principle 5. *A key instructional tool for social learning interventions is the restructuring of the special program environment to elicit and reinforce the social behavior the teacher wishes the student to learn and use.* Although social learning theorists recognize that two people placed in the same environment will seldom behave identically, they stress that the manipulation of environmental contingencies is our most effective tool for reducing variability in behavior. Mischel (1973), for example, says "psychological 'situations' and 'treatments' are powerful to the degree that they lead all persons to construe the particular events the same way, induce *uniform* expectancies regarding the most appropriate response pattern, provide adequate incentives for the performance of that response pattern, and instill the skills necessary for its satisfactory construction and execution" (p. 276). In social learning interventions, it is the task of special teachers to create instructional situations that are powerful in the sense described by Mischel; that is, in which environmental contingencies guide students to produce and maintain approved social behavior. In some cases, the desired performance already exists in the repertoire of the student, and the teacher's problem is to elicit its performance. In other cases, the desired behavior must be taught.

Principle 6. *The goal of social learning interventions is to have students learn, produce, and practice approved behavior at all times.* Some psychodynamic or psychoeducational curricula include activities that permit or encourage the expression of strong emotion by students, guided by the theoretical assumption that "bottling up" feelings produces intrapsychic damage so serious that their release through almost any behavior is therapeutic. The social learning assumption is that such behavior is counterproductive. Why practice behavior that causes one to be labeled as "emotionally disturbed"? In social learning interventions, activities are planned to encourage and support the expression of feelings in socially acceptable ways at all times. Thus, the special teacher designs and structures situations to make it difficult for strong emotions to be expressed in socially disapproved ways; at the same time, the teacher helps students practice socially approved behavior planned to remove the presumed "causes" of those feelings. At other times, approved behavior incompatible with the disapproved behavior is taught on the assumption that if it is sufficiently satisfying to the student, he or she can give up the disapproved behavior without harm.

Principle 7. *Generalization of approved behavior is planned.* The appropriately "powerful" instructional situations created by the teacher may be very different from the situations of the student's usual environment. Behavior learned and practiced in such special settings may not generalize to the everyday environment if the differences are too great (Stokes and Baer, 1977). Social learning theory suggests several ways of dealing with this problem. Meichenbaum (1977) has shown that teaching students cognitive self-regulatory strategies facilitates greater generalization in some cases. Generalization is also facilitated if the special setting is gradually altered to more closely resemble the "real world"; the maintenance of the approved behavior is monitored during such alterations. Special teachers can also work with others to modify destructive or nonsupportive real world environments, but they must remember that their first responsibility is to help the student learn the approved behavior in the special setting.

If the student could have learned the behavior in the regular setting, his or her placement in the special program was premature and inappropriate. The teacher's second responsibility is to help the student use newly learned behavior appropriately in regular settings.

A SOCIAL LEARNING INTERVENTION PROGRAM

The general goal of this social learning intervention program is to elicit and support the performance of approved social behavior in school situations through the establishment of an appropriate educational environment. In teaching to achieve this goal, teachers assess behavior, plan and implement interventions, and evaluate the resulting behavioral changes. These skills will be illustrated in this section of the chapter.

The focus in our discussion is on nonacademic social behavior in school situations, since this is the primary area of difficulty for students labeled "seriously emotionally disturbed." However, a broad definition of social behavior includes skills educators categorize as academic, such as reading and mathematics. Research on social learning has demonstrated that learning can occur through the learner's observation of the behavior of others without any observable performance by the learner, but it is assumed throughout this discussion that an observable performance is necessary to confirm that learning has occurred. Such a performance should be real rather than symbolic. If, for example, the desired performance is "appropriate participation in a group discussion," a verbal (symbolic) description of appropriate participation in a group discussion would not be considered a confirming performance — unless, of course, the objective was *verbally describing* appropriate participation in a group discussion."

Assessment of Behavior

In planning social learning interventions, the teacher is interested in both approved or "positive" behavior and disapproved or "negative" behavior. The central focus of the teacher's analysis is the BCU, a segment of positive or negative behavior in temporal association with its presumed antecedents and consequences. Specifying the behavior of interest, or "target behavior," is the key to beginning an analysis based on the BCU. Thoughts and feelings, the covert cognitive and affective behaviors that accompany an observable performance, as well as antecedent factors and consequent events, are defined in relation to a specific observed behavior. Thus, the first step in assessing student behavior is to define the target behaviors that have priority for educational planning. Once the target behaviors have been defined, related setting factors, thoughts and feelings, and consequent events can be observed and described.

Defining Target Behaviors. The definition of a target behavior is based on observation of the student. F. H. Wood (1980) has discussed a variety of observation procedures useful to classroom teachers, ranging from a simple checklist to frequency records and the use of different time intervals for recording. Examples of two procedures that may be used, a skill sequence checklist and an interval observation schedule, will be discussed here.

The typical skill sequence checklist includes an extensive list of behavior patterns that are checked off by an observer as "characteristic" or "not characteristic" of the student observed to form a summary record of a relatively long period of observation. Although such a checklist can also be completed more frequently (daily or hourly), the typical checklist is both extensive and general and lists many patterns of behavior that are not relevant to the needs of a given student or a particular program. Here is one strategy for making a checklist that will be more useful:

1. Develop a list of task skills of positive social behavior patterns.
2. Arrange the skills in an ordered list that reflects a logical task sequence, moving from basic or simple skills to more complex patterns that incorporate several skills.
3. Start at the beginning of the list and check off the skills demonstrated by the student you are rating. Eventually, you will reach the point at which listed skills are not being performed by the student at an acceptable frequency.
4. Choose the first five or six missing skills as objectives for instruction and maintain a daily summary record of their performance by the student, only periodically checking the student's overall level of skill development against the entire list.

Note that a set of negative or disapproved behaviors is defined implicitly in this process.

Task or skill sequence checklists of this type can be made quite specific and fitted to the characteristics of particular groups of students. The general strategy is not unique to the social learning or any other conceptual model, although the wording of behavior descriptions and their arrangement reflects the developer's perspective.

This procedure was used by M. M. Wood and her colleagues in the development of the Developmental Therapy Objectives Rating Form (DTORF) (1975b, 1979), which is described in Chapter 9, as well as in many individually administered "tests" (checklists) of intelligence and academic and social skills. Although the DTORF items are grouped into developmental stages, the measure has many characteristics of a skill sequence and can if desired be modified for that purpose. Hewett (1968), Stephens (1978), and Hewett and Taylor (1980) have developed skill sequence checklists useful with emotionally disturbed students that are arranged without reference to developmental levels. Stephens's Social Skills

List, based on items chosen by teachers as important, includes such items as:

asking a peer for help

making relevant remarks in conversation with peers

ignoring interruptions of others in a conversation

Hewett and Taylor's ABC's of the IEP is arranged into six levels of learning competence: attention, response, order, exploratory, social, and mastery. The levels are further broken down into skill components and subcomponents. Examples from the social level are:

willingly waits turn

will respond without constant reassurance

takes responsibility for own problems

From a social learning point of view, the main limitation of skill sequence checklists is their failure to provide a picture of the functioning of the student in relation to antecedent and consequent events. Under what conditions is the student quiet or talkative, active or inactive, attending to task or off-task, and interacting positively or negatively with peers? This fuller picture of student behavior can be obtained by using a continuous observation procedure coupled with an exhaustive (covering all behavior) recording system. The more detailed the record, the more difficult it will be for the recorder. F. H. Wood (1973) has developed a simple observation schedule, the Pupil Observation Schedule (POS), Form B, for use by teachers and psychologists in field situations. A sample form is presented in Figure 8.1. Definitions for the categories are provided in Figure 8.2. Notice how the categorized information is supplemented by marginal anecdotal notes that provide a better sense of the context of the behavior. The POS permits an observer to record the occurrence of eight categories of student behavior at thirty-second intervals. All behavior on the checklist is directly observable, but in some cases the observer makes a value judgment about whether the behavior is positive or negative based on inferences about the thoughts and feelings accompanying the behavior. With this type of system, it is useful to summarize the observations as percentages, computed as the number of intervals in which behavior was observed to occur over the total number of intervals in the observation session. Observations should be made at different times and over a series of days to obtain a more complete description of student functioning. Observations should also be made of peer group behavior to establish the degree of uniqueness in the student's behavior (Cullinan and Epstein, 1980).

In the example given (Figure 8.1), Ray is "on task" 55 percent of the time observed and "at place" 90 percent of the time. The POS form shows the pattern of his behavior and of teacher's interaction with him. The activity pattern of the other students is not described except in relation to Ray's behavior, which is a limitation of this procedure from an

FIGURE 8.1
PUPIL OBSERVATION SCHEDULE (FORM B)

Observer ______________________ Date ____________

Description of Student Observed: Ray is eleven years old, average in height and build when compared to the other boys in the classroom. As he moves about, he gives an impression of strength and activity. When observed, he was in a special adjustment class in which he had just been placed because of disruptive behavior in the regular fifth-grade classroom to which he was assigned this fall.

*Description of Other Persons in Setting: Besides the observer, the adults are Ray's teacher and a classroom aide (both female). Ray is sitting at one of four desks that have been grouped together by the teacher near the center of the room (see diagram). All four students at these desks are doing individualized reading seatwork. Bill is twelve; the other two students are eleven.

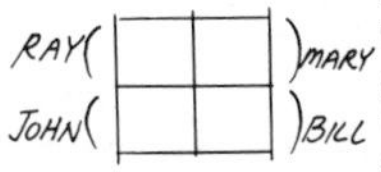

*Description of Setting and Activities: The teacher and aide are working with other students who are seated in cubicles at the sides of the room. Besides a desk in the center of the room, each student has one of these cubicles. Ray had been working for several minutes when the observation began. Five minutes into the session, Ray went to his cubicle.

		1	2	3	4	5	6	7	8	9	10
On Task		✓:	:✓	✓:✓	:	:	:	:✓	:✓	✓:✓	✓:✓
At Place		✓:✓	✓:✓	✓:✓	✓:✓	✓:	:✓ (goes by Mary on way to cubicle)	✓:✓	✓:✓	✓:✓	✓:✓
Positive Verbal Interaction		:X (whispering to Bill)	X:	:	:	:	:	:	:	:	:
Teacher Interaction	(+)	:	:	:	:	:	:	:✓ (goes to cubicle and talks to Ray "OK now you can get to work.")	:	:	:
	(−)	:	✓: (signals to be quiet)	:	:	✓: (tells R to go to cubicle)	:✓	✓:	:	:	:
Noise		✓: (bounces desk top)	:	:✓ (mumbles to self (about work?))	✓:	:	:	:	:	:	✓: (drums on desk with finger)
Negative Verbal Interaction		:	:	:	:	✓: ("Shut up" to Mary)	✓:✓ (threats to Mary)	✓:✓ (complains to teacher)	:	:	:
Negative Physical Contact		:	:	:	:✓ (pushes desk against Mary's)	:✓ (pushes M's chair)	:	:	:	:	:
________ (Other behavior of interest)		:	:	:	:	:	:	:	:	:	:

*During this ten-minute period.

FIGURE 8.2
INSTRUCTIONS FOR USE OF THE PUPIL OBSERVATION
SCHEDULE (FORM B)

Before beginning to observe, the observer should fill in name and date. Running notes about student characteristics, the setting, and the activity can be taken during the observation, but the final statement should be written at the close of the observation.

All boxes (behavior descriptions) needed to describe the performance one or more times of a target behavior pattern by the student being observed during each thirty-second observation period should be marked once with the appropriate symbol in the vertical column for that period. The present form has twenty columns, enough for ten minutes of observation of one student. Use spaces between the lines on the form to write in descriptions of special behaviors noted if not otherwise coded.

Record all verbal and physical interactions as positive unless clearly negative in intent and/or effect on others.

Symbols: A check (√) indicates the occurrence of a nondirected student behavior or, in the interactive categories, the occurrence of behavior involving either the teacher or the group as a whole including the teacher. For some categories, special symbols are used to record frequently occurring specific behavior patterns. These symbols are usually lowercase letters. Use of these special codes is optional.

CATEGORY DEFINITIONS

On Task: Student is "attending to task" or "working." Eyes are directed toward task area. Task area can be away from desk, involve movement, or both. "Work" could be a game or other activity. A student who is not attending to task may be daydreaming, playing, or engaging in some other activity. Try to make a narrative note on the specific nontask activity if time permits.

At Place: Student is at teacher-approved place, usually at desk or table. Buttocks touching chair. Special codes: "T" when student turns head, shoulders, or pelvis 90 degress or more from "correct" task orientation for more than four seconds. "R" when student is rocking in chair so that one or more chair legs leave floor. A narrative note may be useful if "place" is away from usual work area. A student is away from a teacher-approved place when his or her buttocks are off the chair for more than four seconds. The behavior need not be "off task." Make a note if the student leaves the room and resume recording when a student returns.

Positive Verbal Interaction: Positive verbal interaction may be self-initiated or responding. Examples would be when students express verbal support for a

Source: Original version (1973) by Frank H. Wood, Special Education Programs, University of Minnesota. Revised 1979.

ecological perspective (see Chapter 3). We will discuss this example more fully when we describe the further analysis of behavior that is part of the assessment process, and when we discuss intervention strategies.

The POS procedure has been used successfully by resource or consulting teachers as part of their assessment of problem behavior in regular classrooms (Rardin, 1976). Rardin supplemented the pupil categories by adding five categories of teacher behavior: control, organize, discuss, demonstrate, and describe. She also provided space for recording whether the

FIGURE 8.2 *(Continued)*

peer or the teacher, ask constructive questions, give suggestions, offer ideas on topics being discussed, respond to teacher or peer questions, recite, and acknowledge help given by another. Special codes: Mark "X" if a verbalization initiated is positive in intent but comes at the wrong time. If time permits, note specific words and any positive gestures or expressions that accompany students' other behavior.

Teacher Interaction: Teacher interaction with the target student is recorded as either positive or negative. This interaction may be verbal or nonverbal. Although the focus is on an individual student, records of the teacher's behavior directed toward the group of which the student is a part should also be recorded here. Task description and instruction, as well as verbal praise and encouragement, are to be recorded as positive ($+$). Criticism and threats are recorded as negative ($-$). Absence of marks in either of these categories during a single interval is an indication that there was no teacher interaction with the student during that time.

Noise: Noise is recorded whether generated by the use of objects or the voice. Examples of object-generated noise are making a noise with the hands (drumming, pounding, clapping, etc.) or a hand-held object (pencil tapping, noisy scribbling on paper, crumpling paper, etc.). Vocal noise is when a student makes a noise with the mouth not directed specifically at others (humming, singing to self, shouting, mumbling, whistling, etc.). Record the occurrence of noise if, in the observer's judgment, the noise is audible to others in the group.

Negative Verbal Interaction: Negative verbal interaction may be self-initiated or a response to statements by others. Examples of the first area would be student-initiated complaints about or criticism of the behavior of others and student verbal threats. Responding negative verbalizations are those made in response to statements or gestures by others or as part of a continuing dialogue or discussion.

Negative Physical Contact: Student hurts or interferes with the activity of another by touching him or her and his or her work or property. Student attacks another using hands, feet, or object either thrown or held in hand.

Individual Behavior: Space is provided for recording individual student behavior of special interest.

Remember to supplement symbols by jotting in a written description of specific behavior or the wording of a verbalization whenever time permits.

---

teacher attended positively, negatively, or not at all to the target student during each interval. Since teacher behavior is an important environmental contingency for student behavior, a record that establishes a temporal relationship between teacher behavior and student behavior is very useful in assessment using the BCU model (see Table 8.1).

Describing the Observable Contingencies for a Student's Target Behavior. After selecting a target behavior for development or change, the next step is to describe the environmental events hypothesized to be contingent on performance of the approved or disapproved behavior using the BCU model as a framework for analysis. Features of time, space, persons, or things to which the behaver is sensitive can be extremely important contingent events. This is inevitably a somewhat subjective process. The teacher is making hypotheses about the most likely temporal relationships that exist among variables in the environment. Such an analysis for our example is shown in Table 8.2. The variables subject to teacher control will then be observed to see whether or not changes in them produce changes in the target behavior.

Several of Ray's behaviors could be chosen for further analysis. We have chosen his off-task behavior, the periods in minutes 1, 2, 4, 5, 6, and 7 when he was not attending to his work. All off-task behavior took place while he was in the small group; it all involved an interaction with a peer, positive with Bill and negative with Mary. Each episode was followed by peer and teacher attention.

Making Inferences About Nonobservable Factors Influencing Learner Behavior. The social learning approach differs strikingly from the standard behavioral approach by including assessment of the learner's cognitive and emotional functioning, neither of which is observable directly. Teachers

TABLE 8.2
ANALYSIS OF RAY'S BEHAVIOR USING BCU MODEL

	Antecedent events	Behavior	Consequent events
May be known directly through observation	Desk is close to peer's desk. Teacher is in another part of room, talking with other students.	"Off task" 1. plus whispering to Bill 2. plus physical and verbal threats to Mary	1. Bill listens to whispers. 2. Mary starts, cringes, at desk slam, threats. 3. Teacher signals, later talks to Ray about behavior.
May be known indirectly through inference based on observation	Wants peer attention? Wants more activity? Wants teacher attention? Feels work is too hard? Thinks he won't finish work? General plan for behavior is to be "tough"?	Frustration? Boredom? Anger?	Pleased to be "tough guy"? Pleased at peer attention? Pleased at teacher attention?

guided by our social learning principles seek ways to assess students' spoken or written verbalizations about thoughts and feelings, their responsiveness to aspects of the situation, their expectancies and plans, the influence of observations of others being rewarded or punished for their behavior, and their implementation of plans of self-reinforcement. Since many of the students in special classes for the emotionally disturbed do not easily complete paper and pencil measures, an interview procedure is most useful for getting information that helps fill in these cells of the BCU model. (See Table 8.2 for an example.)

All our analysis in the second half of Table 8.2 is the result of inferences based on our observation of Ray's behavior in its environmental context. To remind us that these are inferences, we have marked each with a question mark. Our inferences can be checked through further observations of Ray and interviews that focus on specific instances of his behavior which we have recorded.

As a guide to interviewing students about their behavior, we have adapted the methods of the "life space interview" (Redl, 1959; Morse, 1963) and the "no-lose problem-solving procedure" (Gordon, 1974). The most important feature of such interview procedures is teacher (interviewer) sensitivity to the importance of asking the student to describe his or her responses to the situation to obtain information about contingent thoughts and feelings before the teacher intrudes his or her own comments. Inferences made on the basis of such interviews can be checked against inferences based on observation of student functioning at other times.

Monitoring and Evaluation

Student behavior analyzed into significant BCUs is the focus of the assessment on which instruction is based. A record of student behavior as it changes over time provides the basis for evaluating the effectiveness of instruction in a social learning curriculum. The teacher can choose a method for maintaining such a record that is appropriate for his or her situation, taking into account the expectations of parents and supervisors for reports on student progress and program effectiveness as well as instructional needs. Stephens (1978) and Hewett and Taylor (1980) describe how their behavior sequence checklists can be used to monitor change in student behavior over time.

The Pupil Observation Schedule procedure can also be used periodically to assess the behavior of the student in regular or special class situations. Depending on the observer time available to the teacher, such records can be made one or more times per week on a random basis to maintain a general picture of student functioning. Such a procedure can also be used as a pretest and posttest to provide an objective record of changes in students' behavior before and after leaving the special program.

Standard procedures for recording behavior rates such as those described in Chapter 4 can also be used when they seem appropriate. As mentioned in the discussion of key social learning concepts, the measurement of change focuses on observable behavior. On this point, we are in agreement with the strict behavioral psychologists. Our differences in viewpoint are strongest with regard to whether one should assess and use inferences about thoughts and feelings in planning and carrying out interventions intended to change behavior. We agree with them that to infer a change that cannot be observed is bad practice.

SOCIAL LEARNING INTERVENTIONS

From a social learning perspective, students whose behavior is frequently inappropriate or disordered should not be assumed for that reason to be incapable of behaving in ways that would be approved by teachers. Within a student's repertoire of potential behavior may be approved behavior learned through observing the behavior of others but never performed as well as approved behavior performed infrequently because environmental and personal contingencies do not support it. In helping students with disordered behavior behave in school situations to gain consistent peer and teacher approval or acceptance, teachers need to be able to apply interventions for three different purposes.

The first group of interventions includes those likely to elicit and support approved behavior already in the students' repertoires. Through systematic use of environmental and personal style factors, a teacher can encourage and reward student performance of approved behaviors that are part of the students' repertoires so that they will perform them more frequently in the future. The stress in this group of interventions is on *preventing the occurrence of disapproved behavior* by making it more likely that approved behavior incompatible with disapproved behavior will occur. Nevertheless, problem behavior will occur, so teachers of behaviorally disordered students need a second set of interventions that will enable them *to manage the disapproved behavior and redirect the student to approved behavior*. Finally, some students may not be able to perform as planned by the teacher because they have never mastered the approved behavior. These children are victims of a "behavior deficit." To meet the needs of these behaviorally disordered students, teachers must be able *to teach approved behavior*. Although these three groups of interventions overlap, it is helpful to keep in mind these three distinct tasks which the teacher of seriously emotionally disturbed students must cope with.

Interventions That Elicit and Support Approved Behavior

We cluster interventions that elicit and support approved behavior in a social learning curriculum into two groups. One set of interventions focuses on the planned use of instructional time, space, and the contents of the instructional environment. The other set requires the planned use of the teacher's personal behavior.

Environmental Interventions. Following is a list of principles for structuring the environment to elicit and support approved behavior:

1. Structure the physical environment to support approved behavior.
2. Structure the schedule to provide the appropriate pattern of new, familiar, quiet, and stimulating activities.
3. Match instructional procedures to pupils' levels of development and competence.
4. Match the content of instruction to pupils' interests.

Time, objects in the setting and the arrangement of "space" itself, and methods of instruction are important factors influencing student behavior that are subject to direct control by the teacher. Together with pupil interests and expectancies regarding specific content of the school curriculum, which can be known through inferences based on observation of behavior, these factors are important antecedents to behavior. The skillful teacher, having formed and checked out general working hypotheses about the effects of various combinations of these factors on student behavior, can arrange schedules, the classroom environment, and the curriculum to make approved student behavior likely to occur. The right combination of setting events makes approved behavior "easier" for students than disapproved behavior.

5. Develop peer group support systems.

Polsky (1962), Buckholdt and Gubruin (1979), Vorrath and Brendtro (1974), and Johnson and Johnson (1975) are among those who have documented the powerful influence of the peer group on behavior, an influence that grows stronger for many students as they move into adolescence. Teachers often regard the peer group as a negative influence on student behavior, one which encourages and reinforces disruptive behavior and resistance to teacher authority. But adults may actually create some of these problems by the manner in which we behave toward the student peer group structure. Johnson and Johnson (1975) and McCauley, Hlidek, and Feinberg (1977) have suggested ways to develop patterns of peer group support for teacher-approved behavior that are rewarding to both teachers and students. Peers also provide important models and examples for vicarious student learning.

6. Use relaxation or tension release activities when appropriate.

Spending five to six hours each day with large groups of people, many of whom would not be chosen as friends if school policies provided for choice of associates, is fatiguing and tension-producing for students and teachers. In addition, seriously emotionally disturbed students often come to school tense from the stress of problems unrelated to school and become more tense as they move through the day. Teachers have found it useful to introduce various kinds of tension-reducing activities into the curriculum. Suggestions for relaxation activities that might be adapted are found in Hendricks and Wills (1975), Hendricks and Roberts (1977), and Koeppen (1974). Teachers themselves find practice in voluntary relaxation procedures helpful in warding off excessive fatigue. Such activities have their place in our group of techniques for increasing the probability of approved social behavior in the classroom.

Teacher Interventions.   The teacher is a unique part of the environment, being perceived by students not only as a powerful arranger and source of reinforcement but as a model for behavior. Skillful teachers must be able to make purposeful use of their ongoing behavior in many ways. Following are some principles that suggest what that role should be in the framework of a social learning model:

1. Adopt a style of personal planfulness making use of your personal influence as a social reinforcer and reflecting the characteristics of a good classroom management style defined by Kounin (1970): "withitness," "overlapping," smooth handling of the flow of activities, avoidance of slowdowns, and maintenance of group focus.

Kounin and his colleagues have made a unique contribution to our understanding of social behavior in classroom groups. Through intensive study of film and videotape records of classroom interaction, they selected a group of teacher behaviors highly correlated with student work involvement and low rates of disapproved behavior. Those listed here are especially important in work with seriously behaviorally disordered students. "Withitness" is Kounin's label for teacher behavior that communicates to students that the teacher "knows all" about what is going on in the classroom, even in areas far removed in space from his or her current focus of attention. "Overlapping" is the teacher skill of juggling several activities simultaneously so that all keep up their momentum. The related skill of handling events smoothly describes the skill of moving without jerkiness or stops from one activity to another. Good control of the classroom also seems related to a teacher style that causes each student to feel that he or she is involved at all times in planned activities and is an object of the teacher's attention, a management skill Kounin calls "maintaining group focus." By practicing alertness to subtle cues given by students and avoiding behavior that Kounin found often leads to student inattention and disruptiveness, the teacher does much to create an environment that diminishes the frequency with which problem behavior occurs. Besides the primary report of Kounin's work (1970), a summary of his studies of classroom groups is available in another reference (Kounin, 1975).

2. Make basic classroom rules and informal social contracts explicit.
3. Be aware of your own influence as a model of behavior and model the behavior you wish students to imitate.
4. Label and reward appropriate student behavior so that students become aware of peer models of approved behavior.
5. Support positive pupil expectancies regarding performance capability and outcomes through reinforcement and feedback of information.

These four strategies (numbers 2–5) for preventive behavior management are teacher applications of fundamental behavioral principles. The first reinforces the importance of clarifying for students the largely unwritten social compact that guides relationships between teachers and students. The details of this social compact vary from group to group. Each student and each teacher has idiosyncratic preferences that may influence what is acceptable in matters of dress, language, and social behavior. Students with a history of disordered relationships with others have imperfect or distorted perceptions of the social compact and benefit when it is discussed and "taught." The other three suggestions are reminders of the powerful influence of the teacher as a model of positive, supportive social behavior. Social learning theory stresses the influence of observational learning and the importance of the "means-ends" (behavior-consequence) relationship. Seriously emotionally disturbed students need teacher models whose behavior is fair, consistent, and effective, since this is the behavior we wish our students to learn.

6. Maintain your own mental health through self-regulatory procedures that increase your stress tolerance and permit you to release tensions.

Teaching is a stressful occupation; teaching students whose behavior is disturbing to others much of the time is extremely stressful. School administrators must take responsibility for providing support and respite to teachers of students with special needs to avoid premature "burnout," but teachers can also learn to husband their own energy and derive the maximum benefit from opportunities for relaxation and recreation. Teacher responsiveness to stress is an important antecedent to their response to the stress-producing behavior of their students. The dynamic relationships of the BCU model apply to teachers as well as to students.

Interventions to Manage and Redirect Disapproved Behavior

Although social learning interventions are strategies that are likely to elicit and support approved behavior in the classroom, there will be many times when interventions planned to prevent the occurrence of problem behavior are unsuccessful. As a result, teachers of seriously emotionally disturbed students must be familiar with a range of crisis management procedures that will enable them to control or contain problem behavior and to redirect pupils into approved activities. The general rule in these interventions is to interfere with the student's behavior as lightly and indirectly as possible, to deflect or redirect rather than confront, thereby avoiding the undesirable side effects of more direct interference. Teacher attention, for example, is rewarding to some students even when it is negative in intent. Problem behavior that attracts teacher attention may be repeated. Strong, direct teacher intervention is also arousing for students; it often stimulates escape or attack behavior. This behavior will frequently increase in strength in direct relationship to increases in the intensity of the teacher's interference. For these reasons, the rule to use the least interference required to control or stop student problem behavior is an important guide to efficient crisis management.

A second consideration in crisis management is the implementation of the "incompatible behavior" concept through redirection of student behavior. Thus, one phase of crisis management is control of the problem behavior, and the second phase is redirection of the student to perform an approved behavior that is incompatible with the problem behavior. Although it seems obvious when stated, teachers sometimes forget that this approved behavior must not only be present in the student's repertoire but it must also have been practiced sufficiently that it can be performed without great difficulty. Many attempts at crisis behavior management and redirection founder because we attempt to redirect the student to perform a behavior that is frustrating and may have contributed to the original problem — back to an academic task that is too difficult, for example.

Several techniques useful in controlling and redirecting students' behavior are listed below. The list is based on the authors' personal experience in developing and applying (within the context of the social learning model) ideas from psychologists and educators such as Long and Newman (1976), Redl and Wattenberg (1959), Gnagey (1968), and O'Leary and O'Leary (1977). Except for the O'Learys, these psychologist-educators developed their ideas about interventions in the psychoeducational tradition. The emphasis and goals of such procedures change when they are "translated" to fit the purposes of the social learning intervention program. These crisis management skills are grouped into four different clusters.

Skill 1. *The teacher should be able to redirect problem behavior by changing antecedent events.* The focus here is on minimal restructuring of the environment and minimal direct interference. The procedures are similar to what Long and Newman (1976) call "surface management techniques," but here more attention is given to analysis of the cue and reinforcement aspects of the interventions than in Long and Newman's discussion.

1. Permit behavior without reinforcing it.
2. Nonverbally signal a student to desist from present behavior and direct attention to a previously assigned task.
3. Inhibit the problem behavior by moving close to the student. Such control by proximity often sufficiently alters the environment to cause the student to turn to the assigned task.

Long and Newman (1976, p. 311) and Gnagey (1968, p. 41) speak of "ignoring" problem behavior anticipated to be of short duration when its intensity is less disruptive than more direct teacher interference is likely to be. From a social learning viewpoint, the teacher is more accurately described as perceiving but permitting the behavior, acting on the assumption that if the behavior is not reinforced or punished, it will soon cease. If the behavior persists or begins to increase in intensity, the teacher may need to communicate to the student through nonverbal signals his or her awareness and disapproval of the behavior. These procedures involve subtle readjustments of the antecedent conditions under the teacher's control and depend for their success on the adequacy of the unchanged task and consequent conditions. A task too frustrating (punishing) or reinforcement too weak will render such antecedent-oriented interference futile.

Skill 2.   *The teacher should be able to make program modifications and changes as necessary to manage and redirect problem behavior.* Such modifications require a willingness on the part of the teacher to compromise with the instructional goals originally scheduled for the time by restructuring the environment while work is in progress. The success of such modifications requires that the student possess the skills necessary to complete the modified task. Accompanying environmental changes with verbal comments will facilitate student awareness that the task has been modified so that it can be performed successfully. The assumption underlying this group of interventions is that student frustration with the task (student's low expectancy for successful performance and the resulting low expectancy for reinforcement for success) has contributed to his or her disapproved behavior.

1. Use cognitive intervention techniques such as humor or reassurance to reduce tension and overcome incorrect anticipation of failure.
2. Strengthen student efforts by alerting students to the likelihood of obtaining a desirable reward for task completion.
3. Cue, prompt, and model the needed behavior to facilitate successful performance.
4. Alter the planned schedule to accommodate to student fatigue or lowered tolerance for stress.
5. Alter the length or difficulty of assigned tasks to accommodate to student fatigue or lowered stress tolerance.

6. Use direct verbal appeals for behavior conforming to a previously established contract or set of rules, linked when appropriate to a reminder of the rewards for such conformity. (The teacher should consider whether such an appeal is to be made privately to an individual student or "publicly" to the student and the peer group as a whole.)

These procedures use planned changes in teacher instructional style, time schedule, or task characteristics in an effort to change student responsiveness and expectancies. The changes in the antecedent conditions are much greater than those produced by permitting or signaling, while consequent factors remain relatively unaltered. The focus is more on redirecting the student's behavior than on direct interference with the problem behavior. The success of these interventions is indicated by student movements in the direction of approved behavior. An analysis of such situations using the BCU framework (Table 8.1) helps us see that these changes in our behavior may reinforce the student's problem behavior, however, since they follow its occurrence. This will be much more apt to occur if the existing reinforcing events, which the interventions do not change, are inadequate to support approved behavior. The greater the change in the teacher's plan produced by the student's disapproved behavior, the greater the danger that the change will reinforce rather than redirect that behavior. Teachers who use these procedures without attending systematically to the contingent changes in the flow of student behavior may find that they have unwittingly accelerated the occurrence of problem behavior.

Skill 3.   *The teacher should be able to control and redirect student behavior by combining the use of mildly punishing cognitive interference procedures with changes in antecedent conditions that make the occurrence of approved behavior more likely.* Any of the preceding procedures, which stress altering the antecedents of student behavior in an effort to make the occurrence of approved behavior more likely, may be combined with interference with the student's disapproved behavior. Such combined procedures are required when we estimate that redirection in itself will not be a successful strategy. This group of interventions relies heavily on teacher verbalizations — reprimands, praise, task redirection — and assumes that the student can process such verbal information efficiently. Students must understand what the teacher is talking about to respond appropriately to such interventions.

1. Praise approved behavior while permitting disapproved behavior without reinforcing it.
2. Combine a soft verbal reprimand with reinforcement of the approved behavior of a student model or of behavior previously shown by the target student.

3. Occasionally, make judicious use of a loud verbal reprimand combined with reinforcement of approved behavior.
4. Use a quick "problem-solving interview" to determine the student's self-perceptions of the reasons for the problem behavior and to negotiate a plan for redirection. (The interview should be terminated quickly if the problem seems more extensive than originally perceived or if the interview develops into a verbal power struggle.)

O'Leary and O'Leary (1977) provide well-chosen case study examples of 1, 2, and 3, while 4 is a social learning application of the life space interview technique (Redl, 1959; Morse, 1963). In the interview procedure, used as recommended here, the teacher seeks to get information about the student's perceived "reasons" for engaging in disapproved behavior and to guide a cognitive restructuring of the situation that will support approved behavior without slipping into a continuing reinforcement of student problem behavior. From a social learning viewpoint, prolonged discussion of problem behavior is undesirable because teacher attention tends to reinforce the discussion itself, rather than efficiently redirecting disapproved behavior. Note that, to be most effective, control procedures such as these and those in the next group need to be combined with some of the planned changes in antecedent conditions that have been mentioned earlier.

Skill 4. *The teacher should be able to control and redirect student behavior by combining the use of punishing physical interference procedures with changes in antecedent conditions that make the occurrence of approved behavior more likely.* The likelihood of arousing strong student resistance through interference has increased in each set of the interventions discussed. The likelihood of high strength avoidance or escape behavior by the student is particularly great when direct physical interventions are used. Indeed, so much respondent "disturbed student" behavior may be elicited by physical interference that efforts to redirect the student to approved behavior will be pointless for considerable periods of time. Troubling side effects may also result. The student's avoidance behavior is negatively reinforced and vicariously learned by his or her peers. Finally, the teacher becomes in a sense a "prisoner" of the student, unable to engage in other activity until the avoidance behavior subsides. Because the use of physical interference procedures is so subject to error, they are discussed individually.

1. "Seductive objects" can be removed from easy access in the environment. These are objects that are most likely to function in ways that are incompatible with approved behavior. The term "seductive objects" is Long and Newman's (1976, p. 314). Such objects should not be confiscated permanently if they are the property of the student unless appro-

priate due process procedures are followed. However, when problems of misuse are anticipated, an anticipatory "time-out from use" intervention by the teacher is good practice if it does not stimulate strong defensive behavior from the student. If strong defensive behavior by the student is anticipated, the teacher must weigh the probable benefits to be gained by removing the object against the problems created by the resulting disruption. Also, the removal of the object should be managed so that a disapproved behavior, "the bringing of inappropriate objects," is not inadvertently reinforced.

2. Temporary time-out from reward can be used as a mild punishment for disapproved behavior. Time-out from reward procedures are aversive for most students (Rutherford, 1978; Gast and Nelson, 1977). They cause a target problem behavior to stop, but they may also produce high intensity defensive and escape behavior. Such problems are minimized if time-out procedures are used following patterns that are well established and understood by the students. In general, teachers are advised to practice the use of time-out procedures under the supervision of an experienced teacher before trying them in their own room. Time-out can easily be abusive.

3. Isolation procedures involving removal of the student to a specially prepared unstimulating area for a period of time-out may be necessary when student behavior is highly disruptive or dangerous to self or others. Teachers should not use isolation procedures unless they have been given supervised training in their use and are well informed about the precautions that must be taken to protect students from physical injury or undue emotional stress (F. H. Wood and Lakin, 1978).

4. Teachers should be familiar with the pros and cons of using physical restraint with students and be able to judge when and if appropriate physical restraint procedures are to be used. We do not feel that there is sufficient basis for the psychodynamic hypothesis that some students receive positive emotional gains from being physically held. Therefore, physical restraint is normally used only when necessary to control students who are physically attacking people or objects in the environment. The amount of restraint applied is limited to that necessary for control, and efforts are made to minimize the pain that occurs as a secondary effect. Teachers are advised not to use physical restraint in situations where they may become concerned about their ability to control a student without painful consequences to themselves. When fear of pain is present in the teacher, there is a tendency to begin to inflict pain for defensive purposes.

Because of the concern about misuse, some secondary-level programs that follow a general framework of social learning principles do not permit teachers to use physical interference procedures with students under any circumstances except direct self-defense. When students enter such programs, they are told that the use of physical restraint is not part of the teacher's role, and that should any kind of physical intervention be needed, police officers trained to deal with violent behavior will be called and formal charges will be filed against offending students. It is reasoned that teachers, as models of adult behavior, should not get involved in physical struggles with students.

Interventions to Teach Approved Behavior That Is Missing from the Student's Repertoire

Frequently, the inappropriate behavior of students who are labeled "seriously emotionally disturbed" results from their lack of experience in behaving in ways to win approval. Such students may not respond to important environmental stimuli that could cue them to behave in approved ways, or they may misread stimuli and respond to neutral events such as teacher's instructions as if they are hostile remarks. Aware of their own inadequacy, they may also deliberately offend or unwittingly behave in a way that is disapproved by others. As a result, teachers implementing a social learning curriculum must give attention to the teaching of approved behavior.

The teaching of approved behavior can be highly specific and be guided by objectives such as those that have been discussed in the section on assessment procedures. Techniques to support student learning of approved behavior include writing formal contracts with students (Homme et al., 1970) and practice in simulated situations. When possible, guided practice in real situations is also desirable as an aid to generalization and the elimination of unanticipated difficulties. Besides regular classroom task activities, such experiences as discussion groups, field trips, parties, and interviews with visitors can provide opportunities for such practice.

Some social curriculum materials that can be adapted for use by the teacher of seriously emotionally disturbed students have been produced in recent years. These materials cannot be reviewed at length here, but examples can be found in Stephens (1978); Hewett (1968); Hewett and Taylor (1980); M. M. Wood (1975b); Fagen, Long, and Stephens (1975); Dinkmeyer (1970); and DuPont (1974). Some of this curriculum has been developed following a psychodynamic or psychoeducational perspective. Thus, the teacher seeking to develop a social learning curriculum must expect to do a careful analysis, and modification may be necessary to adapt procedures to the purposes of his or her program. Application of the BCU paradigm (Table 8.1) will be helpful in such an analysis.

One area to which social learning psychologists have given special attention is the learning of self-regulatory behavior. Self-monitoring, self-evaluating, and self-reinforcing and self-punishing techniques are skills that can be learned and applied by students of all ages. Polsgrove (1979) has reviewed the extensive literature on this topic with an eye to its relevance for teachers of seriously emotionally disturbed students. Teachers implementing a social learning curriculum should become familiar with self-regulation procedures and seek opportunities to practice them under the supervision of one familiar with their application.

SUMMARY: APPLYING SOCIAL LEARNING INTERVENTIONS TO RAY'S BEHAVIOR

Returning to our discussion of Ray's behavior (Figure 8.1 and Table 8.2), we note several things. Most of Ray's "off-task" behavior and his inappropriate interactions with his peers took place while he was seated in the group. After he had moved to the cubicle and had his talk with the teacher, he appeared to attend more consistently to his work. This calls our hypothesis about task difficulty into question. The BCU analysis suggests that his behavior may have been reinforced by peer attention, with teacher attention a supplementary reward. However, the fact that he did not behave in ways that might elicit such responses from others after moving to the cubicle prompts attention to antecedent rather than consequent events as key factors in controlling his behavior. Preventative intervention by the teacher, which in this case would be not placing Ray in an unsupervised activity in a group, might make the disapproved behavior less likely to occur. Ray's response to the teacher's crisis management procedure, removal from the group (a mild time-out technique), was more successful, although teacher proximity might have forestalled the push to Mary's chair. In the long run, it may help to plan a contract with Ray focused on his work behavior in the group. If he is sufficiently concerned about remaining in the group, he may be ready to monitor and control his own behavior.

When planning instructional interventions or developing materials, the teacher of seriously emotionally disturbed students who is guided by social learning principles gives first priority to interventions that have a high probability of eliciting and maintaining desired behavior patterns. At the same time, he or she is prepared to manage disapproved behavior should it occur, deflecting or stopping it while using behavioral and cognitive intervention procedures to redirect the student to perform approved behavior. The goal of long-range intervention strategies is to decrease the need for such management and redirection since it is an inefficient use of instructional time.

Instruction based on a social learning perspective is designed to stimulate the performance of approved behavior. Although talking about approved behavior as part of modeling, role playing, rehearsal, or prompting may sometimes facilitate its performance, changes in verbal behavior alone are generally not a major focus in this curriculum. They would be so only when verbal behavior itself is the primary target of instruction.

Teachers following a social learning intervention program plan and teach for the generalization to everyday environments of the approved behavior that becomes typical of their students in the special setting. One reason for the attention given to the cognitive factors in behavior is the hypothesis that cognitive changes facilitate generalization of other behavior. The problem of generalization of approved social behavior to new settings remains critical for this as well as other curricula for seriously disturbed students (Polsgrove, McLeskey, and Rieth, 1980; Stokes and Baer, 1977).

There is no single theory of human behavior that compels general acceptance as a sufficiently close approximation to *the* truth. Teachers of emotionally disturbed and behaviorally disordered students must select from among competing theories the one they find most useful as an aid to planning efficient instructional interventions. "Usefulness" must be measured with reference to our personal feelings and behavioral style as well as the theory's effectiveness in managing problem behavior and teaching approved behavior. Social learning theory blends behavioral and cognitive elements in ways that have proved useful in both laboratory and field situations. In this chapter, we have attempted to demonstrate briefly the utility of interventions based on this theory.

Chapter 9

Developmental Therapy for the Severely Emotionally Disturbed and Autistic

Mary M. Wood
University of Georgia

with

William W. Swan
Office of Special Education
Washington, D.C.

Vera S. Newman
Los Angeles City Unified School District
Los Angeles, California

WHAT IS DEVELOPMENTAL THERAPY?

The Goal of Developmental Therapy

Developmental therapy is a psychoeducational curriculum for severely emotionally disturbed, behaviorally disordered, and autistic children from two to sixteen years of age. The curriculum goal is social and emotional growth. Successful social and emotional development involves meeting the demands of life by *doing, saying, caring,* and *thinking* with a reasonable degree of balance between inner needs and societal expectations (Mussen, Conger, and Kagan, 1969; Segal and Yahraes, 1978; Ziegler and Trickett, 1978). These four processes are used by all children, with varying effectiveness, as they attempt to cope with their experiences. In coping, a child uses his or her available resources — senses, muscles, cognition, communication, attitudes, values, emotions, motivations, and interpersonal skills. When a child is coping successfully, these resources are used effectively, but when these resources are not functioning successfully, the balance between a child's needs and the demands of life is disrupted. The behaviors of emotionally disturbed and behavior disordered children are products of just such an imbalance. Developmental therapy is designed to restore this balance by teaching the child the sequential tasks essential to social and emotional development.

Developmental therapy has been formulated and validated in the field over a ten-year period at the Rutland Center and the University of Georgia by special education teachers, regular education teachers, school psychologists, school social workers, music, art, and recreation therapists, day-care teachers, program evaluators, paraprofessionals, parents, and volunteers. It has proved effective with children from various ethnic and socioeconomic backgrounds who are severely disruptive, withdrawn, psychotic, autistic, multihandicapped, or functionally retarded (Kaufman, Paget, and Wood, 1981; Swan and Wood, 1975; M. M. Wood, 1972, 1975b, 1977, 1978a; M. M. Wood and Swan, 1978).

Aspects of the model have been used successfully in preschool programs, regular elementary and middle schools, special classes, resource rooms, psychoeducational centers, day treatment centers, community mental health centers, day-care centers, Head Start programs, and in residential treatment. It is presently being used in numerous locations in the United States and abroad (Beardsley, 1977; Beardsley and Combs, 1978; Hoyt, 1978; Swan, 1976; N. J. Wood, Wood, and Algeria, 1979).

The Scope of the Curriculum

Developmental therapy has put into practice constructs and research evidence about social and emotional development by translating the four processes of *doing, saying, caring,* and *thinking* into specific sequential tasks in four curriculum areas: behavior, communication, socialization, and (pre)academics. These four curriculum areas are summarized below.

Behavior Is Doing.   Behavior includes the adaptive processes a child uses to cope with the environment. Behavior objectives begin with a child being aware of stimuli in the environment. With awareness, other processes can develop: attending to a stimulus, simple motor responses, body control, recognizing essentials and nonessentials, and participating in routine activities. More advanced behavior processes include impulse control, organizing responses according to the expectations of others, and involvement with rules.

Communication Is Saying.   Communication implies interpersonal processes. For this reason, the area of communication includes all forms of verbal and nonverbal efforts to interact with another child or adult, such as watching and imitating others and producing sounds, verbal approximations, sequences of words, assertive statements, and questions. As communication skills increase, children learn to listen, describe feelings and characteristics of themselves and others, convey information, and express their feelings through words.

Socialization Is Caring. Socialization involves processes that lead a child to positive group experiences and eventually to the use of values in social situations. These processes begin with awareness of adults and peers and develop into cooperative play. Socialization takes on a definitive form when a child has the interpersonal skills for successful interactions with many different people. To do this, the child must have a sense of self, self-confidence, and an interest in others. The processes involved include taking turns, suggesting activities, sharing, participating in what others suggest, recognizing characteristics of others, valuing, developing preferences for friends, supporting others, and eventually participating as an invested member of a group. Through these experiences a child's value system develops.

(Pre)Academics Is Thinking. (Pre)Academics includes processes used in cognitive functioning that contribute to the mastery of academic content. In developmental therapy, academic skills are considered tools for personal enrichment and creative problem-solving. Such processes include eye-hand coordination and perceptual skills, body coordination, memory, discriminating similarities and differences in all sensory modalities, classifying, concept-building, using objects, recognizing details in pictures, and possessing concepts of number and conservation. These basic processes lead to others that are more complex, such as expressive language, recognizing signs and symbols, generalization, and logical and creative problem-solving.

The Developmental Therapy Sequences and Stages

In each of the four curriculum areas of developmental therapy, there are specific hierarchical sequences of tasks. The sequences are delineated in a series of 171 objectives that specify normal developmental milestones in sequential steps for social and emotional development from birth to age sixteen. At key points in the sequences of objectives, general stages of social and emotional development are delineated.

The developmental therapy curriculum specifies the procedures, activities, and general techniques that are needed to teach children to accomplish the objectives. It also describes the characteristics of adults needed by children for their social and emotional development at various stages of development. Table 9.1 contains a summary of developmental therapy stages, overall goals, the adults' roles, techniques, amounts of intervention, and the types of environments and experiences needed for each stage.

Table 9.2 outlines the sequence of social and emotional goals in the four curriculum areas at each stage of development therapy (M. M. Wood, 1972, 1975b). Table 9.3 summarizes the typical characteristics of normal social and emotional development contained in the five stages of the developmental therapy objectives. This information illustrates the qualitative dif-

TABLE 9.1
THE SEQUENTIAL DEVELOPMENTAL THERAPY GOALS
FOR EACH CURRICULUM AREA

	Behavior	*Communication*	*Socialization*	*Academic skills*
Stage I	To trust own body and skills.	To use words to gain needs.	To trust an adult sufficiently to respond to him or her.	To respond to the environment with processes of classification, discrimination, basic receptive language concepts, and body coordination.
Stage II	To successfully participate in routines.	To use words to affect others in constructive ways.	To participate in activities with others.	To participate in classroom routines with language concepts of similarities and differences, labels, use, color, numerical processes of ordering and classifying, and body coordination.
Stage III	To apply individual skills in group processes.	To use words to express oneself in the group.	To find satisfaction in group activities.	To participate in the group with basic expressive language concepts, symbolic representation of experiences and concepts, functional semiconcrete concepts of conservation, and body coordination.
Stage IV	To contribute individual effort to group success.	To use words to express awareness of relationship between feelings and behavior in self and others.	To participate spontaneously and successfully as a group member.	To successfully use signs and symbols in formalized school work and in group experiences.
Stage V	To respond to critical life experiences with adaptive-constructive behavior.	To use words to establish and enrich relationships.	To initiate and maintain effective peer group relationships independently.	To successfully use signs and symbols for formalized school experiences and personal enrichment.

Source: M. M. Wood (Ed.). *Developmental Therapy Objectives: A Self-Instructional Workbook.* Baltimore: University Park Press, 1979, p. 21. Used by permission.

TABLE 9.2
SUMMARY OF DEVELOPMENTAL THERAPY STAGES

Stage I: Responding to the environment with pleasure

General Description:	*Responding and trusting*
Adult's Role:	Arouser and satisfier of basic needs
Techniques:	Body contact and touch; physical intervention; classroom structure and consistent routine; control of materials by teacher; controlled vocabulary
Intervention:	Constant physical contact; caring, arousing
Environment and Experiences:	Routine constant, luring rather than demanding; stimulating, arousing sensory activities

Stage II: Responding to the environment with success

General Description:	*Learning individual skills*
Adult's Role:	Motivator; redirector of old coping behavior to successful outcomes; reflection of success; predictable point of reference
Techniques:	Classroom structure; consistent routine; verbal interaction between lead and support teachers; physical and verbal redirection; holding limits; reflection of action, feelings, and success
Intervention:	Frequent, both physical and verbal; supportive
Environment and Experiences:	Structured, successful exploration; activities leading to self-confidence and organization; communication activities; beginning cooperative activities; simple group experiences

Stage III: Learning skills for successful group participation

General Description:	*Applying individual skills to group procedures*
Adult's Role:	Model for group participation; stimulator and encourager of appropriate group interaction; upholder of limits and group expectations; reflector and interpreter of behavior, feelings, and progress
Techniques:	Redirection; reflection; verbal interaction between lead and

Note: References to chronological age have been deliberately omitted to emphasize that a sequence of development is important rather than a comparison to a norm.

Source: M. M. Wood (Ed.). *Developmental Therapy.* Baltimore: University Park Press, 1975, pp. 7–8. Used by permission.

ferences between the stages, the types of social and emotional tasks included in the developmental therapy objectives, and the sequential nature of social and emotional development.

Assessment and Program Planning

The 171 developmental therapy objectives are the basis for assessment and program planning. These objectives are contained in the Developmental Therapy Objectives Rating Form (DTORF) (M. M. Wood, 1979). The DTORF is used to (1) assess a child's current level of social and emotional development; (2) provide short-term objectives and long-term goals in social and emotional development for the child's Individualized Education Program (IEP); (3) serve as the basis for curriculum planning in the

TABLE 9.2 (*Continued*)

	support teachers; individual life space interviews; predictable structure and expectations; reflector of feelings; predictability; frequent verbal intervention; consistency
Intervention:	Frequent; primarily verbal; group focus
Environment and Experiences:	Group activities that stimulate cooperation, sharing, and beginning friendships; focus on group procedures and expectations; approximate real-life situations and conditions as much as group can tolerate

Stage IV: Investing in group processes

General Description:	*Valuing one's group*
Adult's Role:	Group leader; counselor; reflector of reality
Techniques:	Interpretation of feelings and behavior; individual and group life space interview; reality reflection
Intervention:	Intermittent, approximating real life
Environment and Experiences:	Reality-oriented environment; activities, procedures, and expectations determined by the group; emphasis on group academic learning experiences, role play, field trips, elements of normal competition

Stage V: Applying individual and group skills in new situations

General Description:	*Generalizing and valuing*
Adult's Role:	Counselor, teacher, friend
Techniques:	Normal expectations; relationships between feelings, behaviors, and consequences; nonclinical
Intervention:	Infrequent
Environment and Experiences:	Normal childhood settings; conversations about real-life experiences; support in solving problem situations; independent skill-building

classroom; (4) provide a means to group children according to social and emotional development; and (5) provide a criterion-referenced evaluation system to document child change.

The hierarchical sequence of objectives contained in the DTORF serves teachers, parents, and therapists as a series of guideposts to assist severely emotionally disturbed and autistic youngsters in learning socially appropriate and emotionally satisfying skills.

Teachers conducting developmental therapy use specific intervention strategies, materials, activities, and adult roles according to the DTORF objectives specified for each child. Thus, to reduce the enormous range of individual differences with which a teacher must work, children are grouped according to specific developmental objectives as indicated by each child's rating on the DTORF. In this way, a teacher will have a group of children

TABLE 9.3
SOME CHARACTERISTICS OF SOCIAL EMOTIONAL DEVELOPMENT
IMPORTANT TO DEVELOPMENTAL THERAPY

Developmental therapy stage	Characteristic cognitive style	Major socialization theme	Predominating anxieties and fears	Characteristic play	Examples of typical curriculum themes
One: responding to the environment with pleasure	*Sensory-motor* Kinetic feedback Use of simple objects as tools Association of motor movements to environment by labeling	*Recognition and trust* Relational bonds between child and adult Pleasure and comfort	*Aloneness* Separation Abandonment The unknown Deprivation	*Sensory-based experiences* Awareness and pleasure Sameness Touch Imitation of simple movements Hoarding Repetition Individual regularity	*Tangible things and familiar persons* Food Personal objects Water play Rhythm
Two: responding to the environment with success	*Preschematic and preoperational* Form recognition Primitive symbols Egocentrism Object permanence Exploration and experience through motor activities	*Measuring up and being successful to please adults* Discrimination of good and bad in self — learned from others	Anxieties from previous stages plus: *Inadequacy* Fears loss of acceptance and approval Concern for obtaining needs (physical and emotional) Management of body impulses and drives	*Symbolic play about people and animals* Play is for self Make-believe Imitation of adults Imitation of other children Desires, fears, and impulses projected into play and resolved happily	*Good conquers bad* Child controls, is omnipotent, independent, powerful, and successful Imitates fantasy heroes (the Hulk, Superman, Three Billy Goats Gruff)

Stage	Cognitive	Self-esteem / Social	Fears	Discipline	Play	Themes / Heroes
Three: learning skills for successful group participation	*Schematic and concrete operational*	*Self-esteem Phase I*	Anxieties from previous stages plus:	Restrictions from adults	Problems solved via magic	*Reality situations with heroes, adventures, and things*
	Organization of parts into wholes	Acceptance and appreciation by others is essential	*Guilt*	Fear of being caught	Simple story sequences	Role play and child drama
	Rigid constructs	Measuring up to self-standards set by peers and adults	Fear of loss of love or approval because of personal failings	Fear of punishment	Minimal expression of inner life	Complex story themes resulting in hero (child) looking good to parents and friends
	Decentering begins	"Looking good" in the eyes of others	Fear of failure		Interactions with other children (parallel and interactive play)	Television and movie heroes
		Self is worthy or unworthy	Death fears		Semisymbolic toys	Parents appreciating child
		Self-protective in responses to others	Fear of the unknown		Practice of simple rules	Peers admiring child
		Cooperation	Realistic fears "It could happen . . ."		Rules are respected as adult authority	
			Remote fears		*Organized play with inflexible rules and fairness*	
					Social play	
					Group participation and cooperation	
					Concern over nonconformists	
					Attempts to win	
					Problems solved by others (adults or heroes)	
					Wishes reality-based	
					Experiments with direct power (control) over others	

TABLE 9.3 (Continued)

Developmental therapy stage	Characteristic cognitive style	Major socialization theme	Predominating anxieties and fears	Characteristic play	Examples of typical curriculum themes
			"It might be possible..." Mystical fears "Wouldn't it be terrible if..."	Models mannerisms of powerful people Common rules	Noncompetitive games
Four: investing in group processes	*Dawning realism* Reversibility Conservation Understands consequences of actions	*Self-esteem Phase II* Conforming to societal, accepted values Acceptance in groups Interest in helping others	Anxieties from previous stages plus: *Conflict* Balancing complex inner drives and needs with outer demands of peers and adults Fear of not being accepted by the group vs. expressing self Anxiety over responsibility for independence and making decisions	Same as Stage Three plus: *Problems solved by self and peers* Reading for vicarious experiences Group interactions predominate over child's need to control Interest in roles of others Rules are changed to suit group Experimentation with new experiences Sympathy and awareness of others' needs	*New roles and experiences* Clubs, teams, gangs, and organizations Role play socio-dramas Field trips Movies and television Original writing, diaries, letters Competitive sports Skill sports Day camping Pen pals Instruments and technology Human control of the physical environment

Five: applying in-dividual and group skills in new situations	*Formal operations and pseudorealism* How things work Values assimilated into cognitive style	*Identity* "Who am I?" Personal convictions and values Security from belonging Goals and ideals	Anxieties from all previous stages plus: *Self-image* Concern for body image and dress Sex role doubts Sexual expressions Obtaining affection Doubts of future role and earning capacity Conflict about values governing behavior and decision-making	Respect for rules and justice Desire for equality	*Experiments with alternatives* Changes physical style via dress, mannerisms, eating, drinking, and drug experimentation Daydreams Dates (role-playing relationships) Talking about others Cliques, clubs, and groups Imitation of societal roles via TV, movies, magazines Problems solved by self-interacting with close friends Rules developed and modified in response to situation and need Ideological "causes" Sexual activity Empathy Mutual respect from relationships	*Sports, social, and community activities* Preparing news re-ports, commentaries, and critiques Field trips Volunteer activities to assist others such as Red Cross, hos-pital, and political campaigns, Boy's Club, Scouts Travel Camping Vocational and pre-vocational experi-ences Driving Building Creating Cooking Music Hobbies Futuristic problems Space colonization

TABLE 9.3 (Continued)

Developmental therapy stage	Characteristic cognitive style	Major socialization theme	Predominating anxieties and fears	Characteristic play	Examples of typical curriculum themes
					Living in domed cities
					Hypnosis
					Extrasensory perception
					The Supernatural

Note: Information for this table was taken from the following sources: Developmental therapy stage: M. M. Wood, 1975b, 1979, 1981. Characteristic cognitive style: Flavell 1968, 1977; Lowenfeld, 1957; Lowenfeld and Brittain, 1970; Mischel, 1971; Piaget, 1967; Piaget and Inhelder, 1969; Wolff, 1960, 1972. Major socialization theme: Aronfreed, 1968; Bandura, 1976, 1977b; Bandura and Walters, 1963; Erikson, 1963, 1972, 1977; Kagan and Moss, 1962; Kohlberg, 1976; Loevinger, 1976. Predominating anxieties and fears: Aronfreed, 1968; Fagen and Hill, 1977; A. Freud, 1965, 1973; S. Freud, 1936; Long, Morse, and Newman, 1976. Characteristic play: Bettelheim, 1977; Erikson, 1972, 1977; S. Freud, 1955; Henry, 1956; Loevinger, 1976; Piaget, 1932, 1962. Examples of typical curriculum themes: Bachrach et al., 1978; Williams and Wood, 1977; M. M. Wood, 1981; Torrance, 1979.

Source: M. M. Wood (Ed.). *Developmental Therapy Sourcebook.* Vol. 1. Baltimore: University Park Press, 1981, pp. 4–7. Used by permission.

working on the same objectives, on objectives in the same stage, or both. Table 9.4 provides an example of the DTORF for a specific child, Charlie.

The use of developmental therapy in Charlie's case is illustrated in the following example.

It is arithmetic time. Charlie has individualized worksheets chosen by his teacher to meet his precise current level of academic functioning. A few problems are at his mastery level, to insure success. A few are at the practice level, to insure mastery. And a small, new, problem step has been introduced to make him acquire new learning. While Charlie stays on task, his teacher is teaching a new math concept to another group of children. Charlie raises his hand and waves it frantically back and forth. The teacher doesn't respond, so he shouts out the teacher's name. The teacher ignores Charlie because (1) she is in the midst of an important teaching situation with others; (2) the rule is "Don't interrupt others"; (3) Charlie knows that he must take turns; (4) she doesn't want to reinforce his "disruptive behavior"; and (5) she knows that the worksheets are exactly right for Charlie. Suddenly, Charlie leaps to his feet, turning over his chair in the process. Grabbing his arithmetic worksheets, he tears them savagely into small pieces, throws them on the floor, and bolts for the classroom door.

Is Charlie emotionally disturbed? Hyperactive? Behaviorally disturbed? A "street kid"? Is he perhaps a gifted child frustrated by the monotony of his task? Could he be partially blind? Hearing impaired? Learning disabled? Maybe Charlie is a child without any serious problem at all.

Any child could be in Charlie's position. In the process of growing up, all children are occasionally disruptive, alienated, hyperactive, withdrawn, troubled, nonproductive, or a discipline problem. The difficult job for special educators is to determine when a problem is severe enough for special help. We recognize that when problems are transient, it is both unjustified and damaging to label them. Yet it is through the labeling process that we hope we can identify those youngsters who cope so unsuccessfully that their continuing development is in jeopardy.

What should we look for? Children do not walk in with a sign that says "I am emotionally disturbed." Nor does the presence of any particular behavior predict emotional disturbance. But children do give signals. If we watch for signals and note the context in which they occur, we can begin sifting through the behaviors to determine if a "problem" really is a problem. For example, assume that all children at every age are maturing along certain developmental lines, such as *thinking, participating, communicating, making friends, relating to adults, controlling impulses,* and *meeting society's expectations* ("act your age"). Problems can arise at any point in each dimension. Table 9.5 illustrates how problems may range from mild and transient to severe and devastating.

TABLE 9.4
SAMPLE DEVELOPMENTAL THERAPY OBJECTIVES RATING FORM (DTORF)

Child's Name CHARLIE

Date 10/20/81 Class Stage 3 Raters PARENT, TEACHER, DEVELOPMENTAL THERAPY TCHR

Type Rating (Check One) Baseline _____ X

5th Week _____ 10th Week _____

Behavior

Stage I
- ☑ 0. Indicate awareness
  - ☑ Tactile ☑ Aud. ☑ Motor
  - ☑ Taste ☑ Visual ☑ Smell
- ☑ 1. React by attending
- ☑ 2. Respond by sustained attending
- ☑ 3. Simple stim./motor behavior
- ☑ 4. Complex stim./lmit.
- ☑ 5. Assist in self-help
- ☑ 6. Respond independent play material
- ☑ 7. Indicate recall of routine

Stage II
- ☑ 8. Use play material appropriately
- ☑ 9. To wait/no intervention
- ☑ 10. Participate/sitting; no intervention
- ☑ 11. Participate/movement; no intervention
- ☑ 12. Spontaneous participation

Stage III
- ☒ 13. Complete individual tasks in group
- ☒ 14. Accept success without loss control
- ☒ 15. Awareness/expected conduct vb.
- ☒ 16. Reasons for expectations
- ☒ 17. Tell other/appropriate behavior
- ☒ 18. Refrain inappropriate behavior
  When others inappropriate
- ☒ 19. Control in group

Stage IV
- ☑ 20. Respond appropriately/leader choice
- ☒ 21. Aware of own progress
- ☐ 22. Implement alternative behaviors
- ☐ 23. Flexible/modify procedure
- ☐ 24. New experience with control
- ☐ 25. Provocation with control
- ☐ 26. Interpersonal/group problem solving

Communication

Stage I
- ☑ 0. Produce sounds
- ☑ 1. Attend speaker
- ☑ 2. Respond verbal stimulation/motor behavior
- ☑ 3. Answer/verbal approx.
- ☑ 4. Spontaneous/verbal approx.
- ☑ 5. Recognize wd./to adult
- ☑ 6. Recognize wd./to child
- ☑ 7. Word sequence

Stage II
- ☑ 8. Answer/recognize word
- ☑ 9. Receptive vocabulary
- ☑ 10. Command, question/word sequence
- ☑ 11. Share minimum information/adult
- ☑ 12. Describe characteristics/self, others
- ☑ 13. Share minimal information/child

Stage III
- ☑ 14. Spontaneous description/personal experiences
- ☒ 15. Show feeling response appropriately
- ☒ 16. Participate group discussions/appropriately
- ☒ 17. Describe attributes in self
- ☒ 18. Make positive statement/self
- ☒ 19. Describe attributes/others
- ☒ 20. Recognize others' feelings
- ☐ 21. Verbalize pride/group achievement

Stage IV
- ☐ 22. Channel feelings/non-verbal creativity
- ☐ 23. Same as B21
- ☐ 24. Explain how behavior influences others
- ☐ 25. Verbal praise/support others
- ☐ 26. Verbal feelings spon. approp./gp.
- ☐ 27. Verbal initiate positive relation
- ☐ 28. Spon. express cause-effect/self, others

Socialization

Stage I
- ☑ 1. Aware/others
- ☑ 2. Attend/others' behavior
- ☑ 3. Respond to name
- ☑ 4. Interact/adult non-verbal
- ☑ 5. Solit. play
- ☑ 6. Respond request/come
- ☑ 7. Dem. underst./sing. request
- ☑ 8. Same as C5
- ☑ 9. Same as C6
- ☑ 10. Same as C7
- ☑ 11. Begin emergence/self
- ☑ 12. Contact/adult spontaneous

Stage II
- ☑ 13. Parallel play
- ☑ 14. Same as B9
- ☑ 15. Initiate minimal movement/child
- ☑ 16. sharing activity
- ☑ 17. Interactive play
- ☑ 18. Coop. activity/child in organ. activ.

Stage III
- ☒ 19. Model appropriate behavior/child
- ☒ 20. Share/turns without reminders
- ☒ 21. Lead/demonstrate for group
- ☒ 22. Label situation/simple values
- ☒ 23. Particp. activ./sugges./child
- ☒ 24. Sequence own experiences
- ☒ 25. Develop friendship
- ☒ 26. Seek assistance, praise child
- ☒ 27. Assist others/conforming

Stage IV
- ☐ 28. Show identification/adult role
- ☐ 29. Sequence group experience
- ☐ 30. Spontaneous suggestions to group
- ☐ 31. Aware of others' different actions
- ☐ 32. Respect others' opinions
- ☐ 33. Interest/peer opinions/self
- ☐ 34. Suggest solution to problems
- ☐ 35. Discrim. opposite values
- ☐ 36. Inferences/social situations

Stage I

1. Same as B1
2. Same as B2
3. Same as B3
4. Same as B4
5. Fine/gross motor/24 months
6. Imitate acts of adults
7. Discrim. of objects
8. Same as C3
9. Same as C4
10. Short-term memory/sound, object and people
11. Match object with different/same attri.
12. wrd./label pictures
13. Body coordination/3–4 year level
14. Match identical pictures
15. Recognize body parts
16. Fine-motor coordination/3–4 year
17. Recognize colors

Stage II

18. Recognize use of objects
19. Recognize detail in pictures
20. Recognize different object
21. Count to 5 (1 to 1)
22. Recognize same/different pictures
23. Count to 10 (1 to 1)
24. Eye-hand coordination/5 year level
25. Recognize shapes, symbols, numerals words/same, different
26. Categorize different pictures/similar/assoc.
27. Tell story sequence/pictures
28. Discriminate opposites
29. Body coordination/5 year level
30. Recognize groups to 10
31. Give reasons why

(Pre) Academic

Stage III

32. Eye-hand coordination/left-right/6 year
33. Body-coordination/6 year
34. Read 50 primary words
35. Recognize, write numerals for groups 1–10 (sets/subsets)
36. Write 50 basic words/mem., dictation
37. Recog. and write numerals for groups/100
38. Add, subtract/1–10 (union/sets; commut. prop.)
39. Listen/story/comprehension
40. Read sentences/comprehension
41. Physical skills/games
42. Identify illogical elements
43. Add, subtract/10–20 regroup/place value
44. Write sentences/memory, dictation
45. Multiplication, division to 25
46. Read, write quantitative words
47. Read, write/third grade comprehension
48. Size seriation/relationship

Stage IV

49. Write to communicate
50. Multiply, divide to 81 (prime numbers)
51. Read for pleasure/information
52. Compute money to $10.00
53. Explain story characters
54. Use grammatical rules/writing
55. Same as $35
56. Measurement problems

Stage V

57. Seek others' opinions/current issues
58. Discriminate fact/opinion
59. Recognize/explain illogical ideas
60. Rational numbers/problems
61. Same as B32
62. Use academic tools/citizen, worker

Stage V

27. Seeks work skills
28. Seeks desired role
29. Accept responsibility/self
30. Law/order concepts
31. Participate/group self-governance
32. Apply rational process/problem solving

29. Complex verbal structures/content
30. Verbal conciliatory skills
31. Recognize others' contributions
32. Describe multiple motives/values
33. Spontaneous expression/ideals, values
34. Sustain interper./gp. relations

37. Underst./respect others' feelings
38. Reciprocal skill/multiple roles
39. Personal choices/values
40. Self-understanding/goals
41. Sustain mutual relations

Notes

Parent's Signature

Parent Worker's Signature

Teacher's Signature, Regular Education

Teacher's Signature, Special Education

Source: M. M. Wood. *Developmental Therapy Objectives: A Self-Instructional Workbook* (3rd ed.). Baltimore: University Park Press, 1979, p. 39. Used by permission.

TABLE 9.5
ILLUSTRATIONS OF DIFFERENT LEVELS OF PROBLEMS
ALONG DEVELOPMENTAL LINES

Examples of developmental lines	Sometimes problems are mild, such as when a child:	But sometimes problems are so severe that a child:
Thinking	doesn't understand, makes mistakes, and won't try.	becomes disorganized and no learning occurs.
Participating	wants to watch rather than play.	cannot participate because of withdrawal, nonconstructive activity, or disorganized behavior.
Communicating	doesn't have much to say.	won't or can't talk, or says words that don't make sense.
Making friends	plays alone.	is isolated or made a scapegoat.
Relating to adults	is reserved with adults.	ignores, avoids, or defies adults.
Controlling impulses	has a temper tantrum.	rages, physically attacks others, or destroys materials.
Meeting social expectations	is not "acting his age."	"acts like a baby."

From such an array of possible problems a child might display at home or school, how do parents and teachers determine that a child should be referred? Three questions help us focus on important information bearing on this issue.

Depth: How Unusual or Deviant Is the Child's Behavior?   The question of *depth* involves the severity, or deviancy, of the present behavior. On one hand, the extent to which a child's behaviors vary from the behavior of other children of the same age, race, sex, intelligence, health status, and socioeconomic culture, within the same setting, indicates the seriousness of the disruption in the child's day-to-day adaptations to the environment (Novick et al., 1966). On the other hand, the expectations of teachers, parents, and society vary considerably, and a troublesome behavior may exist only in the eye of the beholder (Lobitz and Johnson, 1975; Rubin and Balow, 1978; Rhodes, 1977). Both perspectives can be accurate. As Pappanikou and Spears (1977, p. 119) suggest, the issue is to "perceive the process from both the child's cognitive life space and that of the practitioner."

Duration: How Long Has the Problem Been Going On?   *Duration* measures are concerned with the time that problem behaviors have persisted.

The reference point can be birth, a critical phase of development, particular events of childhood, or certain ages or grades. Time provides a perspective on a behavioral trend that helps clarify the difficult question of whether a manifest problem indicates a major change or an insignificant fluctuation (Wohlwill, 1976; Rhodes and Paul, 1978). Other time-related measures involve daily, weekly, and monthly patterns of behavior. Analyses of behavior problems through direct observation and measurement often yield rich information about the circumstances surrounding the behavior and its antecedent and consequent events (Fagen and Hill, 1977; Fredricks et al., 1977). This shorter time focus helps us understand how much of a child's daily effort results in positive and how much in negative outcomes. Both time frames are important in determining whether a problem warrants special intervention strategies.

Development: To What Extent Does the Problem Interfere with the Child's Development? Developmental questions assess the impact of a problem on a child's current and future abilities to cope with the tasks of life. At each stage of life the tasks and demands made upon children change. The extent to which a child can meet the demands of one stage and later adapt to the demands of a new stage is an index to his or her general adjustment. According to Gazda (1978),

> the needs of children, preadolescents, adolescents, and adults can be related to their developmental stages of growth and the developmental tasks that confront them. How they cope with or fulfill the tasks is related directly to their level of adjustment and well-being. The developmental tasks . . . with their appropriate coping behaviors serve as excellent guideposts or signals for all those who are responsible for facilitating growth and development. *(p. xiv)*

The implication is that development is the "organizer" — it provides a series of reference points that integrate extensive information about a child's problem behaviors into past, present, and future perspectives. The past history indicates how intractable the problem behavior is; present analysis tells us how the child is presently coping; and projections of the future help us anticipate and prepare for the challenges ahead.

By answering these depth, duration, and development questions, a teacher will generally obtain enough information to determine whether a classroom problem warrants special help. In Charlie's situation, special help proved to be necessary. His teacher noted in his permanent records that severe explosive, disruptive behavior directed toward other children had resulted in several suspensions from school during the previous school year (depth). The teacher also determined that these aggressive outbursts occurred almost daily during the arithmetic period and on the playground. Periods of loss of control lasted only a short time, but they were followed by several hours of sullen withdrawal. His mother told the teacher that he had always been that way (duration). Charlie's teacher and mother were most concerned that his angry aggression and withdrawal were alienating him from the friends and social experiences that are particularly important to the development of children at his age (development). Charlie's teacher and parent agreed that special help was needed, so Charlie was referred for possible special education services. The following summary contains excerpts from the reports of the educational diagnostician, the school psychologist, and the school social worker who made up the diagnostic child study team.

Charlie is a nine-year-old enrolled in the fourth grade. He was referred by his fourth-grade teacher because of inattentiveness, overactivity, need for constant attention, poor persistence on tasks, and aggressiveness toward other children. Other school problems include poor self-concept, inappropriate responses, and a lack of social skills.

Charlie's home life has been very unstable, and this has contributed to his problems. He lives with his mother and maternal grandmother and says he does not get along well with either one. His mother and father were divorced when he was an infant. He saw his father for the next few years on an irregular basis but has not seen him since he was four. He says he remembers him but is ambivalent about whether he wants to see him again. The family lives in the country, and as a result Charlie has no one to play with except a teenage cousin who visits occasionally. His mother has no social life of her own.

Observations of Charlie at school suggest that he tries hard to be part of his group of friends. He continually brags about himself to the other children and threatens them if they do not do as he asks. In contrast, he sometimes resorts to bribery to influence others and will share whatever he has with other children. He seems to need to be the dominant person and control the group. He tries to put down others' suggestions. He also resists attempts to discuss reasons for problem situations or the feelings and views of others. He disclaims any interest in the other children and what they think, which he claims is because he is part of a scientific experiment for mind control. He seems unwilling or unable to describe himself.

Charlie is unable to express his feelings. He can describe how he should behave, even though he is unable to do what he knows is expected. He accuses the children at school of trying to trick him. He responds to them by fighting, playing rough, or talking, all of which get him into trouble. In contrast, his mother says he loves people, treats strangers like friends, shares, and responds well to praise. She sees his problems as resisting discipline, becoming frustrated easily, lack of confidence, temper, obscene language, and jealousy. According to her, when Charlie is angry, he yells, curses, throws things, or stomps and destroys toys.

The fourth-grade teachers and the diagnostic team report somewhat different problems. His teachers feel that the following are high priority problems: attendance, short attention span, perseveration, ritualism, trouble expressing feelings, avoidance of eye contact, manipulation, suspiciousness, arithmetic, and penmanship. The diagnostic team feels that moodiness and resistance to becoming involved appropriately are his major problems. His mother, school teachers, and the diagnostic team agree that aggressiveness towards other children is a major problem.

For enjoyment Charlie says he likes sports (especially Pee Wee baseball), riding his bike, watching TV, and playing with others. He says he enjoys playing games with his mother, but says she is usually too tired, so they just play records and watch TV.

The school administered the WRAT and reported Charlie's grade level achievement as follows: reading, 6.1; spelling, 5.0; and arithmetic, 3.0.

During further educational testing, Charlie seemed comfortable and at ease. He talked freely but volunteered very little information. His performance in academic skill areas appears uneven. In math, he could borrow and carry and knew all the addition and subtraction facts. He wrote his name, address, and birthday from memory, although his writing and drawings were tight and small. Charlie did well on the Woodcock Reading Mastery Test, scoring at the sixth-grade level in Word Identification, at the fifth-grade level on Word Comprehension and Word Attack, and at the third-grade level in Passage Comprehension. Some confusion between left and right was noted during testing.

The results of the psychological testing reported Charlie to be functioning in the superior range of intelligence. On the Stanford-Binet (LM), he achieved an IQ score of 120. His weaknesses seem to be in the areas of social judgment, reasoning, and visual perception, whereas his strengths are in vocabulary, verbal fluency, auditory memory, and conceptualization of relationships. Overall, Charlie feels very inadequate, has a poor self-image, is depressed and anxious, and sees no advantages in using school-related skills.

The psychiatric assessment resulted in a diagnosis of "severe adjustment reaction" with no signs of a thought disorder or neurological problems.

Charlie's IEP

Subsequently, the diagnostic team, fourth-grade teacher, and parent reviewed the assessment results and developed an Individualized Education Program (IEP) for Charlie. This IEP specified that the long-range social and emotional goal was for Charlie to "learn skills for successful group participation" (see stage III in Table 9.1). This long-range goal was divided into goals in the four curriculum areas (see stage III in Table 9.2).

The specific short-term objectives were obtained by using the DTORF (M. M. Wood, 1979).

The developmental therapy goals and objectives used in Charlie's IEP are summarized below.

Short-Term Developmental Therapy Objectives (from the DTORF)

Behavior
Goal: To apply individual skills in group processes.

To complete short, individual tasks with familiar material independent of any teacher intervention (B-13).

To give simple reasons for home, school, and community expectations (B-16).

To refrain from inappropriate behavior when others in the group are losing control (B-18).

To maintain physical and verbal control while participating in group activities including transitions and group play (B-19).

Communication
Goal: To use words to express oneself in the group.

To use words or gestures to show appropriate positive and negative feeling responses to the environment, materials, and people or animals (C-15).

To participate in group discussions in ways not disruptive to the group (C-16).

To describe characteristic attributes, strengths, and problems in self (C-17).

To describe characteristic attributes of others (C-19).

Socialization
Goal: To find satisfaction in group activities.

To model appropriate behavior of another child (S-19).

To participate without inappropriate response in an activity suggested by another child (S-23).

To describe own experiences in the sequence of occurrence (S-24).

To seek assistance or praise from another child (S-26).

Academics

Goal: To participate in the group with basic expressive language concepts, symbolic representation of experiences, numerical concepts of conservation and operations, and body coordination.

To give simple reasons why events occur (A-31).

To identify illogical elements in simple situations (A-42).

To do simple numerical operations of multiplication and division (including arrays) to twenty-five (A-45).

To write for communication of information or feelings to others or self (A-49).

Charlie's initial DTORF, containing the objectives listed above, was presented previously in Table 9.4. This rating was completed by his mother, regular teacher, and developmental therapy teacher working together. A check indicates that these raters agreed that Charlie had mastered the objective. An *X* indicates that Charlie needed to work on the objective. The rating was based on consensus agreement about Charlie's performance on each objective. After the raters marked a maximum of four *X*s in each curriculum area, subsequent objectives not yet mastered were marked *NR* (Not Ready).

Charlie's IEP specified that he would continue to participate in his regular fourth-grade classroom for homeroom period. Then he would attend a stage III developmental therapy class for two and one-half hours each morning. The plan also specified that Charlie would return to his regular fourth-grade class for lunch and the afternoon program. In this way, Charlie was not separated from daily contact with the regular school program and peers.

Charlie's Developmental Therapy Program

Charlie's program in the developmental therapy class, with seven other children all working on stage III objectives, followed this general daily schedule:

9:00– 9:20	Group meeting — planning the day (for the socialization and communication objectives)
9:20– 9:50	Language arts (individual and group work in reading and creative writing for the behavior, academic, and communication objectives)
9:50–10:15	Outside time — physical game skills (for the behavior and socialization objectives)

10:15–10:45   Math
(individual and group work in math processes and problems for the behavior, academic, and socialization objectives)

10:45–11:15   Special time
(creative unit involving role play, music, and art for the behavior, communication, and socialization objectives)

11:15–11:30   Group meeting — reviewing the successes of the day (for the socialization and communication objectives)

The activities, materials, and techniques used by Charlie's developmental therapy teacher were designed to promote progress toward the overall stage III goal and his specific stage III objectives. These procedures are summarized in competency-based teacher evaluation instruments designed for each stage of developmental therapy (Robinson, 1981). Here are examples of items from this instrument illustrating some of the techniques used at stage III*:

Activities are conducted to insure the participation of each child in the group.

Activities provide success and pleasure-producing responses in children.

Activities such as games are designed so that there are no losers and no peer competition.

Activity does not extend beyond peak of motivation.

Before activity begins, teacher "talks through" or demonstrates the activity when necessary so each child will understand the task and enjoy it.

Classroom materials are used for a specific purpose and are chosen as vehicles for the accomplishment of objectives.

Materials are used to increase individual effectiveness in the group.

Group is allowed to control the materials with teacher assistance.

Children know the behaviors expected in each activity.

Teachers have a consistent schedule of activities to follow each day.

Rules are meaningful and reflect developmental objectives.

Classroom rules are few and are stated positively.

Children are prepared for transition time from one activity to another.

Voice modulation and facial expression are effectively used (e.g., calm, quiet voice, animated voice and expression; emphatic, matter-of-fact voice; eye contact).

Each child is frequently contacted by the lead teacher either through verbal or nonverbal techniques.

Control of materials by teacher is used occasionally to calm a group or prevent a child from acting out.

* J. Stafford Robinson, Construction of an instrument to assess the classroom skills of teachers who use developmental therapy with emotionally disturbed students (Doctoral dissertation, University of Georgia, 1981), Appendix.

Excessive external controls, contrived rewards, and token reinforcements are avoided completely or minimized.

Interpersonal forms of praise and rewards are used frequently. (Verbal praise and group activities)

Positive statements rather than negative statements are used.

Punishment is not used.

Small accomplishments are recognized.

Teacher conveys personal recognition of child as an important individual.

The lead and support teachers use verbal exchanges to provide models for interpersonal responses.

The lead teacher is clearly leading.

Redirection is used as a major technique.

Reflection is used as a major technique.

Interpretation is a technique used frequently.

Confrontation is used only when there is certainty of a therapeutic outcome.

Life Space Interviewing (LSI) is used as a major technique with individual children.

Assessment of Charlie's Progress

As noted previously in Table 9.4, Charlie was rated by his regular teacher, his mother, and his developmental therapy teacher when he entered the program. Subsequently, the same team of people rated Charlie at ten-week intervals throughout the year. Each time this rating was undertaken, the team sat down together to review each objective to determine if Charlie has mastered it, if he needed to work on it, or if he was not yet ready to begin work on it. Table 9.6 is a bar graph that summarizes Charlie's progress. Each cell corresponds to an objective. The cells marked in gray are the short-term objectives for that particular time period. Cells marked with slanted stripes are objectives mastered. Unmarked cells indicate objectives for which Charlie is not yet ready.

Several trends are evident from this graph. First, at the baseline rating in the behavior columns, Charlie has difficulty with impulse control, acting out when assigned to individual tasks (B-13) and when others lost control (B-18). He did not convey that he really understood the reasons for the rules (B-16). He also had difficulty during transitions and could not function successfully without a considerable amount of verbal structure from the teacher (B-19). At midyear, Charlie had mastered only one of these objectives (B-16), but by the end of the year he had mastered all of the original behavior objectives except B-19. Since the midyear rating, Charlie had also been working on new objectives in behavior at stage IV; by the end of the school year, he had mastered four additional stage IV behavior objectives. These objectives were age-appropriate for Charlie, which suggested that he no longer needed special services as provided in the developmental therapy classroom.

TABLE 9.6
SUMMARY OF CHARLIE'S PROGRESS ON THE DTORF

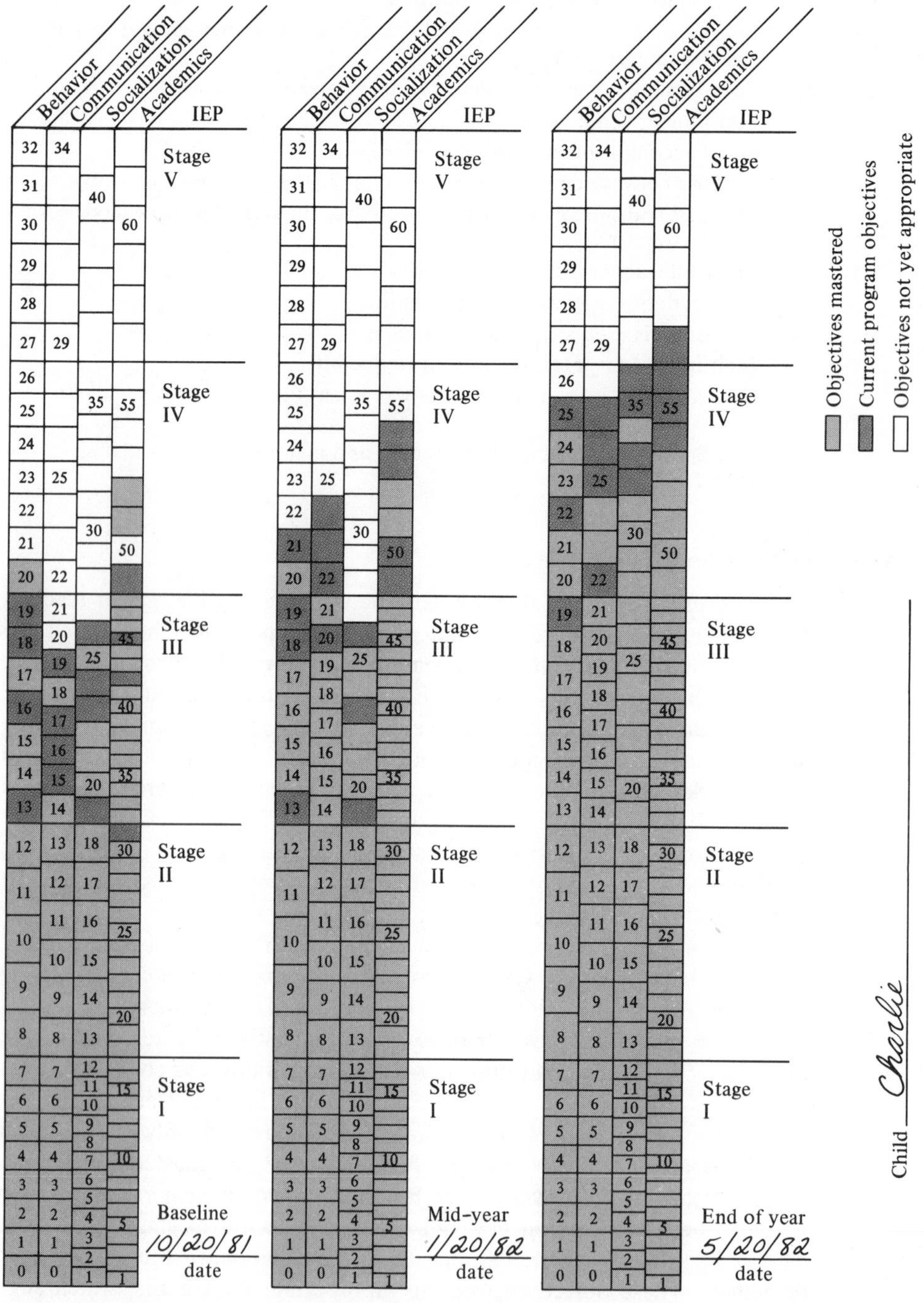

Legend:
- ▨ Objectives mastered
- ▦ Current program objectives
- ☐ Objectives not yet appropriate

Chart 1 — Baseline, date 10/20/81

	Behavior	Communication	Socialization	Academics	IEP
	32	34			Stage V
	31		40		
	30			60	
	29				
	28				
	27	29			
	26				Stage IV
	25		35	55	
	24				
	23	25			
	22		30		
	21			50	
	20	22			
	19	21		45	Stage III
	18	20	25		
	17	19			
	16	18		40	
	15	17 / 16			
	14	15	20	35	
	13	14			
	12	13	18	30	Stage II
	11	12	17		
	10	11	16	25	
		10	15		
	9	9	14		
	8	8	13	20	
	7	7	12 / 11	15	Stage I
	6	6	10		
	5	5	9 / 8		
	4	4	7	10	
	3	3	6 / 5		
	2	2	4	5	Baseline 10/20/81 date
	1	1	3 / 2		
	0	0	1		

Chart 2 — Mid-year, date 1/20/82

Chart 3 — End of year, date 5/20/82

Child _Charlie_

The same trend is evident in the graphs of Charlie's progress in communication. At the time of the baseline rating, he was having problems expressing feelings appropriately (C-15), participating in group discussions appropriately (C-16), and describing characteristics of himself (C-17) and others (C-19). At midyear Charlie had mastered all of the original communication objectives and begun work on four new ones. Three of these (C-22, C-23, and C-24) were in stage IV. By the end of the year, the final communication objective in stage III had been mastered and Charlie was working on communication objectives well into stage IV.

In socialization, Charlie made less dramatic gains from baseline to midyear. At the baseline, he was modeling the inappropriate rather than the appropriate behavior of other children (S-19). He was also learning to participate willingly in activities suggested by another child (S-23), to describe his experiences in sequential steps (S-24), and to seek out other children for support, assistance, and recognition (S-26). At midyear, Charlie had mastered only S-24, so no new socialization objectives were added to his IEP. By the end of the year, however, Charlie's progress was better. He had mastered all of the stage III objectives in socialization and was working on high-level objectives in stage IV. These objectives were related to developing empathy, understanding of others, and skills for reciprocal social interactions.

Similar trends were evident in the academic area. At the baseline, Charlie's major difficulties were with activities in language arts that required insight, such as giving reasons why things happened (A-31), identifying illogical elements (A-42), and writing to communicate personal ideas (A-49). He had already achieved grade level in basic academic skills — reading and writing with third-grade comprehension (A-47) was mastered and he was working on multiplication and division processes (A-45). Charlie made steady progress throughout the year in the academic area. By the end of the year, he was using academic skills as interpersonal tools. This is one of the overall goals for academics in stage IV.

In summary, Charlie's progress on the DTORF reflects a mastery of the social and emotional objectives and goals for stage III and considerable progress in mastering the objectives of stage IV. Socially and emotionally, this was where Charlie should have been for his age and cognitive ability.

HISTORICAL AND THEORETICAL BACKGROUND: WHY USE A DEVELOPMENTAL APPROACH?

Developmental therapy is built on the assumption that everyone, including the severely disturbed and autistic, must accomplish a common array of developmental tasks for social and emotional growth. A second assumption is that these tasks ordinarily occur in a sequence or hierarchy. Although the term "developmental tasks" is often associated with the work of Havinghurst (1972) and others concerned with the sequential nature of mental development, the same term can be used to characterize the nature of social and emotional development. Curriculum and intervention programs for the severely disturbed and autistic constructed from a developmental viewpoint emphasize (1) the systematic designation of social and emotional tasks, (2) the identification of hierarchical sequences for these tasks, and (3) the usefulness of stage guidelines for grouping children to master the tasks. Such an approach seems both logical and relevant. Each of these points is briefly discussed below in relation to developmental therapy.

What Are the Social and Emotional Tasks?

Numerous researchers and theorists have contributed to the identification of specific tasks in social and emotional development. The full range of theory and research on the subject, produced over six decades, could not be adequately reviewed in several volumes. Many theories have influenced developmental therapy significantly. The long-term goals and specific short-term objectives in developmental therapy, for example, outlined in Figures 9.1, 9.2, 9.3, and 9.4 contain sequences of personal, interpersonal, and group experiences identified as elements in the processes of ego development, moral development, social and interpersonal development, motivation, and cognitive development. Each of these is summarized briefly below.

The elements of *ego development* included in the developmental therapy objectives are impulse control, cognitive style, relationship to parents, relationship to peers, rules and social standards, dependence and independence, motivation, inner fantasy life, strategies for problem-solving, and values (Ausubel, 1952; Bobroff, 1960; A. Freud, 1946, 1965, 1973; Henry, 1956; Loevinger, 1976; Mahler, 1968; Mahler, Pine, and Bergman, 1975).

Several principles from the area of *moral development* have been used in the developmental therapy model. First, moral development is an intricate part of emotional development, cognition, and socialization. Second, empathic capacities and multiple-role experiences are necessary for higher stages of moral development. Third, the nature of adult-child interactions is important in moral development (and thus in social and emotional development); these interactions must change in quality as the child develops. Fourth, most behaviors that adults find desirable in children are elements of moral development, reflecting adults' own values. Finally, elements of moral development can be identified, studied experimentally, and traced over a developmental continuum (Boyd and Kohlberg, 1973; Gibbs, 1977; Kohlberg, 1969, 1971, 1976; Kohlberg and Hersh, 1977; Midlarsky and Suda, 1978; Piaget, 1954, 1965; Turiel, 1969).

Social-interpersonal development is also a major component of developmental therapy. It is probably accurate to say that almost all developmental theorists acknowledge the significance of social-interactive elements in human development. There appears to be agreement that feelings, personality, behavior, thought, and values are directly influenced by interactions with people — the social environment. However, each theorist focuses on different aspects of the social-interpersonal domain (Bandura, 1976, 1977b; Erikson, 1956, 1963, 1972, 1977; Flavell, 1968; Kohlberg and Hersh, 1977; Selman, 1976; Selman and Byrne, 1974).

Differences are found because each theorist emphasizes a particular aspect of the social-interpersonal domain. Learning from others, for example, constitutes a major element in the work of Bandura. As a social learning theorist, Bandura explains the acquisition and maintenance of aggressive behaviors as products of observation or direct experience with aggression. Although he has not integrated his constructs into a sequence of development, the elements he emphasizes are important to a model of intervention which seeks to render developmental theory operational. The social learning constructs developed by Bandura and Walters (1963) that are particularly significant for developmental therapy are:

1. The influence of *examples* set by others.
2. The importance of *cognitive processes,* such as memory for images and words and other forms of symbolic functioning.
3. The usefulness of *symbolic modeling* through pictures, words, drama, demonstrations, and role play.
4. The necessity for *direct experience* guided by valued outcomes.
5. The extent to which modeling can be used to influence human behavior, particularly when controlled through *selective attention* to specific aspects.
6. The power of *status,* social derision, and self-contempt as forces which influence behavior significantly.
7. The value of the *vicarious experience* of others' successes and failures.
8. The importance of *self-reinforcement, self-reward, self-censure,* and *self-disengagement* for regulating behavior.

Motivation development, as the psychological force for change, is an essential construct for developmental therapy. The forces which move children to cooperate, participate, interact, and learn are highly personal and complex. They involve feelings, attitudes, emotions, beliefs, and pleasures. These forces are usually concealed for protection, so a teacher must understand the motivations and needs which directly influence the behavior of a specific child to manage the child's behavior for a successful outcome. Once a teacher recognizes the stage of development for a particular child, determining individual patterns of motivation becomes the chief concern (Swanson and Reinert, 1979).

The many "master motivators" suggested by numerous theories include tension-reduction (Rapaport, 1960); avoidance of anxiety (Sullivan, 1953); search for meaning (Fingarette, 1963); equilibration (Piaget, 1977); guilt (Kohlberg and Hersh, 1977); the ideal self as pacer (Loewald, 1962; Baldwin, 1975); competence (White, 1959); achievement (McClelland, 1955); and others. Madsen (1968) compared and contrasted twenty different theories of motivation. Two of the notable conclusions he draws are that (1) motivation works in concert with cognition as a determinant of behavior, and (2) every force that influences behavior is a part of the motivational field. According to Midlarsky and Suda's 1978 review of motivations, these are the forces which promote development: internalization (internal motivation resulting from identification through the reinforcement process, Mowrer, 1960); empathy (resulting from either intrinsic or extrinsic rewards, Rosenhan, 1972); and vicarious rewards (empathy for the positive affect of another, Aronfreed, 1968). Elements from each of these theorists have been included in the developmental therapy objectives and in the teaching strategies specified for each developmental therapy stage.

In addition, Erikson's (1963) psychosocial themes are included in the developmental therapy curriculum as broad categories for motivation in developmental sequence. There are seven major motivational themes in Erikson's sequential schema:

pleasure-pain (trust)

dependence-independence (autonomy and power)

secondary narcissism (imitation and identification)

fears and expectations (initiative)

self-esteem (identification, industry, and activity)

conscience (guilt and conflict)

independence-dependence (identity formation and values)

Principles for guiding *cognitive development,* provided by Piaget and associates, are included in the basic framework of developmental therapy. These principles are summarized below (Inhelder and Piaget, 1964; Piaget, 1967, 1972, 1977; Piaget and Inhelder, 1969; Wolff, 1960, 1972).

1. An optimal learning environment is one which maintains a balance between too much newness (resulting in frustration) and too much sameness (resulting in boredom). Creating such an environment involves knowing the child's current developmental stage of mastery and the next step in the child's developmental sequence.

2. The constraints inherent in a child's cognitive problem-solving abilities are developmental in nature; that is, they are bound by capacities that cannot be accelerated or readjusted on demand. Thus, each expectation established for a child's social, emotional, and interpersonal problem-solving behavior must be based on the child's current cognitive capacity.

3. Piaget's emphasis on personal experience as a child's medium for learning is reflected in the active, creative, and experiential focus of developmental therapy.

4. The emphasis Piaget places on processes rather than content is incorporated into the development therapy objectives in all four curriculum areas and in the management of behavior. Thus, the orientation is on

teaching a child processes which are tools for further coping with all the demands of life — behavioral, communicative, social, and academic.

5. Piaget's emphasis of peer interactions as a major factor in cognitive and moral (social) development has influenced the way developmental therapy is conducted. Adult control begins to decrease during stage I as the emphasis begins the shift toward awareness of peers. This gradual movement continues with systematic decreases in adult control and increases in peer control throughout the stages. Similarly, self-esteem has its roots in stage I in the care and valuing of a child by the adult. This valuing is systematically built into the developmental therapy objectives through a hierarchical sequence of valuing self, valuing peers, and eventually being valued by peers.

Why Is Sequence Important?   Consider the constructs implied in the term "development." The Thorndike-Barnhart dictionary tells us that development is "a gradual unfolding; a working out in detail." Blasi (1976) states that absolute stability or reversibility are two conditions which preclude development. Based on this position, he equates development with structural changes. Structures, Blasi contends, are organizational units ("systems" or "schema") held together by "a set of relations among the elements" (1976, p. 32). Development, then, occurs through changes in or acquisitions to, existing structures.

The process of development, according to theorists, probably occurs like this: First, an existing structure has a homeostatic quality. Second, changes in structures are set in motion when internal, genetic, or environmental demands disrupt the balance, causing disequilibrium. Third, selective assimilation and accommodation occur. Thus, the old structure becomes a new structure. The change occurs in two forms — incremental changes in the previous elements and acquisition of new elements and directions. Thus, the new is linked to the old and a developmental sequence results.

This idea of transformations within stability and continuity has extremely important implications for intervention with emotionally disturbed children: Both cognitive and affective elements of a stable nature already established in a disturbed child may be the foundation upon which changes acquired in an intervention program can be secured. Such changes, when they result in satisfying outcomes, become assimilated into the core of the child's response system. Thus, a spiraling expansion of the child's capacities can occur. Over time, such a process can produce social and emotional growth. Consider impulse control, for example. On a continuum, a child develops from having no control of impulses at birth to having highly sophisticated control systems as an adult. The common characteristic is impulsivity, which occurs during all stages of life. The incremental aspect to this developmental line is the amount of control exercised. These are continuous variables. The strategies for impulse control at various phases of life are the qualitative differences, the developmental tasks. Each developmental task represents a nonlinear change.

Thus, consideration of developmental sequences permits the teacher to identify both individual, qualitative differences and progress on a single, continuous dimension. From individual differences, we obtain information about the unique, current coping strategies of a child at a particular point in time. These short-term fluctuations are important because they represent day-to-day expressions of the individual. From the study of trends, we obtain information about where an individual child is on a continuum of tasks when a program begins, the time it takes to accomplish several developmental sequences, patterns of mastery, and sequences for the future. Such information is extremely useful in the context of preparing, implementing, and evaluating the IEP.

Why Are Stages Important?   From the cumulative study of the milestone trends, patterns, and rates of mastery of many children, stage theorists and researchers have identified commonly shared sequences, patterns of acquisition, and clusters of characteristics which lend themselves to *grouping* by *similarity*. Such clusters are called "stages." Stages simplify the teachers' task of providing instruction to meet the needs of individual children. Stages offer guidelines for grouping children with similar characteristics, thereby allowing teachers to focus their selection of activities, materials, and techniques. Stages also define the changing role of the adult, which is necessary to facilitate social and emotional growth. For an illustration of how children's characteristics cluster into stages, see Table 9.3.

Loevinger (1976) notes that stages are generally named to denote the characteristics most evident at a particular stage. She also cautions about several limitations. One is that the name or number of a stage is only a label. Stages are made up of complex structures, having vast, unique characteristics which both differentiate them from and connect them to previous stages and stages to follow. Another caution is that a child in a particular stage may exhibit remnants of the previous stage while mastering the characteristics predominating at the present stage and manifesting a preview of elements that will merge more fully at the next stage. Piaget (1977) identifies this phenomenon as *décalage*. Turiel (1969) describes this as *stage mixture* and sees it as an important part of developmental transitions.

EVALUATION: VALIDATION OF THE MODEL AND DOCUMENTATION OF CHILD PROGRESS

Both formative and summative evaluation procedures are used in the evaluation system that is criterion-referenced to developmental therapy (Huberty and Swan, 1975; Huberty, Quirk, and Swan, 1973; Swan and Wood, 1975; M. M. Wood and Swan, 1978). The information collected is used for decision-making, so the evaluation processes help maintain the highest possible quality of service to children and families. A second emphasis of the evaluation system is on providing information for continuing refinements and adaptations of the model. This emphasis provides for continuing research into the characteristics of the children receiving developmental therapy.

Although program evaluation systems are somewhat constrained by the need to provide consistency for comparison and decision-making, such systems must also be sufficiently dynamic to meet the program needs of individual children, their families, and their teachers. Evaluation procedures in developmental therapy are based on this requirement for a flexible, responsive system. Continuous review, refinement, and elaboration of the procedures are the top priority.

Program Effectiveness

The developmental therapy model was submitted to the Joint Dissemination Review Panel (JDRP) of the U. S. Office of Education and the National Institute of Education in 1975 and received validation as an effective program (U. S. Office of Education, 1978). The validation criteria used by JDRP are summarized as follows:

> Effectiveness, however, is not defined simplistically. In order for the JDRP to determine that a given product, project, or practice is effective, several conditions must be met. The evidence must be valid and reliable, the effect must be of sufficient magnitude to have educational importance, and it should be possible to reproduce both the intervention and its effect at their sites. *(Tallmadge, 1977, p. 2)*

The ways in which the developmental therapy model has met these effectiveness criteria are described below.

Valid and Reliable Evidence.   Evidence of change in children enrolled in developmental therapy classes is obtained from two instruments, the Referral Form Checklist (RFCL) and the Developmental Therapy Objectives Rating Form (DTORF). These are described below:

1. *The Referral Form Checklist (RFCL).* The RFCL is composed of fifty-four problems stated in terms of behavior, which are drawn from a pool of over 200 referral problems. These problems represent all the referral problems appearing in the records for a two-year period. A review of the literature indicated that these problems were identified in previous investigations of the characteristics of emotionally disturbed children (Peterson and Quay, 1967; Kooi and Schutz, 1965; Schrupp and Gjerde, 1953).

Factor analyses of the RFCL ratings of 194 emotionally disturbed children identified three general factors highly similar to the factorial dimensions of problem behaviors identified by Peterson and Quay (1967): aggressiveness and hostility; apathy and inattentiveness; and anxiety or withdrawal. These factor dimensions occurred similarly among four different groups of raters: parents, teachers, psychologists, and educational diagnosticians (Kaufman, Swan, and Wood, 1979). Using Ebel's (1951) procedures for estimating interobserver reliability, values of .46 to .76 were reported by Huberty, Quirk, and Swan (1973) for ratings by educators and psychologists. Similarly, coefficient alpha reliabilities from .55 to .88 were reported by Morris and Arrant (1978).

2. *The Developmental Therapy Objectives Rating Form (DTORF).* As illustrated in Charlie's case earlier in this chapter, the DTORF is a rating form composed of 171 objectives outlining a series of sequential, developmental milestones for social and emotional growth in four curriculum areas: behavior, communication, socialization, and (pre)academics. The DTORF is used in assessment, program planning, grouping children for classes, identifying short-term objectives for implementing an IEP, and for documenting child change.

A consensus rating procedure involving at least three persons is recommended in using the DTORF (Combs, 1975; M. M. Wood, 1979). Generally, a DTORF rating team includes the lead teacher, a parent, and other support personnel. The rating is intended to reflect a child's performance at home, in school, and in a special program. Each DTORF objective is rated in one of three ways: a check indicates that a developmental therapy objective has been mastered; *X* indicates that an objective needs more work; and *NR* indicates that an objective is not yet ready for attention. A child is rated at enrollment and at regular intervals until he or she no longer needs services or until the end of the school year. Numerical summaries yield before and after averages and percentages of mastery of objectives by individual children or by groups of children.

To explore the hierarchical validity of the DTORF, eighty-seven severely disturbed children at the Rutland Center were evaluated at three different times over a nine-month period. A Guttman-type scalogram analysis yielded an order of objectives similar to that of DTORF objectives in each curriculum area. In addition to these analyses, professionals using the DTORF in other locations were asked to judge each objective for correctness of sequence. Their findings resembled those of the statistical analyses. These studies resulted in the reordering of several objectives in the sequences (Swan and Wood, 1975; M. M. Wood and Swan, 1978).

The idea that the DTORF contains hierarchical sequences in which lower level skills are gradually integrated into new learning at higher levels is also supported by a study of thirty-three severely emotionally disturbed and autistic children who entered a developmental therapy program at stage II. Figure 9.1 illustrates the sequential nature of their gains in the four developmental therapy curriculum areas.

At entry, these thirty-three children had mastered the fewest objectives in behavior and communication. By termination, more than three-fourths of these objectives had been achieved, with the greatest gains occurring in

FIGURE 9.1
PROGRESS OF STAGE II CHILDREN (N = 33)
Average treatment: 27.3 weeks; range: 10–60 weeks.

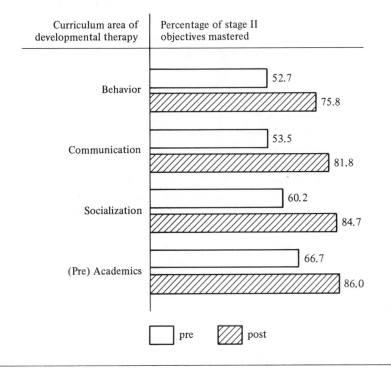

Source: Data from M. M. Wood. *Developmental Therapy.* Baltimore: University Park Press, 1975, Table 3–4. Used by permission.

communication. However, the relative position of the four curriculum areas remained the same. In ascending order of proportion of objectives mastered, the areas were behavior, communication, socialization, and (pre)-academics. This same pattern was repeated when DTORF gains were analyzed according to curriculum area and across four stages of developmental therapy. These results follow the theoretical model of developmental therapy, in which each of the four curriculum areas draws upon the basic skills of the preceding area and stage.

In a study of the reliability of the DTORF, two professionals using the DTORF rated twenty-one severely emotionally disturbed children at the Rutland Center. The mean percentage of agreement was 82 percent (range, 60 percent to 99 percent). Subsequently, four procedures were used to reduce the range of rater variability: (1) examples of mastery of each objective were written; (2) the "consensus rating" of three persons currently working together with the child was emphasized in the directions for using the instrument; (3) a self-instructional workbook was developed for training persons to use the DTORF; and (4) a series of three video training tapes was developed, with the final tape displaying the criterion according to which the trainee's rating is compared with the standard rating for accuracy.

The Effect.   The effect of developmental therapy was first documented by a study of seventy-five severely emotionally disturbed and autistic children. Their average age was 8.7 years at entry (range, 4 to 12.7 years). The mean length of time in treatment was 23.9 weeks (range, 10 to 60 weeks). Each of the children had completed a specified developmental therapy program designed according to individual DTORF profiles. The DTORF data, which showed mastery of objectives according to each child's entry stage, documented that about 80 percent of the entry objectives were mastered by the time of termination. This level of mastery was judged to indicate general mastery of that stage of social and emotional development. The conclusion drawn from this study was that severely disturbed and autistic children do show progress in mastering specified developmental therapy objectives, and that they generally do so in less than a year. This study also verified that it is possible to monitor the progress of children as they master, or fail to master, developmental objectives (Swan and Wood, 1975).

In another study, which used the RFCL to measure reduction of severe problems, the parents of thirty-seven severely disturbed and autistic children ages three to twelve years were asked to rate their children at the beginning and end of their children's developmental therapy programs. Statistically significant reductions in problem behaviors were found (p. < .005). In the same study, a different group of thirty-five children was followed two years after the completion of their programs. The same significant reductions in problems were reported by their parents. The mean length of treatment was 11.5 months (SD 6.3 months) for the first group and 10.0 months (SD 5.8 months) for the second group. Significant reductions in total number of severe problem behaviors were also found to occur regardless of age, sex, race, parents' income, and length of time in treatment (Kaufman, Paget, and Wood, 1981).

Another study reported the progress during one school year of 106 young children with varying handicaps who received developmental therapy in different settings. It should be noted that these children had not completed their programs during the period of the study. The results indicate that the children, regardless of handicapping condition, made gains on the DTORF in all settings: a half-day treatment center with 37 severely emotionally disturbed children, mean age 6 years, 2 months (range, 2 years, 5 months to 8 years); a self-contained, full-day program with 39 autistic children, mean age 6 years, 4 months (range, 4 years, 6 months to 7 years, 11 months); a full-day mainstream program with 20 mixed handicapped youngsters in day care, mean age 4 years, 11 months (range, 2 years, 8 months to 6 years, 7 months); and a half-day mainstreamed Head Start program with 10 emotionally disturbed children, mean age 4 years (range 3 years, 5 months to 4 years, 9 months). With the exception of the autistic group, who began the year in stage I, these children began their programs of developmental therapy objectives in stage II. By the end of the year, all four groups had made their greatest proportion of gains in stage II, generally achieving more than 50 percent of the objectives in each stage II curriculum area. Because the end of stage II is the demarcation between preschool and school-age expectations in developmental therapy, these results suggest that these 106 children were nearing age and performance expectations in each setting (M. M. Wood and Swan, 1978).

Replication of the Model.   Several minimal standards have been designated as necessary for replication of the model:

1. Use of the DTORF with an accuracy score of 75 percent correct or better on the training tapes.
2. Formation of small groups according to each child's developmental therapy stage to implement developmental therapy (averaging six children to a group with two adults).
3. Use of the developmental therapy classroom practices and procedures by teachers, as indicated by a classroom rating of performance of 75 percent or better on the Developmental Therapy Rating Inventory of Teacher Skills (Robinson, 1981).
4. Involvement of a parent and the child's regular classroom teachers in the DTORF ratings and the developmental therapy program whenever possible.
5. Provision for concomitant enrollment of a child in a regular educational setting, if possible, while enrolled in the developmental therapy program (mainstreaming).

As an example of the response of the field to developmental therapy, between 1973 and 1976, seventy-eight new programs were established using the model. These programs served 2,971 severely emotionally disturbed or mixed handicapped youngsters (Swan, 1976). Between 1978 and 1980, approximately fifty-four additional new sites began using the model.

Evidence of Program Effectiveness.   The effectiveness of the developmental therapy model, according to the JDRP criteria, has been documented: The evidence is valid and reliable; the effect is of educational importance in that problems are significantly reduced and are not evident two years later; and the results have been reproduced by others in various settings, in terms of length of time in treatment, types of handicaps, and child progress on the developmental therapy objectives.

SUMMARY: THE CURRENT STATUS OF THE DEVELOPMENTAL THERAPY MODEL

The developmental therapy model is a systematic approach that teachers, paraprofessionals, volunteers, parents, and various mental health professionals find easy to understand and implement. It provides a common language in which each member of a multiprofessional team can contribute. It also has a built-in accountability system, directly referenced to the curriculum and classroom practices, which guides teachers and parents.

There is a philosophy and theory behind the model which teachers and parents understand and endorse. The philosophy emphasizes the aspects of normal social and emotional development inherent in all children. The theoretical foundation is based upon research and theory from developmental psychology, social learning theory, psychodynamic theory, and special education (Hoyt, 1978; M. M. Wood, 1975a, 1975b, 1978b).

The model has been used in varied settings, primarily with children from age two to sixteen, ranging from the severely emotionally disturbed, autistic, or psychotic to those who are functioning in regular school settings. The model also has been used to a limited extent with children who are deaf, orthopedically handicapped, educable retarded, trainable retarded, language delayed, and gifted.

The specified long- and short-term goals in developmental therapy for social and emotional growth are used in planning the Individualized Education Plans (IEPs) mandated by Public Law 94-142 (M. M. Wood, 1975b, 1979). The sequential short-term objectives for social and emotional development, ranging from the most basic motoric and attending responses through a hierarchical series of developmental milestones, are applicable to children up to age sixteen. These objectives provide the curriculum scope and sequence and are the result of testing and modifications which have been conducted over a ten-year period (Swan and Wood, 1975; M. M. Wood, 1979).

The curriculum provides a text of basic instructional methods carefully sequenced to the developmental objectives. This text contains descriptions of the amount of time that instruction should be conducted, as well as schedules and guidelines for the selection of instructional activities. Examples and alternative strategies for obtaining each objective are outlined in detail, as are examples of mastery of each objective. There are numerous descriptions of useful teaching procedures and a detailed account of problems which may result in particular situations and ways to modify them. The curriculum provides a list of instructional materials used to reach developmental therapy goals in each stage of development. Also, the roles of adults at each stage of development are carefully outlined (M. M. Wood, 1975b).

In addition, the curriculum includes four books of methods using fantasy, storytelling, the arts, recreation, music, child drama, sociodrama, adaptive physical education, and play to reach curriculum goals in each stage of development (Purvis and Samet, 1976; Williams and Wood, 1977; M. M. Wood, 1981). Descriptions of home programs and services for parents, especially with very young and autistic children, are also available (Bachrach et al., 1978; M. M. Wood, 1975b).

The criterion-referenced evaluation system has procedures for assessment, establishing baseline developmental objectives, and a periodic program of data collection and program monitoring. Both formative and summative data are used. The child progress aspect uses a preproblem and postproblem checklist and a developmental milestones rating procedure. The instruments have been pilot-tested and shown to be reliable and valid (Huberty and Swan, 1975; Swan and Wood, 1975; M. M. Wood and Swan, 1978). Research studies to evaluate the progress of children two years after developmental therapy is terminated have shown that the number of severe problem behaviors are significantly reduced (Kaufman, Paget, and Wood, 1981). Another indication of effectiveness is that the developmental therapy model is validated by the U. S. Office of Education Joint Dissemination and Review Panel (JDRP) and is designated in *Educational Programs That Work* by the National Diffusion Network as a developer-demonstration project (U. S. Office of Education, 1978).

Finally, there is a training program in developmental therapy for college students and for direct service, supervisor, and leadership personnel. This program has been field-tested for three years, evaluated, and revised (M. M. Wood, 1977, 1978a).

Eventual understanding of the complex nature of emotional disturbance and the education of these handicapped children depends on rigorous and consistent investigation of a variety of models. Such investigations should be based on specification of theoretical constructs and functional and analytic applications. Constructs, theories, and applications should be investigated in many ways. Not only do we need a variety of evaluation strategies, but we also need basic information, such as the rates and patterns of social and emotional progress of both handicapped and nonhandicapped children; particular characteristics of children benefiting from specific treatment approaches; and practices and procedures which seem to produce beneficial results (Ziegler and Trickett, 1978). The limits are those we impose on ourselves. The more open we are to a variety of sets of information about disturbed children, their families, curriculum, and instruction, the more we are able to learn, revise, and develop strategies which can facilitate the development of these children.

As Benjamin Bloom (1978) says about the future improvement of education,

> The answer does not lie in additional funds, new fads, or major sweeping changes in the organization of our educational system. As I see it, the solution lies in our views about students and their learning. These views have grown out of our practices and they will not be changed until we alter these practices. When the changed practices succeed in promoting more effective learning, both teachers and students will change their views. *(p. 563)*

Chapter 10

The Parent Role in Special Education

Ronnie N. Alexander
University of Texas at San Antonio

with

Roger L. Kroth
University of New Mexico

Richard L. Simpson
University of Kansas

Thomas Poppelreiter
Scottsdale, Arizona

Parents are probably the single most neglected source of expertise in educating emotionally disturbed children. The skills and knowledge that parents possess and can provide educators have seldom been recognized. On the one hand, some professionals want parents involved minimally or not at all. As one teacher said, "I don't want them in the room. They distract the children and upset them. They also undo the work we do at school when the child goes home." On the other hand, some professionals feel that all parents should be totally involved in and committed to the educational program philosophy espoused by the program the children are in. These professionals might argue that all parents should attend a series of training sessions and be able to demonstrate the skills of behavior management, filial therapy, developmental therapy, or whatever structure the program uses. The attitude reflected by one extreme is "stay out — you will mess up the program." The other extreme reflects the attitude that "you don't know how, so we will teach you."

Most educators recognize the strong influence that parents have on their children. Parents are with their children two-thirds of every day during the school year and all day for one-fourth of the calendar year. Parents also have the major responsibility for their children from birth until the children can provide for themselves — without summers off or being able to pass the children on to new caregivers. Hobbs (1978) says, "We have to reconceptualize the role of parents. . . . Professional specialists and public school people have deplorably neglected parents in the past. Schools often treat parents a nuisances, but actually they have to be central in any kind of intelligent programming for children. . . . Parents have to be recognized as special educators, the true experts on their children, and professional people — teachers, pediatricians, psychologists, and others — have to learn how to be consultants to parents" (pp. 495–496).

The position proposed by Hobbs would require a novel approach to working with parents. Professionals would need to accept the parents as experts in the educational process. It is doubtful that most professionals would accept this change in roles, since it would put the parents in the role of the authority and the professional in the role of the paid employee. Actually, this role reversal might not change how good programs are run now. Many parents would probably choose to have additional training. They would probably like to have more information, knowledge, and skills, and they might rely on professional judgment, but they could also say they wanted a second opinion, or that they were currently unable to take a short course. Professionals would have to be more cognizant of the strengths and weaknesses of parents and more attuned to their needs.

Since there probably will never be enough professionals to serve the needs of children, either educationally or therapeutically, it makes sense to involve parents actively in the education of their own children. But the involvement will have to be what parents are ready for and be geared to parents' backgrounds. According to Kroth and Scholl (1978),

> an alternative approach is to educate parents to be change agents or educators for their own children. Adherents of the three basic theoretical models, behavioral, psychodynamic, and client-centered, have reported success in using parents in the treatment of their own children.
>
> Since most special educators work closely with psychologists or psychiatrists, there is a temptation to draw on their theoretical positions in working with parents, particularly those of the behavioral or client-centered models. (p. 30)

Although there have been some changes recently, significant parent involvement in their child's educational program remains the exception rather than the rule.

> Attitudes toward parent involvement in the education and socialization of their children, while nearly always officially affirmative and encouraged by school personnel and special education in particular, in reality run the gamut from total dissociation to active participa-

tion and commitment required of parents for their children to receive educational and therapeutic services. *(Clements and Alexander,
1975, p. 1)*

There is a marked increase in concern by school personnel, often expressed with considerable anxiety, about the role, scope, and direction of
parent involvement programs. Recent changes in legislation have required
school personnel to rethink their position regarding parent involvement.
These changes may have a profound effect on the part played by parents
in the schooling of exceptional children during the next decade. This will
not occur if parents and school personnel responsible for educational programs for the handicapped continue to function unilaterally. Perry (1977)
recently stated that we may meet the letter of the new laws and ignore
their spirit and intent. Perry delineated the differences between the laws'
requirements and the actions actually taken by those responsible for carrying out its mandates. Despite the new legislation, professional attitudes will
continue to be the major determinant of parental involvement in their
children's education.

With the signing of the Education of All Handicapped Children's Act
in 1975, an era of mandated involvement between educators and parents
began. This law is the keystone of the new legislation. The law and its implementing regulations provide the framework for a new partnership between parents and teachers, one which will lead, it is hoped, to a far more
productive relationship. Unfortunately, however, after only a short time
both educators and parents have realized that PL 94-142 represents only
a preliminary step toward developing the desired partnership. The formal
due process procedures established by the law will not, by themselves, lead
to effective teamwork. Perhaps more than anything else, PL 94-142 demonstrated that although "involvement" can be mandated, the ingredients
of a successful relationship between parents and educators cannot.

One central ingredient of a successful relationship, trust, can only be
achieved when the parents and teacher work, share, and attempt to meet
the needs of a child together. That trust is a necessary component to the
working relationship has been strongly suggested by a number of parent
educators and teachers (Kroth, 1975; Kroth and Simpson, 1977). Communication between home and school is vital to the operation of a successful educational program for behaviorally disordered children and youth,
and establishing trust is a critical component in building that communication. Educators have the responsibility for identifying techniques for developing trust. Without trust, even the most well-planned program and
well-meaning teacher will not develop effective parent involvement.

Specific techniques and procedures for establishing trust have been
suggested by a number of educators (Kroth and Simpson, 1977); these
have all revolved around convincing parents that they represent a legitimate
source of involvement, information, knowledge, and skill, and that relationships based on cooperative efforts produce the greatest dividends.

PARENT RIGHTS AND RESPONSIBILITIES

The rights of parents, and to a certain extent their responsibilities, are delineated in PL 94-142. A thorough and complete understanding of these rules, regulations, and provisions is necessary for special educators and school personnel because of their role in educating exceptional children. This knowledge is not required of parents. Parents are currently more likely to be uninformed about their rights and the rights of their children under the law than are special education personnel. It remains the responsibility of the school personnel and advocacy groups to provide parents with this information.

Screening and Evaluation

Parents must be informed in writing that their child is being considered or evaluated for special education services. They must give their written consent before such evaluation can begin. Parents must also be apprised of the results and findings of the evaluation and assessment process, and they have the right to question or challenge any part of the evaluation process, findings, or conclusions. In addition, parents have the right to request an evaluation of their child by an agency, organization, or individual outside the school district or education agency. This must be provided at no cost to the parents.

Parents must also be notified in writing of the meeting to evaluate the results of the assessment conducted with their child, and they have the right and the responsibility to discuss any decisions relating to the educational plan for their child. This plan must include both short-term and long-term objectives and plans for evaluation of the therapeutic efforts. School personnel and parents must indicate in writing that they understand what is called for in the educational plan and that they agree or disagree with the plan. If the parent disagrees with the school personnel about what would be best for the child, an appeals process is initiated. If the differences between parents and school personnel about what constitutes an appropriate plan of education for a particular child cannot be resolved through negotiation, a hearing officer is appointed and procedures are instituted to determine what actions are necessary to resolve the problem. During this process the child's educational placement and status remain unchanged. The Individualized Education Program (IEP), which summarizes the assessment data and educational plans, must be reviewed and revised at least annually, and parents must confirm their agreement with the plan and its revisions in writing once a year.

A more complete explanation of the regulations concerning PL 94-142 is provided in the *Federal Register* (DHEW, 1977). PL 94-142 is the focus of the entire October 1977 issue of *Exceptional Children*.

Special educators have an important responsibility to educate parents about these provisions. This should be a first order priority of local and state education agencies and should be facilitated by the office of special education and rehabilitation services.

Some may question the assertion that school personnel should assume the major responsibility of informing parents of their rights and the rights of their children under the law. This hesitancy is understandable when viewed from the perspective of the school district or program administrator concerned about possible litigation by angry or contentious parents. But to reject this responsibility places professionals in the professionally untenable position of not acting in the best interest of the child. The right of the parents to question the plan proposed, to suggest alternatives, or to reject the educators' assumptions and recommendations is a necessary part of accountability for special education.

Advocacy: The Educator's Role

Being the parent of even a well-adjusted child or adolescent is without doubt one of the most difficult jobs an adult can undertake. Constant challenges and problems and considerable stress are almost universally associated with this endeavor. Few parents are prepared for the complexity of the child-rearing task, and most parents occasionally face problems they don't know how to solve or get help with. The situation is more difficult if the child is emotionally disturbed. Consequently, an effective relationship between parent and teacher must include an advocacy component.

Some parents may need support from a person dedicated to meeting the needs of the parent and family and willing to help secure necessary educational, psychological, and social services. This need for advocacy can be met in a variety of ways, including rendering crisis intervention services, working as a community liaison, and being committed to obtaining the most appropriate educational services possible. Crisis intervention measures should be aimed at developing strategies to solve immediate problems created by the emotionally disturbed child or youth, as well as a wider variety of family and social problems. The teacher should be both someone the parents can talk to and a professional capable of securing immediate services to deal with specific problems. The community liaison role requires that the educator be capable of coordinating existing community, federal, and state services to meet the needs of a student or family. These services may include welfare; medical and dental care; child protection; psychological, social, psychiatric, and vocational help; and alternatives to traditional family living. This basic role may be satisfied if the educator can represent the child and parents as primary clients rather than the school administration or board of education. Although difficult, progress will result when such a strategy has been routinely adopted. As part of this process, educators must also be willing to interpret legislation, specifically PL 94-142, to the parents.

Advocacy: The Parents' Role

It is significant that there is no large, formal organization of parents of emotionally disturbed children comparable to the parent organization groups for the retarded (Association for Retarded Citizens), and for the learning disabled (Association for Children with Learning Disabilities), even though emotional disturbance is considered to have a relatively high incidence in the school-age population. A very small proportion of this population, autistic children, has a parent advocacy organization (The National Society for Autistic Citizens) that works to benefit these children, but the majority of emotionally disturbed children have no organized parent group working on their behalf. One can only speculate about why this is so, but it may have to do with outmoded preconceptions and stereotypes about the characteristics of parents of emotionally disturbed children, which make these parents reluctant to work publicly for their children.

Parents of emotionally disturbed children need to work collectively and actively, at the local, state, regional, and national levels, toward obtaining more and better educational and therapeutic services for their children. Without such efforts, behaviorally disordered children will continue to be one of the least adequately served populations in our schools.

PARENTAL NEEDS

There is a tendency on the part of professionals who advocate parental involvement to feel that all parents of exceptional children need everything the professionals have to offer in awareness, knowledge, and skill training. This is reflected in programs in which parents are required to attend conferences, group meetings, and workshops with the implied threat that their children will be dropped from the program if they fail to attend. Although the requirement of full parental participation results from a recognition of the importance of parental involvement in the total treatment program, such a requirement ignores the differing needs and capabilities of parents.

Coletta (1977) discusses the needs of parents in terms of Maslow's needs hierarchy. Since the parents of emotionally disturbed children, like any group of parents, are not a homogeneous group, they possess different skills, needs, and knowledge. Some parents, for instance, work hard to obtain their families' basic needs. Obtaining food, shelter, and clothing can be a major struggle. The economically more secure professional may not realize that asking such a parent to take off work for a meeting may reflect more basic considerations than simply parent interest in their child. It should come as no surprise when a parent who is struggling to meet basic needs does not respond to requests for conferences, or if conferences are mandatory for the child's continuance in the program, comes to the school hostile or anxious. A related point is that even parents who are strongly concerned with the education of their emotionally disturbed children may not want to give school personnel a work phone number for fear that a call from school about their children's problems will cause them embarrassment or even jeopardize their employment. Such anxieties exist in the suburban areas as well as impoverished areas, and with both well-educated and poorly educated parents. Home visits even in apparently wealthy neighborhoods sometimes reveal a type of "poverty." Parents who are out of work and burdened by debt may continue to live in expensive homes, trying to retain their social and economic status, but feeling anxiety, anger, and fear. Preoccupation with these basic needs for survival prevents such parents from becoming fully involved in programs focusing on their emotionally disturbed children's adjustment needs.

More personal anxieties may also affect parents' ability to participate. Some parents are insecure in their parental role and feel guilty for having produced a child with problems. This may be particularly true if the child is classified as emotionally disturbed. Another problem is that taking the child to therapy sessions, working with the child at home, and attending workshops and meetings takes a large amount of time and energy, so that parents have little time for themselves or other members of the family. The price of cooperation with school may be paid at home. As one mother said, "I spent so much time with my child that I almost forgot I had a husband, and then one day I didn't have one." Such stories are quite common.

For some parents, the need for respite from their emotionally disturbed child becomes overwhelming. This is not always viewed sympathetically by the educational community or society. The placement of the child in summer school, summer camp, private schools, or temporarily in institutions may be vital to the mental health of other family members. Educators, however, often say to parents that the child needs time off from school and structures, or that children should be deinstitutionalized rather than institutionalized. This is another situation in which parent needs may be disregarded by well-meaning but insensitive professionals.

The needs of parents vary at different stages in the educational life of their child. A parent of a high school child, for example, reported that she was now able to take advantage of a workshop for parents because her emotionally disturbed child was the only one left at home. She was also ready to share her earlier experiences and feelings about rearing her emotionally disturbed child with parents whose children were younger.

Professionals, then, must analyze the needs and skills of parents as they do those of children. Individualizing services and programs is as important for parents as it is for children if one hopes to obtain optimal levels of parental involvement.

In summary, here are some good working assumptions:

1. Parents care about their children at all ages. There are many valid reasons other than lack of concern to explain why parents do not participate in educational activities deemed worthwhile by professionals.
2. Parents have different needs at different times in their child's life. Thus, their availability for involvement will vary from time to time.
3. Most parents will get involved to some extent. Involvement may range from participation in the development of IEPs to participation in therapy groups.
4. Today, parents have more knowledge about handicapping conditions than ever before. Information has reached most homes via TV and popular articles. Some of the information may be erroneous or misunderstood, but there is a heightened awareness of exceptionality.
5. Schools are providing more services to parents than in previous years. There are more phone calls, notes home, flexibly scheduled conferences, and parent groups than in the past.

PARENT INVOLVEMENT MODELS

Approaches to parent involvement can be characterized or classified in a variety of ways. Lilly (1974) states that parent programs tend to be of three types: behavioral, psychological insight, and experiential. Such a classification system stresses philosophical or theoretical differences.

Karnes and Zurbach (1975) offer a model for structuring a family involvement process that disregards philosophical approach. They describe an administrative framework for involving parents in programs serving their exceptional children. Their family involvement process model delineates steps for deciding who can best meet the needs of the child in accordance with most of the basic assumptions we have listed.

Clements and Alexander (1975) describe a school-based informational model used to formalize parent involvement programs. Their model focuses on how parents can receive information, meet with professionals, and receive functional information and training appropriate to their children's special needs. The informational model system has three phases, for preschool-age, elementary-age, and secondary-age children.

Kroth (1975) suggests a variety of techniques for obtaining information from parents, providing information to parents, problem-solving with parents, disseminating information, counseling individuals, and involving parents in behavior management and instructional processes. Kroth and Simpson (1977) present a system for using parent conferences as a teaching strategy that uses strategies they perceive to be effective with children. Techniques include clarifying and assessing values, establishing trust, using various methods of interviewing, and using evaluation procedures.

PARENT INVOLVEMENT APPROACHES

Cone and Sloop (1973) point out that the inclusion of one or both parents as agents of change in therapy for children has a history almost as long as that of contemporary psychological treatment itself. They cite Guerney (1969), who notes that Freud was a pioneer in this regard in his treatment of the phobias of a five-year-old child.

Client-centered therapies have also involved parents in the therapy process with their children. Guerney (1969) describes examples of teaching parents the principles and procedures of filial therapy, including methods of training parents to act as therapists to their children in play therapy sessions at home.

Psychological insight (Lilly, 1974) approaches that emphasize analysis of the interaction dynamics between parents and children include Gordon's (1970) parent effectiveness training procedures, Auerbach's (1968) group discussion process approaches, and Stewart's (1974) parent and teacher counseling approaches.

Behavioral approaches to parent involvement have also become widely utilized. Clements and Alexander (1975) note that

> concomitant with the recent proliferation of the application of learning theory or behavior modification in clinical, institutional, and classroom settings . . . there has been an increasing interest in teaching parents to modify and manage their children's behavior through the application of behavioral techniques. . . . [This work] include[s] studies in which parent training was conducted in clinical or institutional settings to totally home based training. While the majority of studies are concerned primarily with deviant social behaviors, a number of them have as their focus improved academic performance. Training varied from modeling corrective behavior for parents and using videotape feedback for self-correction to direct instruction and signaling parents to apply specific techniques. Other methods included traditional group meetings and advisement in general application principles as well as the use of prompting, fading, reinforcement, and corrective parent behavior. The accumulated results of these studies demonstrate the efficacy and validity of the incorporation of a learning theory approach by parents in altering their children's interpersonal, social, and academic behavior and suggest the functional viability of direct parent training by teachers through many of the same processes and principles. *(p. 4)*

In addition to the above approaches, a number of packaged audio-visual parent education kits are commercially available (Kroth and Brown, 1978, p. 251):

Many educators are interested in providing parents and staff members with parent education training but do not have the time to develop parent education programs. There are a number of commercial materials available that require a minimum amount of background to use. Usually the materials have guides and manuals for leaders and participants as well as worksheets. These materials require the user to have a tape recorder, phonograph, slide or filmstrip projector. The following kits address various phases of parenting, parent education, or working with parents.

Systematic Training for Effective Parenting by Don Dinkmeyer and Gary D. McDay. American Guidance Service Inc., Circle Pines, N.M. 55014, 1976.

Managing Behavior: A Parent Involvement Program by Richard L. McDowell, B. L. Winch and Assoc., P. O. Box 1185, Torrance, Ca. 90505, 1976. Also distributed by Research Press, Champaign, Il.

Even Love Is Not Enough: Children with Handicaps. Parent Magazine Films, Inc., 52 Vanderbilt Avenue, New York, N.Y. 10017, 1975.

The Art of Parenting by Bill R. Wagonseller, Mary Burnett, Bernard Salzburg, and Joe Burnett. Research Press, Champaign, Il., 1977.

Keeping in Touch with Parents: A Teacher's Best Friend by Leatha Mae Bennett and Ferris O. Henson. Learning Concepts, 2501 N. Lamar, Austin, Tx. 78705, 1977.

Evaluating Parent Involvement Programs

Several methodological problems and unanswered questions in parent intervention research are pointed out by Johnson and Katz (1973). One problem is the need to identify and verify variables in parent training, which includes analyzing different training procedures to determine comparative effectiveness and efficiency. Cone and Sloop (1973), in their review of single- and multiple-family training strategies, concluded that single-family studies have generally involved a higher level of methodological sophistication than have multiple-family group designs. O'Dell (1974) indicates that two methodological problems have continued to be problematic in data on parent involvement: (1) the lack of designs that demonstrate the effects of behavioral treatment relative to other parent counseling approaches, and (2) the lack of adequate control for maturational factors. Methodological concerns in evaluation procedures in parent-teacher conferencing are pointed out by Alexander (1977). These include problems of duration and frequency of evaluation, alteration of measurement instruments and procedures, and research design concerns. Research by Patterson and his colleagues (1974) and O'Dell, Flynn, and Benlolo (1976) also assessed the effectiveness of parent training. Other examples include the work of Bernal and Margolin (1976) and Forehand and King (1977).

Research on the comparative effectiveness of parent involvement programs has only recently been reported (Bernal and Margolin, 1976;

Tavormina, 1975; Martin, 1976; Peed, Roberts, and Forehand, 1977; and O'Dell, Flynn, and Benlolo, 1976). The results of this research are probably best characterized as equivocal at this time. Contradictory findings were reported by Bernal and Margolin (1976) and Tavormina (1975) on results of two forms of parent training, whereas other researchers (Martin, 1976) reported no differences. O'Dell, Flynn, and Benlolo (1976) found differences in the effects of didactic and nondidactic parent training.

Integrating Methodologies with Needs

Although the utility and comparative effectiveness of the approaches to parent involvement cited above have yet to be adequately investigated or demonstrated, a number of observations can be made at this time concerning parent involvement: (1) the choices professionals make in conducting parent training appear to be more a function of philosophy and training than of the demonstrated comparative efficacy of the approach used; (2) a variety of methods and systems exist for implementing parent involvement from a psychological insight or expressive counseling perspective; (3) there are a number of systems for implementing a behavioral approach to parent involvement; and (4) noncategorical approaches to parent involvement that integrate several philosophies and approaches are also available.

Taking into account the availability of a variety of systems and methods of parent involvement, the demonstrated efficacy of several parent involvement approaches, and the face validity and good sense inherent in others, a broader perspective concerning parent involvement seems justified.

Parents, school personnel, and other professionals concerned with parent involvement might profitably choose a method for involving parents on the basis of a particular situation's demands rather than choosing to apply a single system throughout a district with all parents. The latter approach is less likely to serve the variety of purposes and needs for which parent involvement has been indicated.

Processes and instruments, as well as the means used for determining parent involvement needs, deserve careful consideration and analysis when this perspective is adopted. Needs analysis should occur not just with parents of handicapped children, but also with teachers, agencies, organizations, and communities. Kroth and Scholl (1978) offer a number of strategies for assessment of these areas, including a Parent Involvement Assessment Scale. School personnel should assess their own needs and the needs of the parents of the children they serve as a prerequisite to the selection of ways to meet those needs. Special education faculty in schools, individual teachers, and parents might find it profitable to engage in values clarification activities as one means to determine priorities. A needs assessment survey focused on awareness and knowledge levels in the community or among parents of handicapped children at a school or in a district might also be indicated. Frequency counts of types of material provided parents or random samples of particular groups about their knowledge of exceptional children might also be helpful in developing priorities for parent involvement.

Levels of Parent Involvement

Conceptually, parent involvement needs can be delineated by the levels of involvement necessary to meet the needs of areas or domains of children, teachers, parents, other professionals, and the community at large. These parent involvement needs include a need for awareness, a need for knowledge and information, a need for meaningful exchanges and interactions, and a need for skill acquisition and training.

It is no longer believed that there is a single "best" method for working with parents. Previous parent involvement programs were often based on expediency rather than individual needs and lacked systematic evaluation, specifically of short- and long-term goals and objectives. Current parent involvement approaches should be based on individual needs specific to particular communities, parents, and teachers. This proposed process for individualization of parent-teacher involvement is represented graphically in Figure 10.1.

Probably the most common needs of parents and educators can be met without extensive involvement. The needs of some persons or agencies, however, may need to be approached at several levels simultaneously, and reciprocal needs may occur between and among those involved with exceptional children. Needs may also cut across different age groups and types of problems, but it may be expedient and appropriate to use approaches and processes for parent involvement that are superficially very dissimilar. Martin (1976) comments that differences in theoretical approaches should not be exaggerated.

> In part, the difference may simply be a matter of deciding which behavior we want to change — noncompliance, hitting, talking back, withdrawal or crying versus emotional-verbal communication and how to negotiate agreements about conflicts. Do we want to teach children to behave, or improve communication and joint decision-making between parent and child, or both? If we teach communication and conflict resolution skills by behavioral rehearsal and modeling procedures, then the basic methodological difference between the two approaches would seem to vanish, assuming the operational measures of such variables as communication about emotions can be reasonably obtained. *(p. 3)*

An obvious point of departure for the development, selection, and organization of resources is the new public law and regulations concerning parent involvement in programs for handicapped children. At the awareness level, parents need to know that there are laws and regulations pertaining to programs for handicapped children. At the knowledge level, par-

FIGURE 10.1
THE PROCESS OF PARENT-TEACHER INVOLVEMENT

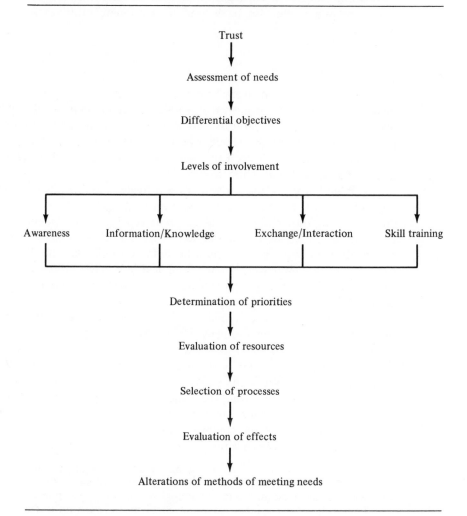

ents need to know their rights and the rights of their child under these laws. Parents and regular and special education teachers need information and knowledge about the concept of the least restrictive educational alternative. Parents, teachers, and administrators need to develop processes for interpersonal interactions that enable them to work effectively with each other. Teachers and parents need programs and resources to develop the skills necessary to devise and evaluate IEPs and to provide individualized instruction. Preservice teacher preparation programs must meet needs that cut across the various levels of involvement and must also take into consideration state regulations governing teacher certification. School districts need to prepare programs of in-service training for administrators, regular class teachers, special educators, and ancillary personnel to meet the state education agency requirements of the new law.

PARENT INVOLVEMENT AT THE SECONDARY LEVEL

Educators at the secondary level often observe that parents do not care about their children. They infer a lack of caring from the fact that the attendance of parents of secondary students at conferences and parent meetings is often below that at other educational levels. In fact, parent group meetings are usually uncommon at the secondary level. There are, however, several reasons for the lack of involvement that are unrelated to caring.

History of Conflict with the Schools

Parents of older emotionally disturbed children often have a long history of negative interactions with school personnel. The telephone calls and notes from the schools they have received have usually concerned their children's disapproved behavior. One mother of a secondary-school-age boy said that a phone ringing during the day sent chills through her body. Another mother reported that a teacher called her home about their secondary-school-age son and identified herself as Johnny's teacher. "What did he do now?" asked the mother. "I just wanted to tell you that Johnny did exceptionally well on a math paper today," the teacher replied. "Are you sure you have the right number?" the parent asked.

Similar reports are common. Building trust and cooperative relationships at the secondary level may take a great deal of persistence on the part of educators. Inexperienced teachers are turned off very quickly by a lack of parental response. Negative parental attitudes based on bad experiences with the school have been overcome by teachers who continued to send letters and notes to parents even when they didn't get responses for a while. Eventually, parents felt secure enough to want to try working with school personnel one more time.

Complex School Structure

Coming to a high school campus today can be overwhelming to a parent. High schools in large cities often have two to three thousand students and more than one hundred faculty members. Buildings are not planned to make public access easy. It is not unusual to have to ask directions from four or five people to find one's way to the office. After arriving at the office, the parent must decide who to speak to among the many vice-principals and counselors. It's not surprising that parents sometimes fear going to the school.

Complex Family Structure

By the time emotionally disturbed children reach the high school level in our society, they are often not living with both original parents. Since more than one quarter of all marriages in the United States end in divorce, and since the incidence of divorce in families with exceptional children is estimated to be two to three times the national rate, there is a good chance that an emotionally disturbed student will be living in a family that has undergone major changes in structure.

Lack of Continuity of Parent Education Programs

Parent education programs at the secondary level may not take into consideration the programs to which parents have been exposed in the past or parent desires for future programming. One family related that they had been trained and retrained in behavior management techniques almost every year from elementary school into high school. Each teacher had offered a program, and being cooperative parents they had participated. At the secondary level, parents may want programs relating to career education for their emotionally disturbed children rather than additional skill training, or they may want skill training to focus on topics more appropriate to older children, such as the self-instructional techniques of Meichenbaum (1974) or the communication skill training of Wagonseller et al. (1977) or Gordon (1970).

Parent Burnout

If their family has included an emotionally disturbed child for thirteen or more years, there is a good chance that parents' resources will be severely depleted. There has been recent public comment on the high rates of turnover among teachers of emotionally disturbed children. It appears that teachers do not continue to work with these children longer than from three to five years. Thus, it is not surprising that parents are exhausted and have lost their enthusiasm for parent programs and high levels of involvement with school personnel by the time their children reach the secondary school. Unlike teachers, parents do not get the summer off, nor do they get to pass the child on to a new set of parents.

Mainstreaming

When special educators mainstream a child with special needs, they tend to drop the parents from supportive services, which makes parents more responsible but provides them with less help. Mainstreaming is an additional source of anxiety for parents of emotionally disturbed students. To adjust, they often need specialized help. Parents of previously mainstreamed children may be used as resource people for parents of children who are in the process of being mainstreamed. Recently, for example, two sets of parents who had successfully taken their child home from a residential center were included in a group of parents who were considering such a move. In this way, the "successful" parents were provided with supportive services and they were able to report to the group some of the trials and tribulations of the move.

Parents of secondary level children can also be used as resource people by parents of children in the last years of elementary school. They can tell the parents of younger children who to turn to for support in the secondary schools and what pitfalls to avoid during the transition. A bonus to such programs is that parents often find it refreshing to help others rather than receive help themselves.

PARENT POWER

Educators and psychologists may have done parents a disservice by stressing the value of democratic family organization, including family meetings for making major decisions. One father said, "If I had taken a vote of the family on whether to make a rather recent move to a city in the southwest, I would have lost four to two or five to one. Now, of course, the family is happy with the move."

In an increasingly complex society, it is difficult for parents to obtain normative data to assist them in setting standards. A few generations ago, when families belonged to smaller communities, they could compare notes informally about such things as bedtime, ownership of cars, and allowances. Now, parents who compare practices find a great range in parental expectations of children. Television shows about families may be the source of standards for students, but these standards may not reflect the real world as viewed by their parents. From a phenomenological point of view, a wide discrepancy between perceptions of the real and the ideal indicates a poor self-concept. It is possible that many parents and their children suffer from poor self-concepts because they compare themselves to television families they consider ideal.

The systematic collection of normative data about child-rearing practices by those interested in parent education could benefit many parents. Such normative data could serve as a basis for comparison with parents' own perceptions. Ideals, however, would still need to be set by the individual families. Such normative data could include such information as hours of television watching, scheduling of activities such as music lessons, and bedtimes.

Overwhelmed by rapid changes in society and unprecedented opportunities for self-expression, some parents have delegated important child-rearing decisions to the children themselves without teaching them responsible behavior. Trying to regain control when things have gone sour after control has been turned over to another is very difficult. The parental struggle to regain control occurs not only in families, but between home and school. The reaffirmation of parents' rights as reflected in PL 94-142 indicates that school personnel should help parents in this endeavor rather than fight them. With rights come responsibilities, and parents should have the responsibility for the care of their children with the support of professionals.

PARENT CENTERS

One way that school systems can assist parents is by establishing parent centers. These centers need not be elaborate, but they should be places where parents can obtain information or meet with other parents. They can be at least partially staffed with volunteers. They can serve as referral services for locating respite care or babysitting services. More extensive centers can provide education programs for parents to attend on a voluntary basis. With declining enrollment in the public schools, most school districts will have a vacant classroom or two that can be converted into a center for parent information and activities.

A FINAL COMMENT ON COMMITMENT

Throughout this chapter, research has been cited indicating the efficacy of various approaches to parent involvement. Resources that have proved to be beneficial in accomplishing parent involvement have been identified, and sources of information and curricula for parent involvement programs have been provided. Models, approaches, and systems for parent involvement have been delineated, and concerns related to specific areas and needs of parent involvement have been discussed. But this information will be of little value if there is no commitment on the part of parents and educators to work together. Low rates of interaction between parents and educators should not be attributed to a lack of technology and knowledge, but to priority problems in our school systems, our lives, and our society. If parents and educators make a commitment to more effective interactions, handicapped children will be served better than ever before. This commitment can be enhanced through professional activities and interpersonal behaviors that engender attitudes of mutual respect and reciprocal reinforcement.

The only treatment that fully satisfies anyone is found not when we tamper with the body but when we touch the soul, and thus each other. The planet is threatened, not because of what we don't know about but because of what we don't care about. While illnesses are man's curse, handicaps (stigmas attached to illness) are his invention, and we have yet to learn the difference. While we still have a lot to learn about illnesses, we have everything to learn about handicaps. You must understand that, even though not all illnesses have effective treatments, all handicaps are preventable and curable. Handicaps are conditions of the soul. *(Blatt, 1978, p. 9)*

References

The Adventures of the Lollipop Dragon. Chicago: Society for Visual Education, 1970.

Alexander, R. Evaluation procedures in parent-teacher conferencing. *Resources in Education,* 1977. (ERIC Document Reproduction Service No. ED 139 152.)

Allen, D. The seven deadly myths of education. *Psychology Today,* 1971, *4,* 71.

Allen, G. J. Case study: implementation of behavior modification techniques in summer camp settings. *Behavior Therapy,* 1973, *4,* 570–575.

Allen, K. E., Hart, B. M., Buell, J. S., Harris, F. R., and Wolf, M. M. Effects of social reinforcement on isolate behavior of a nursery school child. *Child Development,* 1964, *35,* 511–518.

Alpher, R. W. A strategy for teaching remedial mathematics: if I had $1,000,000. . . . In N. J. Long, W. C. Morse, and R. G. Newman, *Conflict in the Classroom* (3rd ed.). Belmont, Ca.: Wadsworth, 1976.

American Psychiatric Association. *Diagnostic and Statistical Manual of Mental Disorders* (2nd ed., DSM-II). Washington, D. C.: American Psychiatric Association, 1968.

American Psychiatric Association. *Diagnostic and Statistical Manual of Mental Disorders* (3rd ed., DSM-III). Washington, D. C.: American Psychiatric Association, 1980.

Apter, S. Applications of ecological theory: toward a community special education model. *Exceptional Children,* 1977, *43,* 336–373.

Aronfreed, J. *Conduct and Conscience.* New York: Academic Press, 1968.

Auerbach, B. *Parents Learn through Discussion: Principles and Practices of Parent Group Education.* New York: John Wiley and Sons, 1968.

Ausubel, D. P. *Ego Development and the Personality Disorders.* New York: Grune & Stratton, 1952.

Axelrod, S., Whitaker, D., and Hall, R. V. The effects of social and tangible reinforcers on the spelling accuracy of special education students. *School Applications of Learning Theory,* 1972, *4,* 4–14.

Ayllon, T., and Azrin, N. H. *The Token Economy: A Motivational System for Therapy and Rehabilitation.* New York: Appleton-Century-Crofts, 1968.

Ayllon, T., Layman, D. N., and Kandel, J. H. A behavioral-educational alternative to drug control of hyperactive children. *Journal of Applied Behavior Analysis,* 1975, *8,* 137–146.

Ayllon, T., and Roberts, M. D. Eliminating discipline problems by strengthening academic performance. *Journal of Applied Behavior Analysis,* 1974, *7,* 71–76.

Ayllon, T., and Wright, P. New roles for the paraprofessional. In S. W. Bijou and E. Ribes-Inesta (Eds.), *Behavior Modification: Issues and Extensions.* New York: Academic Press, 1972.

Azrin, N. H., Flores, T., and Kaplan, S. J. Job finding club: a group-assisted program for obtaining employment. *Behavior Research and Therapy,* 1975, *13,* 17–27.

Bachrach, A. W., Mosley, A. R., Swindle, F. L., and Wood, M. M. *Developmental Therapy for Young Children with Autistic Characteristics.* Baltimore: University Park Press, 1978.

Baer, D. M. Some comments on the structure of the intersection of ecology and applied behavior analysis. In A. Rogers-Warren and S. Warren (Eds.), *Ecological Perspectives in Behavior Analysis.* Baltimore: University Park Press, 1977.

Baer, D. M., Wolf, M. M., and Risley, R. R. Some current dimensions of applied behavior analysis. *Journal of Applied Behavior Analysis,* 1968, *1,* 91–97.

Baldwin, J. J. *Thought and Things: A Study of the Development and Meaning of Thought, or Genetic Logic.* New York: Arno Press, 1975. (Originally published, 1906.)

Ballard, K. D., and Glynn, T. Behavioral self-management in story writing with elementary school children. *Journal of Applied Behavior Analysis,* 1975, *8,* 387–398.

Bandura, A. *Principles of Behavior Modification.* New York: Holt, Rinehart and Winston, 1969.

Bandura, A. *Aggression: A Social Learning Analysis.* Englewood Cliffs, N.J.: Prentice-Hall, 1975.

Bandura, A. Social learning analysis of aggression. In A. Bandura and E. Ribes-Inesta (Eds.), *Analysis of Delinquency and Aggression.* New York: John Wiley and Sons, 1976.

Bandura, A. Self-efficacy: toward a unifying theory of behavioral change. *Psychological Review,* 1977, *84,* 191–215. (a)

Bandura, A. *Social Learning Theory.* Englewood Cliffs, N.J.: Prentice-Hall, 1977. (b)

Bandura, A. The self system in reciprocal determinism. *American Psychologist,* 1978, *33,* 344–358.

Bandura, A., and Walters, R. H. *Social Learning and Personality Development.* New York: Holt, Rinehart and Winston, 1963.

Barclay, J. R. Classroom climate inventory. *Educational and Psychological Measurement,* 1974, *34,* 439–447.

Barker, R. G. *The Stream of Behavior.* New York: Appleton-Century-Crofts, 1963.

Barker, R. G. *Ecological Psychology.* Stanford, Ca.: Stanford University Press, 1968.

Barker, R. G., and Wright, H. F. *Midwest and Its Children.* Evanston, Il.: Row, Peterson and Co., 1954.

Barrish, H. H., Saunders, M., and Wolf, M. M. Good behavior game: effects of individual contingencies for group consequences on disruptive behavior in a classroom. *Journal of Applied Behavior Analysis,* 1969, *2,* 119–124.

Beardsley, A. G. *Rutland Center Outreach Project Annual Report.* Washington, D.C.: Bureau of Education for the Handicapped, 1977, (G00764744).

Beardsley, A. G., and Combs, C. An evaluation system to measure social and emotional growth in handicapped children. *Emphasis,* 1978, *1,* 6–11.

Beck, A. T. *Cognitive Therapy and the Emotional Disorders.* New York: International Universities Press, 1976.

Becker, W. C. *Parents Are Teachers.* Champaign, Il.: Research Press, 1971.

Becker, W. C., Engelmann, S., and Thomas, D. R. *Teaching: A Course in Applied Psychology.* Chicago: Science Research Associates, 1971.

Becker, W. C., Madsen, C. H., Arnold, C. R., and Thomas, D. R. The contingent use of teacher attention and praise in reducing classroom behavior problems. *The Journal of Special Education,* 1967, *1,* 287–307.

Becker, W. C., Thomas, D. R., and Carnine, D. *Reducing Behavior Problems: An Operant Conditioning Guide for Teachers.* Urbana, Il.: ERIC, 1969.

Benoit, R. R., and Mayer, G. R. Time-out: Guidelines for its selection and use. *The Personnel and Guidance Journal,* 1975, *53,* 501–506.

Berkowitz, P., and Rothman, E. Remedial reading for the disturbed child. *The Clearing House,* 1955, *30,* 165–169.

Berkowitz, P., and Rothman, E. *The Disturbed Child: Recognition and Psychoeducational Therapy in the Classroom.* New York: New York University Press, 1960.

Bernal, M. E., and Margolin, G. *Outcomes of Intervention Strategies for Discipline Problem Children.* Paper presented at the meeting of the

Association for Advancement of Behavior Therapy, New York, December 5, 1976.

Bessell, H., and Palomares, U. *Methods in Human Development: Magic Arch Theory Manual*. La Mesa, Ca.: Human Development Training Institute, 1973.

Bettelheim, B. *Love Is Not Enough*. Glencoe, Il.: Free Press, 1950.

Bettelheim, B. *Truants from Life*. Glencoe, Il.: Free Press, 1955.

Bettelheim, B. *The Uses of Enchantment*. New York: Vintage Books, 1977.

Bijou, S. W., Peterson, F. R., Harris, F. R., Allen, K. E., and Johnson, M. S. Methodology for experimental studies of young children in natural settings. *Psychological Record*, 1969, *19*, 177–210.

Blankenship, C. S., and Lovitt, T. C. Story problems: merely confusing or downright befuddling? *Journal for Research in Mathematics Education*, 1976, *7*, 290–298.

Blasi, A. Concept of development in personality theory. In J. Loevinger (Ed.), *Ego Development*. San Francisco: Jossey-Bass, 1976.

Blatt, B. Introduction: the threatened planet. In A. Turnbull and H. R. Turnbull III (Eds.), *Parents Speak Out: Views from the Other Side of the Two-way Mirror*. Columbus, Oh.: Charles E. Merrill, 1978.

Bledsoe, J. C., and Garrison, K. C. *The Self-Concepts of Elementary School Children in Relation to Their Academic Achievement, Intelligence, Interests, and Manifest Anxiety*. Athens: University of Georgia, 1962.

Bloom, B. New views of the learner: implications for instructor and curriculum. *Educational Leadership*, 1978, *37*, 563–576.

Bobroff, A. The stages of maturation in socialized thinking and in the ego development of two groups of children. *Child Development*, 1960, *31*, 321–338.

Bolstad, O. D., and Johnson, S. M. Self-regulation in the modification of disruptive classroom behavior. *Journal of Applied Behavior Analysis*, 1972, *5*, 443–454.

Bornstein, M. T., Bellack, A. S., and Hersen, M. Social-skills training for unassertive children: A multiple-baseline analysis. *Journal of Applied Behavior Analysis*, 1977, *10*, 183–195.

Borton, T. *Reach, Touch, and Teach*. New York: McGraw-Hill, 1970.

Bostow, D. E., and Bailey, J. Modification of severe disruptive and aggressive behavior using brief time-out and reinforcement procedures. *Journal of Applied Behavior Analysis*, 1969, *2*, 31–37.

Bower, E. *Early Identification of Emotionally Handicapped Children in School*. Springfield, Il.: Charles C. Thomas, 1960.

Boyd, D., and Kohlberg, L. The is-ought problem: a developmental perspective. *Zygon*, 1973, 358–372.

Brigham, T. A., Graubard, R. S., and Stans, A. Analysis of the effects of sequential reinforcement contingencies on aspects of composition. *Journal of Applied Behavior Analysis*, 1972, *5*, 421–430.

Broden, M., Beasley, A., and Hall, R. V. In-class spelling performance —

effects of home tutoring by a parent. *Behavior Modification,* 1978, *2,* 511–530.

Broden, M., Hall, R. V., Dunlap, A., and Clark, R. Effects of teacher attention and a token reinforcement system in a junior high school special education class. *Exceptional Children,* 1970, *36,* 341–349.

Broden, M., Hall, R. V., and Mitts, B. The effect of self-recording on the classroom behavior of two eighth-grade students. *Journal of Applied Behavior Analysis,* 1971, *4,* 191–199.

Brooks, R. B., and Snow, D. L. Two case illustrations of the use of behavior-modification techniques in the school setting. *Behavior Therapy,* 1972, *3,* 100–103.

Brophy, J. E., and Good, T. L. *Teacher-Student Relationships: Causes and Consequences.* New York: Holt, Rinehart and Winston, 1974.

Brown, G. I. *Human Teaching for Human Learnings: An Introduction to Confluent Education.* New York: Viking Press, 1971.

Browning, R. M., and Stover, D. O. *Behavior Modification in Child Treatment: An Experimental and Clinical Approach.* Chicago: Aldine Atherton, 1971.

Bryk, A., Meisels, S., and Markowitz, M. Assessing the effectiveness of open classrooms on children with special needs. In S. Meisels (Ed.), *Special Education and Development.* Baltimore: University Park Press, 1979.

Buchard, J., and Tyler, V., Jr. The modification of delinquent behavior through operant conditioning. *Behaviour Research and Therapy,* 1965, *2,* 461–476.

Buckholdt, D., and Gubruin, J. Doing programs: a participant observation study of a residential day treatment center for emotionally disturbed children. In *Caregivers.* New York: Russell Sage Foundation, 1979.

Budd, K., and Baer, D. M. Behavior modification and the law: implications of recent judicial decisions. *The Journal of Psychiatry and Law,* a special reprint, Summer 1976, 171–244.

Buell, J., Stoddard, P., Harris, F., and Baer, D. Collateral social development accompanying reinforcement of outdoor play in a pre-school child. *Journal of Applied Behavior Analysis,* 1968, *1,* 167–168.

Burdett, C. S., and Fox, W. L. *Measurement and Evaluation of Reading Behaviors: Word Recognition, Oral Reading Comprehension.* Austin, Tx.: Austin Writers Group, 1973.

Carroll, A. W. The classroom as an ecosystem. *Focus on Exceptional Children,* 1974, *6,* 1–11.

Cartledge, G., and Milburn, J. F. The case for teaching social skills in the classroom: a review. *Review of Educational Research,* 1978, *1,* 133–156.

Cartwright, C. A., and Cartwright, G. P. *Developing Observation Skills.* New York: McGraw-Hill, 1974.

Casteel, J. D., and Stahl, R. J. *Value Clarification in the Classroom: A Primer.* Santa Monica, Ca.: Goodyear, 1975.

Catania, A. C. The myth of self-reinforcement. *Behaviorism,* 1975, *3,* 192–199.

Cheney, C., and Morse, W. Psychodynamic interventions. In N. Long, W. Morse, and R. Newman (Eds.), *Conflict in the Classroom* (3rd ed.). Belmont, Ca.: Wadsworth, 1976.

Chesler, M., and Fox, R. *Role-Playing Methods in the Classroom.* Chicago: Science Research Associates, 1966.

Christie, L. S., and McKenzie, H. S. Minimum objectives: a measurement system to provide evaluation of special education in regular classrooms. Unpublished manuscript, University of Vermont, 1974.

Clarizio, H. F., and McCoy, G. F. *Behavior Disorders in Children* (2nd ed.). New York: T. Y. Crowell, 1976.

Clark, H. B., Rowbury, T., Baer, A. M., and Baer, D. M. Time-out as a punishing stimulus in continuous and intermittent schedules. *Journal of Applied Behavior Analysis,* 1974, *6,* 443–456.

Clements, J. E., and Alexander, R. N. Parent training: bringing it all back home. *Focus on Exceptional Children,* 1975, *7* (5), 1–12.

Cobb, J. A. Relationship of discrete classroom behaviors to fourth grade academic achievement. *Journal of Educational Psychology,* 1972, *63,* 74–80.

Cobb, J. A., and Hops, H. Effects of academic survival skill training on low achieving first graders. *Journal of Educational Research,* 1973, *67,* 108–113.

Coletta, A. J. *Working Together: A Guide to Parent Involvement.* Atlanta: Humanics Limited, 1977.

Combs, A. W. Humanizing education: the person in the process. In R. R. Leeprer (Ed.), *Humanizing Education.* Washington, D.C.: Association for Supervision of Curriculum Development, 1967.

Combs, C. Developmental therapy curriculum objectives. In M. M. Wood (Ed.), *Developmental Therapy.* Baltimore: University Park Press, 1975.

Cone, J. D., and Sloop, W. E. Parents as agents of change. In A. Jacobs and W. Spradlin (Eds.), *The Group as Agents of Change.* New York: Behavioral Publications, 1973.

Cormier, W. H. Effects of teacher, random, and contingent social reinforcement on the classroom behavior of adolescents. *Dissertation Abstracts International,* 1969, *31,* 1615–1616.

Cruickshank, W., Bentzen, F., Ratzeburg, F., and Tannhauser, M. *A Teaching Method for Brain-Injured and Hyperactive Children.* Syracuse, N.Y.: Syracuse University Press, 1961.

Cruickshank, W. M., and Quay, H. C. Learning and physical environment: the necessity for research and research design. *Exceptional Children,* 1970, *37,* 261–268.

Csapo, M. Modeling and behavior control. *Teaching Exceptional Children,* 1972, *5,* 20–24.

Cullinan, D., Epstein, M. H., and Reimers, C. Social validation: evaluating the effectiveness of interventions with behaviorally disordered pupils. Paper presented at the Topical Conference on the Emotionally Disturbed, Council for Exceptional Children, Minneapolis, Mn., August 1980.

Curwin, R. L., and Fuhrmann, B. S. *Discovering Your Teaching Self.* Englewood Cliffs, N.J.: Prentice-Hall, 1975.

Dale, E. *Building a Learning Environment.* Bloomington, In.: Phi Delta Kappa, 1972.

d'Alelio, W. A. A strategy for teaching remedial language arts: creative writing. In M. J. Long, W. C. Morse, and R. G. Newman (Eds.), *Conflict in the Classroom* (3rd ed.). Belmont, Ca.: Wadsworth, 1976.

Dealing With Causes of Behavior. Lakewood, Oh.: Lakewood City Public School System, 1972.

Deitz, S. M. Current status of applied behavior analysis — Science versus technology. *American Psychologist,* 1978, *33,* 805–814.

Deitz, S. M., and Repp, A. C. Decreasing classroom misbehavior through the use of DRL schedules or reinforcement. *Journal of Applied Behavior Analysis,* 1973, *6,* 457–463.

Dembinski, R. J. Psychoeducational Management of Disruptive Youths. In D. A. Sabatino and A. J. Mauser (Eds.), *Intervention Strategies for Specialized Secondary Education.* Boston: Allyn and Bacon, 1978.

Dembinski, R. J. An investigation of the reliability of the self-control behavior inventory. *Behavioral Disorders,* 1979, *4* (2), 137–142.

Dembinski, R. J., and Tull, D. *Self-Control Behavior Inventory — II.* DeKalb: Northern Illinois University, 1977.

Deno, S. L., and Mirkin, P. K. *Data-Based Program Modification: A Manual.* Minneapolis: Leadership Training Institute/Special Education, University of Minnesota, 1977.

DeRisi, W. J., and Butz, G. *Writing Behavioral Contracts.* Champaign, Il.: Research Press, 1974.

Despert, L. *The Emotionally Disturbed Child — Then and Now.* New York: Brunner, 1965.

Dinkmeyer, D. *Developing Understanding of Self and Others* (DUSO). Circle Pines, Mn.: American Guidance Service, 1970.

Dinoff, M., and Rickard, H. C. Learning that privileges entail responsibilities. In J. D. Krumboltz and C. E. Thoresen (Eds.), *Behavioral Counseling.* New York: Holt, Rinehart and Winston, 1969.

Drabman, R. S., Spitalnik, R., and O'Leary, K. D. Teaching self-control to disruptive children. *Journal of Abnormal Psychology,* 1973, *82,* 10–16.

Drew, C. J. Research on the psychological-behavioral effects of the physical environment. *Review of Educational Research,* 1971, *41,* 447–465.

Dupont, H. (Ed.). *Educating Emotionally Disturbed Children.* New York: Holt, Rinehart and Winston, 1975.

Dupont, H. Toward affective development: teaching for personal development. Proceedings of a Conference on Preparing Teachers to Foster

Personal Growth in Emotionally Disturbed Students. Minneapolis: The University of Minnesota, 1977, 16–28.

Dupont, H., Gardner, O. W., and Brody, D. S. *Toward Affective Development* (TAD). Circle Pines, Mn.: American Guidance Service, 1974.

Ebel, R. I. Estimation of the reliability of ratings. *Psychometrica,* 1951, *16,* 407–424.

Eisenstein, S. R. The effect of contingent guitar lessons on reading behavior. *Journal of Music Therapy,* 1975, *2,* 138–146.

Ellis, A. *Reason and Emotion in Psychotherapy.* New York: Lyle Stuart Press, 1962.

Epstein, M. H., Cullinan, D., and Sabatino, D. A. State definitions of behavior disorders. *The Journal of Special Education,* 1977, *11,* 417–425.

Epstein, M. H., Repp, A. C., and Cullinan, D. Decreasing "obscene" language of behaviorally disordered children through the use of a DRL schedule. *Psychology in the Schools,* 1978, *15,* 419–423.

Erickson, M. *Child Psychopathology: Assessment, Etiology, and Treatment.* Englewood Cliffs, N.J.: Prentice-Hall, 1978.

Erikson, E. H. The problem of ego identity. *Journal of the American Psychoanalytic Association,* 1956, *4,* 56–121.

Erikson, E. H. *Childhood and Society* (2nd ed.). New York: W. W. Norton, 1963.

Erikson, E. H. Play and actuality. In M. W. Piers (Ed.), *Play and Development.* New York: W. W. Norton, 1972.

Erikson, E. H. *Toys and Reasons.* New York: W. W. Norton, 1977.

Eysenck, H. J. (Ed). *Behavior Therapy and the Neuroses: Readings in Modern Methods of Treatment Derived from Learning Theory.* New York: Pergamon Press, 1960.

Fagen, S. A. Psychoeducational management and self-control. In D. Cullinan and M. Epstein (Eds.), *Special Education for Adolescents: Issues and Perspectives.* Columbus, Oh.: Charles E. Merrill, 1979.

Fagen, S. A., and Hill, J. M. *Behavior Management: A Competency-based Manual for Inservice Training.* Washington, D.C.: Psychoeducational Resources, 1977.

Fagen, S. A., and Long, N. J. Before it happens: prevent discipline problems by teaching self-control. *Instructor,* 1976, 42–47. (a)

Fagen, S. A., and Long, N. J. Teaching children self-control: a new responsibility for teachers. *Focus on Exceptional Children,* 1976, *7,* 1–11. (b)

Fagen, S. A., Long, N. J., and Stevens, D. J. *Teaching Children Self-Control: Preventing Emotional and Learning Problems in the Elementary School.* Columbus, Oh.: Charles E. Merrill Co., 1975.

Fairchild, T. N. *Managing the Hyperactive Child in the Classroom.* Austin, Tx.: Learning Concepts, 1975.

Fantini, M., and Weinstein, G. *Toward a Contact Curriculum.* New York: B'nai Brith, 1969.

Fassler, J. *Child's Series on Psychologically Relevant Themes*. Westport, Cn.: Videorecord Corporation of America, 1971.

Feagans, L. Ecological theory as a model for constructing a theory of emotional disturbance. In W. Rhodes and M. Tracy (Eds.), *A Study of Child Variance* (Vol. 1). Ann Arbor: Institute for the Study of Mental Retardation and Related Disabilities, University of Michigan, 1972.

Fenichel, C. Psychoeducational approaches for seriously disturbed children in the classroom. In P. Knoblock (Ed.), *Intervention Approaches in Educating Emotionally Disturbed Children*. Syracuse, N.Y.: Syracuse University Press, 1966.

Fenton, E. The cognitive-developmental approach to moral education. *Social Education,* 1976, *40* (4), 186–193.

Ferritor, D. E., Buckholdt, D., Hamblin, R. L., and Smith, L. The non-effects of contingent reinforcement for attending behavior on work accomplished. *Journal of Applied Behavior Analysis,* 1972, *5,* 1–6.

Ferster, C. B., Culbertson, S., and Boren, M. C. P. *Behavior Principles* (2nd ed.). Englewood Cliffs, N.J.: Prentice-Hall, 1975.

Ferster, C. B., and DeMyer, M. K. A method for the experimental analysis of the behavior of autistic children. *American Journal of Orthopsychiatry,* 1962, *32,* 89–98.

Ferster, C. B., Nurnberger, J. I., and Levitt, E. B. The control of eating. *Journal of Mathematics,* 1962, *1,* 87–109.

Ferster, C. B., and Skinner, B. F. *Schedules of Reinforcement*. New York: Appleton-Century-Crofts, 1957.

Fingarette, H. *The Self in Transformation*. New York: Basic Books, 1963.

Fink, A. H., Glass, R. M., and Guskin, S. L. An analysis of teacher education programs in behavior disorders. *Exceptional Children,* 1975, *42,* 47.

Fink, W. T., and Carnine, D. W. Control of arithmetic errors by informational feedback. *Journal of Applied Behavior Analysis,* 1975, *8,* 461.

Fixsen, D. L., Phillips, E. L., and Wolf, M. M. Achievement Place: the reliability of self-reporting and peer-reporting and their effects on behavior. *Journal of Applied Behavior Analysis,* 1972, *5,* 19–30.

Fixsen, D. L., Phillips, E. L., and Wolf, M. M. Achievement Place: Experiments in self-government with predelinquents. *Journal of Applied Behavior Analysis,* 1973, *6,* 31–47.

Flavell, J. H. *The Development of Role-taking and Communication Skills in Children*. New York: John Wiley and Sons, 1968.

Flavell, J. H. *Cognitive Development*. Englewood Cliffs, N.J.: Prentice-Hall, 1977.

Forehand, R., and King, H. E. Noncompliant children: effects of parent training on behavior and attitude change. *Behavior Modification,* 1977, *1,* 93–108.

Fox, R. G. The effects of peer tutoring on the oral reading behavior of underachieving fourth grade pupils. Unpublished manuscript, University of Kansas, 1973.

Fredericks, H. D., Baldwin, V. L., Grove, D. N., and Moore, W. G. Social skills. In N. G. Haring (Ed.), *Individualized Educational Plans for Severely Handicapped Children and Youth.* Washington, D.C.: Bureau of Education for the Handicapped, 1977.

Frederiksen, L. W., and Frederiksen, C. B. Teacher-determined and self-determined token reinforcement in a special education classroom. *Behavior Therapy,* 1975, *6* (3), 310–314.

Freud, A. *The Ego and the Mechanisms of Defense.* New York: International Universities Press, 1946. (Originally published, 1937.)

Freud, A. Psychoanalysis and education. In *The Psychoanalytic Study of the Child* (Vol. 9). New York: International Universities Press, 1954.

Freud, A. *Normality and Pathology in Childhood: Assessments of Development.* New York: International Universities Press, 1965.

Freud, A. The concept of developmental lines. In S. G. Spair and A. C. Nitsburg (Eds.), *Children with Learning Problems.* New York: Brunner-Mazel, 1973.

Freud, S. *The Problem of Anxiety.* New York: W. W. Norton, 1936.

Freud, S. *Beyond the Pleasure Principle.* London: Hogarth Press, 1955. (Originally published, 1920.)

Freud, S. *On Creativity and the Unconscious.* New York: Harper & Row, 1958. (Originally published, 1925.)

Fullen, M., and Pomfret, A. Research on curriculum and instruction implementation. *Review of Educational Research,* 1977, *47,* 335–397.

Galbraith, R. and Jones, T. Teaching strategies for moral dilemmas. *Social Education,* 1975, *39,* 16–22.

Gallup, G. H. The eleventh annual Gallup poll of public's attitudes toward the public schools. *Phi Delta Kappan,* 1979, *61,* 33–45.

Gallup Poll on Education, October 1976.

Gardner, R. *The Talking, Feeling, and Doing Game.* Cresskill, N.Y.: Creative Therapeutics, 1973.

Garfunkel, F., and Blatt, B. What teachers need to know. In B. Blatt, D. Biklen, and R. Bogdan (Eds.), *An Alternative Textbook in Education.* Denver, Co.: Love Publishing Co., 1977.

Garmezy, N. Vulnerable and invulnerable children: theory, research, and intervention. Master lecture on developmental psychology. American Psychological Association Convention, 1976.

Garmezy, N. DSM-III: never mind the psychologists; is it good for the children? *The Clinical Psychologist,* 1978, *31,* 1–6.

Gast, D. L., and Nelson, C. M. Time out in the classroom: implications for special education. *Exceptional Children,* 1977, *43,* 461–464.

Gazda, G. M. *Group Counseling: A Developmental Approach* (2nd ed.). Boston: Allyn and Bacon, 1978.

Gazda, G. M., Asbury, F. R., Balzer, F. J., Childers, W. C., Dessell, R. E., and Walters, R. P. *Human Relations Development.* Boston: Allyn and Bacon, 1973.

Gentile, J. R., Roden, A. H., and Klein, R. D. An analysis-of-variance model for the intrasubject replication design. *Journal of Applied Behavior Analysis,* 1972, *5,* 193–198.

Gibbs, J. C. Kohlberg's stages of moral development: a constructive critique. *Harvard Educational Review,* 1977, *47,* 43–61.

Gillespie-Silver, P. *Teaching Reading to Children with Special Needs.* Columbus, Oh.: Charles E. Merrill, 1979.

Glass, R. M., and Griffin, J. B. *Response Book: Affective Education.* Bloomington, In.: Indiana University Center for Innovation in Teaching the Handicapped, 1973.

Glasser, W. *Schools Without Failure.* New York: Harper & Row, 1969.

Glover, J. A., and Gary, A. L. *Behavior Modification: Enhancing Creativity and Other Good Behaviors.* Pacific Grove, Ca.: Boxwood Press, 1975.

Glynn, E. L. Classroom applications of self-determined reinforcement. *Journal of Applied Behavior Analysis,* 1970, *3,* 123–132.

Glynn, E. L., Thomas, J. D., and Shee, S. M. Behavioral self-control of on-task behavior in an elementary classroom. *Journal of Applied Behavior Analysis,* 1973, *6,* 105–114.

Gnagey, W. J. *Controlling Classroom Misbehavior.* Washington, D.C.: National Education Association, 1965.

Gnagey, W. J. *The Psychology of Discipline in the Classroom.* New York: Macmillan, 1968.

Goldberg, H. R., and Greenberger, B. *Getting It Together.* Chicago: Science Research Associates, 1973.

Goldstein, H. Construction of a social learning curriculum. *Focus on Exceptional Children,* 1969, *1,* 1–8.

Goodlad, J. Directions of curriculum change. *NEA Journal,* 1966, *55,* 33–37.

Gordon, I. J. *Studying the Child in School.* New York: John Wiley and Sons, 1966.

Gordon, T. *Parent Effectiveness Training.* New York: Wyden, 1970.

Gordon, T. *Teacher Effectiveness Training.* New York: Wyden, 1974.

Gottman, J., and McFall, R. Self-monitoring effects in a program for potential high school dropouts: a time-series analysis. *Journal of Consulting and Clinical Psychology,* 1972, *39* (2), 273–281.

Grannis, J. C., and Schone, V. *First Things.* Pleasantville, N.Y.: Guidance Associates of Pleasantville, N.Y., 1970.

Graubard, P. Children with behavioral disabilities. In L. M. Dunn (Ed.), *Exceptional Children in the Schools* (2nd ed.). New York: Holt, Rinehart and Winston, 1973.

Graubard, P. S., Rosenberg, H., and Miller, M. B. Student applications of behavior modification on teachers and environments. Paper presented at the Second Annual Invitational Conference on Behavior Analysis in Education, University of Kansas, May 1971.

Greenwood, C. R., Walker, H. M., and Hops, H. Some issues in social interaction/withdrawal assessment. *Exceptional Children,* 1977, *43,* 490–501.

Griggs, J. W., and Bonney, M. E. Relationship between "causal" orientation and acceptance of others, "self-ideal self" congruency and mental health changes for fourth and fifth grade children. *The Journal of Educational Research,* 1970, *63,* 471–77.

Grusec, J. Power and the internalization of self-denial. *Child Development,* 1971, *42,* 93–105.

Grusec, J. E., and Skubiski, S. L. Model nurturance, demand characteristics of the modeling experiment and altruism. *Journal of Personality and Social Psychology,* 1966, *4,* 244–252.

Guerney, B. G., Jr. (Ed.). *Psychotherapeutic Agents: New Roles for Non-Professionals, Parents and Teachers.* New York: Holt, Rinehart and Winston, 1969.

Gump, P. V. Operating environments in schools of open and traditional design. In T. G. David and B. D. Wright (Eds.), *Learning Environments.* Chicago: University of Chicago Press, 1974.

Gump, P. V. Ecological psychology and children. In M. Hetherington (Ed.), *Review of Child Development Research* (Vol. 5). Chicago: University of Chicago Press, 1975.

Gump, P. V. Ecological psychologists: critics or contributors to behavior analysis? In A. Rogers-Warren and W. Warren (Eds.), *Ecological Perspectives in Behavior Analysis.* Baltimore: University Park Press, 1977.

Hall, R. V. *Behavior Modification, Volume I: The Measurement of Behavior.* Lawrence, Ks.: H & H Enterprises, 1971.

Hall, R. V. Responsive teaching: focus on measurement and research in the classroom and the home. *Focus on Exceptional Children,* 1971, *3,* 1–7.

Hall, R. V., Fox, R., Willard, D., Goldsmith, L., Emerson, V., Owen, V., Davis, F., and Porcia, E. The teacher as observer and experimenter in the modification of disrupting and talking-out behaviors. *Journal of Applied Behavior Analysis,* 1971, *4,* 141–149.

Hall, R. V., Lund, D., and Jackson, D. Effects of teacher attention on study behavior. *Journal of Applied Behavior Analysis,* 1968, *1,* 1–12.

Hallahan, D. P., and Kauffman, J. M. Labels, categories, behaviors, ED, LD, and EMR reconsidered. *The Journal of Special Education,* 1977, *11,* 139–148.

Hallahan, D. P., and Kauffman, J. M. *Exceptional Children: Introduction to Special Education.* Englewood Cliffs, N.J.: Prentice-Hall, 1978.

Hamachek, D. Characteristics of good teachers and implications for teacher education. *Phi Delta Kappan,* 1969, *50,* 341–345.

Hammill, D. D. Evaluating children for instructional purposes. *Academic Therapy,* 1971, *6* (4), 341–353.

Hanley, E. M. Review of research involving applied behavior analysis in the classroom. *Review of Educational Research,* 1970, *40,* 597–625.

Haring, N. G., and Eaton, M. D. Systematic instructional procedures: an instructional hierarchy. In N. G. Haring et al. (Eds.), *The Fourth R: Research in the Classroom.* Columbus, Oh.: Charles E. Merrill, 1978.

Haring, N. G., and Gentry, N. D. Direct and individualized instructional procedures. In N. G. Haring and R. L. Schiefelbusch (Eds.), *Teaching Special Children.* New York: McGraw-Hill, 1976.

Haring, N. G., Lovitt, T. C., Eaton, M. D., and Hansen, C. L. *The Fourth R: Research in the Classroom.* Columbus, Oh.: Charles E. Merrill, 1978.

Haring, N. G., and Phillips, E. L. *Educating Emotionally Disturbed Children.* New York: McGraw-Hill, 1962.

Haring, N. G., and Whelan, R. J. Experimental methods in education and management. In N. J. Long, W. C. Morse, and R. G. Newman (Eds.), *Conflict in the Classroom.* Belmont, Ca.: Wadsworth, 1965.

Harmin, M., Kirschenbaum, H., and Simon, S. B. Teaching history with a focus on values. *Social Education,* 1969, *33,* 568–570.

Harmin, M., Kirschenbaum, H., and Simon, S. B. The search for values with a focus on math. Conference Proceedings: *Teaching Mathematics in the Elementary School.* Washington, D.C.: National Association of Elementary School Principals, National Education Association, and the National Council of Teachers of Mathematics, 1970, 81–89.

Harmin, M., Kirschenbaum, H., and Simon, S. B. Teaching science with a focus on values. *Science Teacher,* 1970, *37,* 16–20.

Harmin, M., Simon, S. B., and Kirschenbaum, H. *Clarifying Values Through Subject Matter: Applications for the Classroom.* Minneapolis: Winston, 1973.

Harris, V. W., and Hall, R. V. Effects of systematic reinforcement procedures on performance of underachieving high school students. *Educational Technology Research,* NRE Research Series Publication #51, 1973.

Harris, V. W., and Sherman, J. A. Use and analysis of the "good behavior game" to reduce disruptive classroom behavior. *Journal of Applied Behavior Analysis,* 1973, *6,* 405–417.

Harris, V. W., and Sherman, J. A. Homework assignments, consequences, and classroom performance in social studies and mathematics. *Journal of Applied Behavior Analysis,* 1974, *7,* 505–519.

Hart, B. M., Reynolds, N. J., Baer, D. M., Brawley, E. R., and Harris, F. R. Effect of contingent and noncontingent social reinforcement on the co-operative play of a pre-school child. *Journal of Applied Behavior Analysis,* 1968, *1,* 73–76.

Hart, B. M., and Risley, T. R. Establishing the use of descriptive adjectives in the spontaneous speech of disadvantaged school children. *Journal of Applied Behavior Analysis,* 1968, *1,* 109–120.

Harth, R. An ecological service model in special education. Paper presented to the Annual Convention of Teacher Educators for Children With Behavior Disorders, Atlanta, Georgia, November 1975.

Harth, R., and Grosenick, J. K. Project CASA. In J. K. Growenick and R. Harth (Eds.), *Environmental Interventions for Emotionally Disturbed Children and Youth*. Columbia: University of Missouri, 1973.

Harth, R., and Lloyd, S. The effect of ecological strategies on the ability of adolescents to maintain their behavior after being discharged from a state hospital. In L. M. Bullock (Ed.), *Proceedings of the Fall Conference of Teacher Educators for Children with Behavioral Disorders*. Gainesville: University of Florida, 1975.

Hartmann, D. P., and Hall, R. V. The changing criterion design. *Journal of Behavior Analysis*, 1976, *9*, 527–532.

Hartmann, D. P., Shigetomi, C., and Barrias, B. Design considerations in applied behavioral research. Paper presented at the annual meeting of the Midwestern Association of Behavior Analysis, Chicago, Illinois, May 1964.

Hartshorn, E., and Brantley, J. C. Effects of dramatic play on classroom problem-solving ability. *The Journal of Educational Research*, 1973, *66*, 243–246.

Havinghurst, R. J. *Development Tasks and Education* (3rd ed.). New York: David McKay, 1972.

Hawley, R. C. *Human Values in the Classroom: Teaching for Personal and Social Growth*. Amherst, Ma.: Educational Research Associates Press, 1973.

Hawley, R. C., Simon, S. B., and Britton, D. D. *Composition for Personal Growth: Value Clarification Through Writing*. New York: Hart, 1973.

Hein, G. Evaluation in open classrooms: emergence of a qualitative methodology. In S. Meisels (Ed.), *Special Education and Development*. Baltimore: University Park Press, 1979.

Hendricks, G., and Gadiman, J. *Transpersonal Education: A Curriculum for Feeling and Being*. Englewood Cliffs, N.J.: Prentice-Hall, 1976.

Hendricks, G., and Roberts, T. B. *The Second Centering Book*. Englewood Cliffs, N.J.: Prentice-Hall, 1977.

Hendricks, G., and Wills, R. *The Centering Book*. Englewood Cliffs, N.J.: Prentice-Hall, 1975.

Henry, W. *An Analysis of Fantasy*. New York: John Wiley and Sons, 1956.

Hersen, M., and Barlow, D. *Single-Case Experimental Design*. New York: Pergamon Press, 1976.

Hewett, F. M. Teaching speech to an autistic boy through operant conditioning. *American Journal of Orthopsychiatry*, 1964, *35*, 927–936.

Hewett, F. M. Educational engineering with e.d. children. *Exceptional Children*, 1967, *33*, 459–467.

Hewett, F. M. *The Emotionally Disturbed Child in the Classroom*. Boston: Allyn and Bacon, 1968.

Hewett, F. M., and Taylor, F. *The Emotionally Disturbed Child in the Classroom* (2nd ed.). Boston: Allyn and Bacon, 1980.

Hewett, F. M., Taylor, F. D., and Artuso, A. A. The Santa Monica project: evaluation of an engineered classroom design with emotionally disturbed children. *Exceptional Children,* 1969, *35,* 523–529.

Hobbs, N. Helping disturbed children: psychological and ecological strategies. *American Psychologist,* 1966, *21,* 1105–1115.

Hobbs, N. *The Futures of Children.* San Francisco: Jossey-Bass, 1975.

Hobbs, N. Classification options: a conversation with Nicholas Hobbs on exceptional child education. *Exceptional Children,* 1978, *44,* 494–497.

Hoepfner, R., Bradley, P. A., and Doherty, W. J. National priorities for elementary education. CSE Monograph Series in Evaluation, Center for the Study of Evaluation, U.C.L.A., 1973.

Holman, J. The moral risk and high cost of ecological concern in applied behavior analysis. In A. Rogers-Warren and S. F. Warren (Eds.), *Ecological Perspectives in Behavior Analysis.* Baltimore: University Park Press, 1977.

Homme, L. Perspectives in psychology: XXIV. Control of coverants, the operants of the mind. *Psychological Record,* 1965, *15,* 501–511.

Homme, L. *How to Use Contingency Contracting in the Classroom.* Champaign, Il.: Research Press, 1971.

Homme, L., Csanyi, A. P., Gonzales, M. A., and Rechs, J. R. *How to Use Contingency Contracting in the Classroom.* Champaign, Il.: Research Press, 1970.

Hopkins, B. L. Effects of candy and social reinforcement, instructions, and reinforcement schedule learning on the modification and maintenance of smiling. *Journal of Applied Behavior Analysis,* 1968, *1,* 121–130.

Hopkins, B. L., Schutte, R. C., and Garton, K. L. The effects of access to a play room on the rate and the quality of printing and writing of first and second grade students. *Journal of Applied Behavior Analysis,* 1971, *4,* 77–88.

Hops, H. and Cobb, J. A. Initial investigations into academic survival training, direct instruction, and first-grade achievement. *Journal of Educational Psychology,* 1974, *66,* 548–553.

Hops, H., Fleischman, D. H., and Beickel, S. L. *CLASS (Contingencies for Learning Academic and Social Skills): Manual for Teachers.* Eugene, Or.: Center at Oregon for Research in the Behavioral Education of the Handicapped, University of Oregon, 1976.

Howard, A. W. Discipline is caring. *Today's Education,* 1972, *61,* 52–53.

Howell, K. W. Evaluation of behavior disorders. In R. B. Rutherford and A. G. Prieto (Eds.), *Severe Behavior Disorders of Children and Youth.* Reston, Va.: Council for Children with Behavioral Disorders, CEC, 1978.

Howell, K. W. Recent developments in the field of behavior therapy: The evolution of cognitive behavior modification. In R. B. Rutherford and

A. G. Prieto (Eds.), *Current Issues in Severe Behavior Disorders of Children and Youth*. Reston, Va.: Council for Children with Behavioral Disorders, CEC, 1979.

Hoyt, J. H. Georgia's Rutland Center. *American Education,* 1978, *14,* 27–32.

Huber, F. A strategy for teaching cooperative games: let's put back the fun in games for disturbed children. In N. J. Long, W. C. Morse, and R. G. Newman (Eds.), *Conflict in the Classroom* (3rd ed.). Belmont, Ca.: Wadsworth, 1976.

Huberty, C. J., Quirk, J., and Swan, W. W. An evaluation system for a psychoeducational treatment program for emotionally disturbed children. *Educational Technology,* 1973, *13,* 73–80.

Huberty, C. J., and Swan, W. W. Evaluation of programs. In J. Jordan (Ed.), *Early Childhood Education for Exceptional Children — A Handbook of Ideas and Exemplary Practices*. Arlington: Council for Exceptional Children, 1975.

Inhelder, B., and Piaget, J. *The Early Growth of Logic in the Child*. New York: Harper & Row, 1964.

Itard, J. M. G. *The Wild Boy of Aveyron*. Translated by George and Muriel Humphrey. Englewood Cliffs, N.J.: Prentice-Hall, 1962.

Iwata, B. A., and Bailey, J. S. Reward versus cost token systems: an analysis of the effects on students and teacher. *Journal of Applied Behavior Analysis,* 1974, *7,* 567–576.

Jackson, J. M. Structural characteristics of norms. In N. M. Henry (Ed.), *The Dynamics of Instructional Groups*. Chicago: National Society for the Study of Education, 1960.

Jesness, C. F., and DeRisi, V. J. Some variations in techniques of contingency management in a school for delinquents. In J. S. Stumphauzer (Ed.), *Behavior Therapy with Delinquents*. Springfield, Il.: Charles C. Thomas, 1973.

Johns, J. C., Trap, J., and Cooper, J. O. Students' self-recording of manuscript letter strokes. *Journal of Applied Behavior Analysis,* 1977, *10,* 509–514.

Johnson, C. A., and Katz, R. C. Using parents as change agents for their children: a review. *Journal of Child Psychology and Psychiatry,* 1973, *14,* 181–200.

Johnson, D. W., and Johnson, R. T. Instructional goal structure: cooperative, competitive, or individualistic. *Review of Educational Research,* 1974, *44,* 213–239.

Johnson, D. W., and Johnson, R. T. *Learning Together and Alone: Cooperation, Competition, and Individualization*. Englewood Cliffs, N.J.: Prentice-Hall, 1975.

Johnson, D. W., and Johnson, R. T. Effects of cooperation, competition, and individualism on interpersonal attraction among heterogeneous peers.

Paper presented at American Psychological Association Convention, San Francisco, August 1977.

Johnson, L. V., and Bany, M. A. *Classroom Management: Theory and Skill Training*. London: Collier-Macmillan Limited, 1970.

Johnson, M., and Bailey, J. S. Cross-age tutoring: fifth graders as arithmetic tutors for kindergarten children. *Journal of Applied Behavior Analysis,* 1974, *7,* 223–232.

Johnson, S. M., Wahl, G., Martin, S., and Johansson, S. How deviant is the normal child? A behavioral analysis of the preschool child and his family. In R. D. Rubin, J. P. Brady, and J. D. Henderson (Eds.), *Advances in Behavior Therapy* (Vol. 4). New York: Academic Press, 1973.

Jones, R. T., Nelson, R. E., and Kazdin, A. E. The role of external variables in self-reinforcement: a review. *Behavior Modification,* 1977, *1,* 147–178.

Joyce, B., and Harootunian, B. *The Structure of Teaching*. Chicago: Science Research Associates, 1967.

Kagan, J., and Moss, H. A. *Birth to Maturity: A Study of Psychological Development*. New York: John Wiley and Sons, 1962.

Kanfer, F. H. Self-management methods. In F. H. Kanfer and A. P. Goldstein (Eds.), *Helping People Change: A Text Book of Methods*. New York: Pergamon Press, 1975.

Kanfer, F. H. Personal communication, January 1978.

Kanfer, F. H., and Grimm, L. G. Behavioral analysis: selecting target behaviors in the interview. *Behavior Modification,* 1977, *1,* 7–28.

Kanfer, F. H., and Karoly, D. Self-control: a behavioristic excursion into the lion's den. *Behavior Therapy,* 1972, *3,* 398–416.

Kanfer, F. H., and Saslow, G. Behavior diagnosis. In C. M. Franks (Ed.), *Behavior Therapy: Appraisal and Status*. New York: McGraw-Hill, 1969.

Kaplan, L. *Mental Health and Human Relations in Education* (2nd ed.). New York: Harper & Row, 1971.

Karlin, M. S., and Berger, R. *Discipline and the Disruptive Child*. West Nyack, N.Y.: Parker Publishing Co., 1972.

Karnes, M. B., and Zehrbach, R. R. Matching families and services. *Exceptional Children,* 1975, *41,* 545–549.

Kauffman, J. M. Nineteenth century views of children's behavior disorders: historical contributions and continuing issues. *Journal of Special Education,* 1976, *10,* 335–349.

Kauffman, J. M. *Characteristics of Children's Behavior Disorders*. Columbus, Oh.: Charles E. Merrill, 1977.

Kauffman, J. M. An historical perspective on disordered behavior and an alternative conceptualization of exceptionality. In F. H. Wood and K. C. Lakin (Eds.), *Disturbing, Disordered or Disturbed? Perspectives on the Definition of Problem Behavior in Educational Settings*. Minneapolis:

Department of Psychoeducational Studies, University of Minnesota, 1979.

Kauffman, J. M., and Hallahan, D. P. Learning disability and hyperactivity (with comments on minimal brain dysfunction). In B. B. Lahey and A. E. Kazdin (Eds.), *Advances in Clinical Child Psychology* (Vol. 2). New York: Plenum, 1979.

Kaufman, A. S., Paget, K. D., and Wood, M. M. Effectiveness of developmental therapy for severely emotionally disturbed children. In F. H. Wood (Ed.), *Perspective for a New Decade: Education's Responsibility for Behaviorally Disordered Children and Youth.* Reston, Va.: Council for Exceptional Children, 1981.

Kaufman, A. S., Paget, K. D., and Wood, M. M. Validation of a psychoeducational intervention program for severely emotionally disturbed children. In Frank H. Wood (Ed.), *Perspectives for a New Decade: Education's Responsibility for Seriously Disturbed and Behaviorally Disordered Children and Youth.* Reston, Va.: Council for Exceptional Children, 1981.

Kaufman, A. S., Swan, W. W., and Wood, M. M. Dimensions of problem behaviors of emotionally disturbed children as seen by their parents and teachers. *Psychology in the Schools,* 1979, *16,* 207–217.

Kazdin, A. E. *Behavior Modification in Applied Settings.* Homewood, Il.: Dorsey, 1975.

Kazdin, A. E. Assessing the clinical or applied significance of behavior change through social validation. *Behavior Modification,* 1977, *1,* 427–452. (a)

Kazdin, A. E. *The Token Economy: A Review and Evaluation.* New York: Plenum Press, 1977. (b)

Kazdin, A. E. *History of Behavior Modification: Experimental Foundations of Contemporary Research.* Baltimore: University Park Press, 1978.

Kazdin, A. E. *Behavior Modification in Applied Settings* (2nd ed.). Homewood, Il.: Dorsey Press, 1980.

Kazdin, A. E., and Bootzin, R. R. The token economy: an evaluative review. *Journal of Applied Behavioral Analysis,* 1972, *5,* 343–372.

Kazdin, A. E., and Geesey, S. Simultaneous-treatment design comparisons of the effects of earning reinforcers for one's peers versus for oneself. *Behavior Therapy,* 1977, *8,* 682–693.

Kazdin, A. E., and Hartmann, D. P. The simultaneous-treatment design. *Behavior Therapy,* 1978, *9,* 912–922.

Kazdin, A. E., and Kopel, S. A. On resolving ambiguities of the multiple-baseline design: problems and recommendations. *Behavior Therapy,* 1975, *6,* 601–608.

Kazdin, A. E., and Wilson, G. T. *Evaluation of Behavior Therapy: Issues, Evidence, and Research Strategies.* Cambridge, Ma.: Ballinger, 1978.

Kelly, E. The Place for Affective Learning (editorial). *Educational Leadership,* 1965, *22,* 455–457.

Kelly, E. J. *Parent-Teacher Interaction: A Special Educational Perspective.* Seattle, Wa.: Special Child Publications, 1974.

Keogh, B. Working together: a new direction. *Journal of Learning Disabilities,* 1977, *10,* 478–482.

Kifer, R. E., Lewis, M. A., Gree, D. R., and Phillips, E. L. Training predelinquent youths and their parents to negotiate conflict situations. *Journal of Applied Behavior Analysis,* 1974, *7,* 357–364.

Kirby, F. D., and Shields, F. Modification of arithmetic response rate and attending behavior in a seventh-grade student. *Journal of Applied Behavior Analysis,* 1972, *5,* 79–84.

Kirschenbaum, H., and Simon, S. B. Teaching English with a focus on values. *English Journal,* 1969, *58,* 1071–1076.

Knoblock, P. Open education for emotionally disturbed children. *Exceptional Children,* 1973, *39,* (5), 358–365.

Knoblock, P., and Barnes, E. An environment for everyone: autistic and non-disabled children learn together. In S. J. Meisels (Ed.), *Special Education and Development.* Baltimore: University Park Press, 1979.

Knoblock, P., Barnes, E., Apter, S., and Taylor, S. *Preparing Humanistic Teachers for Troubled Children.* Syracuse, N.Y.: Syracuse University Press, 1974.

Knoblock, P., and Goldstein, A. P. *The Lonely Teacher.* Boston: Allyn and Bacon, 1971.

Knoblock, P., and Johnson, J. (Eds.). *The Teaching-Learning Process in Educating Emotionally Disturbed Children.* Syracuse, N.Y.: Syracuse University Press, 1967.

Koeppen, A. S. Relaxation training for children. *Elementary School Guidance and Counseling,* 1974, *9,* 14–21.

Kohlberg, L. Stage and sequence: the cognitive-developmental approach to socialization. In D. A. Goslin (Ed.), *Handbook of Socialization Theory and Research.* Chicago: Rand McNally, 1969.

Kohlberg, L. From is to ought: how to commit the naturalistic fallacy and get away with it in the study of moral development. In T. Mischel (Ed.), *Cognitive Development and Epistemology.* New York: Academic Press, 1971.

Kohlberg, L. Moral stages and moralization: the cognitive developmental approach. In T. Lickone (Ed.), *Moral Development and Behavior: Theory, Research, and Social Issues.* New York: Holt, Rinehart and Winston, 1976.

Kohlberg, L., and Hersh, R. H. Moral development: a review of the theory. *Theory into Practice,* 1977, *16,* 53–58.

Kooi, B. Y., and Schutz, R. E. A factor analysis of classroom disturbance intercorrelations. *American Educational Research Journal,* 1965, *3,* 37–40.

Kounin, J. S. *Discipline and Group Management in Classrooms.* New York: Holt, Rinehart and Winston, 1970.

Kounin, J. S. An ecological approach to classroom activity settings: some methods and findings. In R. A. Weinberg and F. H. Wood (Eds.), *Observation of Pupils and Teachers in Mainstream and Special Education Settings: Alternative Strategies*. Reston, Va.: Council for Exceptional Children, 1975.

Kounin, J. S., and Sherman, L. School environments as behavior settings. *Theory into Practice*, 1979, *18* (3), 145–151.

Krantz, P. J. *Ecological arrangements in the classroom*. Unpublished doctoral dissertation, University of Kansas, Lawrence, Ks., 1974.

Krathwohl, D. R., Bloom, B. S., and Masia, B. B. *Taxonomy of Educational Objectives, Handbook II: Affective Domain*. New York: David McKay, 1964.

Kratochwill, R. R. *Single Subject Research: Strategies for Measuring Change*. New York: Academic Press, 1978.

Kravetz, R. J., and Forness, S. R. The special classroom as a desensitization setting. *Exceptional Children*, 1971, *37*, 389–391.

Kroth, R. L. *Target Behavior*. Olathe, Ks.: Select-Ed., 1973.

Kroth, R. L. *Communicating with Parents of Exceptional Children: Improving Parent-Teacher Relationships*. Denver, Co.: Love Publishing Co., 1975.

Kroth, R. L., and Brown, G. B. Welcome in the parent. *School Media Quarterly*, 1978, *6*, 246–252.

Kroth, R. L., and Scholl, G. T. *Getting Involved with Parents*. Reston, Va.: Council for Exceptional Children, 1978.

Kroth, R. L., and Simpson, R. L. *Parent Conferences as a Teaching Strategy*. Denver, Co.: Love Publishing Co., 1977.

Kroth, R. L., Whelan, R., and Stables, J. Teacher application of behavior principles in home and classroom environments. *Focus on Exceptional Children*, 1970, *2* (3), 1–10.

Lahey, B. B., McNees, M. P., and Brown, C. C. Modification of deficits in reading for comprehension. *Journal of Applied Behavior Analysis*, 1973, *6*, 475–480.

Lahey, B. B., McNees, M. P., and McNees, C. M. Control of an obscene "verbal tic" through time-out in an elementary school classroom. *Journal of Applied Behavior Analysis*, 1973, *6*, 101–104.

Laten, S., and Katz, G. A. A theoretical model for the assessment of adolescents: the ecological/behavioral approach. Madison, Wi.: Madison Public Schools, 1975.

Leitenberg, H. The use of single-case methodology in psychotherapy research. *Journal of Abnormal Psychology*, 1973, *82*, 87–101.

Lewin, K. *A Dynamic Theory of Personality*. New York: McGraw-Hill, 1935.

Lewin, K., Lippitt, R., and White, R. K. Patterns of aggressive behavior in experimentally created social climates. *Journal of Social Psychology*, 1939, *10*, 271–299.

Lewis, Clayton D. In J. Kauffman and C. Lewis (Eds.), *Teaching Children with Behavior Disorders: Personal Perspectives.* Columbus, Oh.: Charles E. Merrill, 1974.

Lewis, H., and Streitfeld, H. *Growth Games.* New York: Harcourt, Brace, Jovanovich, 1970.

Lewis, W. W. Project Re-ED: educational intervention in discordant child rearing systems. In E. L. Cowen, E. A. Gardner, and M. Zax (Eds.), *Emergent Approaches to Mental Health Problems.* New York: Appleton-Century-Crofts, 1967.

Lewis, W. W. Ecological planning for disturbed children. *Childhood Education,* 1970, *46,* 306–310.

Lilly, D. L. Dimensions in parent programs: an overview. In J. Grimm (Ed.), *Training Parents to Teach — Four Models.* 1st Chance for Children (Vol. 3). Chapel Hill, N.C.: Technical Assistance Development Systems, 1974.

Limbacher, W. J. *Dimensions of Personality: Here I Am.* Dayton, Oh.: G. A. Pflaum, 1969.

Limbacher, W. J. *Dimensions of Personality: Becoming Myself.* Dayton, Oh.: G. A. Pflaum, 1970.

Lindsley, O. R. Direct measurement and prosthesis of retarded behavior. *Journal of Education,* 1964, *147,* 62–81.

Litow, L., and Pumroy, D. K. A brief review of classroom group-oriented contingencies. *Journal of Applied Behavior Analysis,* 1975, *8,* 341–347.

Lloyd, S. Project ACE: working with and maintaining disturbed adolescents in their natural settings. In J. K. Grosenick and R. Harth (Eds.), *Environmental Interventions for Emotionally Disturbed Children and Youth.* Columbia: University of Missouri at Columbia, 1973.

Lobitz, G. K., and Johnson, S. M. Normal vs. deviant children: a multi-method comparison. *Journal of Abnormal Child Psychology,* 1975, *3,* 353–374.

Loevinger, J. *Ego Development.* San Francisco: Jossey-Bass, 1976.

Loewald, H. W. The superego and the ego-ideal II: superego and time. *International Journal of Psychoanalysis,* 1962, *43,* 264–268.

Long, B. *The Journey to Myself: A Curriculum in Psychology for Middle Schools.* Austin, Tx.: Steck-Vaughn, 1974.

Long, N. J., and Fagen, S. A. Therapeutic management: a psychoeducational approach. In G. Brown, R. McDowell, and J. Smith (Eds.), *Educating Adolescents with Behavior Disorders.* Columbus, Oh.: Charles E. Merrill, 1981.

Long, N. J., Morse, W. C., and Newman, R. G. *Conflict in the Classroom* (2nd ed.). Belmont, Ca.: Wadsworth, 1971.

Long, N. J., Morse, W. C., and Newman, R. G. (Eds.). *Conflict in the Classroom: The Education of Children with Problems* (3rd ed.). Belmont, Ca.: Wadsworth, 1976.

Long, N. J., and Newman, R. G. The teacher's handling of children in conflict. *Bulletin of the School of Education.* Bloomington, In.: Indiana University, 1961.

Long, N. J., and Newman, R. G. Managing surface behavior of children in school. In N. J. Long, W. C. Morse, and R. G. Newman (Eds.), *Conflict in the Classroom: The Education of Children with Problems* (3rd ed.). Belmont, Ca.: Wadsworth, 1976.

Long, N. J., Kauffman, M. J. M., Lewis, C. D. (Eds.), *Teaching Children with Behavior Disorders: Personal Perspectives.* Columbus, Oh.: Charles E. Merrill, 1974.

Lovaas, O. I. A program for the establishment of speech in psychotic children. In J. K. Wing (Ed.), *Early Childhood Autism.* New York: Pergamon Press, 1966.

Lovaas, O. I., and Koegel, R. L. Behavior therapy with autistic children. In C. E. Thoresen (Ed.), *Behavior Modification in Education.* Chicago: University of Chicago Press, 1973, 230–258.

Lovaas, O. I., Schaeffer, B., and Simmons, J. W. Building social behavior in autistic children by use of electric shock. *Journal of Experimental Research in Personality,* 1965, *1,* 99–109.

Lovitt, T. C. Self-management projects with children with behavioral disabilities. *Journal of Learning Disabilities,* 1973, *6,* 138–150.

Lovitt, T. C. Applied behavior analysis and learning disabilities. *Journal of Learning Disabilities,* 1975, *8* (7), 42–43.

Lovitt, T. C. Applied behavior analysis techniques and curriculum research: implications for instruction. In N. G. Haring and R. L. Schiefelbusch (Eds.), *Teaching Special Children.* New York: McGraw-Hill, 1976.

Lovitt, T. C. Arithmetic. In N. G. Haring, T. C. Lovitt, M. D. Eaton, and C. L. Hansen (Eds.), *The Fourth R: Research in the Classroom.* Columbus, Oh.: Charles E. Merrill, 1978, 127–166.

Lovitt, T. C., and Curtiss, K. A. Academic response rate as a function of teacher and self-imposed contingencies. *Journal of Applied Behavior Analysis,* 1969, *2,* 49–53.

Lovitt, T. C., Eaton, M., Kirkwood, M., and Pelander, J. Effects of various reinforcement contingencies on oral reading rate. In E. A. Ramp and B. L. Hopkins (Eds.), *A New Direction for Education: Behavior Analysis.* Lawrence: University of Kansas Press, 1971.

Lovitt, T. C., Schaff, M., and Sayre, E. The use of direct and continuous measurement to evaluate reading materials and pupil performance. *Focus on Exceptional Children,* 1970, *2,* 1–11.

Lowenfeld, V. *Creative and Mental Growth* (3rd ed.). New York: Macmillan, 1957.

Lowenfeld, V., and Brittain, W. L. *Creative and Mental Growth* (5th ed.). New York: Macmillan, 1970.

Lyon, H. *Learning to Feel — Feeling to Learn.* Columbus, Oh.: Charles E. Merrill, 1971.

McAllister, L. W., Stachowiak, J. G., Baer, D. M., and Conderman, L. The application of operant conditioning techniques in a secondary school classroom. *Journal of Applied Behavior Analysis,* 1969, *2,* 277–285.

McCauley, R. W., Hlidek, R., and Feinberg, F. Impacting social interactions in classrooms: the classroom management and relationship program. In F. H. Wood (Ed.), *Preparing Teachers to Foster Personal Growth in Emotionally Disturbed Students.* Minneapolis: University of Minnesota, Department of Psychoeducational Studies, 1977.

McClelland, D. *Studies in Motivation.* New York: Appleton-Century-Crofts, 1955.

McDowell, R. *Program Designs for Teachers of the Behaviorally Disordered.* Santa Fe, N.M.: State Department of Education, Division of Special Education, 1975.

MacFarlane, J., Allen, L., and Honzik, M. *A Developmental Study of the Behavior Problems of Normal Children Between Twenty-one Months and Fourteen Years.* Berkeley: University of California Press, 1954,

McLaughlin, R. F. Self-control in the classroom. *Review of Educational Research,* 1976, *46* (4), 631–663.

McLeskey, J., Rieth, H. J., and Polsgrove, L. The implications of response generalization for improving the effectiveness of programs for learning disabled children. *Journal of Learning Disabilities,* 1980, *13* (5), 287–290.

Madsen, C. H., Becker, W. C., and Thomas, D. R. Rules, praise, and ignoring: elements of elementary classroom control. *Journal of Applied Behavior Analysis,* 1968, *1,* 139–150.

Madsen, K. B. *Theories of Motivation.* Kent, Oh.: Kent State University Press, 1968.

Mager, R. F. *Preparing Instructional Objectives.* Belmont, Ca.: Fearon, 1962.

Mahler, M. S. *On Human Symbiosis and the Vicissitudes of Individualization.* (Vol. I: Infantile psychosis.) New York: International Universities Press, 1968.

Mahler, M. S., Pine, F., and Bergman, A. *The Psychological Birth of the Human Infant: Symbiosis and Individualism.* New York: Basic Books, 1975.

Mahoney, M. J. *Cognition and Behavior Modification.* Cambridge, Ma.: Ballinger, 1974.

Mahoney, M. J. Reflections of the cognitive-learning trend in psychotherapy. *American Psychologist,* 1977, *32,* 5–13.

Maloney, K. B., and Hopkins, B. L. The modification of sentence structure and its relationship to subjective judgment of creativity in writing. *Journal of Applied Behavior Analysis,* 1973, *6,* 425–434.

Mantz, G. A mental health unit for fourth and fifth grades. *The Journal of School Health,* 1969, *39,* 658–661.

Martin, B. *Bill Martin's Freedom Books*. Glendale, Ca.: Bowmar Publishing Co., 1970.

Martin, B. *Brief Family Intervention: Effectiveness and the Importance of Including Father*. Paper presented at the meeting of the Association for Advancement of Behavior Therapy, New York, December 5, 1976.

Maslow, A. *Motivation and Personality*. New York: Harper & Row, 1970.

Maslow, A. *A Memorial Volume*. Belmont, Ca.: Brooks/Cole Publishing Co., 1972.

Maturity: Growing up Strong. Englewood Cliffs, N.J.: Scholastic Book Services, 1972.

Mehrabian, A. *Public Places and Private Spaces*. New York: Basic Books, 1976.

Meichenbaum, D. M. *Cognitive Behavior Modification*. New York: Plenum Press, 1977.

Meichenbaum, O. H. Self-instructional methods. In F. G. Kanfer and A. P. Goldstein (Eds.), *Helping People Change*. London: Pergamon Press, 1974.

Menninger, K. *The Vital Balance*. New York: Viking Press, 1963.

Mercer, J. The meaning of mental retardation. In R. Koch and J. Dobson (Eds.), *The Mentally Retarded Child and His Family*. New York: Brunner/Mazel, 1971.

Mercer, J. *Labeling the Mentally Retarded: Clinical and Social System Perspectives on Mental Retardation*. Berkeley: University of California Press, 1973.

Mercer, J., and Lewis, J. *SOMPA Conceptual and Technical Manual*. New York: The Psychological Corporation, 1978.

Midlarsky, E., and Suda, W. Some antecedents of altruism in children: theoretical and empirical perspectives. *Psychological Reports, 1978, 43,* 187–208.

Miller, L., Hampe, E., Barrett, C., and Noble, H. Children's deviant behavior within the general population. *Journal of Consulting and Clinical Psychology, 1971, 37,* 16–22.

Mischel, T. Piaget: cognitive conflict and the motivation of thought. In T. Mischel (Ed.), *Cognitive Development and Epistemology*. New York: Academic Press, 1971.

Mischel, W. *Personality Assessment*. New York: John Wiley and Sons, 1968.

Mischel, W. Toward a cognitive social learning reconceptualization of personality. *Psychological Review, 1973, 80,* 252–283.

Montgomery, P. A., and Van Fleet, D. S. Evaluation of behavioral and academic changes through the Re-ED process. *Behavioral Disorders, 1978, 3* (2), 136–146.

Moos, R. H. *Evaluating Educational Environments*. San Francisco: Jossey-Bass, 1979.

Moos, R. H., and Trickett, E. J. *Classroom Environment Scale*. Palo Alto, Ca.: Consulting Psychologists Press, 1974.

Morales v. Truman, 364 F. Supp. 166 (E.D. Texas, 1973). In R. Martin, *Legal Challenges to Behavior Modification*. Champaign, Il.: Research Press, 1975.

Morris, J. D., and Arrant, D. Behavior ratings of emotionally disturbed children by teachers, parents, and school psychologists. *Psychology in the Schools,* 1978, *15,* 450–455.

Morse, W. C. Diagnosing and guiding relationships between group and individual class members. In N. M. Henry (Ed.), *The Dynamics of Instructional Groups*. Chicago: National Society for the Study of Education, 1960.

Morse, W. C. Working paper: Training teachers in life space interviewing. *American Journal of Orthopsychiatry,* 1963, *33,* 727–730.

Morse, W. C. The mental hygiene viewpoint on school discipline. *The High School Journal,* 1965, *37,* 396–401.

Morse, W. C. Education of maladjusted and disturbed children. In N. Long, W. Morse, and R. Newman (Eds.), *Conflict in the Classroom* (2nd ed.). Belmont, Ca.: Wadsworth, 1971.

Morse, W. C. The crisis or helping teacher. In N. Long, W. Morse, and R. Newman (Eds.), *Conflict in the Classroom* (3rd ed.). Belmont, Ca.: Wadsworth, 1976. (a)

Morse, W. C. The helping teacher/crisis teacher concept. *Focus on Exceptional Children,* 1976, *8* (4), 1–11. (b)

Morse, W. C., and Munger, R. L. *Bibliography: Helping Children with Feelings, Affective-Behavioral Science Education, and Resources for the Developing Self-Schools*. Ann Arbor: University of Michigan, 1975.

Mowrer, O. H. *Learning Theory and Behavior*. New York: John Wiley and Sons, 1960.

Mussen, P. H., Conger, J. J., and Kagan, J. *Child Development and Personality* (3rd ed.). New York: Harper & Row, 1969.

Newberg, N. The impact of affective education in the Philadelphia School System. In A. Alschuler (Ed.), *New Directions in Psychological Education* (Educational Opportunities Forum). Albany: New York State Department of Education, 1969.

Newcomer, P. L. Special education services for the "mildly handicapped": beyond a diagnostic and remedial model. *The Journal of Special Education,* 1977, *11,* (2), 153–165.

Newcomer, P. L. *Understanding and Teaching Emotionally Disturbed Children*. Boston: Allyn and Bacon, 1980.

Newcomer, P. L., Larsen, S., and Hammill, D. Research on psycholinguistic training: critique and guidelines — a response. *Exceptional Children,* 1975, *42* (3), 144–148.

New York Association of Retarded Citizens vs. Rockefeller, 357 F. Supp.

(E. D. New York, 1973). In R. Martin, *Legal Challenges to Behavior Modification*. Champaign, Il.: Research Press, 1975.

Nordquist, V. M. The modification of a child's enuresis: some response-response relationships. *Journal of Applied Behavior Analysis,* 1971, *4,* 241–247.

Novick, J., Rosenfeld, E., Block, D. A., and Dawson, D. Ascertaining deviant behavior in children. *Journal of Consulting Psychology,* 1966, *30,* 230–238.

O'Dell, S. Training parents in behavior modifications: a review. *Psychological Bulletin,* 1974, *81,* 418–433.

O'Dell, S., Flynn, J. M., and Benlolo, L. T. *A Comparison of Parent Training Techniques in Child Behavior Modification.* Paper presented at the meeting of the Association for the Advancement of Behavior Therapy, New York, December 5, 1976.

Ojemann, R. Incorporating psychological concepts in the school curriculum. *Journal of School Psychology,* 1967, *5,* 195–204.

O'Leary, K. D., and Becker, W. C. Behavior modification of an adjustment class: a token reinforcement program. *Exceptional Children,* 1967, *33,* 637–642.

O'Leary, K. D., Becker, W. C., Evans, M. B., and Saudergas, R. A. A token reinforcement program in a public school: a replication and systematic analysis. *Journal of Applied Behavior Analysis,* 1969, *2,* 3–13.

O'Leary, K. D., and Drabman, R. Token reinforcement programs in the classroom: a review. *Psychological Bulletin,* 1971, *75* (6), 379–398.

O'Leary, K. D., and O'Leary, S. G. *Classroom Management: The Successful Use of Behavior Modification* (2nd ed.). New York: Pergamon Press, 1977.

O'Leary, S. G., and O'Leary, K. D. Behavior modification in the school. In H. Leitenberg (Ed.), *Handbook for Behavior Modification and Behavior Therapy*. Englewood Cliffs, N.J.: Prentice-Hall, 1976.

Osman, J. A rationale for using clarification in health education. *Journal of School Health,* 1973, *43,* 621–623.

Packard, R. G. The control of "classroom attention": a group contingency for complex behavior. *Journal of Applied Behavior Analysis,* 1970, *3,* 13–28.

Pappanikou, A. J., and Spears, J. J. The educational system. In A. J. Pappanikou and J. M. Paul (Eds.), *Mainstreaming Emotionally Disturbed Children*. Syracuse, N.Y.: Syracuse University Press, 1977.

Park, C. *The Siege*. Boston: Little, Brown and Company, 1967.

Parker, J. C., and Rubin, L. J. *Process as Content: Curriculum Design and the Application of Knowledge*. Chicago: Rand McNally, 1966.

Pastor, D., and Swap, S. An ecological study of emotionally disturbed preschoolers in special and regular classes. *Exceptional Children,* 1978, *45* (3), 213–215.

Pate, J. Emotionally disturbed and socially maladjusted children. In L. M. Dunn (Ed.), *Exceptional Children in the Schools.* New York: Holt, Rinehart and Winston, 1963.

Patterson, G. R. An application of conditioning techniques to the control of a hyperactive child. In L. P. Ullmann and L. Krasner (Eds.), *Case Studies in Behavior Modification.* New York: Holt, Rinehart and Winston, 1965. (a)

Patterson, G. R. A learning theory approach to the treatment of the school phobic child. In L. P. Ullmann and L. Krasner (Eds.), *Case Studies in Behavior Modification.* New York: Holt, Rinehart and Winston, 1965. (b)

Patterson, G. R. Interventions for boys with conduct problems: multiple settings, treatments, and criteria. *Journal of Consulting and Clinical Psychology,* 1974, *42,* 471–481.

Patterson, G. R. The aggressive child: victim or architect of a coercive system? In L. A. Hamerlynk, L. C. Handy, and E. J. Mash (Eds.), *Behavior Modification and Families.* New York: Brunner/Mazel, 1975.

Paul, G. L. Outcome of systematic desensitization. I: Background procedures, and uncontrolled reports of individual treatment. In C. M. Franks (Ed.), *Behavior Therapy: Appraisal and Status.* New York: McGraw-Hill, 1969. (a)

Paul, G. L. Outcome of systematic desensitization, II: controlled investigations of individual treatment, technique variations, and current status. In C. M. Franks (Ed.), *Behavior Therapy: Appraisal and Status.* New York: McGraw-Hill, 1969. (b)

Pavlov, I. P. *Conditioned Reflexes: An Investigation of the Physiological Activity of the Cerebral Cortex.* (G. V. Anrep, Ed. and trans.). London: Oxford University Press, 1927.

Peed, S., Roberts, M., and Forehand, R. Evaluation of the effectiveness of a standardized parent training program in altering the interaction of mothers and their noncompliant children. *Behavior Modification,* 1977, *1,* 323–350.

Perry, H. Up front with the president. *Exceptional Children,* 1977, *44* (1), 5.

Peter, L. *Prescriptive Teaching.* New York: McGraw-Hill, 1965.

Peterson, D. Behavior problems of middle childhood. *Journal of Consulting Psychology,* 1961, *25,* 205–209.

Peterson, D. R., and Quay, H. C. *Behavior Problem Checklist.* Champaign, Il.: Children's Research Center, University of Illinois, 1967.

Phillips, E. L. Achievement Place: token reinforcement procedures in a homestyle rehabilitation setting for "predelinquent" boys. *Journal of Applied Behavior Analysis,* 1968, *1,* 213–224.

Phillips, E. L., Phillips, E. A., Fixsen, D. L., and Wolf, M. M. Achievement Place: modification of the behaviors of predelinquent boys within a token economy. *Journal of Applied Behavior Analysis,* 1971, *4,* 45–59.

Phillips, E. L., Phillips, E. A., Fixsen, D. L., and Wolf, M. M. *The*

Teaching-Family Handbook. Lawrence, Ks.: University Printing Service, 1972.

Phillips, E. L., Phillips, E. A., Wolf, M. M., and Fixsen, D. L. Achievement Place: development of the elected manager system. *Journal of Applied Behavioral Analysis,* 1973, *6,* 541–561.

Piaget, J. *The Construction of Reality in the Child.* New York: Basic Books, 1954.

Piaget, J. *Play, Dreams, and Imitation in Children.* New York: W. W. Norton, 1962.

Piaget, J. *The Moral Judgment of the Child.* New York: Free Press, 1965. (Originally published, 1932.)

Piaget, J. *Six Psychological Studies.* New York: Random House, 1967.

Piaget, J. Some aspects of operations. In M. W. Piers (Ed.), *Play and Development.* New York: W. W. Norton, 1972.

Piaget, J. *The Development of Thought: Equilibration of Cognitive Structures.* New York: Viking Press, 1977.

Piaget, J., and Inhelder, B. *The Psychology of the Child.* New York: Basic Books, 1969.

Polsgrove, L. Self-control: methods for child training. *Behavioral Disorders,* 1979, *4* (2), 116–130.

Polsgrove, L., Rieth, H. J., Friend, J., and Cohen, R. An analysis of the various instructional procedures on the oral reading performance of high school special education students. *Monograph in Behavior Disorders* (CCBD), No. 3, 1980.

Polsky, H. W. *Cottage Six: The Social System of Delinquent Boys in Residential Treatment.* New York: Russell Sage Foundation, 1962.

Popham, W. J. *Criterion-Referenced Measurement.* Englewood Cliffs, N.J.: Prentice-Hall, 1978.

Popham, W. J., and Husek, T. R. Implications of criterion-referenced measurement. *Journal of Educational Measurement,* 1969, *1,* 1–9.

Premack, D. Reinforcement theory. In D. Levine (Ed.), *Nebraska Symposium on Motivation: 1965.* Lincoln: University of Nebraska, 1965.

Prieto, A., and Rutherford, R. An ecological assessment technique for behaviorally disordered and learning disabled children. *Behavioral Disorders,* 1977, *2* (3), 169–175.

Proshansky, E., and Wolfe, M. The physical setting and open education. *School Review,* 1974, *82,* 557–574.

Proshansky, H. M. Theoretical issues in environmental psychology. *School Review,* 1974, *82,* 541–556.

Purvis, J., and Samet, S. *Music in Developmental Therapy.* Baltimore: University Park Press, 1976.

Quay, H. C. Dimensions of personality in delinquent boys as inferred from the factor analysis of case history data. *Child Development,* 1964, *35,* 479–484.

Quay, H. C., Morse, W. C., and Cutler, R. L. Personality patterns in pupils in special classes for the emotionally disturbed. *Exceptional Children,* 1966, *32,* 297–301.

Quay, H. C., and Werry, J. S. Patterns of aggression, withdrawal and immaturity. In H. C. Quay and J. S. Werry (Eds.), *Psychopathological Disorders of Childhood.* New York: John Wiley and Sons, 1972.

Rapaport, D. Psychoanalysis as a developmental psychology. In B. Kaplan and S. Wapner (Eds.), *Perspectives in Psychological Theory.* New York: International Universities Press, 1960.

Rardin, C. A. Comparison of the utility of two classroom observation systems as diagnostic-assessment tools. Unpublished MA colloquium paper, Department of Psychoeducational Studies, University of Minnesota, 1976.

Rardin, C. A. A special education mainstream elementary program for behavior and emotion problem students. In F. H. Wood (Ed.), *Preparing Teachers to Develop and Maintain Therapeutic Educational Environments.* Minneapolis: Department of Psychoeducational Studies, University of Minnesota, 1978.

Raths, L., Harmin, M., and Simon, S. *Values and Teaching.* Columbus, Oh.: Charles E. Merrill, 1966.

Redl, F. Strategy and techniques of the life space interview. *American Journal of Orthopsychiatry,* 1959, *29,* 1–18.

Redl, F. It's about time. *Reiss-Davis Clinic Bulletin,* 1964, *1* (1), 2.

Redl, F. Designing a therapeutic classroom environment for disturbed children: the milieu approach. In M. P. Knoblock (Ed.), *Intervention Approaches in Educating Emotionally Disturbed Children.* Syracuse, N.Y.: Syracuse University Press, 1966. (a)

Redl, F. *When We Deal with Children.* New York: Free Press, 1966. (b)

Redl, F. The concept of the life-space interview. In N. J. Long, W. C. Morse, and R. G. Newman (Eds.), *Conflict in the Classroom* (3rd ed.). Belmont, Ca.: Wadsworth, 1976. (a)

Redl, F. The concept of a therapeutic milieu. In M. N. Long, W. Morse, and R. Newman (Eds.), *Conflict in the Classroom* (3rd ed.). Belmont, Ca.: Wadsworth, 1976. (b)

Redl, F., and Wattenberg, W. W. *Mental Hygiene in Teaching* (2nd ed.). New York: Harcourt, 1959.

Redl, F., and Wineman, D. *Children Who Hate.* New York: Fress Press, 1951.

Redl, F., and Wineman, D. *Controls from Within.* New York: Free Press, 1952.

Redl, F., and Wineman, D. *The Aggressive Child.* New York: Free Press, 1954.

Reed, J. Parents/Re-ED: partners in re-education. *Behavioral Disorders,* 1978, *3* (2), 92–94.

Reiber, J. L., Schilmoeller, G. L., and LeBlanc, J. M. The use of self-control to maintain attending of pre-school children after self-counting procedures. In T. A. Brigham, R. Hawkins, J. W. Scott, and T. F. McLaughlin (Eds.), *Behavior Analysis in Education.* Dubuque, Iowa: Kendall/Hunt, 1976.

Repp, A. C. Observations of a day at Bicetre. *Journal of Applied Behavior Analysis,* 1977, *10,* 548.

Reynolds, N. C., and Balow, B. Categories and variables in special education. *Exceptional Children,* 1972, *38,* 357–366.

Rezmierski, V., and Kotre, J. A limited literature review of theory of the psychodynamic model. In W. Rhodes and M. Tracy (Eds.), *A Study of Child Variance* (Vol. 1). Ann Arbor: University of Michigan Press, 1974.

Rhodes, W. C. The disturbing child: A problem of ecological management. *Exceptional Children,* 1967, *33,* 449–455.

Rhodes, W. C. A community participation analysis of emotional disturbance. *Exceptional Children,* 1970, *36* (5), 309–314.

Rhodes, W. C. Beyond abnormality into the mainstream. In A. J. Pappanikou and J. L. Paul (Eds.), *Mainstreaming Emotionally Disturbed Children.* Syracuse, N.Y.: Syracuse University Press, 1977.

Rhodes, W. C., and Paul, J. L. *Emotionally Disturbed and Deviant Children.* Englewood Cliffs, N.J.: Prentice-Hall, 1978.

Rhodes, W., and Tracy, M. (Eds.). *A Study of Child Variance* (Vol. 1: Theories). Ann Arbor: University of Michigan, 1972. (a)

Rhodes, W. C., and Tracy, M. L. (Eds.). *A Study of Child Variance* (Vol. II: Interventions). Ann Arbor: University of Michigan, 1972. (b)

Rich, H. L. Behavior disorders and school: a case of sexism and racial bias. *Behavioral Disorders,* 1977, *2,* 201–204.

Rich, H. L. A model for educating the emotionally disturbed and behaviorally disordered. *Focus on Exceptional Children,* 1978, *10* (3), 1–11.

Rich, H. L. Teachers' perceptions of motor activity and related behaviors in elementary resource students. *Exceptional Children,* 1978, *45,* 210–211.

Rie, H. Historical perspective of concepts of child psychopathology. In H. E. Rie (Ed.), *Perspectives in Child Psychopathology.* Chicago: Aldine Atherton, 1971.

Rieth, H. J., Axelrod, S., Anderson, R., Hathaway, F., Wood, K., and Fitzgerald, C. Influence of distributive practice and daily testing on weekly spelling tests. *Journal of Educational Research,* 1974, *68,* 73–77.

Rieth, H. J., Polsgrove, L., Raia, S., Patterson, N., and Buchman, K. The use of free time to increase the reading achievement of three students placed in programs for behavior disordered children. *Behavior Disorders,* 1977, *3* (1), 45–54.

Rimland, B. Psychogenesis vs. biogenesis: the issues and the evidence. In

S. C. Plog and R. B. Edgerton (Eds.), *Changing Perspectives in Mental Illness*. New York: Holt, Rinehart and Winston, 1969.

Risley, R. R., and Twardosz, S. Suggested guidelines for the humane management of the behavior problems of the retarded. Unpublished paper, Florida Department of Health and Rehabilitative Services, Division of Retardation, 1974.

Risley, T. R., and Wolf, M. Establishing functional speech in echolalic children. In H. M. Sloane, Jr., and B. D. MacAulay (Eds.), *Operant Procedures in Remedial Speech and Language Training*. Boston: Houghton Mifflin, 1968.

Robinson, E. J. Reliability and validity study of the Developmental Therapy Verification Form. Unpublished paper, Division for Exceptional Children, University of Georgia, 1977.

Rogers-Warren, A. Planned change: ecobehaviorally based interventions. In A. Rogers-Warren and S. F. Warren (Eds.), *Ecological Perspectives in Behavior Analysis*. Baltimore: University Park Press, 1977.

Rogers-Warren, A., and Baer, D. M. Correspondence between saying and doing: teaching children to share and praise. *Journal of Applied Behavior Analysis,* 1976, *9,* 335–354.

Rogers-Warren, A., and Warren, S. F. The developing ecobehavioral psychology. In A. Rogers-Warren and S. F. Warren (Eds.), *Ecological Perspectives in Behavior Analysis*. Baltimore: University Park Press, 1977.

Rosenhan, D. L. Learning theory and prosocial behavior. *Journal of Social Issues,* 1972, *28,* 151–163.

Rosenhan, D. L., and White, G. M. Observation and rehearsal as determinants of pro-social behavior. *Journal of Personality and Social Psychology,* 1967, *5,* 424–431.

Rosenthal, R., and Jacobson, L. *Pygmalion in the Classroom*. New York: Holt, Rinehart and Winston, 1968.

Ross, A. O. *Psychological Disorders of Children: A Behavioral Approach to Theory, Research, and Therapy*. New York: McGraw-Hill, 1974.

Rubin, R. A., and Balow, B. E. Prevalence of teacher identified behavior problems: a longitudinal study. *Exceptional Children,* 1978, *45,* 102–111.

Rutherford, R. B. Theory and research on the use of aversive procedures in the education of moderately behaviorally disordered and emotionally disturbed children and youth. In F. H. Wood and K. C. Lakin (Eds.), *Punishment and Aversive Stimulation in Special Education: Legal, Theoretical and Practical Issues in Their Use with Emotionally Disturbed Children and Youth*. Minneapolis: Department of Psychoeducational Studies, University of Minnesota, 1978.

Salter, A. *Conditioned Reflex Therapy: The Direct Approach to the Reconstruction of Personality*. New York: Creative Age Press, 1949.

Salvia, J., and Ysseldyke, J. E. *Assessment in Special and Remedial Education*. Boston: Houghton Mifflin, 1978.

Santagrossi, D. A., O'Leary, K. D., Romanczyk, R. G., and Kaufman, K. F. Self-evaluation by adolescents in a psychiatric hospital school token program. *Journal of Applied Behavior Analysis,* 1973, *6,* 277–288.

Sarason, I. G., and Ganzer, V. J. Developing appropriate social behaviors of juvenile delinquents. In J. D. Krumboltz and C. E. Thorsen (Eds.), *Behavioral Counseling.* New York: Holt, Rinehart and Winston, 1969.

Sarason, I. G., and Ganzer, V. J. Modeling and group discussion in the rehabilitation of juvenile delinquents. *Journal of Counseling Psychology,* 1973, *20,* 442–449.

Schmuck, R. Some aspects of classroom social climate. *Psychology in the Schools,* 1966, *3,* 59–65.

Schoggen, P. Environmental forces in the everyday lives of children. In R. G. Barker (Ed.), *The Stream of Behavior.* New York: Appleton-Century-Crofts, 1953.

Schrank, J. *Teaching Human Beings 101 Subversive Activities for the Classroom.* Boston: Beacon Press, 1972.

Schrupp, M. H., and Gjerde, C. M. Teacher growth in attitudes toward behavior problems of children. *Journal of Educational Psychology,* 1953, *44,* 203–214.

Schulman, J. L., Ford, R. C., and Bush, P. A classroom program to improve self-concept. *Psychology in the Schools,* 1973, *10,* 481–487.

Schulman, J. L., Ford, R. C., Bush, P., and Kaspar, J. C. Evaluation of a classroom program to alter friendship practices. *The Journal of Educational Research,* 1973, *67,* 99–102.

Schultz, E. W., Heuchert, C., and Stampf, S. M. *Pain and Joy in School.* Champaign, Il.: Research Press, 1973.

Schultz, E. W., Hirshoren, A., Manton, A., and Henderson, R. Special education for the emotionally disturbed. *Exceptional Children,* 1971, *38,* 313–319.

Schultz, E. W., Silvia, J., and Feinn, J. Prevalence of behavioral symptoms in rural elementary school children. *Journal of Abnormal Child Psychology,* 1974, *2,* 17–24.

Schumaker, J. B., Hovell, M. F., and Sherman, J. A. An analysis of daily report cards and parent-managed privileges in the improvement of adolescents' classroom performance. *Journal of Applied Behavior Analysis,* 1977, *10,* 449–464.

Schwartzrock, S., and Whenn, C. G. *The Coping With Series.* Circle Pines, Mn.: American Guidance Service, 1973.

Segal, J., and Yahraes, H. Protecting children's mental health. *Children Today,* 1978, *7,* 23–25.

Seguin, E. *Idiocy and Its Treatment by the Physiological Method.* New York: Brandow, 1866.

Selman, R. L. Toward a structural analysis of developing interpersonal relations concepts: research with normal and disturbed preadolescent boys. In *Minnesota Symposia on Child Psychology*. Minneapolis: University of Minnesota Press, 1976.

Selman, R. L., and Byrne, D. F. A structural-developmental analysis of levels of role taking in middle childhood. *Child Development, 1974, 45,* 803–806.

Shaftel, F., and Shaftel, G. *Role-Playing for Social Values: Decision Making in the Social Studies.* Englewood Cliffs, N.J.: Prentice-Hall, 1967.

Simon, A., and Boyer, E. G. *Mirrors for Behavior* (3 vols.). Philadelphia: Research for Better Schools, 1967, 1970a, and 1970b.

Simon, S. B., Howe, L. W., and Kirschenbaum, H. *Values Clarification: A Handbook of Practical Strategies for Teachers and Students.* New York: Hart, 1972.

Simon, S. B., and O'Rourke, R. D. *Developing Values with Exceptional Children.* Englewood Cliffs, N.J.: Prentice-Hall, 1977.

Skiba, E. A., Pettigrew, L. E., and Alden, S. E. A behavioral approach to the control of thumb-sucking in the classroom. *Journal of Applied Behavior Analysis, 1971, 4,* 121–125.

Skinner, B. F. *Science and Human Behavior.* New York: Free Press, 1953.

Smith, D. D., and Lovitt, T. C. The influence of instructions and reinforcement contingencies on children's abilities to compute arithmetic problems. Paper presented at the Fifth Annual Conference on Behavior Analysis in Education, University of Kansas, October 1974.

Smith, R. M., Neisworth, J. T., and Greer, J. G. *Evaluating Educational Environment.* Columbus, Oh.: Charles E. Merrill, 1978.

Solomon, R. W., and Wahler, R. G. Peer reinforcement control of classroom problem behavior. *Journal of Applied Behavior Analysis, 1973, 6,* 49–56.

Sommer, R. Classroom layout. *Theory into Practice, 1977, 16,* 174–175.

Sprinthall, N. A cognitive developmental curriculum: the adolescent as a psychologist. *Counseling and Values, 1974, 18,* 94–101.

Stenhouse, L. The humanities curriculum project: the rationale. *Theory into Practice, 1971, 10,* 154–163.

Stephens, T. M. *Directive Teaching of Children with Learning and Behavioral Handicaps.* Columbus, Oh.: Charles E. Merrill, 1975.

Stephens, T. M. *Social Skills in the Classroom.* Columbus, Oh.: Cedars Press, 1978.

Stewart, J. C. *Counseling Parents of Exceptional Children: Principles, Problems and Procedures.* New York: MSS Information Corporation, 1974.

Stiles, C. A strategy for teaching remedial reading: I'm not gonna read and you can't make me! In N. J. Long, W. C. Morse, and R. G. Newman (Eds.), *Conflict in the Classroom* (3rd ed.). Belmont, Ca.: Wadsworth, 1976.

Stokes, T., and Baer, D. An implicit technology of generalization. *Journal of Applied Behavior Analysis, 1977, 10,* 349–367.

Strain, P. S., Cooke, T. P., and Appolloni, T. *Teaching Exceptional Children: Assessing and Modifying Social Behavior.* New York: Academic Press, 1976.

Strain, P. S., Shores, R. E., and Kerr, M. M. An experimental analysis of "spill over" effects of the social interaction of behaviorally handicapped pre-school children. *Journal of Applied Behavioral Analysis, 1976, 9,* 31–40.

Strain, P. S., and Timm, M. A. An experimental analysis of social interaction between a behaviorally disordered pre-school child and her classroom peers. *Journal of Applied Behavior Analysis, 1974, 7,* 583–590.

Strain, P. S., and Wiegerink, R. The social play of two behaviorally disordered preschool children during four activities: a multiple baseline study. *Journal of Abnormal Child Psychology, 1975, 3,* 61–70.

Strain, P. S., and Wiegerink, R. The effects of sociodramatic activities on social interaction among behaviorally disordered pre-school children. *The Journal of Special Education, 1976, 10,* 71–76.

Strauss, A., and Lehtinen, L. *Psychopathology and Education of the Brain-Injured Child.* New York: Grune & Stratton, 1947.

Stuart, R. B. Behavioral contracting within families of delinquents. *Journal of Behavior Therapy and Experimental Psychiatry, 1971, 2,* 1–11.

Stuart, R. B., and Lott, L. A. Behavioral contracting with delinquents: a cautionary note. *Journal of Behavior Therapy and Experimental Psychiatry, 1972, 3,* 161–169.

Sullivan, H. S. *The Interpersonal Theory of Psychiatry.* New York: W. W. Norton, 1953.

Sulzbacher, S. I., and Houser, J. E. A tactic to eliminate disruptive behaviors in the classroom: group contingent consequences. *American Journal of Mental Deficiency, 1968, 73,* 88–90.

Sulzer-Azaroff, B., and Mayer, G. R. *Applied Behavior Analysis Procedures with Children and Youth.* New York: Holt, Rinehart and Winston, 1977.

Swan, W. W. Three year final performance report: outreach assistance for utilization of the Rutland Center-Developmental Therapy model. Washington, D.C.: Bureau of Education for the Handicapped/HCEEP, December 1976 (IEG007305585).

Swan, W. W., and Wood, M. M. Making decisions about treatment effectiveness. In M. M. Wood (Ed.), *Developmental Therapy.* Baltimore: University Park Press, 1975.

Swanson, H. L., and Reinert, H. R. *Teaching Strategies for Children in Conflict.* St. Louis: C. V. Mosby Co., 1979.

Swap, S. Disturbing classroom behaviors: a developmental and ecological view. *Exceptional Children, 1974, 41,* 163–172.

Swap, S. The ecological model of emotional disturbance in children: a status report and proposed synthesis. *Behavioral Disorders,* 1978, *3* (3), 186–196.

Tallmadge, G. K. *The Joint Dissemination Review Panel IDEABOOK.* Mountain View, Ca.: RMC Research Corp., 1977.

Tavormina, J. B. Relative effectiveness of behavioral and reflective group counseling with parents of mentally retarded children. *Journal of Counseling and Clinical Psychology,* 1975, *43,* 22–31.

Tharp, R. G., and Wetzel, J. R. *Behavior Modification in the Natural Environment.* New York: Academic Press, 1969.

Thomas, A., Chess, S., and Birch, H. *Temperament and Behavior Disorders in Children.* New York: New York University Press, 1968.

Thomas, A., and Chess, S. *Temperament and Development.* New York: Brunner/Mazel, 1977.

Thomas, D. R., Becker, W. C., and Armstrong, M. Production and elimination of disruptive classroom behavior by systematically varying teacher's behavior. *Journal of Applied Behavior Analysis,* 1968, *1,* 35–45.

Thoresen, C. E., and Mahoney, M. J. *Behavioral Self-Control.* New York: Holt, Rinehart and Winston, 1974.

Thorndike Barnhardt World Book Dictionary, Field Enterprises Educational Corp., Chicago, 1964.

Torrance, E. P. *The Search for Satori and Creativity.* Buffalo, N.Y.: Creative Education Foundation, 1979.

Trap, J. J., Milner-Davis, P., Joseph, S., and Cooper, J. O. The effects of feedback and consequences on transitional cursive letter formation. *Journal of Applied Behavior Analysis,* 1978, *11,* 381–393.

Turiel, E. Developmental processes in the child's moral thinking. In P. Mussen, J. Langer, and M. Covington (Eds.), *Trends and Issues in Developmental Psychology.* New York: Holt, Rinehart and Winston, 1969.

Turkewitz, H., O'Leary, K., Ironsmith, M. Generalization and maintenance of appropriate behavior through self-control. *Journal of Consulting Clinical Psychologists,* 1975, *43,* 577–583.

Ullmann, L. P., and Krasner, L. (Eds.). *Case Studies in Behavior Modification.* New York: Holt, Rinehart and Winston, 1965.

U. S. Department of Health, Education, and Welfare, Office of Education. Education of handicapped children: implementation of Part B of the Education of the Handicapped Act. *Federal Register, 42* (163), August 23, 1977, Part II, 42474–42518.

U. S. Department of Health, Education, and Welfare, Office of Education, Bureau of Education for the Handicapped, State Program Implementation Studies. *Progress Toward a Free Appropriate Public Education: A Report to Congress on the Implementation of Public Law 94–142: The Education For All Handicapped Children Act.* Washington, D.C.: 1979.

U. S. Office of Education, National Institute of Education Far West Laboratory, *Educational Programs That Work,* 1978. (Contract #300-77-415), 8–21.

U. S. Office of Education. *Estimated Number of Handicapped Children in the United States, 1976–79.* Washington, D.C.: U. S. Office of Education, 1979.

Vorrath, H. H., and Brendtro, L. K. *Positive Peer Culture.* Chicago: Aldine, 1974.

Wagonseller, B. R., Burnett, M., Salzberg, B., and Burnett, J. *The Art of Parenting.* Champaign, Il.: Research Press, 1977.

Wahler, R. G. Setting generality: some specific and general effects of child behavior therapy. *Journal of Applied Behavior Analysis,* 1969, *2,* 239–246.

Wahler, R. G., and Cormier, W. H. The ecological interview: a first step in outpatient child behavior therapy. In J. M. Stedman, W. F. Patton, and K. F. Waton (Eds.), *Clinical Studies in Behavior Therapy with Children, Adolescents and Their Families.* Springfield, Il.: Charles C. Thomas, 1973.

Wahler, R. G., House, A., and Stambaugh, E. *Ecological Assessment of Child Problem Behavior.* New York: Pergamon Press, 1976.

Wahler, R. G., Winkel, G. H., Peterson, R. F., and Morrison, D. C. Mothers as behavior therapists for their own children. *Behavior Research and Therapy,* 1965, *3,* 113–124.

Walker, H. M. *Walker Problem Behavior Identification Checklist.* Los Angeles: Western Psychological Corporation, 1970.

Walker, H. M., and Buckley, N. K. The effects of reinforcement, punishment and feedback upon academic response rate. *Psychology in the Schools,* 1972, *9,* 186–193. (a)

Walker, H. M., and Buckley, N. K. Programming generalization and maintenance of treatment effects across time and across settings. *Journal of Applied Behavior Analysis,* 1972, *5,* 209–224. (b)

Walker, H. M., and Hops, H. The use of group and individual reinforcement contingencies in the modification of social withdrawal. In L. A. Hamerlynck, L. C. Handy, and E. J. Mash (Eds.), *Behavior Change: Methodology, Concepts, and Practice.* Champaign, Il.: Research Press, 1973.

Walker, H. M., and Hops, H. Increasing academic achievement by reinforcing direct academic performance and/or facilitative nonacademic responses. *Journal of Educational Psychology,* 1976, *68,* 218–225.

Walker, H. M., and Hops, H. Use of normative peer data as a standard for evaluating classroom treatment effects. *Journal of Applied Behavior Analysis,* 1976, *9,* 159–168.

Walker, H. M., Hops, H., and Fiegenbaum, E. Deviant classroom behavior as a function of combinations of social and token reinforcement and cost contingency. *Behavior Therapy,* 1976, *7,* 76–88.

Walker, H. M., Hops, H., and Johnson, S. M. Generalization and maintenance of classroom treatment effects. *Behavior Therapy,* 1975, *6,* 188–200.

Walker, H. M., Mattson, R. H., and Buckley, N. K. The functional analysis of behavior within an experimental classroom. In W. C. Becker (Ed.), *An Empirical Basis for Change in Education.* Chicago: Science Research Associates, 1971.

Wallace, G., and Kauffman, J. M. *Teaching Children with Learning Problems.* Columbus, Oh.: Charles E. Merrill, 1978.

Wallace, G., and Larsen, S. C. *Educational Assessment of Learning Problems: Testing for Teaching.* Boston: Allyn and Bacon, 1978.

Watson, J. B., and Rayner, R. Conditioned emotional reactions. *Journal of Experimental Psychology,* 1920, *3,* 1–14.

Webster's Third New International Dictionary. Springfield, Ma.: G. and C. Merriam Co., 1971.

Wehling, L. J., and Charters, W. W. Dimensions of beliefs about the teaching process. *American Educational Research Journal,* 1969, *6,* 7–30.

Weinstein, G., and Fantini, M. D. *Toward Humanistic Education: A Curriculum of Affect.* New York: Praeger Publishers, 1970.

Weinstein, L. Project Re-ED schools for emotionally disturbed children: effectiveness as viewed by referring agencies, parents, and teachers. *Exceptional Children,* 1969, *35* (9), 703–711.

Whelan, R. J. The emotionally disturbed. In E. L. Meyer (Ed.), *Exceptional Children and Youth: An Introduction.* Denver, Co.: Love Publishing Co., 1978.

White, O. R. Personal communication, 1978.

White, O. R., Billingsley, F., and Munson, R. Evaluation of the daily progress of severely and profoundly handicapped pupils. Paper presented at the meeting of the American Association for the Education of the Severely and Profoundly Handicapped, Baltimore, Md., 1978.

White, O. R., and Haring, N. G. *Exceptional Children: A Multimedia Training Package.* Columbus, Oh.: Charles E. Merrill, 1976.

White, O. R., and Liberty, K. A. Behavioral assessment and precise educational measurement. In N. G. Haring and R. L. Schiefelbusch (Eds.), *Teaching Special Children.* New York: McGraw-Hill, 1976.

White, R. Motivation reconsidered: the concept of competence. *Psychological Review,* 1959, *66,* 297–333.

Wiederholt, J. L., Hammill, D. D., and Brown, V. *The Resource Teacher.* Boston: Allyn and Bacon, 1978.

Willems, E. P. Sense of obligation to high school activities as related to school size and marginality of student. *Child Development,* 1967, *38,* 1247–1260.

Willems, E. P. Planning a rationale for naturalistic research. In E. P. Willems and H. L. Raush (Eds.), *Naturalistic Viewpoints in Psychological Research*. New York: Holt, Rinehart and Winston, 1969.

Willems, E. P. Some radical proposals in ecological psychology. Paper presented to the Third Annual Mardi Gras Symposium, Louisiana State University, Baton Rouge, February 24, 1971.

Willems, E. P. Behavioral technology and behavioral ecology. In A. Rogers-Warren and S. F. Warren (Eds.), *Ecological Perspectives in Behavior Analysis*. Baltimore: University Park Press, 1977.

Williams, G., and Wood, M. M. *Developmental Art Therapy*. Baltimore: University Park Press, 1977.

Winett, R. A., and Winkler, R. C. Current behavior modification in the classroom: be still, be quiet, be docile. *Journal of Applied Behavior Analysis,* 1972, *5,* 499–504.

Wohlwill, J. F. The age variable in psychological research. In N. S. Endler, L. R. Boulter, and H. Osser (Eds.), *Contemporary Issues in Developmental Psychology* (2nd ed.). New York: Holt, Rinehart and Winston, 1976.

Wolf, M. M. Social validity: the case for subjective measurement, or how applied behavior analysis is finding its heart. *Journal of Applied Behavior Analysis,* 1978, *11,* 203–214.

Wolf, M. M., Hanley, E. L., King, L. A., Lachowicz, J., and Giles, D. K. The timer-game: a variable interval contingency for the management of out-of-seat behavior. *Exceptional Children,* 1970, *37,* 113–117.

Wolff, P. H. The developmental psychologies of Jean Piaget and psychoanalysis. *Psychological Issues,* 1960, *2,* 5–179.

Wolff, P. H. Operational thought and social adaptation. In M. W. Piers (Ed.), *Play and Development*. New York: W. W. Norton, 1972.

Wolpe, J. *Psychotherapy Reciprocal Inhibition*. Stanford, Ca.: Stanford University Press, 1958.

Wolpe, J. Cognition and causation in human behavior and its therapy. *American Psychologist,* 1978, *33,* 437–446.

Wood, F. H. *Pupil Observation Schedule*. Minneapolis: Department of Psychoeducational Studies, University of Minnesota, 1973. Revised 1979. (Copy available from the author: 106 Pattee Hall, 150 Pillsbury Dr., S.E., Minneapolis, Mn. 55455.)

Wood, F. H. Observing skills for teachers. In M. C. Reynolds (Ed.), *Social Environment of the Schools*. Reston, Va.: Council for Exceptional Children, 1980.

Wood, F. H., and Lakin, K. C. (Eds.). *Punishment and Aversive Stimulations in Special Education: Legal, Theoretical, and Practical Issues in Their Use with Emotionally Disturbed Children and Youth*. Minneapolis: University of Minnesota, Department of Psychoeducational Studies, 1978.

Wood, M. M. (Ed.). *The Rutland Center Model for Treating Emotionally Disturbed Children.* Athens: Technical Assistance Office to the Georgia Psychoeducational Center Network, 1972.

Wood, M. M. A developmental curriculum for social and emotional growth. In D. L. Lillie (Ed.), *Early Childhood Education: An Individualized Approach to Developmental Instruction.* Chicago: Science Research Associates, 1975. (a)

Wood, M. M. (Ed.). *Developmental Therapy.* Baltimore: University Park Press, 1975. (b)

Wood, M. M. The developmental therapy training program: review of the component for teachers of children with autistic characteristics. In F. H. Wood (Ed.), *Proceedings of a conference on preparing teachers for severely emotionally disturbed children with autistic characteristics.* Minneapolis: University of Minnesota Department of Psychoeducational Studies, 1977.

Wood, M. M. *An Instructional Model for Inservice Training: Final Performance Report.* Washington, D.C.: Bureau of Education for the Handicapped, 1978 (G0077–01379). (a)

Wood, M. M. The psychoeducational model. In N. B. Enzer and K. G. Goin (Eds.), *Social and Emotional Development: The Pre-Schooler.* New York: Walker and Co., 1978. (b)

Wood, M. M. (Ed.). *The Developmental Therapy Objectives: A Self-Instructional Workbook* (3rd ed.). Baltimore: University Park Press, 1979.

Wood, M. M. (Ed.). *Developmental Therapy Sourcebook* (Vol. 1 and 2). Baltimore: University Park Press, 1981.

Wood, M. M. and Swan, W. W. A developmental approach to educating the disturbed young child. *Behavioral Disorders,* 1978, *3,* 197–209.

Wood, N. J., Wood, M. M., and Alegria, A. The economics of special education in a developing country. In A. Fink (Ed.), *International Perspectives on Futures in Special Education.* Arlington: Council for Exceptional Children, 1979.

Worell, J., and Nelson, C. M. *Managing Instructional Problems: A Case Study Workbook.* New York: McGraw-Hill, 1974.

Wright, H. F. *Recording and Analyzing Child Behavior.* New York: Harper & Row, 1967.

Wyatt v. *Stickney,* 344 F. Supp. (M. D. Alabama, 1972). In R. Martin, *Legal Challenges to Behavior Modification.* Champaign, Il.: Research Press, 1975.

Ylvisaker, P. Beyond '72: Strategies for schools. *Saturday Review of Education,* 1972, *55,* 33–34.

Ysseldyke, J. E., and Salvia, J. Diagnostic-prescriptive teaching: two models. *Exceptional Children,* 1974, *41,* 181–185.

Zeilberger, J., Sampen, S. E., and Sloane, H. N., Jr. Modification of a child's problem behaviors in the home with the mother as a therapist. *Journal of Applied Behavior Analysis,* 1968, *1,* 47–53.

Ziegler, E., and Trickett, P. K. I.Q., social competence, and evaluation of early childhood intervention programs. *American Psychologist,* 1978, *33,* 789–798.

Zimmerman, E. H., and Zimmerman, J. The alteration of behavior in a special classroom situation. *Journal of the Experimental Analysis of Behavior,* 1962, *5,* 59–60.

Zimmerman, J., and Bayden, N. T. Punishment of S responding of humans in conditional match-to-sample by time-out. *Journal of the Experimental Analysis of Behavior,* 1963, *6,* 589–597.

Zimmerman, J., and Feister, C. B. Intermittent punishment of S responding in matching-to-sample. *Journal of Experimental Analysis of Behavior,* 1963, *6,* 349–356.

Index

359